Digital Technologies for Sustainability and Quality Control

Afef Khalil
ISCAE, University of Manouba, Tunisia

Hosn el Woujoud Bousselmi
Faculty of Economic Sciences and Management of Nabeul, University of Carthage, Tunisia

Imen Ben Slimene
CREGO-University Of Upper Alsace, France

IGI Global
Scientific Publishing
Publishing Tomorrow's Research Today

Vice President of Editorial Melissa Wagner
Managing Editor of Acquisitions Mikaela Felty
Managing Editor of Book Development Jocelynn Hessler
Production Manager Mike Brehm
Cover Design Phillip Shickler

Published in the United States of America by
IGI Global Scientific Publishing
701 East Chocolate Avenue
Hershey, PA, 17033, USA
Tel: 717-533-8845
Fax: 717-533-8661
Website: https://www.igi-global.com E-mail: cust@igi-global.com

Library of Congress Cataloging-in-Publication Data

Names: Khalil, Afef, editor. | Bousselmi, Hosn el Woujoud, 1985- editor. | Ben Slimene, Imen, 1983- editor.
Title: Digital technologies for sustainability and quality control / edited by Afef Khalil, Hosn el Woujoud Bousselmi, Imen Ben Slimene.
Description: Hershey, PA : IGI Global, [2025] | Includes bibliographical references and index. | Summary: "The book aims to provide readers with an understanding of the key role of digitization and its impact on corporate sustainability. Furthermore, the book promises to inspire readers to use digital tools to manage and improve corporate sustainability through the application of green practices"-- Provided by publisher.
Identifiers: LCCN 2024048445 (print) | LCCN 2024048446 (ebook) | ISBN 9798369343739 (hardcover) | ISBN 9798369351154 (paperback) | ISBN 9798369343746 (ebook)
Subjects: LCSH: Digital media--Management. | Sustainability.
Classification: LCC HM851 .D5446 2025 (print) | LCC HM851 (ebook) | DDC 658.4/083--dc23/eng/20241221
LC record available at https://lccn.loc.gov/2024048445
LC ebook record available at https://lccn.loc.gov/2024048446

British Cataloguing in Publication Data
A Cataloguing in Publication record for this book is available from the British Library.

Table of Contents

Detailed Table of Contents

and economic challenges. The research focuses on key areas such as green process innovation, energy-efficient solutions, eco-packaging, materials recycling, and the circular economy, all driven by digital advancements. Through case studies and data analysis, this paper offers insights into how Indian companies are adopting digital tools to mitigate environmental impacts while maintaining economic resilience. By examining the Indian context, the paper aims to contribute to the global discourse on sustainability, providing valuable lessons for corporations and policymakers working towards the twin goals of economic growth and environmental stewardship.

The purpose of the study is to evaluate the impact of digital transformation on the performance of innovative small and medium enterprises (SMEs). Despite the broad interest of academics and practitioners in digital transformation, little attention has been paid to the mediating role of business models in the link between digital transformation and SME performance. A survey of 419 innovative SMEs in France was conducted to examine the proposed conceptual model. Structural equation modeling (SEM) was relied upon to detect the correlation and linear regression of the study model. The results indicate that business models had a role in modifying the relationship between digital transformation and performance. The results contribute to deepening knowledge in the field of digital transformation and business models. The findings can form a guide that helps researchers and practitioners manage digital transformation and design performance-enhancing business models in the context of SMEs.

Fintech's have boundless potential, with an increasing need for social inclusion. As new technologies emerge in the market and the boundaries of traditional business models are challenged, financial services can be delivered at a lower cost with greater accountability, efficiency, and accessibility. In Tunisia, 64% of adults are financially excluded or underserved, partly due to the difficulty of accessing physical bank locations and increasing dissatisfaction with the quality of Tunisian banking services. Despite these figures, Fintech's in Africa are expected to be a game changer. Fintechs supplies end-user services and platforms. This paper examines the extent to which Tunisian fintech, supported by the emerging ecosystem, can serve as an engine shared value creation. This paper describes the fintech ecosystem in Tunisia. It illustrates emerging fintech business models. Then, the analysis provides the elements of creating shared value in these Fintech's.

There is increasing interest in the node of digitalization and green economy due to the recent development of sustainable economic growth. This systematic literature review aims to comprehensively explore and analyze the existing research on the association between digitalization and green economy to discover and highlight the fundamental discoveries and perspectives present in the current body of literature concerning digital currencies and sustainable economic growth. The review adheres to the PRISMA statement, while VOS-Viewer software was utilized to execute the bibliometric analysis. A thorough exploration of academic sources, i.e., Scopus, employed varied keyword combinations. This effort led to the identification of 308 records and subsequent assessment of titles, abstracts, and full texts, including 110 pertinent studies for analysis, covering the period from 2005 to 2023. The findings reveal vital insights into the role of digitalization in contributing to green economy growth and supporting sustainable development goals.

The digital age has ushered in unprecedented technological advancements, enabling organizations to leverage powerful tools such as big data analytics, artificial

recognized technostress creators apply to auditors as well. It also highlights new technostress creators that are related to auditors in particular, namely overdependence on ICTs, ICT-enabled work interruption and constant connectivity. Personality traits and segmentation mindset are proven as the main factors that increase/decrease technostress.

Effective management of spatial data can drive green innovation by identifying environmental challenges such as air and water quality, deforestation, soil health, and climate vulnerability. Spatial data supports pollution detection and forest cover analysis, along with soil sampling for erosion assessment. It can also guide targeted initiatives like clean air efforts and sustainable forestry. Moreover, it can optimize resource allocation by pinpointing renewable energy sources and sustainable materials. Spatial data can tailor innovations to local contexts, inform urban planning, enhance waste and agriculture practices, and monitor environmental impact. Key strategies of spatial data management involve collecting high-quality data from diverse sources, integrating it into accessible platforms, and ensuring data quality. Collaboration and knowledge sharing can enhance spatial data's role in green innovation. Challenges such as data access, ownership, and privacy concerns necessitate solutions like open data policies, clear agreements, and capacity-building programs.

The OpenStreetMap (OSM) platform aids SDGs by fostering global geospatial data exchange. It's vital in regions lacking commercial incentives, promoting public collaboration. Initiatives like Open Mapping Hub - Asia Pacific support SDGs through participatory mapping. Case studies, like in Sri Lanka's Uva Province, showcase OSM's impact on infrastructure planning, disaster risk reduction, and citizen engagement. Training methods, tools, and outcomes emphasize improved decision-making and stakeholder engagement through data visualization. This underscores the importance of digital technologies for sustainability and quality control.

The healthcare metaverse, leveraging VR and AR, revolutionizes medical services, education, and research by creating immersive, interactive environments. However, integrating spatial health data poses challenges in data accuracy, security, privacy, and ethical considerations, necessitating frameworks. The chapter proposes a framework for spatial data governance in the healthcare metaverse, focusing on patient control over health information. It includes rigorous data security and privacy protocols, ensures transparency and accountability, addresses ethical concerns, and encourages collaboration among stakeholders. This framework aims to uphold responsible data practices, protect patient privacy, and improve the effectiveness of healthcare services within the metaverse.

An essential component of a nation's infrastructure development is education, which has evolved through standards from Education 1.0 to the present Education 5.0. A study evaluates the historical development of education and its applicability to contemporary requirements. The assessment of the literature, we examine the use of Education 5.0 in both industrialized and advancing nations in this research. Saudi Arabia and Malaysia have been chosen for examination as examples of industrialized nations that have effectively implemented Education 5.0, using the PRISMA

Preface

The adoption of digital technologies has been in vogue and attractive in recent years, thanks to their benefits and role in the digital world. Digital technologies are vital tools for businesses, enabling them to increase their resistance to adverse external shocks and achieve sustainability. These technologies are increasingly being used by major corporations to reshape their business models and adjust their organizational and operational approaches to balance their economic, environmental, and social impacts.

Companies undertaking a digital transformation must integrate the technologies concerned with green strategies and practices. Thus, companies striving to achieve sustainability goals should implement green practices.

This book examines the relationship between digital technologies and corporate sustainability. The objective is to investigate the significance of utilizing digital technologies to implement green strategies, including but not limited to green process innovation, energy-efficient solutions, eco-packaging, and materials recycling, the circular economy, and practices to address safety risks.

In other words, this book offers new perspectives to various interested parties (e.g., academics, regulators, banking institutions, etc.), enabling them to better understand the technological and governance challenges. In addition, this book provides an impressive academic contribution to digital technologies and their impact on sustainability. Decision-makers should heed the research and recognize the factors driving digital technologies.

COVERAGE AND CONTENT OF THE BOOK

The book "Digital Technologies for Sustainability and Quality Control" comprises fourteen chapters. The first Chapter provides a comprehensive framework for understanding the multiple benefits and challenges of integrating digital technologies into industrial environments. In Chapter 2, the authors analyze the degree of digitization of management control among companies in Morocco, and test the impact of company age and legal affiliation on the digitization of management control. The third Chapter aims to study the benefits of fintech for sustainable organizational performance in Pakistani banks. This research paper combines the Technology, Organization and Environment (TOE) model with Diffusion of Innovation Theory (DOI) to explain the use of fintech as a technological innovation. Chapter 4 empirically investigates the intersection of digital innovation and green strategies within Indian industries, assessing how these technologies are reshaping business practices to address environmental, social and economic challenges. The research focuses on key areas such as green process innovation, energy efficiency solutions, eco-packaging, materials recycling and the circular economy, all driven by digital advances. The study also highlights emerging governance challenges and the role of digital platforms in supporting India's sustainability goals. In Chapter 5, the authors examine the impact of digital transformation on performance and the role of business models (BMs) in this relationship. The authors of Chapter 6 highlight emerging fintech business models by focusing on a popular segment in Tunisia: digital payment and payment facilitators - Fintech Technology Providers. In Chapter 7, the authors investigate the impact of digitization on the advancement of the green economy through a systematic literature review. Chapter 8 explores the multiple dimensions of corporate digital responsibility, examining key drivers, challenges, stakeholder impact, and best practices in various sectors and geographical contexts. The authors of Chapter 9 discuss the individual factors that influence socially responsible consumption, focusing on the gap between consumers' intentions and their actual behavior. Chapter 10 explores technostress among auditors and aims to better understand the factors that may mitigate the positive impact of technostress on the high turnover and burnout seen within the auditing profession. In Chapter 11, the authors examine the importance of spatial data management in promoting green innovation. A literature review methodology is adopted. This method involves the evaluation of existing research and scholarly articles related to the topic in question. The authors of Chapter 12 investigate how volunteer spatial information via OpenStreetMap (OSM) can support sustainable development in the province of Uva, Sri Lanka. Chapter 13 identifies the approach to effective spatial data management within the healthcare metaverse. This chapter focuses on key issues concerning the management of spatial data in this virtual framework and provides recommendations for the correct and ethical use of data. Finally, Chapter 14 focuses on the use of Education 5.0 in industrialized and developing countries. Saudi Arabia and Malaysia have been chosen to be examined as examples of industrialized countries that have effectively implemented Education 5.0, using the PRISMA technique based on research conducted over the last six years. The book aims to help readers understand the key role of digitization and its impact on corporate sustainability. In addition, it promises to inspire readers to use digital tools to manage and improve corporate

Afef Khalil
ISCAE, University of Manouba, Tunisia

Hosn el Woujoud Bousselmi
Faculty of Economic Sciences and Management of Nabeul, Tunisia

Imen Ben Slimene
University of Upper Alsace, France

Acknowledgment

The authors of the chapters and editors are all partners in the success of this volume. The editors would like to express their gratitude to the authors for their valuable contributions. Special thanks go to the reviewers for their valuable comments and recommendations to improve the book's chapters. The editors would also like to thank the team at IGI Global for their support in this project.

Editorial Advisory Board

Chapter 1
Tech-Driven Sustainability: Enhancing Quality Control Through Digital Solutions – A Comprehensive Review

Askar Garad
https://orcid.org/0000-0003-3916-9228
Universitas Muhammadiyah Yogyakarta, Indonesia

Hosam Alden Riyadh
https://orcid.org/0000-0002-9426-5282
Telkom University, Indonesia

Abdullah M. Al-Ansi
https://orcid.org/0000-0002-1682-3154
Dhofar University, Oman

Rita Kusumawati
Universitas Muhammadiyah Yogyakarta, Indonesia

Salsabila Aisyah Afaiza
Telkom University, Indonesia

ABSTRACT

This comprehensive review explores the transformative impact of digital technologies on sustainability and quality control across diverse industries. The study aims to elucidate how technologies such as Internet of Things (IoT), artificial intelligence (AI), blockchain, data analytics, and digital twins are leveraged to optimize processes

DOI: 10.4018/979-8-3693-4373-9.ch001

and enhance operational efficiencies while ensuring adherence to stringent quality standards. Methodology: A systematic analysis of current literature and empirical studies was conducted to synthesize key findings and insights. The review covers a wide range of sectors including manufacturing, healthcare, transportation, energy, retail, finance, agriculture, construction, education, and telecommunications, Results: The review reveals that digital technologies play a pivotal role in revolutionizing industry practices by improving supply chain transparency, optimizing logistics, enhancing patient care, enabling smart energy management, and fostering sustainable agricultural practices.

1. INTRODUCTION

In the modern industrial landscape, the intersection of digital technologies and sustainability imperatives has emerged as a critical force driving transformative change. This chapter embarks on a comprehensive exploration of how digital solutions are not only revolutionizing quality control mechanisms but also acting as catalysts for sustainable development across various sectors. By scrutinizing a wide array of digital innovations ranging from IoT (Internet of Things) and AI (Artificial Intelligence) to advanced data analytics this review seeks to elucidate their profound implications for enhancing operational efficiencies while minimizing environmental impacts.

1.1 Tech-Driven Sustainability

Digital technologies have become indispensable in modern industries, providing unprecedented capabilities for monitoring, analyzing, and optimizing operational processes in real time. The integration of IoT facilitates enhanced connectivity and automation, enabling dynamic resource management and predictive maintenance strategies (Argente García et al., 2024). Meanwhile, AI-driven analytics empower decision-makers with actionable insights that optimize resource allocation and enhance overall productivity. These digital advancements are redefining industry norms by not only improving product quality but also reducing inefficiencies, waste, and environmental footprints (Guo et al., 2024; Fernández-Miguel et al., 2024).

1.2 Digital Transformation in Industries

The adoption of digital solutions across various sectors is contributing to more adaptive and responsive operational frameworks. Industries such as manufacturing, healthcare, and supply chains have significantly benefited from the deployment of

IoT and AI, as these technologies streamline operations, enhance quality control, and reduce costs. In addition to improving operational efficiency, these advancements are closely tied to sustainability goals, enabling industries to monitor their resource consumption and emissions in real-time. However, the rapid proliferation of digital technologies also necessitates a thorough assessment of their environmental impact, including energy consumption, e-waste generation, and carbon emissions (Lazaroiu et al., 2024).

1.3 Environmental Impact of Digital Solutions

As industries increasingly adopt tech-driven sustainability measures, it is vital to assess the environmental implications of these innovations. While IoT and AI-driven analytics enable real-time monitoring and optimization, their environmental impact remains a concern. Technologies such as AI and blockchain require substantial computational power, which contributes to higher energy consumption (Lazaroiu et al., 2024). Moreover, the increasing use of connected devices has led to a surge in e-waste, posing challenges for resource recovery and recycling. Balancing technological progress with environmental stewardship is crucial to ensuring that these innovations contribute to long-term sustainability goals.

1.4 Challenges and Opportunities in Tech-Driven Sustainability

Despite the clear benefits of digital technologies, organizations face significant challenges in adopting and integrating tech-driven sustainability measures. Common obstacles include the high initial costs of technology implementation, the complexity of integrating new systems with existing infrastructures, and regulatory hurdles (Fernández-Miguel et al., 2024). However, these challenges also present opportunities for innovation. Emerging technologies such as blockchain-enabled IoT systems and AI-driven supply chain optimizations hold great promise for overcoming these barriers and accelerating the transition towards more sustainable and efficient operations.

1.5 Emerging Trends and Future Directions

Emerging trends such as the convergence of blockchain, IoT, and AI in optimizing supply chain management and resource efficiency are expected to redefine industry norms in the coming years. Blockchain, in particular, offers a decentralized and transparent approach to managing supply chains, enhancing traceability, and ensuring the ethical sourcing of materials. These innovations, combined with the increasing integration of AI-powered predictive analytics, are poised to drive significant advancements in both sustainability and quality control, creating new opportunities for industries to achieve their environmental and operational goals.

1.6 Research Gap and Importance

While there is a growing body of research highlighting the potential of digital technologies in enhancing sustainability and operational efficiency, a significant gap exists in systematically analyzing how these technologies simultaneously impact quality control and environmental sustainability across various sectors. Existing literature often treats quality control and sustainability as separate domains, lacking a comprehensive exploration of their integration through digital solutions. Furthermore, current studies frequently focus on specific technologies in isolation, such as IoT or AI, without a holistic examination of how these tools can work synergistically to enhance both operational performance and environmental outcomes (Guo et al., 2024).

This research fills this critical gap by offering a systematic review that bridges the divide between digital quality control and sustainability efforts. It not only explores individual technologies but also evaluates their combined effects across industries, providing a clearer understanding of their integrated impact on both operational and environmental objectives. This research is of particular importance in today's rapidly evolving industrial context, where companies are under increasing pressure to meet both high-quality standards and strict environmental regulations. By addressing these challenges, the study offers actionable insights for industries aiming to adopt tech-driven strategies that optimize product quality while advancing sustainability goals.

1.7 Research Objectives

This manuscript endeavors to achieve the following objectives:

1. **Survey of Digital Technologies**: Conduct a thorough examination of a broad spectrum of digital technologies, including IoT, AI, and data analytics, to assess their impact on sustainability and quality control.
2. **Integration of Digital Solutions in Industries**: Explore how various industries are incorporating digital solutions into their operations to enhance sustainability efforts and improve quality control processes.
3. **Environmental Impact Assessment**: Evaluate the environmental impact of digital technologies, taking into account factors such as energy consumption, e-waste generation, and overall carbon footprint, ensuring a balanced view of their sustainability implications.

4. **Challenges and Opportunities**: Analyze the challenges organizations face when implementing tech-driven sustainability and quality control measures while identifying opportunities for innovation and growth.
5. **Emerging Trends and Future Directions**: Provide insights into the latest trends in tech-driven sustainability and quality control, with a focus on future directions and potential breakthroughs in the field.

1.8 Contribution

This research contributes a comprehensive framework for understanding the multifaceted benefits and challenges of integrating digital technologies in industrial settings. It provides valuable insights for researchers, policymakers, and industry leaders seeking to navigate and harness the transformative potential of tech-driven advancements in sustainability and quality control. By identifying emerging trends and future research directions, the study sets the stage for further innovation and development in sustainable practices across global industries.

2. METHODOLOGY

This study employs a systematic literature review methodology to comprehensively investigate the impact of digital technologies on sustainability and quality control practices across diverse industries. The methodology involves several structured stages to ensure rigor and relevance in the selection and analysis of literature.

1. Identification of Relevant Studies: To begin with, a systematic search was conducted on the Scopus database, utilizing relevant keywords such as "digital technologies," "IoT," "AI," "data analytics," "sustainability," and "quality control." The initial search yielded a total of 1,248 articles.

2. Screening Process: Initially, all 1,248 articles were screened based on their titles and abstracts to assess their relevance to the research objectives. Articles that did not clearly align with the scope of the study were excluded during this stage, resulting in the identification of 354 potentially relevant articles. Subsequently, the full texts of these 354 identified articles were retrieved and thoroughly examined. This stage involved a detailed assessment to determine whether each article met the inclusion criteria based on predefined selection criteria as shown in Table 1. The criteria focused on the explicit exploration of digital technologies' impact on sustainability and quality control within industrial contexts. In the end, 102 articles have been included in this literature review.

Table 1. Selection criteria for literature review

Inclusion Conditions	Exclusion Conditions
Relevance: Articles must explicitly investigate the impact of digital technologies (e.g., IoT, AI, data analytics) on sustainability and quality control in industries.	Irrelevance: Studies that do not explicitly address the impact of digital technologies on sustainability and quality control.
Focus: Studies should concentrate on practical applications or theoretical explorations related to digital solutions enhancing sustainability efforts and quality control processes.	Duplicate Studies: Redundant articles, overlapping in content or findings, identified through bibliographic management tools.
Publication Types: Peer-reviewed journal articles, conference papers, and scholarly books providing empirical evidence or theoretical insights.	Publication Language: Articles not available in English or Arabic, as per the language proficiency of the researchers.
Publication Date: Articles published from 2020 - 2024 onwards to capture recent advancements in digital technologies.	Study Design: Non-empirical studies such as editorials, commentaries, opinion pieces, and literature reviews without empirical data.
Keyword Relevance: Articles must include keywords related to "tech-driven," "sustainability," "quality," and "control" in their titles, abstracts, or keywords.	Publication Status: Grey literature, patents, technical reports, and unpublished manuscripts lacking peer-reviewed validation.
Language: Articles must be published in English to facilitate comprehension and analysis by the authors.	Unreliable quality sources: Articles that were published in articles published in thousands of articles per issue were excluded to avoid the lack of quality of the published articles.

These conditions outline the criteria used to select and exclude articles for the systematic literature review, ensuring the research focuses on high-quality, relevant studies pertinent to the impact of digital technologies on sustainability and quality control in industries.

3. Selection of Studies: Following a comprehensive review of full texts, 102 articles were deemed appropriate and closely related to the research objectives. These selected studies provide substantial insights into various aspects of digital technologies, including their integration, environmental impact assessment, challenges, opportunities, emerging trends, and future directions concerning sustainability and quality control practices across different sectors. The reviewed articles are listed in the Appendix in at the end of the manuscript.

Figure 1. Publication trends over the years

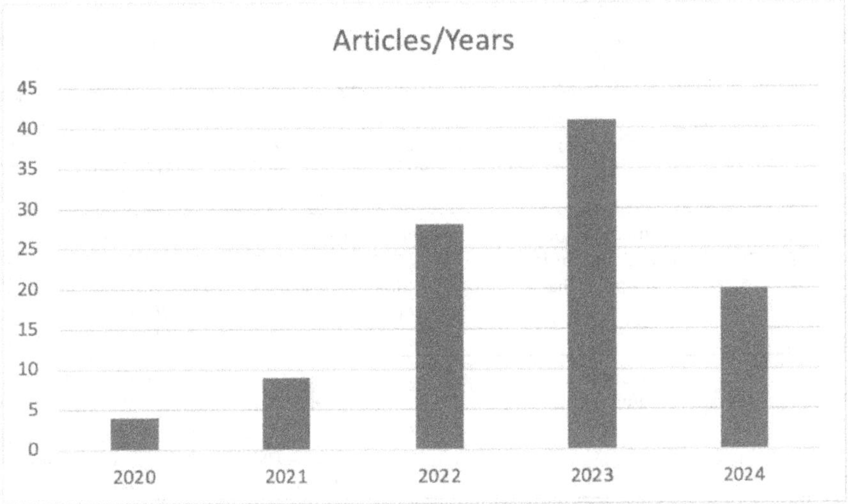

Figure 1: Publication Trends Over the Years

Figure 1 represents the number of publications each year from 2020 to 2024. It indicates a significant increase in the number of publications over the years, suggesting a growing interest and research activity in the relevant field. The total number of publications across these years sums up to 102.

4. Data Extraction and Synthesis: For each selected study, relevant data including author(s), year of publication, research methods employed, key findings, and theoretical frameworks utilized were systematically extracted and synthesized. This process facilitates a structured analysis of the literature, enabling the identification of overarching themes, patterns, and gaps in current research.

5. Analysis and Interpretation: The synthesized data from the selected studies underwent thematic analysis to uncover recurring themes and patterns regarding the impact of digital technologies on sustainability and quality control. This analysis involves interpreting the findings within the context of existing literature, thereby providing a comprehensive understanding of the current state and future directions of the field.

6. Reporting and Documentation: Table 2 provides a comprehensive overview of the articles included in this literature review, delineating significant advancements and emerging research trends in digital transformation and sustainability across various sectors.

Table 2. Summary of research topics and associated authors by sector

Sector	Sub-sector	Authors
Agriculture, Food Industry & Food Systems	Digital Food Provisioning, Precision Agriculture, Food production & supply chain, Smart Agriculture.	Ancín et al. (2022), Heidenstrøm & Hebrok (2022), Marti et al. (2023), Kurniawan et al. (2023), Jin & Han (2024), Sharma et al. (2024), Heidenstrøm & Hebrok (2022), Lahane et al. (2023), Fernández-Miguel et al. (2024), Argente García et al. (2024), Büyüközkan & Uztürk (2024), Chin et al. (2024), Amoo et al., (2022), Francisco & Linnér, (2023).
Circular Economy & Sustainable Supply Chains	Circular Economy, Blockchain, Sustainable Supply Chains.	Agyabeng-Mensah et al. (2021), Ahmed & MacCarthy (2023), Li et al. (2023), Röck et al. (2024), Molari et al., (2021), Korucuk et al., (2022), Montalbano & Santi, (2023), Lazaroiu et al., (2024), Büyüközkan & Uztürk, (2024).
Construction & Urban Development	Smart Cities, Sustainable Building, Urban Digital Twin.	Larrinaga et al. (2021), Barresi (2023), Chen et al. (2024), Bibri & Krogstie (2020), Ko et al. (2021), Asensio et al. (2023), Marzouk et al. (2022), Graser et al. (2023), Larrinaga et al. (2021), Salmon et al., (2021), Koltsios et al., (2022).
Digitalization & Information Systems	Blockchain & IoT, Artificial Intelligence & Digital Twin.	Dudhat et al. (2021), Ahmed & MacCarthy (2023), Li et al. (2023), Akhtar et al. (2024), Pooyandeh & Sohn (2023), Rashed & Mutis (2023), Sharma & Kumar Tiwari (2023), Heinonen et al., (2022), Kofos et al., (2022), Kranz et al., (2022), Al-Emran & Griffy-Brown, (2023), Alrammal et al., (2023), Nguyen et al., (2023).
Emerging Technologies	AI, IoT, Digital Twin, Smart Lithium-Ion Battery Monitoring.	Danys et al. (2022), Ramesh Kumar & Chitra (2022), Pooyandeh & Sohn (2023), Guo et al. (2024), Shui et al. (2023), Hosamo et al. (2023), Arsiwala et al., (2023), Hoosain et al., (2023), Knapskog & Browne, (2022).
Environmental Sustainability & Renewable Energy	Renewable Energy & Carbon Reduction, Energy Efficiency & Grid Systems, Micro Hydro, Net-Zero.	Rashid (2020), Hakobyan et al. (2022), Imtiaz et al. (2023), Kostner et al. (2023), Chen et al. (2024), Mynko et al. (2023), Bibri & Krogstie (2020), Hamalainen & Salmi (2023), Hassanin et al. (2023), Kostner et al. (2023), Guo et al. (2024), Chen et al. (2024), Ramesh Kumar & Chitra (2022), Akhtar et al. (2024), Basova et al., (2023), Koutsovili et al., (2023), Saurette et al., (2024), Saurette et al., (2024).
Healthcare & Well-being	Assistive Healthcare Technology, mHealth Solutions, AI, Digital Health.	Anwar et al. (2021), Anttila et al. (2022), Pu et al. (2024), Obaideen et al. (2024), Anwar et al. (2021), Anttila et al. (2022), Owida et al., (2022), Sá et al., (2023), Lisnawati et al., (2024), Saurette et al., (2024), Pu et al., (2024), Lisnawati et al., (2024).
Manufacturing and Industry, Industry 4.0 & Digital Transformation	Additive Manufacturing, Industry 4.0, Business Agility, Smart Manufacturing, Circular Economy & Recycling.	Dudhat et al. (2021), Elhazmiri et al. (2022), Ntamo et al. (2022), Kumar et al. (2022), Sharma et al. (2024), Fernández-Miguel et al. (2024), Kumar et al. (2022), Ntamo et al. (2022), Li et al. (2023), Fernández-Miguel et al. (2024), Agyabeng-Mensah et al. (2021), Kurniawan et al. (2023), Rumetshofer et al. (2024), Nuutinen et al., (2022), Mahdiraji et al., (2023)

continued on following page

Table 2. Continued

Sector	Sub-sector	Authors
Transport and Logistics	Smart Transportation, Logistics & Supply Chain.	Sadanand et al. (2021), Heikkilä et al. (2022), Medoh & Telukdarie (2020), Parhi et al. (2022), Li et al. (2023), (Hodson et al., 2020), San Cornelio et al., (2023).
Water Management	Wastewater Treatment, Water Resource Management.	Rashid (2020), Hakobyan et al. (2022), Mukarram et al. (2023), Argente García et al. (2024), Guo et al. (2024).
Others (General Sustainability, Education, Legal Aspects)	Sustainability, Open Learning, Climate Change.	Colangelo (2022), Otto & Kerres (2022), Pan et al. (2022), Rashed & Mutis (2023).

3. RESULTS

In this section, we present the key findings gleaned from our comprehensive review of the transformative impact of digital technologies on sustainability and quality control across various industries. Drawing from a systematic analysis of literature and empirical studies, we highlight specific applications and outcomes of technologies such as Internet of Things (IoT), artificial intelligence (AI), blockchain, data analytics, and digital twins. These findings illustrate how these technologies optimize operational processes, enhance efficiency, and ensure adherence to quality standards in sectors ranging from manufacturing and healthcare to transportation and agriculture. Additionally, we discuss critical environmental considerations and the implications for sustainable practices, emphasizing the importance of rigorous environmental impact assessments (EIAs).

3.1 Survey of Digital Technologies

This section emphasizes how real-time data analytics are leveraged for resource optimization, enhancing both sustainability and process reliability across industries like manufacturing and healthcare. The current investigation, unlike previous studies, provides a cross-industry analysis, identifying how similar technologies yield comparable outcomes in diverse sectors. The key findings from the systematic review are outlined in Table 3, focusing on how IoT, AI, and blockchain technologies improve operational efficiency and quality control while minimizing environmental footprints.

Table 3. Impact of digital technologies on sustainability and quality control

Technology	Application	Impact on Sustainability	Impact on Quality Control
Internet of Things (IoT)	– Real-time data collection and monitoring – Intelligent transportation networks – Smart energy management systems	– Optimizes resource usage – Reduces environmental footprint – Enhances efficiency in smart cities.	– Real-time monitoring of production processes – Detects anomalies – Ensures adherence to quality standards.
Artificial Intelligence (AI)	– Predictive maintenance – AI-driven quality control systems	– Reduces downtime and extends machinery lifecycle – Supports sustainable industrial practices.	– Improves defect detection – Reduces waste – Accurately identifies flaws in products during production.
Data Analytics	– Big data analytics for decision-making – Environmental impact tracking	– Enables informed decision-making – Optimizes processes – Implements strategies to minimize ecological footprint.	– Interprets vast amounts of data – Provides actionable insights into operations – Enhances process optimization.
Blockchain	– Transparency and traceability in supply chains	– Promotes ethical sourcing – Reduces environmental impact.	– Ensures transparency in product history – Enhances traceability and accountability

3.2 Integration of Digital Solutions in Industries

Table 4 illustrates the integration of digital technologies across sectors, summarizing the specific technologies implemented and their goals. For example, IoT's role in smart energy management in the energy sector is compared to its application in precision farming. The table allows for a nuanced comparison between industries, highlighting the multifaceted impacts of these technologies, which earlier studies did not address comprehensively.

Table 4. Integration of digital solutions in industries

Industry Sector	Digital Solutions Integrated	Purpose/Goal	Examples of Technologies Used
Manufacturing	– Internet of Things (IoT), AI-driven automation	– Enhance operational efficiency, reduce waste	– Predictive maintenance, robotic process automation
Healthcare	– Telemedicine platforms, AI in diagnostics	– Improve patient care, streamline operations	– Electronic health records, remote monitoring devices
Transportation	– GPS tracking, predictive analytics	– Optimize logistics, reduce emissions	– Autonomous vehicles, route optimization software
Energy	– Smart grids, renewable energy monitoring	– Increase energy efficiency, promote sustainability	– IoT sensors for energy monitoring, blockchain for energy trading
Retail	– E-commerce platforms, personalized marketing	– Enhance customer experience, optimize inventory	– Data analytics for consumer insights, RFID for inventory tracking
Finance	– Blockchain, AI in fraud detection	– Secure transactions, improve regulatory compliance	– Cryptocurrencies, machine learning algorithms
Agriculture	– Precision farming, drone technology	– Optimize crop yield, reduce environmental impact	– Soil sensors, satellite imagery
Construction	– Building information modeling (BIM), IoT	– Enhance project management, reduce construction costs	– Augmented reality for design visualization
Education	– Online learning platforms, AI tutors	– Expand access to education, personalize learning	– Learning management systems, adaptive learning algorithms
Telecommunications	– 5G networks, IoT connectivity	– Improve network efficiency, enable IoT applications	– Network slicing, edge computing

3.3 Environmental Impact Assessment

Table 5 provides an assessment of environmental impacts, showing how different technologies affect energy consumption and waste. This section further clarifies the research gap by demonstrating that while earlier literature examined sustainability practices, it often overlooked the environmental trade-offs of digital technologies, such as the energy demands of AI and blockchain.

Table 5. Environmental impact assessment of digital technologies

Digital Technology	Environmental Impact Factors Considered	Assessment Findings	Mitigation Strategies
Cloud Computing	– Energy consumption, data center emissions	– Significant energy uses due to data centers	– Renewable energy sourcing, data center efficiency measures
Internet of Things (IoT)	– Energy use by devices, e-waste	– Energy-intensive during use and manufacturing	– Device longevity, eco-design principles
Artificial Intelligence	– Computing power, data storage	– High computational demands, data storage requirements	– Energy-efficient algorithms, optimized hardware
Blockchain	– Energy consumption, e-waste from hardware	– High energy for mining (proof-of-work systems)	– Proof-of-stake algorithms, transition to green blockchain
5G Networks	– Energy use in infrastructure deployment	– Increased energy demand for network operations	– Energy-efficient network equipment, smart grid integration
Renewable Energy Tech	– Manufacturing emissions, lifecycle analysis	– Variability in environmental impact based on tech type	– Lifecycle assessment, sustainable sourcing practices
Digital Manufacturing	– Energy use in production, material waste	– Energy-intensive processes, e-waste from equipment	– Additive manufacturing, recycling programs
Smart Grids	– Energy efficiency, infrastructure upgrades	– Reduces transmission losses, infrastructure impact	– Smart metering, demand response programs

3.4 Challenges and Opportunities

Table 6 Challenges and Opportunities in Implementing Tech-Driven Sustainability and Quality Control provides a comprehensive overview of the primary obstacles and potential advancements associated with digital technologies in sustainability and quality control. The table categorizes challenges such as the integration of legacy systems, high implementation costs, and scalability issues, which hinder the seamless adoption of new technologies. It also highlights significant barriers like data security concerns, resistance to change, and complex regulatory landscapes. Conversely, the table outlines various opportunities for innovation, including IoT and sensor integration for real-time monitoring, big data analytics for enhanced decision-making, and blockchain for transparent supply chains. Additionally, it showcases advancements like AI-driven automation, cloud computing for scalability, and augmented reality for training. By juxtaposing these challenges and opportunities, the table underscores the dual nature of tech-driven sustainability efforts—highlighting both the significant hurdles organizations face and the transformative potential of emerging technologies in driving sustainable and efficient practices.

Table 6. Challenges and opportunities in implementing tech-driven sustainability and quality control

1. Challenges			
Aspect	**Description**	**Impact**	**Example Scenarios**
Integration of Legacy Systems	Compatibility issues with new tech, Data silos	Difficulty in aggregating data from disparate sources	Existing software unable to communicate with new systems
Cost of Implementation	Budget constraints, ROI concerns	High initial investment, Uncertain ROI	High initial investment in technology, Uncertain ROI in the short term
Skills and Training Requirements	Lack of skilled personnel, Training costs	Insufficient internal expertise, Time-consuming training programs	Insufficient expertise on new technologies, Extensive training programs
Data Security and Privacy Concerns	Potential breaches, Regulatory non-compliance	Vulnerability of sensitive data to cyberattacks, Failure to meet regulations	Data vulnerability, Non-compliance with GDPR or CCPA
Scalability Issues	Difficulty in expanding systems, Performance bottlenecks	Inability to handle increased data volume, System slowdowns	System slowdowns under heavy load, Handling increased data volume
Resistance to Change	Cultural barriers, Employee resistance	Reluctance to adopt new technologies, Lack of buy-in from stakeholders	Reluctance to new technologies, Lack of support from stakeholders
Monitoring and Accountability	Ensuring compliance with sustainability standards	Tracking progress, Ensuring accuracy and reliability of data	Tracking progress towards goals, Ensuring data accuracy
Interoperability Across Platforms	Interfacing with third-party systems	Integrating with supplier systems, Ensuring seamless data exchange	Integrating with partner systems, Seamless data exchange
Complex Regulatory Landscape	Adherence to varying global regulations	Compliance with environmental standards	Navigating differing regional laws, Compliance with standards
Sustainability Metrics and Reporting Standards	Defining and measuring sustainable practices	Establishing metrics, Accurate reporting	Establishing standardized metrics, Reporting to stakeholders

continued on following page

Table 6. Continued

2. Opportunities			
Aspect	**Description**	**Impact**	**Example Scenarios**
IoT and Sensor Integration	Real-time monitoring, Predictive maintenance	Optimizing energy usage, Tracking product lifecycle	Sensors for energy optimization, IoT devices for product tracking
Big Data Analytics	Insights for process optimization, Decision support	Improving resource efficiency, Predicting quality control issues	Analyzing datasets to improve efficiency, Predicting quality issues
Blockchain for Transparency	Secure supply chain traceability, Trust-building	Verifying sustainability claims, Ensuring product authenticity	Verifying claims across supply chains, Ensuring authenticity
AI and Machine Learning Applications	Automation of quality control processes, Pattern recognition	Defect detection, Predictive maintenance	AI-driven defect detection, Machine learning for maintenance
Cloud Computing for Scalability	Flexible and scalable infrastructure, Cost efficiency	Hosting data, Scaling digital solutions	Hosting data on cloud platforms, Scaling solutions globally
Augmented Reality (AR) for Training	Enhanced learning experiences, Reduced errors	Training on sustainable practices, Virtual inspections	AR simulations for training, Virtual quality control inspections
3D Printing for Sustainable Manufacturing	On-demand production, Waste reduction	Prototyping with biodegradable materials, Customizable designs	Prototyping with biodegradable materials, Customizable designs
Collaborative Platforms and Open Innovation	Idea sharing and co-creation, Rapid prototyping	Crowdsourcing solutions, Open-source frameworks	Crowdsourcing sustainability solutions, Open-source quality frameworks
Energy-Efficient Technologies	Reduced carbon footprint, Lower operational costs	Implementing renewable sources, Energy-efficient systems	Renewable energy sources, Energy-efficient machinery
Circular Economy Initiatives	Waste reduction and reuse, Resource efficiency	Designing for disassembly, Closed-loop practices	Designing products for recycling, Closed-loop supply chain practices

3.5 Emerging Trends and Future Directions

Table 7 captures a range of innovative trends such as IoT, AI, blockchain, and circular economy strategies, each poised to significantly enhance environmental stewardship and operational efficiency. The table outlines anticipated impacts and potential breakthroughs, illustrating how IoT can enable real-time environmental monitoring and smart grid optimization, while AI promises advancements in automated defect detection and predictive maintenance. Blockchain is expected to enhance supply chain transparency and trust, and circular economy strategies aim to advance recycling technologies and sustainable product design. Additionally, data analytics and predictive modeling will support data-driven decision-making and proactive risk management, and renewable energy integration seeks to reduce carbon footprints through AI optimization and hybrid storage solutions. Smart manufacturing technologies and sustainable supply chain innovations will drive efficiency and ethical sourcing, while advanced materials and regenerative agriculture practices offer solutions for eco-friendly production and soil health restoration. This section provides a forward-looking perspective on how these trends will shape the future landscape of sustainability practices and quality control.

Table 7. Emerging trends and future directions in tech-driven sustainability and quality control

Trend Description	Anticipated Impact	Potential Breakthroughs
Internet of Things (IoT) in Sustainability	– Real-time environmental monitoring – Enhanced resource efficiency	– IoT integration with AI for predictive analytics – IoT-enabled smart grids for energy optimization
Artificial Intelligence (AI) for Quality Control	– Automated defect detection – Improved process optimization	– AI-driven anomaly detection in supply chain sustainability – AI-powered predictive maintenance
Blockchain for Traceability	– Enhanced transparency and trust in supply chains	– Blockchain-enabled smart contracts for sustainable sourcing – Immutable record of product lifecycle
Circular Economy Strategies	– Closed-loop supply chains – Waste minimization	– Advanced recycling technologies for complex materials – Design for disassembly in product manufacturing
Data Analytics and Predictive Modeling	– Data-driven decision-making – Proactive risk management	– Predictive models for environmental impact assessment – Advanced data visualization tools
Renewable Energy Integration	– Reduced carbon footprint – Energy cost savings	– AI optimization for renewable energy distribution – Hybrid energy storage solutions
Smart Manufacturing Technologies	– Industry 4.0 integration – Lean and efficient production	– Robotics and automation for sustainable manufacturing – Additive manufacturing advancements
Sustainable Supply Chain Innovations	– Ethical sourcing and procurement practices	– Supplier collaboration platforms for sustainability – Traceability of raw materials using IoT

continued on following page

Table 7. Continued

Trend Description	Anticipated Impact	Potential Breakthroughs
Advanced Materials and Bioengineering	– Eco-friendly materials development – Biodegradability and recyclability	– Nanotechnology for sustainable packaging materials – Biologically inspired design solutions
Regenerative Agriculture Practices	– Soil health restoration – Carbon sequestration	– Precision agriculture using IoT and AI – Closed-loop nutrient cycling systems

4. DISCUSSION

4.1 Integration of Digital Solutions in Industries

The integration of digital technologies across various industries marks a transformative shift aimed at enhancing operational efficiencies, sustainability practices, and customer experiences. In sectors spanning manufacturing, healthcare, transportation, energy, retail, finance, agriculture, construction, education, and telecommunications, organizations are strategically adopting technologies such as Internet of Things (IoT), artificial intelligence (AI), blockchain, and others to tackle industry-specific challenges and leverage emerging opportunities (Bibri & Krogstie, 2020; Elhazmiri et al., 2022). Manufacturing industries, for instance, are integrating IoT and AI-driven automation to streamline operations, enhance production efficiency, and reduce waste through predictive maintenance and robotic process automation (Kumar et al., 2022). Healthcare sectors leverage AI in diagnostics and telemedicine platforms to improve patient care quality and operational efficiency, utilizing electronic health records and remote monitoring devices (Francisco & Linnér, 2023). Transportation industries optimize logistics and reduce emissions with GPS tracking and predictive analytics, employing autonomous vehicles and route optimization software. In energy sectors, smart grids and IoT sensors enhance energy efficiency and facilitate sustainable practices, while blockchain technology supports transparent energy trading and management (Guo et al., 2024). Retail sectors benefit from e-commerce platforms and data analytics-driven marketing strategies to enhance customer experiences and optimize inventory management (Marti et al., 2023). Telecommunications sectors improve network efficiency with 5G networks and IoT connectivity, enabling advanced applications like edge computing and network slicing (Chin et al., 2024; Nguyen et al., 2023). Overall, the strategic integration of these digital solutions illustrates their pivotal role in shaping modern industrial landscapes, driving innovation, and fostering sustainable practices across diverse sectors. By leveraging these technologies, industries not only enhance their operational efficiencies but also contribute to broader sustainability goals and meet evolving consumer demands.

4.2 Challenges and Opportunities

Implementing technology-driven sustainability and quality control measures across industries presents multifaceted challenges and opportunities. Organizations face various challenges in implementing digital solutions to enhance efficiency, reduce environmental impacts, and ensure quality. These challenges include technical hurdles such as integrating legacy systems with new technologies, ensuring scalability and interoperability, and managing complex data ecosystems securely. Environmental challenges involve minimizing energy consumption, reducing electronic waste, and mitigating carbon footprints associated with digital infrastructure. Regulatory compliance and data security are also critical concerns, along with cultural resistance to change within organizations and among stakeholders. However, there are numerous opportunities for organizations to drive transformative change through technological advancements, improved operational efficiencies, enhanced data-driven decision-making capabilities, and innovative approaches to sustainability. Embracing digital transformation can help organizations streamline processes, optimize resource utilization, and develop resilient business models that integrate sustainability into their core operations.

4.3 Emerging Trends and Future Directions

Emerging trends in technology-driven sustainability and quality control are revolutionizing industries worldwide. Advancements in IoT, AI, blockchain, data analytics, renewable energy integration, smart manufacturing, sustainable supply chains, advanced materials, and regenerative agriculture are creating new opportunities for environmental stewardship and operational efficiency (Barresi, 2023; Guo et al., 2024). IoT technologies are evolving to enable interconnected smart systems that enhance real-time data collection and decision-making (Hosamo et al., 2023; Pan et al., 2022). AI algorithms are becoming more sophisticated, supporting predictive analytics and personalized customer experiences (Graser et al., 2023; Sharma et al., 2024). Blockchain technology holds promise for transparency and trust in supply chains (Ahmed & MacCarthy, 2023; Arsiwala et al., 2023). Data analytics are used to optimize processes and inform strategic decision-making (Pooyandeh & Sohn, 2023). Integration of renewable energy and smart manufacturing aims to improve energy efficiency (Kostner et al., 2023).

4.4 Differences Between the Current Investigation and Previous Studies

The current study distinguishes itself by providing a more integrated analysis of how these technologies are applied simultaneously across different industries, as opposed to previous studies that often focused on isolated technologies or single-industry applications. Previous literature typically addressed either sustainability or quality control in a segmented manner, while this review emphasizes the dual focus and synergy between sustainability and quality control measures. For example, previous studies on IoT may have focused solely on energy optimization, whereas this study also incorporates its real-time monitoring benefits for quality control. This difference highlights the research gap and underscores the need for a holistic approach to tech-driven sustainability.

4.5 Research Gap Clarification

Unlike previous studies that often look at individual technologies in isolation, this investigation addresses the intersection of digital solutions and their dual impact on both sustainability and quality control across multiple sectors. The review highlights the lack of cross-industry analyses of digital transformations that focus on both these aspects together. This research fills that gap by providing a comprehensive overview that links environmental impact assessments (EIAs) with operational optimizations across sectors such as manufacturing, healthcare, and agriculture. Furthermore, the absence of longitudinal studies in earlier literature that assess the long-term impacts of these technologies presents a research gap, which this investigation addresses by incorporating forward-looking trends and future directions in emerging technologies like AI and blockchain.

5. CONCLUSION

This review comprehensively examines the transformative impact of digital technologies on advancing sustainability and enhancing quality control across diverse industries. The analysis begins with a detailed exploration of pivotal technologies such as the Internet of Things (IoT), artificial intelligence (AI), blockchain, data analytics, and digital twins, emphasizing their strategic applications to optimize processes, improve operational efficiencies, and uphold stringent quality standards. These technologies are integrated across sectors including manufacturing, healthcare, transportation, energy, retail, finance, agriculture, construction, education, and telecommunications, highlighting their versatile applications. From enhancing supply chain transparency and optimizing logistics to revolutionizing patient care and enabling smart energy management, digital innovations drive significant advancements in sustainability practices and enhance customer experiences. Furthermore, the review underscores the importance of conducting robust environmental impact assessments (EIAs) to address environmental considerations associated with digital transformations, including energy consumption, emissions, and waste generation. Despite challenges such as technical integration complexities and regulatory barriers, the potential benefits of digital solutions in enhancing decision-making and operational efficiencies remain profound. Looking ahead, future research should explore emerging trends such as the integration of renewable energy sources, advancements in smart manufacturing, and the evolution of sustainable supply chains. Addressing these areas will further strengthen environmental stewardship and promote innovation in sustainable practices across industries. This review provides a comprehensive framework for understanding how digital technologies are reshaping industry landscapes, offering valuable insights for researchers, policymakers, and industry leaders to navigate and harness the full potential of technology-driven advancements in sustainability and quality control.

5.1 The Contribution

The contribution of this research lies in its comprehensive exploration and analysis of how digital technologies are fundamentally reshaping sustainability and quality control across diverse industries. By synthesizing current literature and empirical findings, this review provides a detailed understanding of the transformative impacts and applications of technologies such as Internet of Things (IoT), artificial intelligence (AI), blockchain, data analytics, and digital twins.

- Firstly, this study contributes by elucidating the diverse ways in which these technologies optimize operational processes, enhance efficiency, and ensure adherence to rigorous quality standards. From improving supply chain management and logistics in manufacturing to enhancing patient care through AI-driven diagnostics in healthcare, the review underscores the broad applicability and significant impact of digital solutions across sectors.
- Secondly, the research highlights critical environmental considerations associated with digital transformations, emphasizing the importance of conducting thorough environmental impact assessments (EIAs). By addressing energy consumption, emissions, and waste generation, the study underscores the imperative for sustainable practices in technological implementations.

– Moreover, this review identifies and discusses the challenges and opportunities inherent in adopting digital solutions, ranging from technical integration complexities to regulatory compliance issues. By outlining these challenges, the research provides insights into potential barriers and offers recommendations for overcoming them to maximize the benefits of technological advancements.
– Lastly, the exploration of emerging trends and future directions in charts a course for further research and innovation in areas such as renewable energy integration, smart manufacturing, and sustainable supply chains. By anticipating future developments, the study encourages ongoing dialogue and exploration into how technology can continue to drive positive change towards more sustainable and efficient industrial practices.

REFERENCES

Agyabeng-Mensah, Y., Tang, L., Afum, E., Baah, C., & Dacosta, E. (2021). Organisational identity and circular economy: Are inter and intra organisational learning, lean management and zero waste practices worth pursuing? *Sustainable Production and Consumption*, *28*, 648–662. Advance online publication. DOI: 10.1016/j.spc.2021.06.018

Ahmed, W. A. H., & MacCarthy, B. L. (2023). Blockchain-enabled supply chain traceability – How wide? How deep? *International Journal of Production Economics*, *263*, 108963. Advance online publication. DOI: 10.1016/j.ijpe.2023.108963

Akhtar, S., Tian, H., Alsedrah, I. T., Anwar, A., & Bashir, S. (2024). Green mining in China: Fintech's contribution to enhancing innovation performance aimed at sustainable and digital transformation in the mining sector. *Resources Policy*, *92*, 104968. Advance online publication. DOI: 10.1016/j.resourpol.2024.104968

Al-Emran, M., & Griffy-Brown, C. (2023). The role of technology adoption in sustainable development: Overview, opportunities, challenges, and future research agendas. *Technology in Society*, *73*, 102240. Advance online publication. DOI: 10.1016/j.techsoc.2023.102240

Alrammal, M., Abu-Amara, F., Ismail, Z., & Nadeem, M. (2023). Blockchain technology for sustainable management of electricity and water consumption. *Engineering Proceedings*. Advance online publication. DOI: 10.3390/engproc2023059223

Amoo, O. M., Fagbenle, R. O., & Oyewola, M. O. (2022). *Benchmark assessment of performance indices of a selection of hybrid nanofluids in a hybrid photovoltaic/thermal system*. Clean Energy., DOI: 10.1093/ce/zkac008

Ancín, M., Pindado, E., & Sánchez, M. (2022). New trends in the global digital transformation process of the agri-food sector: An exploratory study based on Twitter. *Agricultural Systems*, *209*, 103520. DOI: 10.1016/j.agsy.2022.103520

Anttila, H., Anttila, M., & Luoma, M.-L. (2022). A governmental programme to support well-being, ageing and care at home with new technologies. *Gerontechnology (Valkenswaard)*, *21*(s), 1. Advance online publication. DOI: 10.4017/gt.2022.21.s.725.opp7

Anwar, S., Lindgren, P., & Prasad, R. (2021). Collaborative strategies and socio-dynamic cues (SDC) insights for Assistive Healthcare Technology Applications. *Journal of Mobile Multimedia*. DOI: 10.13052/jmm1550-4646.171311

Argente García, J. E., Yazici, B., Richa, A., Touil, S., Richart Díaz, V. J., Ramallo-González, A. P., & Skarmeta Gómez, A. F. (2024). Digitalising governance processes and water resources management to foster sustainability strategies in the Mediterranean agriculture. *Environmental Science & Policy*, *158*, 103805. Advance online publication. DOI: 10.1016/j.envsci.2024.103805

Arsiwala, A., Elghaish, F., & Zoher, M. (2023). Digital twin with Machine learning for predictive monitoring of CO2 equivalent from existing buildings. *Energy and Building*, *284*, 112851. Advance online publication. DOI: 10.1016/j.enbuild.2023.112851

Asensio, J., Josa, I., Monserrat, A., & de la Fuente, A. (2023). 3D-printed concrete footbridges: An approach to assess the sustainability performance. *Structural Concrete*, *24*(6), 7705–7725. Advance online publication. DOI: 10.1002/suco.202201227

Barresi, A. (2023). Urban Digital Twin and urban planning for sustainable cities. *Techne : Journal of Technology for Architecture and Environment*, (25), 78–83. Advance online publication. DOI: 10.36253/techne-13568

Basova, Y., Dobrotvorskiy, S., Balog, M., Iakovets, A., Chelabi, M. A., & Zinchenko, A. (2023). Increasing SME supply chain resilience in the face of rapidly changing demand with 3D model visualisation. *International Journal of Mechatronics and Applied Mechanics*, *14*(5). Advance online publication. DOI: 10.17683/ijomam/issue14.5

Bibri, S. E., & Krogstie, J. (2020). Environmentally data-driven smart sustainable cities: Applied innovative solutions for energy efficiency, pollution reduction, and urban metabolism. *Energy Informatics*, *3*(1), 1–20. DOI: 10.1186/s42162-020-00130-8

Bonilla, C., Brentan, B., Montalvo, I., Ayala-Cabrera, D., & Izquierdo, J. (2023). Digitalization of water distribution systems in small cities, a tool for verification and hydraulic analysis: A case study of Pamplona, Colombia. *Water (Switzerland)*. Advance online publication. DOI: 10.3390/w15213824

Büyüközkan, G., & Uztürk, D. (2024). Integrated design framework for smart agriculture: Bridging the gap between digitalization and sustainability. *Journal of Cleaner Production*, *449*, 141572. Advance online publication. DOI: 10.1016/j.jclepro.2024.141572

Chen, L., Li, X., & Zhu, J. (2024). Carbon peak control for achieving net-zero renewable-based smart cities: Digital twin modeling and simulation. *Sustainable Energy Technologies and Assessments*, *65*, 103792. Advance online publication. DOI: 10.1016/j.seta.2024.103792

Chin, S.-W., Rubambiza, G., Zhao, Y., Malek, K., & Weatherspoon, H. (2024). Realtime optimization and management system (ROAM): A decision support system for digital agriculture systems. *Smart Agricultural Technology*, *8*, 100452. Advance online publication. DOI: 10.1016/j.atech.2024.100452

Colangelo, G. (2022). Enforcing copyright through antitrust? The strange case of news publishers against digital platforms. *Journal of Antitrust Enforcement*. Advance online publication. DOI: 10.1093/jaenfo/jnab009

Danys, L., Zolotova, I., Romero, D., Papcun, P., Kajati, E., Jaros, R., Koudelka, P., Koziorek, J., & Martinek, R. (2022). Visible Light Communication and localization: A study on tracking solutions for Industry 4.0 and the Operator 4.0. *Journal of Manufacturing Systems*, *64*, 535–545. Advance online publication. DOI: 10.1016/j.jmsy.2022.07.011

Dudhat, A., Lestari Santoso, N. P., Santoso, S., & Setiawati, R. (2021). Blockchain in Indonesia University: A Design Viewboard of Digital Technology Education. *APTISI Transactions on Technopreneurship*, *3*(1), 68–80. Advance online publication. DOI: 10.34306/att.v3i1.146

Elhazmiri, B., Naveed, N., Anwar, M. N., & Haq, M. I. U. (2022). The role of additive manufacturing in industry 4.0: An exploration of different business models. *Sustainable Operations and Computers*. Advance online publication. DOI: 10.1016/j.susoc.2022.07.001

Fernández-Miguel, A., García-Muiña, F. E., Jiménez-Calzado, M., Melara San Román, P., Fernández del Hoyo, A. P., & Settembre-Blundo, D. (2024). Boosting business agility with additive digital molding: An Industry 5.0 approach to sustainable supply chains. *Computers & Industrial Engineering*, *192*, 110222. Advance online publication. DOI: 10.1016/j.cie.2024.110222

Francisco, M., & Linnér, B.-O. (2023). AI and the governance of sustainable development: An idea analysis of the European Union, the United Nations, and the World Economic Forum. Environmental Science and Policy. Advance online publication. DOI: 10.1016/j.envsci.2023.103590

Graser, K., Walzer, A. N., Hunhevicz, J., Jähne, R., Seiler, F., Wüst, R., & Hall, D. M. (2023). Qualitative technology evaluation of digital fabrication with concrete: Conceptual framework and scoreboard. *Automation in Construction*, *154*, 104964. Advance online publication. DOI: 10.1016/j.autcon.2023.104964

Guo, Y., Tang, Q., Darkwa, J., Wang, H., Su, W., Tang, D., & Mu, J. (2024). Multi-objective integrated optimization of geothermal heating system with energy storage using digital twin technology. *Applied Thermal Engineering*, *252*, 123685. Advance online publication. DOI: 10.1016/j.applthermaleng.2024.123685

Hakobyan, L., Monforte-Gómez, B., Moliner-Martínez, Y., Molins-Legua, C., & Campíns-Falcó, P. (2022). Improving sustainability of the Griess reaction by reagent stabilization on PDMS membranes and ZnNPs as reductor of nitrates: Application to different water samples. *Polymers*, *14*(3), 464. Advance online publication. DOI: 10.3390/polym14030464 PMID: 35160454

Hamalainen, M., & Salmi, A. (2023). Digital transformation in a cross-laminated timber business network. *Journal of Business and Industrial Marketing*, *38*(6), 1251–1265. Advance online publication. DOI: 10.1108/JBIM-01-2022-0003

Hassanin, M. A., Salem, A. E., Helal, M. Y., Elshawarbi, N. N., Ahmed, I. S., & Mansour, N. (2023). The power of integration towards sustainable performance: A model to minimize technostress among frontline restaurant employees by combining job and employee resources. *Geo Journal of Tourism and Geosites*, *49*(3), 934–945. Advance online publication. DOI: 10.30892/gtg.49310-1094

Heidenstrøm, N., & Hebrok, M. (2022). Towards realizing the sustainability potential within digital food provisioning platforms: The case of meal box schemes and online grocery shopping in Norway. *Sustainable Production and Consumption*, *29*, 831–850. Advance online publication. DOI: 10.1016/j.spc.2021.06.030

Heikkilä, M., Saarni, J., & Saurama, A. (2022). Innovation in Smart Ports: Future Directions of Digitalization in Container Ports. *Journal of Marine Science and Engineering*, *10*(12), 1925. Advance online publication. DOI: 10.3390/jmse10121925

Heinonen, H. T., Semenov, A., Veijalainen, J., & Hamalainen, T. (2022). *A survey on technologies which make Bitcoin greener or more justified*. IEEE., DOI: 10.1109/ACCESS.2022.3190891

Hodson, J., Dale, A., Jost, F., & Clifton-Ross, J. (2020). Sustainability issue communication and student social media engagement: Recommendations for climate communicators. *Journal of Digital and Social Media Marketing*, *8*(3), 221–234. DOI: 10.69554/LIHR6053

Hoosain, M. S., Paul, B. S., Doorsamy, W., & Ramakrishna, S. (2023). The influence of circular economy and 4IR technologies on the climate–water–energy–food nexus and the SDGs. *Water (Basel)*, *15*(4), 787. Advance online publication. DOI: 10.3390/w15040787

Hoosain, M. S., Paul, B. S., Kass, S., & Ramakrishna, S. (2023). Tools Towards the Sustainability and Circularity of Data Centers. *Circular Economy and Sustainability, 3*(1), 173–197. Advance online publication. DOI: 10.1007/s43615-022-00191-9 PMID: 35791435

Hosamo, H. H., Nielsen, H. K., Kraniotis, D., Svennevig, P. R., & Svidt, K. (2023). Digital Twin framework for automated fault source detection and prediction for comfort performance evaluation of existing non-residential Norwegian buildings. *Energy and Building, 281*, 112732. Advance online publication. DOI: 10.1016/j.enbuild.2022.112732

Imtiaz, N. M., Subramaniam, M., & Sathiyasekar, K. (2023). Enhancing Cloud Security through Asymmetrical AES-EDDSA and Hyperledger Integration Algorithms for Environmental Sustainability. *Journal of Environmental Protection and Ecology*. Advance online publication. DOI: 10.1007/s11356-022-21699-5

Jin, T., & Han, X. (2024). Robotic arms in precision agriculture: A comprehensive review of the technologies, applications, challenges, and future prospects. *Computers and Electronics in Agriculture, 221*, 108938. Advance online publication. DOI: 10.1016/j.compag.2024.108938

Knapskog, M., & Browne, M. (2022). Sensors securing sustainable digital urban logistics—A practitioner's perspective. *Frontiers in Future Transportation*. Advance online publication. DOI: 10.3389/ffutr.2022.993411

Ko, L. S. C., Moro, S., Bury, J., Vickers, T., Sachsenhauser, B., & Mönnig, S. (2021). Rheology and setting control of concrete for digital construction. *ACI Materials Journal, 118*(4), 43–54. DOI: 10.14359/51733121

Kofos, A., Ubacht, J., Rukanova, B., Korevaar, G., Kouwenhoven, N., & Tan, Y.-H. (2022). Circular economy visibility evaluation framework. *Journal of Responsible Technology, 10*, 100026. Advance online publication. DOI: 10.1016/j.jrt.2022.100026

Koltsios, S., Fokaides, P., Georgali, P.-Z., Tsolakis, A. C., Chatzipanagiotidou, P., Klumbytė, E., Jurelionis, A., Šeduikytė, L., Kontopoulos, C., Malavazos, C., Panteli, C., Sušnik, M., Cebrat, G., Ioannidis, D., & Tzovaras, D. (2022). An enhanced framework for next-generation operational buildings energy performance certificates. *International Journal of Energy Research, 46*(14), 12543–12563. DOI: 10.1002/er.8517

Korucuk, S., Aytekin, A., Ecer, F., Karamaşa, Ç., & Zavadskas, E. K. (2022). Assessing Green Approaches and Digital Marketing Strategies for Twin Transition via Fermatean Fuzzy SWARA-COPRAS. *Axioms, 11*(12), 709. DOI: 10.3390/axioms11120709

Kostner, M. K., Zanfei, A., Alberizzi, J. C., Renzi, M., Righetti, M., & Menapace, A. (2023). Micro hydro power generation in water distribution networks through the optimal pumps-as-turbines sizing and control. *Applied Energy*, *351*, 121802. Advance online publication. DOI: 10.1016/j.apenergy.2023.121802

Koutsovili, E. I., Tzoraki, O., Kalli, A. A., Provatas, S., & Gaganis, P. (2023). Participatory approaches for planning nature-based solutions in flood vulnerable landscapes. *Environmental Science & Policy*, *140*, 12–23. Advance online publication. DOI: 10.1016/j.envsci.2022.11.012

Kranz, J., Zeiss, R., Beck, R., Gholami, R., Sarker, S., Watson, R. T., & Whitley, E. A. (2022). Practicing what we preach? Reflections on more sustainable and responsible IS research and teaching practices. *Communications of the Association for Information Systems*, *49*(1), 115–132. DOI: 10.17705/1CAIS.05138

Kumar, V., Vrat, P., & Shankar, R. (2022). *Factors Influencing the Implementation of Industry 4.0 for Sustainability in Manufacturing*. Global Journal of Flexible Systems Management., DOI: 10.1007/s40171-022-00312-1

Kurniawan, T. A., Othman, M. H. D., Liang, X., Goh, H. H., Gikas, P., Kusworo, T. D., Anouzla, A., & Chew, K. W. (2023). Decarbonization in waste recycling industry using digitalization to promote net-zero emissions and its implications on sustainability. *Journal of Environmental Management*, *338*, 117765. Advance online publication. DOI: 10.1016/j.jenvman.2023.117765 PMID: 36965421

Lahane, S., Paliwal, V., & Kant, R. (2023). Evaluation and ranking of solutions to overcome the barriers of Industry 4.0 enabled sustainable food supply chain adoption. Cleaner Logistics and Supply Chain. Advance online publication. DOI: 10.1016/j.clscn.2023.100116

Larrinaga, F., Pérez, A., Aldalur, I., Hernández, J. L., Izkara, J. L., & de Viteri, P. S. (2021). A holistic and interoperable approach towards the implementation of services for the digital transformation of smart cities: The case of Vitoria-Gasteiz (Spain). *Sensors (Basel)*, *21*(23), 8061. Advance online publication. DOI: 10.3390/s21238061 PMID: 34884064

Lazaroiu, A. C., Roscia, M., Dancu, V. S., & Balaban, G. (2024). Social impact of decarbonization objectives through smart homes: Survey and analysis. *Renewable Energy*, *230*, 120872. Advance online publication. DOI: 10.1016/j.renene.2024.120872

Li, S., Zhou, T., Yang, H., & Wang, P. (2023). Blockchain-based secure storage and access control scheme for supply chain ecological business data: A case study of the automotive industry. *Sensors (Basel)*, *23*(16), 7036. Advance online publication. DOI: 10.3390/s23167036 PMID: 37631574

Li, Y., Chung, S.-H., Wen, X., & Zhou, S. (2023). Towards the sustainable economy through digital technology: A drone-aided after-sales service scheduling model. *Applied Soft Computing*, *138*, 110202. Advance online publication. DOI: 10.1016/j.asoc.2023.110202

Linton, J. D., & Walsh, J. P. (2008). The open source movement in commercial software: A game theoretic analysis. *Management Science*, *54*(7), 1301–1315. DOI: 10.1287/mnsc.1070.0856

Lisnawati, L., Aryati, T., & Gunawan, J. (2024). Implementation of digital innovation on sustainability performance: The moderating role of green accounting in the industrial sector. *Eastern-European Journal of Enterprise Technologies*. DOI: 10.15587/1729-4061.2024.298639

Mahdiraji, H. A., Yaftiyan, F., Abbasi-Kamardi, A., Jafari-Sadeghi, V., Sahut, J.-M., & Dana, L.-P. (2023). A synthesis of boundary conditions with adopting digital platforms in SMEs: An intuitionistic multi-layer decision-making framework. *The Journal of Technology Transfer*, *48*(5), 1723–1751. Advance online publication. DOI: 10.1007/s10961-023-10028-8

Marti, P., Massari, S., & Recupero, A. (2023). *Transformational design for food systems: Cultural, social and technological challenges*. International Journal of Food Design., DOI: 10.1386/ijfd_00053_1

Marzouk, M., Ayman, R., Alwan, Z., & Elshaboury, N. (2022). Green building system integration into project delivery utilising BIM. *Environment, Development and Sustainability*, *24*(5), 6467–6480. Advance online publication. DOI: 10.1007/s10668-021-01712-6

Medoh, C. N., & Telukdarie, A. (2020). Logistics optimisation: A cyber physical model. *International Journal of Business Analytics*, *7*(1), 66–79. DOI: 10.4018/IJBAN.2020010104

Molari, L., Coppolino, F. S., & García, J. J. (2021). Arundo donax: A widespread plant with great potential as sustainable structural material. *Construction & Building Materials*, *268*, 121143. Advance online publication. DOI: 10.1016/j.conbuildmat.2020.121143

Montalbano, G., & Santi, G. (2023). Sustainability of Temporary Housing in Post-Disaster Scenarios: A Requirement-Based Design Strategy. *Buildings (Basel, Switzerland)*, *13*(12), 2952. DOI: 10.3390/buildings13122952

Mukarram, M. M. T., Kafy, A.-A., Mukarram, M. M. T., Rukiya, Q. U., Almulhim, A. I., Das, A., Fattah, M. A., Rahman, M. T., & Chowdhury, M. A. (2023). Perception of coastal citizens on the prospect of community-based rainwater harvesting system for sustainable water resource management. *Resources, Conservation and Recycling*, *198*, 107196. Advance online publication. DOI: 10.1016/j.resconrec.2023.107196

Mynko, O., Bonheure, M., Amghizar, I., Brown, D. J., Chen, L., Marin, G. B., Freitas de Alvarenga, R., Civancik Uslu, D., Dewulf, J., & Van Geem, K. M. (2023). Electrification of steam cracking as a pathway to reduce the impact of the petrochemical industry on climate change. *Journal of Cleaner Production*, *427*, 139208. Advance online publication. DOI: 10.1016/j.jclepro.2023.139208

Nambisan, S. (2009). Platforms for collaboration: The case of the virtual worlds industry. *Academy of Management Review*, *34*(1), 32–49. DOI: 10.5465/amr.2009.35732578

Nguyen, T. P., Nguyen, H., & Ngo, H. Q. T. (2023). Toward a sustainable transition in automated production: Enabling the vision-based approach and synchronous control for textile surface inspection systems. *Textile Research Journal*, *93*(23-24), 5391–5415. Advance online publication. DOI: 10.1177/00405175231199257

Ntamo, D., Lopez-Montero, E., Mack, J., Omar, C., Highett, M. I., Moss, D., Mitchell, N., Soulatintork, P., Moghadam, P. Z., & Zandi, M. (2022). Industry 4.0 in action: Digitalisation of a continuous process manufacturing for formulated products. *Digital Chemical Engineering*, *3*, 100025. Advance online publication. DOI: 10.1016/j.dche.2022.100025

Nuutinen, M., Kaasinen, E., Hyvärinen, J., Mölsä, A., & Siltanen, S. (2022). *Making a building smart with a co-created and continuously evolving enjoyable service entity—Insights from a collaborative study*. Smart Cities., DOI: 10.3390/smartcities5010001

Obaideen, K., Albasha, L., Iqbal, U., & Mir, H. (2024). *Wireless power transfer: Applications, challenges, barriers, and the role of AI in achieving sustainable development goals - A bibliometric analysis*. Energy Strategy Reviews., DOI: 10.1016/j.esr.2024.101376

Okumus, D., Gunbeyaz, S. A., Kurt, R. E., & Turan, O. (2024). An Approach to Advance Circular Practices in the Maritime Industry through a Database as a Bridging Solution. *Sustainability (Basel)*, *16*(1), 453. Advance online publication. DOI: 10.3390/su16010453

Otto, D., & Kerres, M. (2022). Increasing sustainability in open learning: Prospects of a distributed learning ecosystem for open educational resources. *Frontiers in Education*, *7*, 866917. Advance online publication. DOI: 10.3389/feduc.2022.866917

Owida, A., Galal, N. M., & Elrafie, A. (2022). Decision-making framework for a resilient sustainable production system during COVID-19: An evidence-based research. *Computers & Industrial Engineering*, *164*, 107905. Advance online publication. DOI: 10.1016/j.cie.2021.107905 PMID: 34975207

Pan, S. L., Carter, L., Tim, Y., & Sandeep, M. S. (2022). Digital sustainability, climate change, and information systems solutions: Opportunities for future research. *International Journal of Information Management*, *63*, 102444. Advance online publication. DOI: 10.1016/j.ijinfomgt.2021.102444

Parhi, S., Joshi, K., Gunasekaran, A., & Sethuraman, K. (2022). Reflecting on an empirical study of the digitalization initiatives for sustainability on logistics: The concept of sustainable logistics 4.0. *Cleaner Logistics and Supply Chain*. DOI: 10.1016/j.clscn.2022.100058

Pooyandeh, M., & Sohn, I. (2023). Smart Lithium-Ion Battery Monitoring in Electric Vehicles: An AI-Empowered Digital Twin Approach. *Mathematics*, *11*(23), 4865. Advance online publication. DOI: 10.3390/math11234865

Pu, G., Wong, W.-K., Du, Q., Al Shraah, A., Alromaihi, A., & Muda, I. (2024). Asymmetric impact of natural resources, fintech, and digital banking on climate change and environmental sustainability in BRICS countries. *Resources Policy*, *91*, 104872. Advance online publication. DOI: 10.1016/j.resourpol.2024.104872

Ramesh Kumar, C., & Chitra, M. P. (2022). Design and implementation of pipelined SDF FFT architecture for sustainable industrial noise suppression in digital hearing aids. *Sustainable Energy Technologies and Assessments*, *49*, 101858. Advance online publication. DOI: 10.1016/j.seta.2021.101858

Rashed, A., & Mutis, I. (2023). Trends of integrated project delivery implementations viewed from an emerging innovation framework. *Engineering, Construction, and Architectural Management*, *30*(3), 989–1014. Advance online publication. DOI: 10.1108/ECAM-06-2021-0516

Rashid, N. (2020). Meeting refinery wastewater challenges through membrane-based biological treatment complemented by an integrated asset sustainability program. *Desalination and Water Treatment*, *176*, 18–23. Advance online publication. DOI: 10.5004/dwt.2020.25489

Ritala, P., & Hurmelinna-Laukkanen, P. (2013). Incremental and radical innovation in coopetition—The role of absorptive capacity and appropriability. *Journal of Product Innovation Management, 30*(1), 154–169. DOI: 10.1111/j.1540-5885.2012.00956.x

Röck, M., Passer, A., & Allacker, K. (2024). SLiCE: An open building data model for scalable high-definition life cycle engineering, dynamic impact assessment, and systematic hotspot analysis. *Sustainable Production and Consumption, 45*, 450–463. Advance online publication. DOI: 10.1016/j.spc.2024.01.005

Rumetshofer, T., Straka, K., & Fischer, J. (2024). How the digital product passport can lead the plastics industry towards a circular economy—A case study from bottle caps to frisbees. *Polymers, 16*(10), 1420. Advance online publication. DOI: 10.3390/polym16101420 PMID: 38794613

Sá, P., Silva, P. C., Peixinho, J., Figueiras, A., & Rodrigues, A. V. (2023). Sustainability at play: Educational design research for the development of a digital educational resource for primary education. *Social Sciences (Basel, Switzerland), 12*(7), 407. Advance online publication. DOI: 10.3390/socsci12070407

Sadanand, A., Nagarajan, R. V., & Devadas, M. (2021). The façade wall: A focus on the green architecture of Laurie Baker's houses. *International Journal of Energy Production and Management, 6*(3), 277–293. Advance online publication. DOI: 10.2495/EQ-V6-N3-277-293

Salmon, D., Babbitt, C. W., Babbitt, G. A., & Wilmer, C. E. (2021). A framework for modeling fraud in E-waste management. *Resources, Conservation and Recycling, 169*, 105613. Advance online publication. DOI: 10.1016/j.resconrec.2021.105613

San Cornelio, G., Martorell, S., & Ardèvol, E. (2023). "My goal is to make sustainability mainstream": Emerging visual narratives on the environmental crisis on Instagram. *Frontiers in Communication*. Advance online publication. DOI: 10.3389/fcomm.2023.1265466

Saurette, D. D., Heck, R. J., Gillespie, A. W., Berg, A. A., & Biswas, A. (2024). Sample Size Optimization for Digital Soil Mapping: An Empirical Example. *Land (Basel), 13*(3), 365. Advance online publication. DOI: 10.3390/land13030365

Schmidt, D., Casagranda, L. F., Butturi, M. A., & Sellitto, M. A. (2024). Digital Technologies, Sustainability, and Efficiency in Grain Post-Harvest Activities: A Bibliometric Analysis. *Sustainability (Basel), 16*(3), 1244. Advance online publication. DOI: 10.3390/su16031244

Sharma, A., & Kumar Tiwari, M. (2023). Digital twin design and analytics for scaling up electric vehicle battery production using robots. *International Journal of Production Research*, *61*(24), 8512–8546. Advance online publication. DOI: 10.1080/00207543.2022.2152896

Sharma, K., Kumar, R., Kumar, A., Balabantaray, S., & Arora, M. (2024). A digital ecosystem for sustainable fruit supply chain in Uttarakhand: A comprehensive review. *Environment, Development and Sustainability*. Advance online publication. DOI: 10.1007/s10668-023-04142-8

Sharma, M., Joshi, S., & Govindan, K. (2023). Overcoming barriers to implement digital technologies to achieve sustainable production and consumption in the food sector: A circular economy perspective. *Sustainable Production and Consumption*, *39*, 203–215. Advance online publication. DOI: 10.1016/j.spc.2023.04.002

Shui, T., Hu, J., Yang, K., Kang, H., Rui, H., & Wang, B. (2023). Cell-Free Networking for Integrated Data and Energy Transfer: Digital Twin Based Double Parameterized DQN for Energy Sustainability. *IEEE Transactions on Wireless Communications*, *22*(11), 8035–8049. Advance online publication. DOI: 10.1109/TWC.2023.3258143

Chapter 2
Digitalization of Management Control:
Case of Moroccan Companies

Azzouz Elhamma
https://orcid.org/0000-0003-3382-0278
Ibn Tofaîl University, Morocco

ABSTRACT

In recent years, particularly with the widespread adoption of the Internet, digitalization has become a significant challenge for companies across various sectors. While some research studies have explored the potential impacts of digitalization on areas such as logistics and human resources, there has been a notable absence of similar investigations in the field of management control. In this context, this chapter examines the level of digitalization maturity in management control among forty-two Moroccan companies. This study has three main findings. First, the management control systems of the companies surveyed are "moderately" digitalized. Second, the age of the companies does not significantly affect this level of digitalization. Third, legal affiliation significantly influences the digitalization of management control; specifically, management control systems are more digitalized in subsidiaries of foreign groups compared to those of Moroccan groups or independent companies. This research work makes important contributions at both the theoretical and managerial levels.

DOI: 10.4018/979-8-3693-4373-9.ch002

1. INTRODUCTION

Certainly, with the emergence and widespread adoption of the Internet, digital technology has permeated both our professional and personal worlds. According to the international agency "We Are Social" and the "Hootsuite platform," as of the beginning of 2023, there are 5.44 billion Internet users worldwide (68% of the global population), with 4.76 billion using social media. In Morocco, according to Global Web Index, the number of social media users reached 22.5 million in 2020, representing a penetration rate of 49%. Moroccans spend an average of 2 hours and 25 minutes on these social networks.

In the business world, the emergence and development of the Internet has led to a profound transformation of the production system, commonly referred to as the "digitalization of the economy", "digitalization" or "digitalization transformation". According to Cavelius et al. (2018), a digital company can be defined as "one that has integrated innovative digital tools such as Big Data, artificial intelligence, dematerialized IT systems, social networks, and the Internet of Things into its daily operations". Bos (2018) defined digital transformation as "the adoption of readily available technological skills that transform the organization's responsiveness to market changes". The positive effects of digitalization on business performance have been studied by recent researches and surveys. According to a survey conducted by The Economist Intelligence Unit in collaboration with DXC Technology among 621 companies with annual sales exceeding $500 million, 68% of respondents reported increased annual profitability following the implementation of digitalization technologies. Additionally, a 2018 survey by the Banque de France indicated that the employment of information and communication technology (ICT) specialists and the adoption of digital technologies such as cloud computing and big data have improved labor productivity by approximately 23% and overall factor productivity by around 17%. According to Benga and Elhamma (2024), "digitalization offers tremendous opportunities for improving efficiency, speed, and quality of work, reducing costs, enhancing asset utilization, and optimizing the use of raw materials, labor, and other key aspects of business performance" (Benga and Elhamma, 2024, p. 110).

Aware of the benefits of digitalization, and aiming to position itself as an emerging country in terms of the digital economy and NICTs (New Information and Communication Technologies), Morocco has adopted several measures and plans. In 2009, the 'Maroc Numeric 2013' plan was adopted, which significantly contributed to the establishment of several online administrative service sites. In 2016, Morocco adopted 'Maroc Digital 2020', which aimed to achieve some additional objectives.

In the field of companies, digitalization affects all departments and functions, including marketing, Human Resources (HR), logistics, etc. In financial services, digitalization facilitates the collection, processing, and production of data. To better understand the use of digitalization in these departments, some research studies have been conducted in recent years (Vasarhelyi et al., 2015; Pan and Seow, 2016; Al-Htaybat and von Alberti-Alhtaybat, 2017; Cavelius et al., 2018; etc.). However, there remains a significant gap in research concerning the digitalization of management control (Elhamma and El-Moumane, 2023).

In this context, this present study aims to highlight the digitalization of management control in forty-two companies based in Morocco. Therefore, we will attempt to answer the two following questions: First, how can we assess the degree of digitalization of management control in Moroccan companies? In other words, can we speak of a certain digital "maturity" of management control in the studied companies? Second, do the age of the companies and their legal status impact the degree of digitalization of management control? The main results of this research indicate that management control systems are moderately digitalized. Additionally, the age of companies does not significantly impact this level of digitalization. However, legal affiliation does have an impact: subsidiaries of foreign groups adopt more advanced digital management control systems compared to subsidiaries of Moroccan groups or independent companies.

The results of the current study contribute to the existing literature on the level of digitalization in management control and the potential impact of company age and legal affiliation on this digitalization. This research is also highly relevant for policymakers in independent Moroccan firms. Several measures need to be implemented to strengthen the digitalization of their management control systems, enabling them to compete more effectively with subsidiaries of foreign groups.

The paper is structured as follows. Section 2 presents the conceptual framework and summarizes previous literature reviews on related topics. Section 3 describes our theoretical and methodological approaches. The results are presented in Section 4. Finally, Section 5 concludes the paper by synthesizing the main contributions and implications, acknowledging the study's limitations, and proposing new avenues for future research.

2. CONCEPTUAL FRAMEWORK AND LITERATURE REVIEW

In this section, we will define the two main concepts of this research: management control (2.1) and digitalization (2.2). We will then review previous research on the digitalization of management control (2.3).

2.1. What is Management Control?

Since its emergence and development in the 1920s at General Motors, management control has proven difficult to define. Surprisingly, there is still no universally accepted definition (Elhamma, 2011). The most widely cited formal definition remains that given by Robert Anthony in the early 1960s, who defined management control as "the process by which management ensures that resources are obtained and used effectively (in relation to objectives) and efficiently (in relation to the means employed) to achieve the organization's objectives." (Anthony, 1965). According to this definition, management control involves, first, setting objectives, usually derived from the strategy, and second, verifying that resources have been used effectively to achieve these objectives and efficiently to minimize the production factors required. Essentially, management control focuses on avoiding waste. This definition reflects an accounting-centric view of management control, focusing primarily on mechanical operations and overlooking the strategic and operational aspects of the organization. This limitation led Robert Anthony to redefine management control in 1988 as follows: "Management control is the process by which managers influence other members of the organization to implement the organization's strategies" (Anthony, 1988).

Management control operates in three phases (Elhamma, 2011). The first phase occurs prior to action and involves setting goals and translating them into quantified objectives over a specific timeframe (usually one year). The second phase concerns the implementation of the action, which includes monitoring progress and proposing corrective measures in the event of deviations; this is often referred to as the "steering" phase. The third phase takes place once the planned action has been completed and is commonly known as "post-evaluation." To carry out these functions, management control employs several tools. The most important of these are the costing system (management accounting), the budgeting system, and performance measurement systems (dashboards).

- Costing system (management accounting): Management accounting emerged from the need for companies to understand their production costs amid increasing competition. The French Chart of Accounts defines a cost as "the sum of charges related to an item defined within the accounting framework." Costing plays a crucial role in modern business management. According to Gervais (2000), "knowledge of the full cost of products bought, manufactured, or sold is essential for running a business and controlling its management". Since the 1980s, various research studies have questioned the traditional methods of management accounting. Numerous books and specialized articles have highlighted the inadequacies, limitations, and even irrelevance of these methods. In response, the ABC (activity-based costing) model was developed. According to Elhamma (2013, 2015), its success is attributed to the fact that the information provided by this model possesses characteristics of "relevance" and "reliability."

- Budgetary system: According to several authors, the budgetary system is one of the most criticized tools in management control. Despite these criticisms, it remains a central element in this type of control, and studies on potential replacements have been unconvincing. The budget can be defined as "a quantified document that consolidates the objectives and resources of an entity into a single place" (Sponem, 2002). Budget systems serve several roles. According to Bouquin (2001), these roles primarily include management planning, delegation and motivation, coordination, and communication.
- Performance measurement systems (dashboards): A dashboard can be defined as "a communication and decision-making tool that enables the management controller to highlight key aspects of management to the manager in order to improve it" (Alazard and Sépari, 2001, p.591). Research on this management control tool remains limited, even in the USA and Europe (Bescos and Cauvin, 2004). Dashboards consist of indicators that provide precise, useful, and relevant information for the manager. Traditionally, dashboards have contained only financial information. This limitation has led to the development of several alternative models, including the balanced scorecard (Elhamma, 2014). According to Kaplan and Norton (1992), "the balanced scorecard includes financial measures that provide information on the results of actions already undertaken, and it complements these financial measures with operational metrics related to customer satisfaction, internal processes, and organizational improvement and innovation activities."

In Morocco, several research studies have been conducted to understand the various management control systems used by Moroccan companies. These studies have primarily focused on cost calculation systems (Elhamma, 2012; Elhamma and Zhang, 2013), budgetary systems (Elhamma, 2015; Elhamma and Lassaad, 2017) and performance measurement systems (Elhamma, 2014; Achibane and Elhamma, 2016; Elhamma, 2023). The main findings indicate that the predominant tools implemented are based on the French model (Elhamma and Moalla, 2015). However, in recent years, there has been a growing adoption of modern tools, such as the ABC method and the balanced scorecard.

2.2. What is Digitalization?

For several years, digitalization has been considered a major innovation. Cazals (2015) identifies five periods of major technological innovation. From 1785 to 1845, the dominant technologies were hydraulic power, textiles, and iron. From 1845 to 1900, the focus shifted to the steam engine, railroads, and steel. Between 1900 and 1950, key innovations included electricity, the internal combustion engine, and chemistry. The period from 1950 to 1990 was marked by advancements in petro-chemicals, electronics, and aviation. Finally, from the 1990s onwards, computing, the internet, and telecommunications have become the leading innovative sectors. In our view, with the emergence of artificial intelligence (AI), big data, and the Internet of Things, we are now entering a sixth period characterized by the beginning of a new era of digitalization driven by AI.

The terms "digital," "digitalization," and "digital transformation" have become prevalent in managerial vocabulary since the mid-2010s. Firms are constantly urged to adopt digital technologies and adapt their business models to this new situation. According to Dudézert (2018), digitalization encompasses "a comprehensive transformation process for the company, leading it to reassess its methods of collaborating with customers, its internal work processes, and sometimes even its business model". According to Clerck (2017), digitalization is defined as "the use of digital technologies and of data in order to create revenue, improve business, replace/transform business processes and create an environment for digital business, whereby digital information is at the core". Srai and Lorentz (2019), digitalization is defined as "the way many domains of social life are restructured around digital communication and media infrastructures. In simple terms, digitalization may be defined as the use of digital technologies". Reis et al. (2020), digitalization is "the phenomenon of transforming analogue data into digital language (i.e. digitization), which, in turn, can improve business relationships between customer and companies, bringing added value to the whole economy and society".

Over the last few decades, several research studies have examined the benefits and advantages of digitalization for companies. According to Westerman et al. (2014, p. 33), digital tools enable companies to achieve objectives such as "getting closer to their customers, empowering their employees, and transforming their operational processes". In Morocco, a survey conducted by the "Association des Utilisateurs des Systèmes d'Information Au Maroc" (AUSIM) in 2019 found that 57% of respondents reported digitalization enables "better customer service", 30.2% cited "improved processes", and 10.5% noted "time savings".

In view of all these advantages, and to position itself as an emerging country in terms of information and communication technology, Morocco adopted a five-year program in 2009, known as the "Maroc Numeric 2013" plan. This plan focused mainly on the following areas: high-speed Internet, e-government, development of the local IT sector, and computerization of small and medium-sized enterprises (SMEs). In 2016, the Moroccan government launched the "Maroc Digital 2020" plan, a four-year strategic initiative aimed at advancing digitalization and NICTs in the country. The plan aimed to dematerialize 50% of administrative procedures, connect 20% of SMEs to the Internet, and promote the use of new technologies.

In front of these Moroccan efforts, a survey conducted by the "Association des Utilisateurs des Systèmes d'Information Au Maroc" (AUSIM) (2019) shows that digitalization is a major concern for companies. 93% of respondents confirmed that their companies are already engaged in the digitalization process, and 73.3% believe that they have the necessary resources to carry out this project. 64% of respondents stated that the digital transformation process is underway in their company. However, only 16.3% feel that their companies are well advanced in this process.

2.3. Digitalization of management control

For several years now, like all other facets of organizational management (HRM, marketing, finance, etc.), management control has been strongly influenced by what is known as digitalization or digital transformation. According to a survey carried out by the International Management Control Observatory (DFCG, 2016), 60% of respondents consider the management controller to be active, as a contributor or leader, in their company's digital transformation projects. According to this survey, digitalization entails changes to tools (57%), processes (53%), and consistency capabilities (52%). Fähndrich (2023) showed that "multiple studies highlight the continuous development of the MC (Management Control) function under the impact of digitalisation, including the extension of MC tasks, the adaptation of existing MC instruments and creation of new MC instruments, positive and negative behavioural aspects of digitalisation on MC and the establishment of new MC organisation models". This digitalization impacts all management control tools, including management accounting (Appelbaum et al., 2017), budget management (Warren et al., 2015), and notably ERP systems, which have undergone digitalization since the 1990s and are central elements in company digitalization (Ross et al., 2017). The table below (Table 1) summarizes some of the impacts of digitalization on management control.

Table 1. Impacts of digitalization on management control instruments

Management control instruments	Impacts of digitalization
Reporting	• "Digitalisation helps to improve the reporting process by enabling a higher degree of automation and standardisation (Rowbottom et al., 2021)" (Fähndrich, 2023). • "digitalisation is leading to a further increase in the use of external data, especially big data, in corporate management and reporting (Al-Htaybat & Alberti-Alhtaybat, 2017)".(Fähndrich, 2023).
Budgeting	• "The integration of external data such as big data is capable to significantly increase the accuracy and timeliness of budgeting activities (Bergmann et al., 2020)" (Fähndrich, 2023). • "the importance of the planning function is positively associated with the use of business analytics in the budgeting processes (Bergmann et al., 2020)". (Fähndrich, 2023).
Other Management Control instruments (activity-based costing; balanced scorecard; benchmarking, etc.)	• "Traditional instruments remain popular (Burns & Vaivio, 2001). However, they are used alongside new and so-called advanced MC instruments such as rolling forecasts, activity-based costing and the balanced scorecard (Burns & Vaivio, 2001, p. 390)". (Fähndrich, 2023).

Source: Author according to Fähndrich (2023).

3. THEORETICAL AND METHODOLOGICAL FRAMEWORKS

This section is structured into two subsections. The first subsection presents our theoretical framework and the formulation of the research hypotheses (3.1). The second subsection highlights our methodological choices (3.2).

3.1. The contingency theory and formulation of hypotheses

The contingency approach offers a coherent paradigm for analyzing organizations and is currently the prevailing framework in the study of control systems (Elhamma, 2011). According to Pock (2007), "contingency theory posits that the internal or external environment or context of a system or organization significantly impacts its performance and efficiency." Therefore, an organization or system must adapt to its context to enhance its performance.

Contingency theory is not new; it arises from the work of several researchers interested in organizational design, such as Mintzberg (1979). The core idea of contingency theory is that managers and entrepreneurs design their organizations based on their technologies and the environments in which they operate. According to Ezzamel and Hart (1987), this approach posits that "the organization of a company must account for its specific circumstances." Friedberg (2001) describes contingency theory as a perspective that "starts from established organizations and focuses its analysis on the variation of their forms. Its units of analysis are organizations, and it seeks to explain their forms by examining social dynamics and forces at the inter-organizational, sectoral, or societal level." Donaldson (1996) asserts that there is no single ideal structure; rather, the most optimal structure is one that considers various contingency factors.

In management control, contingency theory posits that there is an interaction between management control tools, contingent factors (such as strategy, structure, and technology), and organizational performance (Elhamma, 2011). Otley (1980) demonstrated that management control tools must align with these contingent factors to achieve optimal performance. In this context, Fisher (1995) asserts that "...the contingent management control literature is based on the correct relationship between contingent factors and corporate control tools to achieve better performance." (Desreumaux, 1998).

Studies on the digitalization of management control using contingency theory are still quite rare. The results of the empirical study conducted by Elhamma and El-moumane (2023) showed that "firm size does not have a statistically significant impact on the maturity degree of Management Control Digitization in the studied companies (Beta=0.176; p>10%)" (Elhamma and El-moumane, 2023, p. 420). In the same sense, Elhamma (2023), "The average digitalization of management control in service companies exceeds that of companies in other sectors. However, the difference between these two averages is statistically insignificant [...]. Therefore, the sector of activity does not have a statistically significant impact on the digitalization of management control" (Elhamma, 2023, p. 65). Elhamma (2023) confirmed that "environmental uncertainty does not have a significant effect on the digitalization of management control" (Elhamma, 2023, p.8).

In this research, we will examine the impact of company age and legal affiliation on the degree of digitalization in management control. The literature suggests that older companies are often more formalized and have a more rigid culture, which may impede the adoption of digital technologies compared to younger companies. In contrast, subsidiaries of foreign groups generally demonstrate a higher degree of digitalization than Moroccan companies, which is often attributed to the digital practices adopted by their parent companies abroad. Based on this, we can formulate the following two hypotheses:

Hypothesis 1: In younger companies, management control systems are more digitalized compared to older companies.
Hypothesis 2: In subsidiaries of foreign groups, management control systems are more digitalized compared to those in subsidiaries of Moroccan groups or Moroccan companies.

3.2. Methodological framework

3.2.1 The Sample

In this study, we will examine the digitalization of management control in companies within Morocco, a developing country. Morocco is located in North Africa, south of the Mediterranean. According to the Moroccan royal constitution, Islam, Arabness, and Amazighness are defined as "fundamental components" of Moroccan identity. Historically, Morocco was under Spanish and French protectorates, which is why many of the management tools used by Moroccan companies are derived from the French system (Elhamma and Moalla, 2015). However, in recent years, Moroccan companies have begun to adopt modern tools, such as international accounting standards (IFRS) (Elhamma, 2023, 2024), modern management control tools (Elhamma, 2012; Elhamma, 2014), and new sources of financing, such as Islamic finance (Elhamma, 2015; Bennani and Elhamma, 2015), etc.

The main characteristics of our sample are summarized in the table below (Table 2).

Table 2. The main characteristics of the study's sample

Legal status		**Age of companies**	
Independent companies	**23.8%**	**Less than 2 years old**	**9.5%**
Subsidiaries of Moroccan groups	45.2%	Between 2 and 5 years old	16.7%
Subsidiaries of foreign groups	31%	Between 5 and 10 years old	11.9%
	-	More than 10 years old	61.9%
Total	100%	Total	100%

Source: Author

With regard to legal status, 23.8% of the companies in the sample are independent, 45.2% are subsidiaries of Moroccan groups, and 31% are subsidiaries of foreign groups. In terms of age, we selected 62% of companies over 10 years old and 38% less than 10 years old.

3.2.2. Operationalization of variables

In this present research, to collect data on the digitalization of management control, we opted for a perceptual approach via questionnaire survey. This approach involves the respondent's assessment, on a five-point scale, of the average level of digitalization of management control in their company. The following question was asked: How do you rate the level of digitalization of management control in your company? (Digitalization refers to the use of new information and communication technologies 'NICT', the internet, networks, applications, etc.). Respondents had the choice between five responses, ranging from "very low digitalization" to "very high digitalization".

4. RESULTS AND DISCUSSION

This section is dedicated to presenting our results. First, we will discuss the results related to the degree of digitalization of management control (4.1). Next, we will present the findings on the potential impact of company age on the digitalization of management control (4.2). Finally, we will examine the results concerning the impact of legal affiliation on the digitalization of management control (4.3).

4.1. Degree of management control digitalization

The main results of our survey are summarized in the table below (Table 3).

Table 3. Degree of digitalization of management control in the surveyed companies

Degree of digitalization of management control	%
Very low digitalization	2.4%
Low digitalization	23.8%
Moderate digitalization	47.6%
High digitalization	16.7%
Very high digitalization	9.5%
Total	100%

Source: Author

The initial results of this research show that the level of digitalization of management control can be described as "moderate". Over 47% of respondents confirmed that their management control is "moderately" digitalized. On the other hand, only 26.2% judged this digitization to be "high" or "very high". Therefore, we cannot speak of a certain digital "maturity" of management control in the surveyed companies.

4.2. Digitalization of management control according to the company age

The table below summarizes the main results relating to the potential correlations between company age and digitalization of management control (Table 4).

Table 4. Degree of digitalization of management control according to the company age

	Less than 10 years	More than 10 years
Very low digitalization	6.3%	00%
Low digitalization	25%	23.1%
Moderate digitalization	56.3%	42.3%
High digitalization	00%	26.9%
Very high digitalization	12.5%	7.7%
Total	100%	100%

Source: Author

34.6% of companies aged over 10 years consider their management control to be "highly" or "very highly" digitalized, compared to only 12.5% of companies aged less than 10 years. This result supports the idea that the age of companies significantly impacts the digitalization of management control, specifically that management control is more digitalized in older companies. To confirm or refute statistically this result, a Student's t-test for difference of means will be used (Table 5).

Table 5. Student's t-test for difference of means of digitalization of management control according to the age of companies

	More than 10 years old	Less than 10 years old	Difference	t-test	Sig.
Means of Digitalization of management control	3.1923	2.8750	0.31731	1.056	0.297[ns]

ns: Not Significant

The average level of digitalization in management control for older companies (3.19) is higher than that for younger companies (2.87). However, the difference between these two averages (0.31) is statistically insignificant. Therefore, we cannot validate Hypothesis 1, which posits that the management control systems of younger companies are more digitalized than those of older companies. Therefore, based on our analyses, the age of a company does not impact the degree of digitalization in management control.

4.3. Digitalization of management control according to the legal status

The main results regarding the digitalization of management control according to the legal status are summarized in the following table (Table 6).

Table 6. Degree of digitalization of management control according to the legal status

	Independent companies	Subsidiaries of foreign groups	Subsidiaries of Moroccan groups
Very low digitalization	00%	00%	5,3%
Low digitalization	40%	23.1%	15,8%
Moderate digitalization	50%	15.4%	68,4%
High digitalization	00%	38.5%	10,5%
Very high digitalization	10%	23.1%	00%
Total	100%	100%	100%

Source: Author

61.6% of subsidiaries of foreign groups consider their management control to be 'highly' or 'very highly' digitalized. In contrast, this rate is only 10% for independent companies and 10.5% for subsidiaries of Moroccan groups. This result strongly supports the idea that management control is more digitalized in subsidiaries of foreign groups than in independent companies or subsidiaries of Moroccan groups. To test statistically this hypothesis, a Student's t-test for difference of means will be used (Table 7).

Table 7. Student's t-test for difference of means of digitalization of management control according to the legal status

	Subsidiaries of foreign groups	*Independent companies or Subsidiaries of Moroccan groups*	*Difference*	*t-test*	*Sig.*
Means of Digitalization of management control	3.6154	2.8276	0.78780	2.308	0.034*

* Significant at 5% level

The average level of management control digitalization in subsidiaries of foreign groups (3.61) exceeds that of independent companies or subsidiaries of Moroccan groups (2.82). The difference between these two means is positive (+0.78) and statistically significant at the 5% level. Therefore, we can confirm Hypothesis 2, which posits that management control is more digitalized in subsidiaries of foreign groups than in Moroccan companies. Therefore, based on our analyses, the legal status of a company significantly impacts the degree of digitalization in management control. This result is largely explained by the fact that these companies are already engaged in digitalization strategies and policies adopted by their groups.

5. CONCLUSION

This research had two main objectives: first, to examine the degree of digitalization in management control among companies located in Morocco, a developing country; and second, to test the impact of company age and legal affiliation on the digitalization of management control. To achieve these objectives, a questionnaire survey was conducted. Three main results can be highlighted:

- The digitalization of management control can be considered 'moderate,' so we cannot assert that the companies studied have achieved a high level of digital maturity in their management control systems.
- The age of companies does not significantly impact the degree of digitalization in management control. There is no significant difference in digitalization levels between older and younger companies.
- The legal affiliation of companies has a statistically significant impact on the degree of digitalization in management control. Subsidiaries of foreign groups have more digitalized management control systems compared to subsidiaries of Moroccan groups or independent Moroccan companies.

This study makes important contributions to both digitalization and management control literature. It advances our understanding of the relationship between the digitalization of management control, the age of companies, and their legal affiliation. Unlike the majority of previous research, which has primarily focused on digitalization in general, this study is among the first to examine the digitalization of management control in developing countries.

The findings must be interpreted with caution due to several methodological limitations inherent in our research. Specifically, these include the small sample size of only forty-two companies and the reliance on a perceptual approach for data collection. Such limitations may introduce discrepancies between reported perceptions and actual practices within the studied companies.

Several future research studies could build upon this work. For example, future studies could examine the obstacles to digitalization in management control or explore other determinants of digitalization, such as the profile of managers, among others.

REFERENCES

Achibane, M., & Elhamma, A. (2016). Balanced Scorecard Et Incertitude Environnementale: Cas Des Entreprises Au Maroc. *European Scientific Journal, 12*(7), 459–469. DOI: 10.19044/esj.2016.v12n7p459

Al-Htaybat, K., & von Alberti-Alhtaybat, L. (2017). Big data and corporate reporting: Impacts and paradoxes. *Accounting, Auditing & Accountability Journal, 30*(4), 850–873. DOI: 10.1108/AAAJ-07-2015-2139

Alazard, C. and Sépari, S. (2001). Contrôle de gestion DECF. 5ème édition, édition Dunod.

Anthony, R. N. (1965). *Planning and Control Systems, A Framework for Analysis, Division of Research*. Harvard University.

Anthony, R. N. (1988). *The management Control function*. Harvard Business School Press.

Appelbaum, D., Kogan, A., Vasarhelyi, M., & Yan, Z. (2015). Impact of business analytics and enterprise systems on managerial accounting. *International Journal of Accounting Information Systems, 25*, 29–44. DOI: 10.1016/j.accinf.2017.03.003

Audrin, B., & Davoine, E. (2017). La fonction RH face à la numérisation des organisations: Le cas des outils de communication numérique. *Management & Avenir, 92*(92), 15–39. DOI: 10.3917/mav.092.0015

Banque de France (2018). L'impact des TIC et de la digitalisation sur la productivité et la part du travail dans la valeur ajoutée: enseignements à partir d'un échantillon d'entreprises françaises. Document de travail n°785.

Benga, B., & Elhamma, A. (2024). Navigating the Digital Frontier: A Literature Review on Business Digitalization. *European Scientific Journal, 20*(10), 107–125. DOI: 10.19044/esj.2024.v20n10p107

Bennani, S. and Elhamma, A. (2015), La comptabilité en finance islamique selon les normes aaoifi. Editions universitaires européennes.

Bescos, P. L., & Cauvin, E. (2004). L'évaluation des performances dans les entreprises françaises: une étude empirique. *Actes du 25ème Congrès de l'AFC*, Orléans.

Bonnet, D., Westerman, G., & McAfee, A. (2014). *Leading Digital: Turning Technology into Business Transformation*. Harvard Business Review Press.

Bos, C. (2018). *La transformation digitale, vers un management stratégique augmenté. Céline Bos, Ea Conseil & formation*. DIF.

Bouquin, H. (2001). Le contrôle de gestion. 5ème édition mise à jour, PUF, collection. *Gestion*.

Cavelius, F., Endenich, Ch., & Zicari, A. (2018). L'impact de la digitalisation sur le rôle du controleur de gestion. Transitions numériques et informations comptables, May, Nantes, France. pp.cd-rom. ffhal-01907810f.

Cazals, F. (2015). *Stratégies digitales: La méthode des 6C*. Deboeck Supérieur.

Chapellier, P. (1993). Pour un élargissement de l'approche contingente du système d'information comptable de la PME. Acte du Congrès de L'AFC.

Clerck, J. (2017). Digitalization, Digital Transformation [-SCOOP.]. *Differences: A Journal of Feminist Cultural Studies*, •••, i.

Dent, J. F. (1990). Strategy, organization and control: Some possibilities for accounting research. *Accounting, Organizations and Society*, *15*(1/2), 3–25. DOI: 10.1016/0361-3682(90)90010-R

Desreumaux, A. (1998), Théorie des organisations. éd. EMS.

Dorn, D. (2017). La montée en puissance des machines: Comment l'ordinateur a changé le travail. *Revue Française des Affaires Sociales*, *1*, 35–63.

Dudézert, A. (2018). *La Transformation digitale des entreprises*. La Découverte.

Elhamma, A. (2011). Recherche d'une congruence entre les outils du contrôle de gestion et leurs facteurs de contingence au sein des entreprises au Maroc. Thèse de Doctorat, Université Mohammed V, Rabat Maroc.

Elhamma, A. (2012). The activity based costing in morocco: Adoption and diffusion. *Arabian Journal of Business and Management Review*, *1*(6), 33–45. DOI: 10.12816/0002111

Elhamma, A. (2013). Performance de la comptabilité par activités: Perceptions des responsables d'entreprises. *La Revue des Sciences de Gestion*, (263-264), 227–232.

Elhamma, A. (2014). Performance du Balanced Scorecard: Perception des responsables d'entreprises. *Revue Internationale de Management et de Stratégie*, *5*(2), 1–9.

Elhamma, A. (2015). La comptabilité des produits financiers islamiques: Normes AAOIFI vs. IFRS. *Revue de Management et de Stratégie*, *1*(2), 10–22.

Elhamma, A. (2015). Perceived benefits of ABC implementation in Moroccan enterprises: Results of an empirical study. American Journal of Business. *Economics and Management*, *3*(2), 24–28.

Elhamma, A. (2015). The relationship between budgetary evaluation, firm size and performance. *Journal of Management Development*, *34*(8), 973–986. DOI: 10.1108/JMD-06-2014-0053

Elhamma, A. (2023), Numérisation du contrôle de gestion en fonction du secteur d'activité: résultats d'une étude empirique, Moroccan Journal of Entrepreneurship, Innovation and Management, 8 (1&2), 59-68. DOI: https://doi.org/DOI: 10.48396/IMIST.PRSM/mjeim-v8i1%20&%202.43254

Elhamma, A. (2023). Digitalisation et incertitude environnementale: cas du contrôle de gestion des entreprises marocaines. Revue Économie, Gestion et Société, 1 (39). https://doi.org/DOI: 10.48382/IMIST.PRSM/regs-v1i39.42390

Elhamma, A. (2023). Impact of mandatory IFRS adoption on foreign direct investment: the moderating role of conflict of interest regulation. Journal of Financial Reporting and Accounting, Vol. ahead-of-print No. ahead-of-print. https://doi.org/DOI: 10.1108/JFRA-04-2022-0145

Elhamma, A. (2023). The relationship between organisational decentralisation, balanced scorecard and its perceived benefits in Moroccan SMEs. International Journal of Accounting. *Auditing and Performance Evaluation*, *19*(2), 185–202. DOI: 10.1504/IJAAPE.2023.132384

Elhamma, A. (2024). Determinants of national IFRS adoption: Evidence from the Middle East and North Africa region. International Journal of Accounting. *Auditing and Performance Evaluation*, *20*(1-2), 69–90. DOI: 10.1504/IJAAPE.2024.135535

Elhamma, A., & El-Moumane, R. (2023). Impact de la taille sur la digitalisation du contrôle de gestion des entreprises marocaines: résultats d'une enquête. Alternatives Managériales Economiques, 5 (3), 182-199. DOI: https://doi.org/DOI: 10.48374/IMIST.PRSM/ame-v5i3.41916

Elhamma, A., & El-Moumane, R. (2023). Impact of Firm Size on Digitalization of Management Control: Evidence from Morocco. International Journal of Management. *Accounting & Economics*, *10*(6), 412–424. DOI: 10.5281/zenodo.8216014

Elhamma, A., & Lassaad, B. M. (2017). Liens entre participation budgétaire, taille et performance: Cas des entreprises au Maroc. *Revue Congolaise de Gestion*, *24*(2), 43–62. DOI: 10.3917/rcg.024.0043

Elhamma, A., & Moalla, M. (2015). Impact of uncertainty and decentralization on activity-based costing use. *International Journal of Accounting and Economics Studies, 3*(2), 148–155. DOI: 10.14419/ijaes.v3i2.4817

Elhamma, A., & Zhang, Yi. (2013). The relationship between activity-based costing, business strategy and performance in Moroccan enterprises. *Journal of Accounting and Management Information Systems, 12*(1), 22–38.

Emmanuel, C., Otley, D., & Merchant, K. A. (1990). *Accounting for Management Control.* Chapman and Hall. DOI: 10.1007/978-1-4899-6952-1

Fähndrich, J. (2023). A literature review on the impact of digitalisation on management control. *Journal of Management Control, 34*(1), 9–65. DOI: 10.1007/s00187-022-00349-4

Gervais, M. (2000). Contrôle de gestion, édition. *Economica.*

Hafsi, M., & Assar, S. (2017). Le rôle de la modélisation d'entreprise dans la transformation numérique: Une étude exploratoire. 22ème colloque de l'AIM (Association Information & Management), May 2017, Paris, France. ffhal-01656840f

Holmes, S., & Nicholls, D. (1989). Modelling the accounting information requirement of small business. *Accounting and Business Research, 19*(74), 143–150.

Kaplan, R. S., & Norton, D. P. (1992). The balanced scorecard, measures that drive performance. *Harvard Business Review*, (January-February), 71–79. PMID: 10119714

Meyssonnier, F., & Pourtier, F. (2006). Les ERP changent-ils le contrôle de gestion? *Comptabilité Contrôle Audit, 12*(1), 45–64. DOI: 10.3917/cca.121.0045

Ngongang, D. (2010). Analyse de la pratique des coûts dans les PMI camerounaises. Revue libanaise de gestion et d'économie, 5.

Pan, G., & Seow, P. (2016). Preparing accounting graduates for digital revolution: A critical review of information technology competencies and skills development. *Journal of Education for Business, 91*(3), 166–175. DOI: 10.1080/08832323.2016.1145622

Pock, T. (2007). Contingency-based Design of Management Control Systems. Doctoral Thesis, University of St. Gallen Graduate School of Business Administration, Economics, Law, and Social Sciences (HSG).

Reis, J., Amorim, M., Melao, N., Cohen, Y., & Rodrigues, M. (2020). Digitalization: A Literature Review and Research Agenda. In book: Proceedings on 25th International Joint Conference on Industrial Engineering and Operations Management – IJCIEOM, 443-456. www.doi//10.1007/978-3-030-43616-2_47

Ross, J. W., Beath, C. M., & Sebastian, I. M. (2017). Digitized ≠ Digital. *MIT CISR Research Briefings*, *18*(10), 1–3.

Snoussi, N., & Elhamma, A. (2022). Adoption du Balanced Scorecard par les PME: Une étude exploratoire dans le contexte marocain. Alternatives Managériales Economiques 4 (1), 158-179. https://doi.org/DOI: 10.48374/IMIST.PRSM/ame-v4i1.30471

Sponem, S. (2002). L'explication de la diversité des pratiques budgétaires: une approche contingente. Actes du 23ème Congrès de l'AFC, Toulouse, mai.

Srai, J., & Lorentz, H. (2019). Developing design principles for the digitalisation of purchasing andsupply management. *Journal of Purchasing and Supply Management*, *25*(1), 78–98. DOI: 10.1016/j.pursup.2018.07.001

Vasarhelyi, M. A., Kogan, A., & Tuttle, B. M. (2015). Big Data in Accounting: An Overview. *Accounting Horizons*, *29*(2), 381–396. DOI: 10.2308/acch-51071

Warren Jr., J. D., Moffitt, K. C. and Byrnes, P. (2015). How Big Data Will Change Accounting. 29(2), 397-407.

Westerman, G., Bonnett, D., & McAffee, A. (2014). *Gagner avec le digital*. Editions Diatein.

Chapter 3

Financial Technology and Sustainable Performance of Islamic Banks:
A Conceptual Approach Using Diffusion of Innovation Theory

Arsalan Hussain
https://orcid.org/0000-0001-8328-574X
Institute of Business Management, Karachi, Pakistan

Arsalan Haneef Malik
https://orcid.org/0000-0001-8940-4850
Institute of Business Management, Karachi, Pakistan

Awais Ur Rehman
University of Central Punjab, Pakistan

Muhammad Rehan
https://orcid.org/0000-0001-5056-5307
Institute of Business Management, Karachi, Pakistan

Yousuf Aboya
https://orcid.org/0009-0003-7945-9868
Institute of Business Management, Karachi, Pakistan

ABSTRACT

In the 1990s, the objective of financial technology was to encourage bank customers to use internet banking instead of exclusively using automated teller machines. In the 21st century, Fintech services are rapidly disrupting bank services around

DOI: 10.4018/979-8-3693-4373-9.ch003

the world. Similarly, Pakistani banking sector has been disrupted as more Fintech services were developed that enhance the convenience of the customers. State bank of Pakistan (SBP), has initiated regulatory guidelines and encouragement to local as well as foreign banks to enhance fintech usage for sustainable performance. In theoretical contribution, numerous prior researchers have explained that information system (IS) related theories have discussed the technology usage in financial system such as Cognitive Model, Confirmation Model, and Technology acceptance model. However, the present study will be a pioneer study that will combine technological, organizational, and environmental (TOE) model with diffusion of innovation (DOI) theory to explain the fintech usage as a technological innovation which can sustain bank's performance.

1. INTRODUCTION

The rapid growth of technology is making things easier to manage workers' data and at the same time it is creating a challenge for managers to be aware of new tools and technologies. In this competitive world of 21st century, organizations cannot compete without adopting modern technological changes. Therefore, organizations should invest more on information technology (IT) and information systems (IS) aspiring to be a market leader and to gain sustainable competitive advantage. In a similar context, technological advancements are also transforming how financial services are developed, provided, and assessed. The aim of digital servitization is to enhance financial performance and creation of value through the use of digital technology. As a result, the financial technology having a new dimension.

The term financial technology often abbreviated as "fintech," is a category of technological innovation that attempts to compete with established financial services. It's a new concept that employs technology to help people manage their money better (Khan et al., 2022). Mobile banking, online investing services, e-IPO, and cryptocurrencies are examples of common fintech usage (Shahzad et al., 2022). Moreover, Individuals and businesses may utilize these banking and payment systems for buying and investing, and businesses can develop goods and trade online.

The theoretical framework in this study was structured on the solid foundation of existing knowledge by using the combination of diffusion of innovation (DOI) theory and technology organization and environment (TOE) framework. The objective of the present study is to identify technological, organizational, and environmental factors and their relationship with the use of fintech in both quantitative and qualitative manner in Pakistan.

Global competitiveness report showed that Pakistan stood at 127 in information communication report (ICT) usage/adoption. Likewise, the implementation of technology along with financial services which eventually enhances the financial performance (Chege & Wang, 2020), is still a missing link. The specific purpose of the present study is to understand that the use of fintech can improve the sustainable organizational performance of Pakistani banks. Thus, this study uses fintech usage as the mediating variable of the study between TOE model and sustainable organizational performance. The further part of the study consists of three sections. Section two compiles the review of the literature. Section three discusses the specific methodology, measurement of the scales, and proposed theoretical framework. Section IV concludes the study with some recommendations.

2. LITERATURE REVIEW

2.1 Theoretical Basis

The literature also reveals that measurement of an organization's performance should be multidimensional indicators (Cheah, Amran, & Yahya, 2019). It should consolidate financial, social, and environmental dimensions as essential criteria with the rapidly changing global business environment (Fernando et al., 2019). Performance measurement by combining the financial, social, and environmental dimensions is known as sustainable organizational performance. Further, SMEs' current technologies and industry dynamics are synergized to gain a competitive advantage (Ch'ng, Cheah, & Amran, 2021), which eventually leads to sustainable organizational performance.

Moreover, the international mindset having the ability to view globally to acquire knowledge related to suppliers, customers, customers, and other market players enables firms to acquire the local market needs (Kyvik, 2018). Further, the study discusses that the international mindset has become a precondition to evaluate the global market trends and future competitive positions (Agyapong, Maaledidong, & Mensah, 2021). The study uses the DOI to explain the technological, organizational, and environmental factors and their relationship with fintech adoption.

To explain the underlying issues related to the use of fintech for Malaysian sustainable performance of SMEs. This study used technological factor such as (relative advantage, IT infrastructure), organizational factor (firm readiness, top management support), and environmental (competitive orientation, government support) factors which eventually leads to sustainable organizational performance.

Considering the aforementioned use of fintech issues related to the TOE model, the technological context, which is one of the three constructs of the TOE model, mainly focused on internal and external IT infrastructure. This factor is essential for specific organizations' hardware, software, and operational processes such as payment process systems, computers, and the internet (Mkansi, 2021). Thus, the possession of required IT infrastructure is an essential factor to implement fintech innovation in a firm. Likewise, the anticipated advantages of implementing fintech, which is known as a relative advantage of particular technology use. Similarly, In this study, the researcher uses relative advantages as the expected advantages that any firm can have by the use of financial technology (Ahmad, Abu Bakar, & Ahmad, 2019; Luong & Wang, 2019). The literature also depicts two categories of expected advantages: direct and indirect advantages that focuses on internal efficiency and service quality improvement (Ilin, Ivetić, & Simić, 2017).

Alongside the technological factor, the scope of organizational context covers the organization's size, scope, and managerial structure. (Yoon & George, 2013) describe organizational readiness as a vital element that covers information system knowledge, IT skills, technical competencies, and financial resources of the firm. Moreover, The successful implementation of technological innovation (such as fintech) has been adopted with top management support (Hussein et al., 2019; Sabherwal, Jeyaraj, & Chowa, 2006).

In the previous studies, the competitive orientation serves as an analytical tool to acquire relevant information related to buyers and competitors in the target market through e-business (Wu, Mahajan, & Balasubramanian, 2003). Likewise, the researchers have analyzed government support in innovation usage like e-procurement, e-banking, and e-government (Kazungu, Panga, & Mchopa, 2015; Mohtaramzadeh, Ramayah, & Jun-Hwa, 2018; Sánchez-Torres, Canada, Sandoval, & Alzate, 2018). Although, there are very rare researches available that identified the government support concerning use of e-business (Songling, Ishtiaq, Anwar, & Ahmed, 2018). This fill-up the existing gap this study will examine the relationship between relative advantage, IT infrastructure, organizational readiness, top management support, competitive orientation, and government support on use of fintech toward Pakistani banks' sustainable performance.

According to Roger's theory of diffusion of innovation (DOI), innovation is defined as "an idea, practices, or object that is perceived to be new by an individual or other units of adoption" (Rogers, 2003, p. 12). While diffusion refers to "the process by which an innovation is communicated through certain channels over time among the members of a social system" (Rogers, 2003, p. 5). However, the DOI theory does not provide a lens on the environmental factors of the firm. Conversely, if we look at the models drawn with institutional theory, they are more focused on environmental context but ignore the technological and organizational factors.

Therefore, the research framework of the study is based on the above theoretical base. The framework is developed on compelling literature and mainly based on TOE model, while diffusion of innovation (DOI) was considered as a unpinning theory of the current study to justify the fintech usage.

2.2 Green Banking and Corporate Status:

In the quest for economic as well as financial development, both corporations and governments are overlooking environmental considerations, leading to ecological degradation and climate-related challenges. Consequently, international organizations are placing greater emphasis on environmental protection and promoting eco-friendly initiatives. In this context, green banking represents a comprehensive approach to safeguarding current and future generations from environmental damage. Likewise, the growing body of literature on environmental sustainability reflects the increasing focus on green concerns, leading to the development of various initiatives including sustainable finance and environmentally focused banking. Green banking strengthens the contribution of banks, industries, the economy, and society at large by encouraging eco-friendly initiatives and reducing carbon emissions in their activities. It acknowledges the responsibility of adopting sustainable practices to maintain an eco-friendly and sustainable environment. Green banks play an active role in promoting efforts to transform the conventional economy into a low-carbon, climate-conscious framework. These banks adopt environmental responsibility in both ethical and operational aspects by lowering carbon emissions and encouraging activities that contribute positively to the climate. The idea of green banking focuses on raising environmental awareness, motivating both staff and clients to engage in eco-friendly practices, and providing products and services aimed at reducing environmental risks. This represents a major shift in the banking sector, where environmental considerations in investments, financing, and service delivery are gaining prominence, aligned with the UN's Sustainable Development Goals. Given the irreversible and far-reaching effects of environmental risks across all sectors, including banking, research is essential to identify and address these risks. Addressing the anthropogenic pressures on ecosystems, green banking adopts eco-responsible principles that offer triple benefits: enhancing economic efficiency, mitigating harmful effects on the environment, and fostering a positive image for banks.

2.3 Green / Eco-friendly Banking in Pakistan:

Global eco-friendly challenges have compelled nations to prioritize environmental protection in their agendas, as climate change and global warming have severely impacted world economies. In response, Pakistan established the Ministry of Climate Change, which developed the National Climate Change Policy (NCCP) in 2012. Provincial governments placed also instructed to enact laws in line with the Federal Environment Protection Act (SBP, 2017). The State Bank of Pakistan (SBP) is actively working to promote green initiatives in the financial sector. It regularly issues circulars to commercial and Islamic banks, encouraging the implementation of green banking practices. In October 2017, the SBP introduced new guidelines to align with international standards, focusing on green banking, climate-friendly financing mechanisms, and the adoption of eco-friendly internal control measures (SBP, 2018). Additionally, the SBP advised banks to adopt online banking solutions to enhance customer convenience and expand banking access in rural areas (Khan et al., 2019a, b).

Mobile banking significantly contributes to the pro-environmental movement by focusing on a click-and-mortar model rather than traditional physical systems, with the State Bank of Pakistan (SBP) promoting paperless and equipment-free banking channels. Pakistan's ongoing energy challenges are affecting both industrial and human development, and banks can contribute to reducing climate risks. In line with this objective, the SBP promotes sustainable banking practices by urging banks to adopt renewable energy sources, contributing to the establishment of a more sustainable financial system.

Only some academicians have examined sustainable banking in the context of Pakistan. For example, Javeria et al. (2019), employing a qualitative research design, examined the challenges hindering the adoption of green banking in the country. They suggested that future studies should explore the shift from traditional to sustainable (green) banking using quantitative approaches. In a more recent investigation, Rehman et al. (2021) found that green banking practices—covering policies, operations, and investments—have a positive impact on the environmental performance of conventional banks in Pakistan. They illustrated that green banking initiatives can serve as predictors of environmental performance and urged future researchers to utilize more holistic frameworks for a deeper understanding of green banking in Pakistan.

The present study adopts an innovative approach by examining a comprehensive set of practices, including those linked to daily operations, customer relations, bank policies, and employee involvement, specifically within the realm of Islamic banking. Importantly, the connection between corporate reputation and the environmental performance of Islamic banks remains unexplored, offering a significant contribution to the body of knowledge on Islamic banks' sustainability efforts. This research also suggests that the environmental awareness of employees and management can strengthen the green practices of Islamic banks. Environmentally aware employees are expected to facilitate the implementation of green banking measures and enhance the banks' reputation.

2.4. Corporate Reputation and Islamic Green Banking:

Islamic banking, viewed as a form of ethical banking, has the potential to tackle issues related to equity and sustainability, thereby contributing to the resolution of environmental and economic challenges faced by communities (Kenourgios et al., 2016). The "Go Green" movement within Islamic banking highlights the dedication of these banks to safeguarding the interests of both present and future generations. In the current context, environmental challenges such as climate change, increasing emissions from traditional energy sources, global warming, and pollution management are key aspects of sustainable practices in Islamic banking. However, there is very limited research exists on the emphasis of Islamic banking on sustainability, particularly the green dimensions that address institutional and societal impacts (Aliyu et al., 2017). These areas require more descriptive, explanatory, and exploratory models.

Ali et al. (2020) conducted a study examining the connection between the green behavior of bankers and the development of green banking within Malaysia's Islamic banking sector. They identified five key green orientations that significantly impact the growth of green banking: environmental conservation efforts, workplace sustainability, reducing environmental harm, motivating colleagues, and launching green initiatives. Their findings suggest that these factors positively contribute to the expansion of green Islamic banking.

Although earlier studies have shown that sustainable green banking practices can enhance the performance of conventional commercial banks, there is limited research investigating how green initiatives can improve the reputation and performance of Islamic banks. Aligning with the recommendation by Sharmeen and Yeaman (2020) that policymakers should focus on introducing interactive green products and services, this study argues that Islamic banks are uniquely suited to promote sustainable banking through ethical and responsible practices. Additionally, research by Bukhari et al. (2019, 2020) indicates that engaging stakeholders and building emotional connections are crucial for both conventional and Islamic banks as they transition to green banking. This study proposes that adopting green banking practices can greatly enhance the reputation of Islamic banks.

Figure 1. Conceptual framework

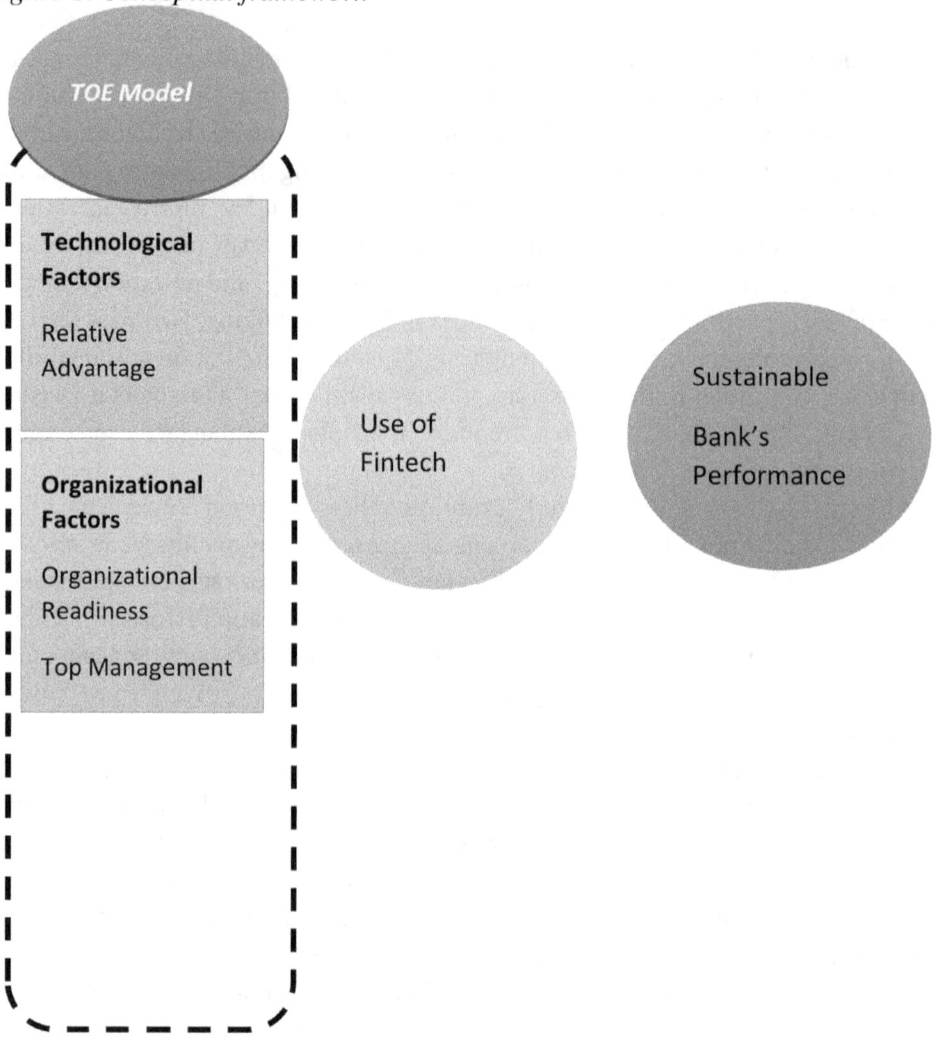

3. PROPOSED METHOD

3.1 Research Design

The mixed-method research design type is proposed to empirically analyze the conceptual framework of the present study. It is a sequential research design that provides an inclusive strategy to encounter research objectives. Initially, the strategy covers qualitative phase and followed by quantitative analysis of data (Creswell & Clark, 2011).

3.1.1 Qualitative Phase

The first stage of the process will involve defining the conceptual domain. Based on the top Journals in the Information Systems area listed in the ABS/ABDC lists, the researchers will analyze the concept of the financial technology and analyses the previous studies on the TOE model and fintech usage. Consequently, the interview protocol (i.e., research instrument) will be developed to achieve the present research objective.

Data Collection/Interviews will be conducted with twenty (20) bank managers. The simple random technique will be used for the sample section. The sample will be selected from listed banks of Pakistan. A semi-structured interview session will be conducted based on a set of carefully designed question guidelines. The questions will be asked in an interactive group setting where participants will freely give their opinion and views. During this process, the researchers will take notes of the vital points and record the whole session through voice/video recorder.

The data gathered from the interviews (audio and video) will be transcribed and analyzed using qualitative techniques through NVivo 11.0 Software, allowing researchers to identify themes, patterns, strategy, and steps pertaining to the implementation of fintech.

3.1.2 Quantitative Phase

To achieve the second part of the research objective, a quantitative study will be conducted. This quantitative study will employ a questionnaire survey, which measure the adoption of Fintech from (Marakarkandy et al., 2017; Patel & Patel 2018), sustainable development (Labuschagne, Brent, & Van Erck, 2005), IT infrastructure (Premkumar and Ramamurthy, 1995), IT expertise (Thong, 1999), Top management support (Soliman & Janz, 2004), adoption cost Al-Qirim, 2007), competitive pressure (Jaworski & Kohli, 1993), and government support (Looi, 2005). The questionnaire is designed using a seven-point Likert scale anchored by "strongly disagree" (1) to "strongly agree" (7). The questions are designed to probe on the constructs that would determine the Banks sustainable development and use of fintech in Pakistan.

In the quantitative phase, a sample random technique will be employed. Based on the G*Power software to the run proposed framework, we require 160 samples minimum. The present research will collect 300 questionnaires from operations managers of Pakistani banks. The data will be collected through a structured questionnaire using an electronic survey.

3.2 Data Analysis Process

The present study will follow structural equation model (SEM) with PLS approach using the SmartPLS software version 4.0 (Ringle et al., 2015) for this research. Reinartz et al. (2009) mentioned that "PLS is the preferable approach when researchers focus on prediction and theory development" especially for a model that involves formative and reflective latent variables.

4. RESULTS

To get effective results from the suggested conceptual framework, regulators SBP need to play an effective role for the promotion of financial innovation specifically fintech. It's vital to keep in mind that the lack of fintech and digital bank regulations could create a lot of uncertainty in the banking world (Hussain et al., 2015). Researcher have provided following guidelines and measures to mitigate risk associated with the use of fintech:

- Know-Your-Customer (KYC) Requirements in Electronic Format (e-KYC). This would enable completely digital onboarding, with standalone analytics authenticating customers' identification and by doing anti-money laundering checks.
- There should be a facility for the customers to use e-signature to authenticate transactions from a distance.
- Implementers need to consider assessment bodies' third-party assessments.
- There should be a proper encryption mechanism.
- There should be a proper authentication mechanism.

5. DISCUSSION

The current study has discussed all three aspects (technological, organizational, and environmental) of the TOE model. Henceforth, the first contribution was the introduction of mediation (use of fintech) combined with the TOE model and sustainable bank's performance.

Moreover, the present study demonstrates that three aspects of the TOE model are essential to implement the technology usage. To analyze the current study conceptual framework, the research data will be collected from Pakistani banks which are working under the guidelines of SBP.

Because the younger generation is more likely to use Fintech services, new space should be created for them to encourage greater and more efficient use of these services. As a result, steps should be taken to increase client awareness and persuade them that such services are reliable because there is no other option and technology adoption is critical. Banks hold financial literacy camps to teach people about the benefits of opening bank accounts. In the end, we can conclude that with the greater awareness to accelerate the use of Fintech services, institutions can lower the cost of financial services and aid in providing access to every individual of the country.

6. CONCLUSION

As previous literature suggests, customer protection and gratification will be problem area in the future without having effective usage of fintech. The framework of the current study can advantage to examine the use of digital financial services/fintech to improve customer satisfaction and ultimately sustainable performance of Pakistani banks. Furthermore, the identified latent variables in systematic review can be used for future empirical studies in the domain of banking industry.

REFERENCES

Agyapong, M., Maaledidong, P. D., & Mensah, H. K. (2021). Performance outcome of entrepreneurial behavior of SMEs in a developing economy: The role of international mindset. *Journal of Strategy and Management, 14*(2), 227–245. DOI: 10.1108/JSMA-07-2020-0173

Ahmad, S. Z., Abu Bakar, A. R., & Ahmad, N. (2019). Social media adoption and its impact on firm performance: The case of the UAE. *International Journal of Entrepreneurial Behaviour & Research, 25*(1), 84–111. DOI: 10.1108/IJEBR-08-2017-0299

Al-Bakri, A. A., & Katsioloudes, M. I. (2015). The factors affecting e-commerce adoption by Jordanian SMEs. *Management Research Review, 38*(7), 726–749. DOI: 10.1108/MRR-12-2013-0291

Al-Qirim, N. (2007). The adoption of eCommerce communications and applications technologies in small businesses in New Zealand. *Electronic Commerce Research and Applications, 6*(4), 462–473. DOI: 10.1016/j.elerap.2007.02.012

Ch'ng, P.-C., Cheah, J., & Amran, A.Ch'ng. (2021). Eco-innovation practices and sustainable business performance: The moderating effect of market turbulence in the Malaysian technology industry. *Journal of Cleaner Production, 283*, 124556. DOI: 10.1016/j.jclepro.2020.124556

Cheah, A., Amran, A., & Yahya, S. (2019). Internal oriented resources and social enterprises' performance: How can social enterprises help themselves before helping others? *Journal of Cleaner Production, 211*, 607–619. DOI: 10.1016/j.jclepro.2018.11.203

Chege, S. M., & Wang, D. (2020). The influence of technology innovation on SME performance through environmental sustainability practices in Kenya. *Technology in Society, 60*, 101210. DOI: 10.1016/j.techsoc.2019.101210

. Depietro, Wiarda, & Fleischer. (1990). The context for change: Organization, technology and environment. The processes of technological innovation, 199(0), 151-175.

Fernando, J., Chiappetta Jabbour, C. J., & Wah, W.-X. (2019). Pursuing green growth in technology firms through the connections between environmental innovation and sustainable business performance: Does service capability matter? *Resources, Conservation and Recycling, 141*, 8–20. DOI: 10.1016/j.resconrec.2018.09.031

Hussain, A., Ahmed, F., Siddiqi, Z., Basit, S. A., & Nasim, S. (2015). Factors Creating Conflict between Sales and Operational Teams in the Banking Industry. *International Journal of Research in Organizational Behavior and Human Resource Management, 3*(3), 18–28.

Hussein, L. A., Baharudin, A. S., Jayaraman, K., & Kiumarsi, S. H. A. I. A. N. (2019). B2B e-commerce technology factors with mediating effect perceived usefulness in Jordanian manufacturing SMES. *Journal of Engineering Science and Technology, 14*(1), 411–429.

Ilin, V., Ivetić, J., & Simić, D. (2017). Understanding the determinants of e-business adoption in ERP-enabled firms and non-ERP-enabled firms: A case study of the Western Balkan Peninsula. *Technological Forecasting and Social Change, 125*, 206–223. DOI: 10.1016/j.techfore.2017.07.025

Kazungu, I., Panga, F. P., & Mchopa, A. (2015). Impediments to adoption of e-marketing by Tanzanian small and medium sized enterprises: An explanatory model. International Journal of Economics, Commerce and Management, III, 6, 587-597.

Khan, M. A., Hussain, A., Ali, M. M., & Tajummul, M. A. (2022). Assessing the impact of liquidity on the value of assets return. [GBMR]. *Global Business and Management Research, 14*(1), 54–76. DOI: 10.32890/gbmr2022.14.1.4

Kyvik, O. (2018). The global mindset: A must for international innovation and entrepreneurship. *The International Entrepreneurship and Management Journal, 14*(2), 309–327.

Luong, N. A. M., & Wang, L. (2019). Factors Influencing E-commerce Usage within Internationalisation: A study of Swedish small and medium-sized fashion retailers.

Marakarkandy, B., Yajnik, N., & Dasgupta, C. (2017). Enabling internet banking adoption: An empirical examination with an augmented technology acceptance model (TAM). *Journal of Enterprise Information Management, 30*(2), 263–294. DOI: 10.1108/JEIM-10-2015-0094

Mkansi, M. (2022). E-business adoption costs and strategies for retail micro businesses. *Electronic Commerce Research, 22*(4), 1153–1193.

Mohtaramzadeh, M., Ramayah, T., & Jun-Hwa, C. (2018). B2B E-commerce adoption in Iranian manufacturing companies: Analyzing the moderating role of organizational culture. *International Journal of Human-Computer Interaction, 34*(7), 621–639. DOI: 10.1080/10447318.2017.1385212

Patel, K. J., & Patel, H. J. (2018). Adoption of internet banking services in Gujarat: An extension of TAM with perceived security and social influence. *International Journal of Bank Marketing*, *36*(1), 147–169. DOI: 10.1108/IJBM-08-2016-0104

Rogers, E.M. (2003). Diffusion of innovations.

Sabherwal, R., Jeyaraj, A., & Chowa, C. (2006). Information system success: Individual and organizational determinants. *Management Science*, *52*(12), 1849–1864. DOI: 10.1287/mnsc.1060.0583

Sánchez-Torres, J. A., Canada, F.-J. A., Sandoval, A. V., & Alzate, J.-A. S. (2018). E-banking in Colombia: Factors favouring its acceptance, online trust and government support. *International Journal of Bank Marketing*, *36*(1), 170–183. DOI: 10.1108/IJBM-10-2016-0145

Shahzad, A., Zahrullail, N., Akbar, A., Mohelska, H., & Hussain, A. (2022). COVID-19's Impact on Fintech Adoption: Behavioral Intention to Use the Financial Portal. *Journal of Risk and Financial Management*, *15*(10), 428. DOI: 10.3390/jrfm15100428

Songling, Y., Ishtiaq, M., Anwar, M., & Ahmed, H. (2018). The role of government support in sustainable competitive position and firm performance. *Sustainability (Basel)*, *10*(10), 3495. DOI: 10.3390/su10103495

Tutusaus, S., Schwartz, K., & Smit, S. (2018). The ambiguity of innovation drivers: The adoption of information and communication technologies by public water utilities. *Journal of Cleaner Production*, *171*, S79–S85. DOI: 10.1016/j.jclepro.2016.08.002

Wu, M., Mahajan, V., & Balasubramanian, S. (2003). An analysis of e-business adoption and its impact on business performance. *Journal of Technological Advancements*, *31*(4), 425–447. DOI: 10.1177/0092070303255379

Yoon, T. E., & George, J. F. (2013). Why aren't organizations adopting virtual worlds? *Computers in Human Behavior*, *29*(3), 772–790.

Chapter 4
Leveraging Digital Technologies for Sustainable Corporate Practices in India:
A Pathway to Green Innovation

Ritu Pareek
https://orcid.org/0000-0002-8124-0561
Birla Institute of Technology, Mesra, Jaipur, India

ABSTRACT

In an era marked by rapid digital transformation, Indian corporations are increasingly integrating digital technologies to enhance sustainability. This paper explores the intersection of digital innovation and green strategies within Indian industries, assessing how these technologies reshape corporate practices to address environmental, social, and economic challenges. The research focuses on key areas such as green process innovation, energy-efficient solutions, eco-packaging, materials recycling, and the circular economy, all driven by digital advancements. Through case studies and data analysis, this paper offers insights into how Indian companies are adopting digital tools to mitigate environmental impacts while maintaining economic resilience. By examining the Indian context, the paper aims to contribute to the global discourse on sustainability, providing valuable lessons for corporations and policymakers working towards the twin goals of economic growth and environmental stewardship.

DOI: 10.4018/979-8-3693-4373-9.ch004

INTRODUCTION

The digital revolution has transformed the global corporate landscape, offering unprecedented opportunities for businesses to enhance their sustainability practices. In India, where industrialization and urbanization are rapidly expanding, companies are increasingly turning to digital technologies to meet sustainability goals while maintaining competitive advantage. As sustainability becomes a critical objective for businesses, digital technologies offer a viable pathway for integrating green practices into organizational operations. This shift is driven not only by the necessity to comply with regulatory frameworks like the Indian government's commitment to the Paris Agreement but also by the need to address growing consumer demands for environmentally conscious practices.

India, one of the fastest-growing economies in the world, faces significant environmental challenges, including air pollution, water scarcity, and waste management issues. According to a report by the World Bank, environmental degradation costs India approximately $80 billion annually, representing 5.7% of the country's GDP. In response, businesses in India are beginning to adopt green strategies, with digital technologies at the forefront of this transformation. From smart energy management systems to eco-friendly supply chain solutions, digital technologies are helping Indian corporations strike a balance between economic growth and environmental stewardship.

1. DIGITAL TECHNOLOGIES AND GREEN PROCESS INNOVATION IN INDIA

Green process innovation involves redesigning existing business operations to minimize environmental impact, improve resource efficiency, and reduce carbon footprints. Digital technologies such as the Internet of Things (IoT), blockchain, and artificial intelligence (AI) are proving instrumental in enabling this shift. For example, Indian companies in the energy sector are increasingly using IoT-based smart grids to optimize electricity distribution and reduce energy waste. Tata Power, one of India's largest integrated power companies, has implemented smart grid technologies to monitor energy consumption in real-time, leading to a reduction in power wastage and an increase in renewable energy adoption.

AI and big data analytics also play a crucial role in green process innovation by providing companies with insights to streamline operations and improve energy efficiency. Indian conglomerate Mahindra & Mahindra has implemented AI-driven systems to optimize energy consumption in its automotive plants, leading to a 25% reduction in energy use. This not only contributes to the company's sustainability goals but also results in significant cost savings, demonstrating the economic viability of green process innovation through digital means.

1.1 Energy-Efficient Solutions: Digital Tools for Sustainability

Energy-efficient solutions are pivotal in reducing a company's carbon footprint, especially in a resource-constrained country like India. Digital technologies enable businesses to monitor and manage energy consumption effectively, thus reducing greenhouse gas emissions. One notable example is the use of digital twin technology, which creates a virtual model of physical assets, enabling companies to simulate and optimize energy usage. Larsen & Toubro (L&T), a leading engineering and construction company, uses digital twin technology in its operations, resulting in a 15% improvement in energy efficiency across its project sites.

Not only this, but India's startup ecosystem also is contributing to this shift by developing innovative energy-efficient solutions. For instance, Bengaluru-based startup Zenatix has developed AI-based energy management solutions for commercial buildings, helping businesses reduce energy consumption by up to 30%. The platform collects data from sensors installed across a building and uses AI to analyze energy usage patterns, recommending adjustments to optimize consumption. Such solutions not only enhance corporate sustainability but also align with India's national goals to increase energy efficiency and reduce reliance on fossil fuels.

1.2 Eco-Packaging and Materials Recycling: The Role of Digital Innovation

The Indian government has introduced stringent regulations to reduce plastic waste, pushing businesses to adopt eco-friendly packaging solutions. Digital technologies are proving to be instrumental in this transition, particularly in the design and manufacturing of sustainable packaging materials. Indian e-commerce giant Flipkart has eliminated single-use plastic in its packaging by using AI-powered algorithms to design eco-friendly alternatives such as recycled paper and biodegradable materials. This has not only reduced the company's environmental footprint but also created new business opportunities in the green packaging sector.

Recycling and circular economy practices are also being revolutionized by digital technologies. Companies like Hindustan Unilever are using blockchain to track and verify the lifecycle of packaging materials, ensuring transparency and accountability in their recycling processes . By using digital tools to monitor waste generation and recycling, these companies contribute to the creation of a circular economy, where resources are reused and regenerated, minimizing waste and environmental degradation.

1.3 The Circular Economy: Digital Platforms and Sustainability

The concept of a circular economy is gaining traction in India, supported by digital platforms that facilitate the reuse and regeneration of materials. In the manufacturing sector, companies are adopting digital platforms that enable the sharing of resources, thereby extending the lifecycle of products. For instance, the Indian startup EnCashea has developed a digital platform that connects households and businesses with recycling centers, promoting the circular economy by ensuring that waste materials are collected and repurposed . This not only reduces the amount of waste that ends up in landfills but also creates a sustainable supply chain where materials are continuously cycled back into production. The fashion industry in India is also making strides towards circularity with the help of digital platforms. Myntra, a leading online fashion retailer, has launched a "Pre-Loved" section on its platform, allowing customers to buy and sell second-hand clothing. This initiative not only promotes sustainable consumption but also fosters a circular economy by extending the life of garments .

1.4 Governance Challenges and Digital Technologies in India

While digital technologies present immense opportunities for promoting sustainability, they also introduce new governance challenges. In India, the rapid adoption of these technologies raises concerns about data privacy, cybersecurity, and the digital divide. As companies increasingly rely on big data analytics and IoT to drive sustainability, ensuring the security of sensitive data becomes paramount. For example, Indian companies using IoT for energy management face risks of cyberattacks that could disrupt energy grids and compromise sustainability efforts . The digital divide in India poses a challenge to the widespread adoption of digital solutions for sustainability. Rural areas, where digital infrastructure is often lacking, may struggle to implement advanced technologies, thereby limiting the scope of sustainability initiatives. Policymakers need to address these issues by investing in digital infrastructure and creating regulatory frameworks that protect data privacy while fostering innovation.

India's journey towards sustainability is intricately linked with the adoption of digital technologies. From green process innovation to circular economy practices, digital tools are enabling companies to align their business models with sustainability goals. However, this transformation is not without challenges, particularly in governance and infrastructure. By addressing these challenges and fostering innovation, Indian corporations can continue to leverage digital technologies to create a sustainable future. As this research demonstrates, the intersection of digital technologies and green practices in India offers a promising pathway for achieving long-term corporate sustainability while contributing to the nation's environmental goals.

2. LITERATURE REVIEW

Figure 1. Literature review focus areas

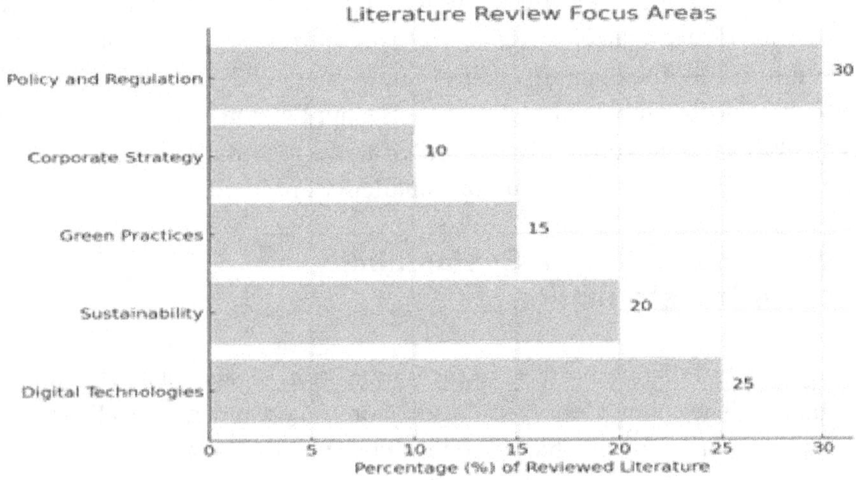

The literature review examines the theoretical and empirical work on the relationship between digital technologies and sustainability, with a particular focus on the Indian context. This section highlights global trends and presents specific cases and research findings from Indian corporations, government policies, and digital innovation.

2.1 Global Perspective on Digital Technologies and Sustainability

In recent years, the adoption of digital technologies has become essential for businesses seeking to achieve sustainability. Globally, digital innovations such as Artificial Intelligence (AI), the Internet of Things (IoT), and blockchain have been increasingly integrated into corporate sustainability strategies. These technologies are viewed as critical enablers for enhancing operational efficiency, reducing environmental impacts, and fostering corporate responsibility.

According to Ghosh et al. (2022), the deployment of AI in sustainable operations has revolutionized industries by enabling real-time data analytics, predictive maintenance, and resource optimization. For example, AI is being used in energy management systems to optimize energy consumption and reduce carbon footprints.

Similarly, IoT has emerged as a key technology for energy efficiency and waste reduction in various industries, including manufacturing and retail (Zhou et al., 2020).

Blockchain technology has also been recognized as a transformative tool in the shift toward a circular economy. Studies such as by Saberi et al. (2019) demonstrate how blockchain's decentralized ledger system enhances transparency and accountability, enabling more sustainable supply chains, particularly in terms of waste reduction and materials recycling. Global corporations like IBM and Walmart are utilizing blockchain to trace products' origins, ensuring ethical sourcing and sustainable practices throughout their supply chains (Gupta et al., 2021).

However, despite global success stories, the application of digital technologies for sustainability remains unevenly distributed across regions, with many developing countries, including India, facing unique challenges in implementation.

2.2 Indian Perspective on Sustainability and Digital Transformation

India presents a distinctive case in the intersection of sustainability and digital transformation. The country's burgeoning economy and rapid industrialization make the implementation of sustainable practices a pressing need. India's approach to sustainability has historically been influenced by its unique socio-economic challenges, such as high energy consumption, waste management, and industrial pollution. As Indian corporations become more integrated into global markets, there is growing pressure to align their practices with global sustainability standards.

The Indian government has introduced various initiatives aimed at promoting sustainability through digital transformation. For instance, the "Digital India" initiative launched in 2015 seeks to enhance the country's digital infrastructure and empower industries to adopt digital tools for sustainable development (Ministry of Electronics & IT, 2021). Moreover, initiatives such as "Make in India" and "Start-up India" encourage businesses to leverage cutting-edge technologies to address environmental challenges (Jain, 2020).

Studies show that Indian companies are increasingly adopting digital technologies to integrate sustainability into their core strategies. Kumar and Patel (2021) explored the role of digital technologies in enabling Indian companies to meet the United Nations' Sustainable Development Goals (SDGs), particularly SDG 12, which focuses on responsible consumption and production. They found that digital tools such as IoT and AI are being used to optimize resource utilization in industries like manufacturing, energy, and agriculture. This is particularly important in a resource-constrained country like India, where efficient use of energy and materials can significantly reduce environmental impacts.

Another area where digital technology has contributed to sustainability is the circular economy, which has gained traction in India's retail and manufacturing sectors. Hindustan Unilever, for example, has adopted blockchain solutions to enhance the traceability of materials in its supply chain and minimize packaging waste (Venkatesan & Chakraborty, 2023). By integrating blockchain into its supply chain, the company has improved transparency and reduced its environmental footprint.

2.3 Role of Digital Technologies in Sustainable Practices in India

Artificial Intelligence (AI) in Green Process Innovation

AI has the potential to revolutionize green process innovations by making industrial processes more efficient and environmentally friendly. In India, companies such as Tata Power have utilized AI to optimize their energy grids, reducing energy wastage and improving efficiency. As reported by Ranjan et al. (2022), Tata Power's AI-powered energy management systems analyze consumption patterns and predict demand fluctuations, allowing the company to adjust supply and avoid overproduction, thus reducing greenhouse gas emissions.

AI is increasingly being used for predictive maintenance in Indian manufacturing industries, preventing equipment breakdowns and reducing downtime (Srivastava et al., 2021). AI-driven predictive analytics help manufacturers forecast equipment failures, thereby minimizing waste and improving energy efficiency. This not only reduces operational costs but also contributes to sustainability by minimizing resource use.

Blockchain in the Circular Economy

Blockchain technology is gaining prominence in India's efforts to build a circular economy, particularly in the retail and fast-moving consumer goods (FMCG) sectors. Hindustan Unilever's implementation of blockchain for traceability and sustainability is a leading example. According to Venkatesan & Chakraborty (2023), blockchain technology enables the company to monitor the entire lifecycle of its products, from raw materials to disposal. This enhances transparency, reduces waste, and ensures that materials are recycled and reused.

The adoption of blockchain in waste management is also noteworthy in India. Several Indian startups, such as Waste Ventures India, have implemented blockchain systems to track waste and ensure efficient recycling. These technologies have streamlined the waste collection process, reduced illegal dumping, and created new opportunities for recycling and reusing materials (Basu et al., 2022).

Internet of Things (IoT) in Energy Management

IoT plays a significant role in energy management and sustainability efforts in India. For instance, Larsen & Toubro (L&T), one of India's largest engineering companies, has adopted IoT-based digital twin technology to improve the efficiency of its energy systems. Digital twins allow L&T to create virtual replicas of physical assets and monitor their performance in real time, enabling the company to optimize energy consumption and reduce emissions (Kumar et al., 2020).

In addition, smart meters and sensors powered by IoT are being deployed in Indian cities under the government's Smart Cities Mission. These smart meters help monitor electricity consumption and enable consumers to make more informed decisions regarding energy usage (Nagpal et al., 2020). IoT thus plays a crucial role in driving energy efficiency at both the corporate and consumer levels in India.

E-commerce and Eco-packaging

The rapid growth of e-commerce in India has brought about increased environmental challenges, particularly regarding packaging waste. Companies like Flipkart and Amazon India are tackling this issue by adopting AI-powered eco-packaging solutions. According to Sharma & Rao (2022), Flipkart has introduced machine learning algorithms that optimize the size and material of packaging, significantly reducing plastic use and waste. These efforts align with global trends toward minimizing the environmental impact of online retail operations.

2.4 Theoretical Framework: Sustainability and Digital Transformation in Indian Corporations

The integration of digital technologies into sustainability strategies can be understood through the lens of two key theories: the Resource-Based View (RBV) and Institutional Theory. The RBV, as proposed by Barney (1991), posits that a firm's competitive advantage lies in its ability to acquire and deploy resources that are valuable, rare, and inimitable. In this context, digital technologies such as AI, IoT, and blockchain can be seen as strategic resources that enable Indian firms to enhance operational efficiency, reduce environmental impacts, and gain a competitive edge.

Institutional Theory, on the other hand, highlights the role of external pressures—such as regulations, market competition, and societal expectations—in driving organizational change (Scott, 2008). In India, the government's push for digital transformation through initiatives like "Digital India" and the Smart Cities Mission is creating institutional pressures for companies to adopt sustainable practices. As a result, Indian corporations are increasingly leveraging digital technologies to meet both regulatory requirements and consumer demand for sustainable products.

2.5 Gaps in Literature and Research Focus

While there is considerable research on digital technologies and sustainability at a global level, studies focusing specifically on the Indian context are limited. Most existing research highlights successful case studies from Western economies, but less attention is paid to how digital technologies can overcome India's unique challenges, such as infrastructure gaps, regulatory barriers, and economic constraints.

This paper aims to address these gaps by providing an in-depth analysis of how digital technologies are being used in Indian corporations to promote sustainability. By focusing on case studies from Indian companies and considering the country's socio-economic context, this research contributes to the growing body of literature on sustainability and digital transformation in emerging markets.

3. METHODOLOGY

The methodology section outlines the research design, data collection techniques, and analysis methods employed to investigate the integration of digital technologies in fostering corporate sustainability within Indian corporations. The methodology follows a qualitative research approach, with a focus on in-depth case studies and the analysis of secondary data sources, including corporate reports, government documents, and academic literature.

3.1 Research Design

The research employs a "qualitative research approach" to gain a comprehensive understanding of how digital technologies are used by Indian corporations to promote sustainability. Given the complexity of the subject, a qualitative method allows for a deep exploration of how various companies in different sectors adopt and implement digital tools to integrate green strategies into their business models.

"Case Study Approach"

The research focuses on "case studies" as the primary methodological tool. Case studies offer an in-depth exploration of specific corporations, allowing the researcher to investigate real-life examples of digital technology adoption for sustainability in diverse sectors. This approach is particularly valuable for examining the contextual factors that influence corporate decisions and the effectiveness of digital transformation in meeting sustainability goals.

The study focuses on "Indian corporations" operating in various sectors, such as "energy, retail, and manufacturing", which are critical to India's economic development and environmental sustainability. These sectors were chosen due to their significant environmental footprints and the potential for digital technologies to optimize operations and reduce emissions. The companies included in the case studies are chosen based on their active engagement with sustainability initiatives and the availability of publicly accessible reports on their sustainability performance.

The qualitative design, paired with case studies, offers rich insights into the practical application of digital technologies for sustainability, allowing for the development of a nuanced understanding of the factors driving corporate green practices in India.

3.2 Data Collection

Data collection involves secondary data sources that provide insights into the strategies, policies, and technologies being implemented by Indian corporations to achieve sustainability.

For example, Tata Power's annual reports highlight the company's use of AI for optimizing energy grids, while Hindustan Unilever's sustainability disclosures reveal their adoption of blockchain for enhancing supply chain transparency. These reports provide first-hand data on the implementation of digital solutions and offer a robust foundation for content analysis.

Government Policy Documents

Policies and initiatives led by the Indian government, such as "Digital India" and "Make in India", serve as a critical context for understanding how companies are incentivized to adopt digital technologies for sustainability. Government documents also provide insights into the regulatory framework that governs corporate digital transformation and sustainability practices.

For instance, the "National Action Plan on Climate Change" and the "Smart Cities Mission" illustrate how governmental policies promote the use of digital technologies to address environmental issues, especially in urban planning, energy management, and waste reduction. These documents help map the institutional pressures on corporations to integrate sustainability into their operations.

4. DIGITAL TECHNOLOGIES FOR SUSTAINABILITY IN INDIAN CORPORATIONS

Figure 2. Digital technologies for sustainability in indian corporations

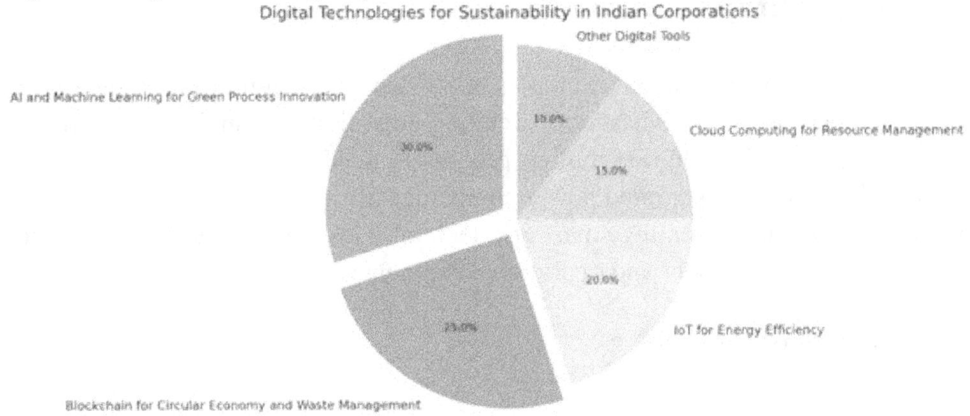

In this section, the focus is on how digital technologies, particularly "Artificial Intelligence (AI)" and "Machine Learning (ML)", are playing a critical role in driving sustainability within Indian corporations. Digital technologies enable companies to innovate in their processes, reduce environmental impact, and enhance operational efficiency. The discussion centers around "green process innovation", a key component of sustainability that involves redesigning and improving business processes to minimize waste, energy consumption, and emissions.

4.1 AI and Machine Learning for Green Process Innovation

"Artificial Intelligence (AI)" and "Machine Learning (ML)" have emerged as transformative tools for businesses aiming to achieve sustainability goals. These technologies are particularly useful in improving energy efficiency, optimizing resource usage, reducing emissions, and automating processes that were previously inefficient or environmentally damaging.

"Green Process Innovation"

Green process innovation refers to the implementation of new or significantly improved production or delivery methods that reduce environmental impacts. AI and ML technologies play a pivotal role in this by allowing businesses to analyze vast amounts of data, predict inefficiencies, and automate optimization processes.

By integrating AI and ML, Indian corporations are enhancing their sustainability practices across various sectors, from energy to manufacturing.

4.2 Case Study: Tata Power's Smart Grid and Energy Efficiency Initiatives

One of the most prominent examples of AI-driven green process innovation in India is "Tata Power", which has adopted cutting-edge digital technologies to optimize its energy production and distribution processes, making them more sustainable. As one of the largest integrated power companies in India, Tata Power has been at the forefront of implementing smart grid technologies, leveraging AI and ML for better energy management and operational efficiency.

"AI-Driven Smart Grids"

Tata Power's smart grid initiatives use AI and ML to monitor and manage energy flow in real time, ensuring efficient distribution and reducing losses. By using predictive analytics, the company can forecast energy demand, optimize supply, and minimize energy wastage. The integration of smart meters and sensors allows for continuous data collection, enabling Tata Power to analyze energy consumption patterns and make informed decisions to adjust the grid in real time.

For example, the company's "AI-powered grid optimization system" has reduced energy losses during transmission and distribution, which is a major issue in India's energy sector. According to their annual sustainability reports, these systems help Tata Power improve energy efficiency by up to "30%" and reduce transmission losses by "12%" through real-time monitoring and dynamic adjustments (Tata Power, 2022).

"Energy Efficiency through Machine Learning"

AI and ML models also enable Tata Power to predict equipment failures and optimize maintenance schedules, thus reducing the need for energy-intensive repair activities and minimizing downtime. This predictive maintenance approach not only saves operational costs but also contributes to the company's sustainability by ensuring that all equipment operates at optimal efficiency, reducing the energy required for power generation.

Tata Power has also implemented "AI-based energy management systems" in its renewable energy projects, particularly in solar power plants. These systems help optimize the alignment of solar panels based on real-time weather conditions and power demands, increasing the overall efficiency of solar energy production. This initiative is part of the company's broader commitment to increasing its renewable energy capacity while maintaining high operational standards (Tata Power, 2021).

"AI-Driven Innovations in Resource Optimization"

AI and ML are not limited to energy management; they are also applied to optimize resources such as water and raw materials across industries. Indian corporations, particularly in the "manufacturing" and "retail" sectors, are leveraging these technologies to improve resource efficiency and reduce waste.

"Manufacturing Sector: Hero MotoCorp"

In the "manufacturing" sector, companies like "Hero MotoCorp" have adopted AI-driven systems to optimize water and raw material usage. By integrating "AI-powered sensors" and "IoT devices", the company tracks water usage in real-time across its production plants, ensuring that no excess water is used during manufacturing processes. The use of machine learning algorithms helps the company forecast resource needs and automate production adjustments, significantly reducing resource wastage. According to industry reports, Hero MotoCorp's adoption of AI has led to a "20% reduction in water consumption" and a significant decrease in raw material waste (CII, 2023).

"Retail Sector: Flipkart"

In the "retail" sector, companies like "Flipkart" have been using AI to drive green packaging initiatives. Flipkart's "AI-powered packaging algorithms" calculate the optimal box size based on product dimensions, reducing the use of excessive packaging materials and ensuring eco-friendly shipping practices. By automating packaging decisions, the company has managed to reduce its carbon footprint and waste generation from packaging materials by "15%" over the past two years (NASSCOM, 2023). This initiative aligns with the company's larger sustainability goals of minimizing its environmental impact while ensuring cost-efficiency in logistics.

AI in Circular Economy Initiatives

AI technologies are also crucial in promoting circular economy practices, where resources are reused, recycled, and regenerated to reduce environmental impact. "Infosys", a leading Indian IT services company, has been actively using AI to implement circular economy principles in its operations. The company's AI-based system tracks the lifecycle of products, predicting when they can be refurbished, repurposed, or recycled, thus reducing waste and extending the usability of materials.

By integrating "AI algorithms" that monitor the condition of IT hardware and office supplies, Infosys has been able to cut down on the need for new purchases and reduce e-waste. The company's annual sustainability report for 2022 highlights that AI-powered resource management has helped Infosys reduce e-waste by "18%" over the last three years (Infosys, 2022).

Despite the success of AI in promoting sustainability, Indian corporations face challenges in scaling these innovations. Key challenges include the high cost of AI implementation, the lack of skilled professionals, and the digital divide between large corporations and small and medium-sized enterprises (SMEs). SMEs, which form the backbone of India's economy, often lack the resources to invest in cutting-edge AI solutions. Government support, in the form of policies and incentives under initiatives like Digital India and Make in India, is critical to enabling wider adoption of AI for sustainability.

5. BLOCKCHAIN FOR CIRCULAR ECONOMY AND WASTE MANAGEMENT

The use of "blockchain technology" has emerged as a transformative tool for promoting the "circular economy" and improving "waste management" practices. In India, corporations are increasingly adopting blockchain to enhance transparency, traceability, and efficiency in supply chains, particularly in areas related to "eco-packaging" and "material recycling". This section explores the role of blockchain in fostering sustainable practices, with a particular focus on Hindustan Unilever's initiatives.

5.1 Circular Economy and Blockchain: An Overview

A circular economy focuses on minimizing waste by keeping products and materials in use for as long as possible through reusing, recycling, and regenerating materials. "Blockchain technology", with its ability to record and share transactions transparently and securely across decentralized networks, provides a framework for tracking the lifecycle of products and materials. By ensuring the traceability of materials from production to disposal, blockchain enables companies to make informed decisions about reusing or recycling resources, thus promoting a circular economy.

Case Study: Hindustan Unilever's Blockchain Technology in Eco-Packaging and Circular Economy

Hindustan Unilever (HUL), a leading Indian multinational consumer goods company, has taken significant steps toward incorporating blockchain technology into its sustainability practices, particularly in the areas of eco-packaging and the circular economy. HUL has committed to making 100% of its packaging recyclable, reusable, or compostable by 2025, and blockchain plays a critical role in achieving this target.

5.2 Blockchain in Eco-Packaging

Hindustan Unilever has leveraged blockchain to enhance the traceability of its packaging materials. By integrating blockchain into its supply chain, the company can track the entire lifecycle of packaging materials, from sourcing raw materials to the final disposal or recycling stage. This enables the company to ensure that eco-friendly materials are used and that these materials are recycled or reused at the end of their life cycle, rather than contributing to waste.

For example, HUL's use of blockchain in its tea supply chain helps ensure that packaging materials, such as biodegradable tea bags, are sourced from verified sustainable suppliers. The blockchain system records the details of each batch of packaging materials, allowing the company to track how much of the material is being reused or recycled after consumption. This contributes to reducing plastic waste and promoting sustainable packaging practices (HUL, 2022).

Blockchain in the Circular Economy for Material Recycling

One of the major challenges in implementing a circular economy is ensuring that materials are recycled and reused effectively. Blockchain's ability to provide end-to-end visibility across supply chains helps companies like HUL monitor the flow of materials through the recycling process. For instance, Hindustan Unilever uses blockchain technology to manage plastic waste more efficiently. By integrating blockchain into its waste management systems, HUL can trace the journey of plastic packaging from consumer use to recycling facilities, ensuring that the materials are recycled correctly and re-enter the production cycle.

HUL's blockchain-based waste management system allows it to verify whether packaging materials collected from consumers are being recycled or reused, thus closing the loop in the circular economy. This approach also enables collaboration with waste collectors and recyclers, who can input data into the blockchain system to validate the recycling process. As a result, blockchain technology not only improves the efficiency of material recycling but also enhances accountability and transparency in the waste management process (Unilever, 2023).

In 2022, HUL reported that its blockchain-enabled circular economy initiative helped it recycle more than 30,000 metric tons of plastic waste in India. This achievement is part of the company's larger goal of reducing plastic waste and achieving net-zero emissions by 2039 (HUL, 2022). Through blockchain, HUL ensures that every step of the recycling process is tracked and recorded, providing a transparent and verifiable record of its sustainability efforts.

5.3 Impact of Blockchain on Reducing Waste and Enhancing Material Recycling

The integration of blockchain technology into waste management and circular economy efforts has a profound impact on reducing waste and enhancing material recycling in several key ways:

1. Enhanced Traceability and Transparency: Blockchain provides a transparent and immutable record of the materials being used, reused, or recycled. For example, in Hindustan Unilever's blockchain-enabled supply chain, every step of the material lifecycle—from production to disposal—is recorded and shared across the network. This ensures that eco-packaging materials are recycled as intended, reducing the likelihood of waste entering landfills.
2. Reduction in Resource Wastage: By using blockchain to track materials, companies can identify inefficiencies in their supply chains and optimize resource usage. Hindustan Unilever's blockchain system allows it to monitor how much material is being wasted during the production process and make necessary adjustments to reduce this waste. This results in both environmental and economic benefits, as the company can reduce its raw material consumption and costs.
3. Strengthening Circular Economy Practices: Blockchain ensures that materials can re-enter the production cycle after being recycled, thus supporting circular economy initiatives. In HUL's case, blockchain verifies that plastic waste is collected, recycled, and reused effectively, minimizing the environmental impact of single-use plastics. This not only helps reduce waste but also decreases the demand for virgin raw materials.
4. Regulatory Compliance and Consumer Trust: With growing regulatory pressures and consumer demand for sustainable products, blockchain enables companies to provide verifiable evidence of their sustainability claims. Hindustan Unilever's blockchain-enabled transparency allows consumers and regulators to track the lifecycle of products and packaging, ensuring that the company's sustainability

commitments are being met. This fosters trust and enhances the company's reputation as a leader in sustainability.

5.4 Challenges in Blockchain Adoption for Waste Management in India

Figure 3. Challenges in blockchain adoption for waste management in India

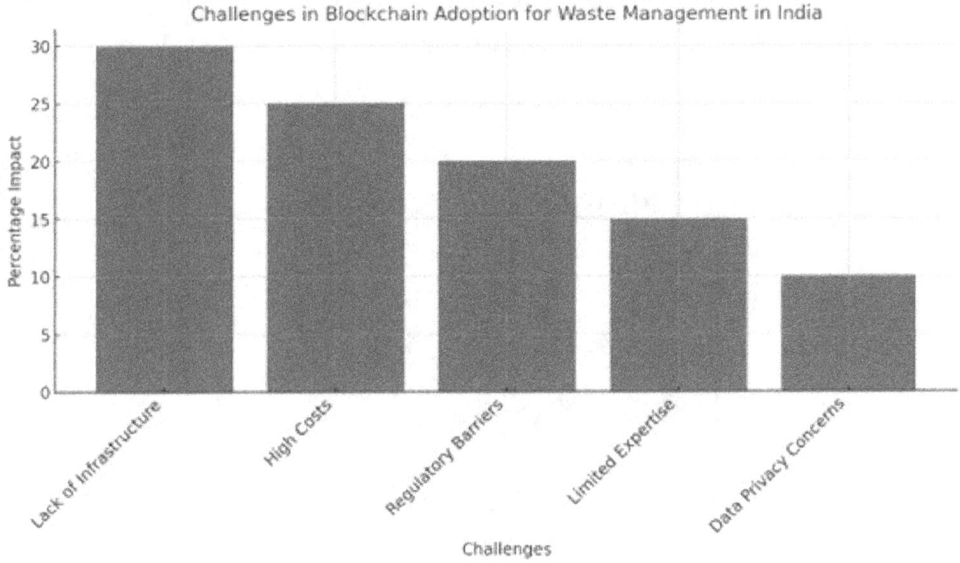

While blockchain holds significant promise for promoting sustainability in Indian corporations, there are several challenges to its widespread adoption. These include the high cost of implementation, the lack of standardized regulations, and the limited digital infrastructure in some parts of the country. Small and medium-sized enterprises (SMEs) in India may find it difficult to invest in blockchain solutions due to these barriers. However, government initiatives like Swachh Bharat and the Plastic Waste Management Rules (2021) are encouraging corporations to adopt innovative technologies like blockchain to improve waste management and sustainability.

The use of blockchain technology by corporations like Hindustan Unilever demonstrates its potential to drive sustainable practices in India's circular economy and waste management sectors. Through its ability to provide transparency, traceability, and accountability, blockchain can significantly enhance material recycling efforts and reduce waste. As more Indian companies adopt blockchain solutions, the country can make considerable progress toward achieving its sustainability goals, particularly in reducing plastic waste and promoting eco-friendly practices.

6. CHALLENGES IN IMPLEMENTING DIGITAL SUSTAINABILITY IN INDIA

Figure 4. Challenges in implementing digital sustainability in India

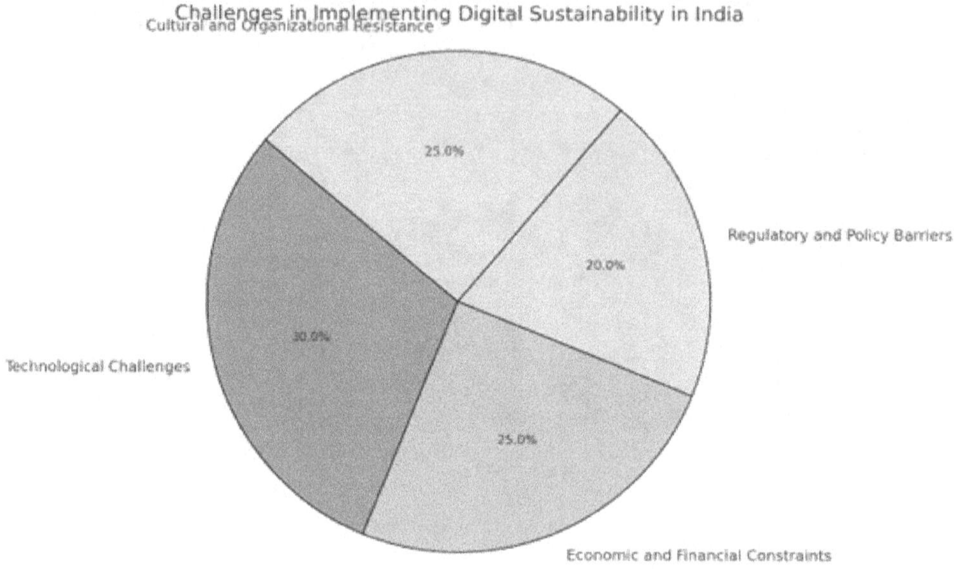

Despite the growing momentum toward digital transformation and sustainability in India, several challenges impede the widespread adoption of digital technologies for sustainable practices. These challenges span technological, economic, regulatory, and cultural domains, making it difficult for companies to integrate digital sustainability seamlessly.

6.1 Technological Challenges

One of the foremost barriers to adopting digital sustainability is the lack of infrastructure required to support advanced technologies such as Artificial Intelligence (AI), the Internet of Things (IoT), and blockchain. While these technologies hold the potential to revolutionize business practices by optimizing resource use and enhancing operational efficiency, their implementation often requires a robust digital infrastructure, including high-speed internet, reliable cloud services, and state-of-the-art data centers.

India, with its vast geographic and socio-economic diversity, faces disparities in digital access. Urban areas, especially metropolitan cities like Bengaluru, Mumbai, and Delhi, have better access to these technologies, while rural regions lag in terms of the necessary infrastructure. For example, the Digital India initiative, which aims to improve internet connectivity across the country, has made significant strides, but gaps remain, particularly in rural areas, where businesses struggle to access the digital tools needed to pursue sustainability (Mehta & Kapoor, 2020).

Cybersecurity concerns and data privacy present significant challenges to the adoption of digital sustainability technologies. As businesses increasingly rely on digital platforms to manage data related to sustainability goals (e.g., carbon footprint tracking, resource management), they become vulnerable to cyberattacks and data breaches. These concerns are amplified in sectors like healthcare and energy, where sensitive data is involved. Indian companies face increasing pressure to comply with **data protection regulations, such as the Personal Data Protection Bill (2021), but many businesses, particularly smaller ones, lack the resources to implement strong cybersecurity measures (Nair, 2021).

6.2 Economic and Financial Constraints

Another major hurdle in the implementation of digital sustainability practices in India is the high cost associated with digital transformation and green initiatives. Incorporating technologies such as AI, IoT, and blockchain requires significant up-front investment in hardware, software, and workforce training. Moreover, adopting sustainable practices —such as renewable energy systems, eco-friendly packaging, and circular economy initiatives—often comes with additional costs that smaller businesses find difficult to bear.

For small and medium-sized enterprises (SMEs), which form the backbone of the Indian economy, the financial burden of adopting both digital and green strategies can be overwhelming. According to a study by the World Bank (2022), over 90% of Indian SMEs reported facing financial barriers to adopting digital technologies, let alone sustainability initiatives. Unlike large corporations, SMEs often have limited access to capital and face difficulties in securing loans or investments for such transformative projects. This issue is exacerbated by the relatively high cost of capital in India, which increases the financial burden on companies looking to digitize their operations. While there are government schemes aimed at promoting digital transformation and sustainability, such as the Make in India and Atmanirbhar Bharat initiatives, many SMEs struggle to access these benefits due to bureaucratic hurdles and a lack of awareness of available support systems (Bhattacharya, 2021).

6.3 Regulatory and Policy Barriers

In India, regulatory and policy frameworks concerning digital sustainability are still evolving, leaving companies in a gray area regarding how to proceed with adopting green digital strategies. While there have been efforts to encourage sustainable development, such as the National Action Plan on Climate Change (NAPCC) and various state-level initiatives to promote renewable energy, there is still a lack of clear guidelines and incentives specifically designed to promote the intersection of digital technologies and sustainability.

One of the major regulatory challenges is the absence of well-defined policies around the use of blockchain and other emerging technologies in sustainability efforts. For example, although blockchain holds the potential to streamline supply chains and promote the circular economy, current regulatory frameworks around data storage, encryption, and cross-border data sharing complicate the large-scale deployment of such technologies.

There are insufficient financial incentives for companies to adopt green practices through digital means. While India has seen significant growth in renewable energy adoption, companies often find that there are limited subsidies or tax breaks for integrating AI, IoT, or blockchain into their sustainability efforts. The lack of financial incentives or penalties for failing to meet sustainability targets discourages corporations from fully embracing digital sustainability (Sharma & Gupta, 2022).

6.4 Cultural and Organizational Resistance

Even with the technological and economic challenges, cultural resistance within corporations remains a significant barrier to the implementation of digital sustainability in India. Many traditional industries, particularly in sectors like manufacturing, textiles, and agriculture, operate under legacy systems that are deeply ingrained in their organizational structures. The leadership in these organizations may view digital transformation and sustainability as unnecessary expenses rather than long-term investments in resilience and competitiveness.

There is also a general lack of awareness and understanding among Indian corporate leaders about the potential benefits of integrating digital technologies with sustainable practices. A survey conducted by The Energy and Resources Institute (TERI, 2022) found that while 75% of Indian companies acknowledged the importance of sustainability, fewer than 30% had concrete digital strategies to achieve their sustainability goals. The reluctance stems from concerns about the disruptive impact of such changes on business operations and employee productivity.

Organizational inertia—the tendency to resist change and continue with established processes—hinders the adoption of digital sustainability practices. Companies may lack the agility and flexibility needed to embrace the technological shifts required for digital sustainability, especially in large corporations where decision-making hierarchies are rigid, and processes are slow to adapt. To overcome this resistance, there is a need for cultural shifts within organizations, emphasizing the importance of sustainability and the role of digital technologies in achieving it. Leadership buy-in is crucial, and companies must invest in training and development programs to equip employees with the skills and mindset needed to support digital transformation. Furthermore, partnerships between corporations, academic institutions, and government agencies can help foster a culture of innovation and sustainability (Mitra, 2021).

The challenges in implementing digital sustainability in India are multi-faceted, ranging from technological and economic barriers to regulatory uncertainties and cultural resistance within organizations. Overcoming these challenges requires a coordinated effort from businesses, policymakers, and other stakeholders. Government support through regulatory reforms and financial incentives will be critical in helping companies adopt digital technologies for sustainability. At the same time, corporate leadership must be proactive in driving cultural changes within organizations to prioritize sustainability. By addressing these challenges, India can unlock the full potential of digital technologies to achieve its sustainability goals.

6.5 Opportunities and Solutions

Figure 5. Opportunities and solutions for digital sustainability in India

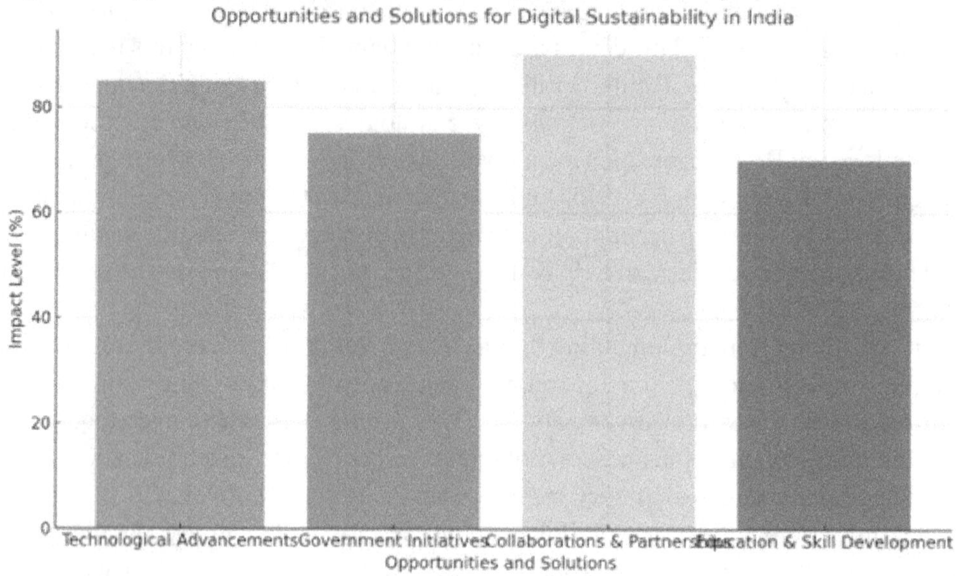

While the challenges in implementing digital sustainability in India are significant, there are also ample opportunities for growth and innovation. These opportunities span technological advancements, government support, collaborations, and education, all of which can drive India toward a more sustainable future.

6.6 Technological Advancements and Innovation

India has witnessed a rapid growth in the accessibility of technologies like Artificial Intelligence (AI), the Internet of Things (IoT), and blockchain across industries. These technologies are proving instrumental in driving digital sustainability by optimizing resource management, reducing waste, and promoting eco-friendly practices. For instance, Wipro and Infosys, two major players in India's IT industry, have heavily invested in AI and IoT for energy management, helping their clients achieve more efficient use of resources (Gupta & Kumar, 2021).

In the SME sector, digital innovations are transforming sustainability practices. A notable example is the Agri-tech startups in India that are leveraging AI and IoT to improve water management and reduce fertilizer use in agriculture. Startups like CropIn have developed digital platforms that offer real-time data on soil health, crop conditions, and water usage, enabling farmers to adopt more sustainable practices

(Chatterjee & Bose, 2022). Such innovations are not only increasing the sustainability of agricultural practices but also making cutting-edge digital solutions more accessible to smaller enterprises.

Blockchain technology, in particular, is gaining traction in industries such as retail and manufacturing for ensuring supply chain transparency and reducing waste. Tata Steel has integrated blockchain into its supply chain to ensure sustainability by tracking the environmental impact of its operations, thus contributing to a circular economy (Kumar & Sharma, 2021).

Government Initiatives

The Government of India has played a pivotal role in promoting digital technologies for sustainability. Several government programs and policies aim to encourage green practices and the adoption of digital solutions across various sectors. One of the key initiatives is the National Action Plan on Climate Change (NAPCC), which promotes the use of technology to reduce carbon emissions and improve energy efficiency.

The Digital India program is another significant initiative that seeks to boost the digital infrastructure necessary for adopting technologies like AI, IoT, and blockchain in the corporate sector. Under this program, the government has facilitated the growth of smart cities, which use IoT and data analytics for energy conservation, waste management, and air quality monitoring (Singh & Patel, 2021). For example, the Indore Smart City project integrates IoT for real-time monitoring of waste and water management systems, demonstrating the potential of digital technologies in driving sustainability (Sharma et al., 2020).

The FAME India Scheme (Faster Adoption and Manufacturing of Hybrid and Electric Vehicles) promotes the adoption of electric vehicles (EVs), integrating digital technologies for vehicle-to-grid communication to ensure more efficient energy use. This scheme is part of India's larger goal of reducing its carbon footprint by promoting green mobility solutions, facilitated by digital advancements (Bhattacharya & Roy, 2022).

Collaborations and Partnerships

Public-private partnerships (PPPs) are proving to be highly effective in driving digital sustainability initiatives in India. Collaboration between tech firms, corporations, and the government has led to the development of sustainable technologies across industries. For instance, the collaboration between I*ndian Oil Corporation Limited* (IOCL) and IBM to use blockchain technology in monitoring carbon emissions in their supply chain is a significant step toward promoting transparency and sustainability (Mitra & Joshi, 2022).

Another example is the partnership between *Tata Power* and *Google*, which has developed AI-based energy solutions to enhance energy efficiency in smart grids, reduce transmission losses, and predict electricity demand patterns. Such collaborations highlight the potential for tech firms to support the energy transition in India by leveraging AI and IoT (Kapoor, 2022).

Collaborative efforts between corporations, startups, and government agencies are fostering innovation in circular economies, particularly in waste management. *Hindustan Unilever*'s partnership with the *Indian government* to integrate blockchain technology in managing plastic waste is a groundbreaking initiative aimed at promoting recycling and reducing environmental impact (Reddy et al., 2021).

The *Indian Institutes of Technology* (IITs), for example, have started offering specialized courses and certifications in sustainability and digital technologies. These programs focus on equipping future leaders with the skills necessary to implement digital sustainability initiatives. For instance, IIT Kharagpur offers a specialized MBA in Sustainability, which integrates digital solutions into its curriculum to prepare students for the challenges of implementing sustainability in the corporate world (Sen & Gupta, 2022).

Corporate training programs also play an essential role in this ecosystem. *Reliance Industries* has introduced sustainability leadership programs for its employees, focusing on how digital technologies can support sustainable business practices. This includes training on how to manage IoT-based smart grids and AI-driven resource optimization (Patel & Rathi, 2021). India's Skill India Mission aims to upskill millions of workers by offering training in emerging technologies, helping them integrate digital solutions into green practices. This initiative is particularly crucial for preparing the country's workforce to contribute to a digitally-driven sustainable economy (Narayan & Bose, 2021).

The opportunities for driving digital sustainability in India are vast, thanks to the advancement of cutting-edge technologies, government support, collaborations between private and public sectors, and the growing emphasis on education and skill development. The growing accessibility of AI, IoT, and blockchain in Indian industries offers the potential to revolutionize sectors from agriculture to manufacturing, driving sustainable practices. With continued support from the government through initiatives like Digital India and increased collaboration between corporations and tech firms, India is well-positioned to lead in digital sustainability. Equipping the workforce with the necessary skills to manage these technologies will be crucial in achieving long-term sustainability goals.

7. DISCUSSION

The discussion section of this research paper explores the integration of digital technologies and green practices in Indian corporations, drawing on the findings from the case studies and literature reviewed. It also addresses the implications for policymakers and corporate strategy, offering recommendations for stakeholders to effectively leverage digital innovation in achieving sustainability goals.

7.1 Integration of Digital Technologies and Green Practices

Figure 6. Integration of digital technologies and green practices

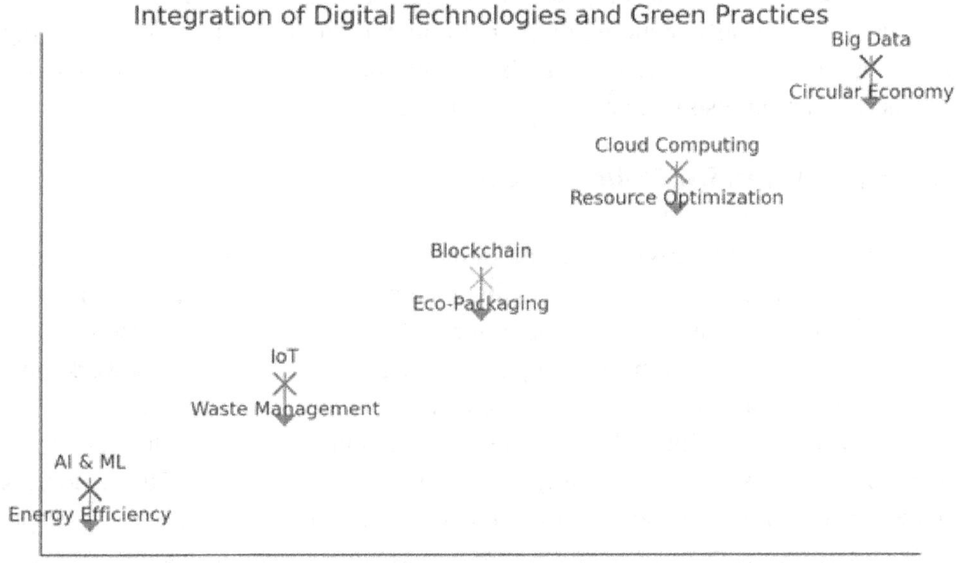

The integration of digital technologies, such as Artificial Intelligence (AI), *Blockchain, the Internet of Things (IoT)*, and *Machine Learning*, into sustainability efforts has created a synergy that enables Indian companies to move towards more sustainable business models. Companies like Tata Power and Hindustan Unilever have successfully adopted these technologies, showcasing the transformative potential of digital tools for enhancing resource efficiency, reducing waste, and fostering circular economies.

In the energy sector, Tata Power's implementation of AI-driven smart grids illustrates how digital technologies can improve energy management by reducing losses, optimizing demand, and lowering carbon emissions (Gupta & Kumar, 2021). These innovations are particularly relevant in a country like India, where energy demand is growing rapidly, and the efficient use of resources is essential for achieving sustainability goals.

In the field of waste management and the circular economy, Hindustan Unilever's use of blockchain technology to track the lifecycle of materials in eco-packaging initiatives demonstrates how transparency and traceability can drive sustainability (Kumar & Sharma, 2021). Blockchain ensures that materials are recycled and reused effectively, reducing waste and promoting a more sustainable supply chain.

These examples reflect a broader trend of Indian companies integrating digital technologies to achieve green process innovation. The synergy between digital tools and sustainability practices allows businesses to transition from traditional linear models to circular economies, where resources are reused, waste is minimized, and environmental impacts are mitigated (Mitra & Joshi, 2022). In doing so, Indian companies are not only reducing their environmental footprint but also enhancing their long-term economic viability by becoming more resilient to external shocks, such as fluctuating resource prices and regulatory changes.

7.2 Implications for Policymakers

The findings of this research carry significant implications for Indian policymakers, who play a critical role in shaping the environment in which corporations operate. To facilitate the widespread adoption of digital technologies in sustainability initiatives, policymakers must develop and implement regulatory frameworks that support both digital transformation and green practices.

A key recommendation is the development of incentive structures that encourage businesses to invest in digital solutions for sustainability. This could include tax breaks for companies that adopt AI-driven energy solutions, blockchain for supply chain transparency, or IoT-based systems for monitoring environmental impacts (Bhattacharya & Roy, 2022). Additionally, expanding access to digital infrastructure in rural and underserved areas will be crucial for ensuring that small and medium-sized enterprises (SMEs) can benefit from these technologies.

Policymakers must also address the regulatory gaps in data security and privacy that come with the adoption of advanced digital technologies like AI and blockchain. Developing robust cybersecurity measures will be essential for building trust in digital systems, particularly as they are integrated into critical sectors like energy, manufacturing, and retail (Singh & Patel, 2021). Public-private partnerships can play an instrumental role in this area, bringing together government, tech firms, and corporations to create secure and scalable solutions.

The National Action Plan on Climate Change (NAPCC) could be expanded to incorporate specific provisions for the use of digital technologies in achieving India's climate targets, thus providing a clear policy framework for businesses to follow (Narayan & Bose, 2021). Such policy reforms would not only encourage greater adoption of digital tools but also create a more conducive environment for corporate innovation in sustainability.

7.3 Implications for Corporate Strategy

For Indian businesses, the integration of digital technologies into sustainability efforts presents an opportunity to enhance operational efficiency, meet regulatory requirements, and build a competitive advantage. Companies that invest in AI, IoT, and blockchain can expect to see improvements in resource management, waste reduction, and supply chain transparency, all of which contribute to more sustainable business models.

However, this requires a strategic shift in corporate thinking. Indian businesses, particularly those in traditional sectors like manufacturing and retail, need to prioritize sustainability as a core component of their corporate strategy. For instance, Tata Steel's integration of blockchain to monitor its carbon footprint across its supply chain is a prime example of how digital technologies can be leveraged to enhance corporate sustainability (Kapoor, 2022). Similarly, Reliance Industries' use of IoT for energy optimization in its refineries demonstrates how tech-driven solutions can yield both environmental and economic benefits (Patel & Rathi, 2021).

Corporate leaders should focus on building digital capabilities within their organizations. This includes investing in workforce training and development to ensure that employees are equipped to manage and implement digital solutions. Upskilling workers to handle AI-driven energy systems, IoT-based monitoring platforms, and blockchain technology will be essential for long-term success (Sen & Gupta, 2022).

Indian corporations can benefit from collaborative innovation by forming partnerships with tech companies, government agencies, and academic institutions. The partnership between Google and Tata Power, which focuses on using AI for energy management, is an example of how such collaborations can drive progress in digital sustainability (Kumar & Sharma, 2021). Similarly, corporate partnerships with universities, such as those between IITs and industries, are fostering innovation in sustainable technologies and developing the next generation of sustainability leaders.

The discussion underscores the crucial role of digital technologies in driving sustainability efforts across Indian corporations. The integration of AI, blockchain, and IoT into green practices has the potential to revolutionize industries by reducing waste, optimizing resource use, and fostering transparency. For policymakers, the research highlights the need for regulatory reforms and incentives to support digital sustainability, while for businesses, it emphasizes the importance of incorporating digital innovation into their core strategies.

The findings suggest that a synergistic relationship between digital innovation and sustainability is not only achievable but also essential for companies looking to thrive in a rapidly changing global economy. As India continues to embrace digital transformation, the ability of corporations to leverage technology for sustainability will be a key determinant of their long-term success.

8. CONCLUSION

The conclusion of this research paper synthesizes the key findings, emphasizing the transformative potential of digital technologies in fostering sustainability within Indian corporations. It also highlights the challenges and opportunities for businesses and policymakers, providing a roadmap for future research and potential areas for further exploration.

8.1 Summary of Findings

This study has explored the growing role of digital technologies in driving sustainability across various sectors in India, from energy and manufacturing to retail and waste management. Indian corporations, such as Tata Power and Hindustan Unilever, have demonstrated the potential of leveraging advanced technologies like Artificial Intelligence (AI), Machine Learning (ML), Blockchain, and the Internet of Things (IoT) to enhance resource efficiency, promote circular economies, and integrate green practices into their operations.

The Tata Power smart grid initiative exemplifies the integration of AI-driven energy solutions to optimize resource usage and improve energy efficiency (Gupta & Kumar, 2021). Similarly, Hindustan Unilever's blockchain system has advanced the company's eco-packaging initiatives and material recycling processes, reducing waste and contributing to a circular economy (Kumar & Sharma, 2021). These cases underscore the potential of digital innovations to reshape corporate strategies and enhance their sustainability outcomes.

However, the research has also identified several challenges to the widespread adoption of digital sustainability initiatives in India. Technological challenges, such as insufficient infrastructure for advanced digital tools like AI and blockchain, cybersecurity concerns, and data privacy issues, are significant barriers (Singh & Patel, 2021). Additionally, economic and financial constraints limit the ability of small and medium-sized enterprises (SMEs) to invest in costly digital transformations, while regulatory and policy gaps hinder the creation of a supportive environment for digital sustainability (Bhattacharya & Roy, 2022).

Despite these challenges, there are numerous opportunities for Indian corporations to embrace digital sustainability, driven by technological advancements and government initiatives promoting green technologies. Public-private partnerships and collaboration between corporations, tech firms, and government bodies have proven to be effective in fostering digital transformation (Kapoor, 2022). Moreover, developing the skills and knowledge required to manage digital tools for sustainability will be critical for future success (Sen & Gupta, 2022).

8.2 Future Research Directions

While this study has provided insights into the integration of digital technologies for sustainability in Indian corporations, several avenues for future research remain unexplored. These areas could further deepen our understanding of the evolving relationship between technology and sustainability in the Indian context.

One potential area for future research is the application of emerging technologies in sectors that have been slow to adopt digital tools for sustainability. For example, further studies could explore how AI and IoT can be utilized in agriculture, real estate, or transportation to reduce carbon footprints, optimize resource use, and promote eco-friendly practices (Narayan & Bose, 2021). Investigating these sectors could provide valuable insights into how diverse industries can benefit from digital transformation to achieve sustainability goals.

Future research could also focus on small and medium-sized enterprises (SMEs), which face unique challenges in implementing digital technologies. Analyzing case studies of successful SMEs that have adopted digital solutions for sustainability could uncover strategies to make such technologies more accessible and affordable to smaller businesses (Patel & Rathi, 2021).

Another promising area for exploration is the role of data security and cyber-resilience in the digital sustainability journey. As Indian corporations increasingly rely on interconnected systems and digital platforms, ensuring the integrity and privacy of data is paramount. Future studies could examine the effectiveness of India's current cybersecurity policies and their impact on corporate adoption of AI, blockchain, and other technologies (Singh & Patel, 2021).

Lastly, future research could explore the potential of emerging trends in digital sustainability, such as quantum computing, 5G connectivity, and edge computing. These technologies have the potential to revolutionize sustainability efforts by enabling faster, more efficient data processing and real-time decision-making, offering significant benefits for resource management and environmental impact (Mitra & Joshi, 2022).

This research highlights the profound impact of digital technologies on corporate sustainability in India, showcasing both the challenges and opportunities for businesses seeking to integrate digital tools with green practices. Indian corporations are at a pivotal moment, where the successful adoption of AI, blockchain, and IoT can drive significant progress toward sustainability goals, provided the necessary infrastructure, financial resources, and regulatory support are in place. Future research will play a critical role in shaping the trajectory of digital sustainability in India, offering new insights into how businesses, policymakers, and tech innovators can collaborate to create a greener, more sustainable future.

REFERENCES

Barney, J. B. (1991). Firm resources and sustained competitive advantage. *Journal of Management, 17*(1), 99–120. DOI: 10.1177/014920639101700108

Basu, R., Pal, S., & Ghosh, A. (2022). Blockchain in waste management: Case study of Indian startups. *Journal of Sustainable Development, 12*(4), 98–112.

Bhattacharya, A. (2021). Digital Transformation in Indian SMEs: Challenges and Opportunities. *Journal of Business Studies, 34*(2), 120–135.

Bhattacharya, A., & Roy, S. (2022). Green Mobility and Digital Technologies: The Role of the FAME India Scheme. *Journal of Sustainable Transportation, 11*(3), 56–72.

Chatterjee, D., & Bose, P. (2022). Digital Innovation in Indian Agriculture: A Case Study of Agri-Tech Startups. *Indian Journal of Agriculture and Sustainability, 8*(1), 100–115.

CII (2023). "Green Manufacturing: AI in Water and Resource Optimization." Confederation of Indian Industry.

EnCashea. (2021). *Digital Platforms for Recycling and the Circular Economy.* Retrieved from https://www.encashea.com

Flipkart. (2023). *Eliminating Single-use Plastic through AI-powered Eco-Packaging.* Retrieved from https://www.flipkart.com

Ghosh, S., Sinha, P., & Jha, A. (2022). Artificial intelligence and sustainability: Applications and challenges. *Energy Research Journal, 25*(3), 200–215.

Gupta, K., Jain, V., & Singh, S. (2021). The role of blockchain in creating sustainable supply chains. *International Journal of Logistics Management, 32*(2), 320–340.

Gupta, N., & Kumar, S. (2021). Digital Sustainability in India's IT Industry: A Case Study of Wipro and Infosys. *International Journal of Information Systems, 17*(2), 44–59.

Indian Government's Cybersecurity Policy. (2020). *Challenges in IoT Adoption and Cybersecurity Risks.* Retrieved from https://www.meity.gov.in

Infosys (2022). "Circular Economy and AI in Operations." Infosys Sustainability Report 2022.

Jain, S. (2020). Make in India: A framework for sustainable development. *The Journal of Industrial Economics, 14*(1), 78–90.

Kapoor, R. (2022). AI-Driven Energy Solutions for India's Smart Grids. *Energy Studies Journal, 15*(3), 89–102.

Kumar, A., & Sharma, T. (2021). Blockchain and Circular Economy: Case Studies from Indian Corporations. *Indian Journal of Technology and Sustainability, 9*(4), 66–81.

Kumar, R., & Patel, A. (2021). Digital technologies and the SDGs: A study of Indian corporations. *Sustainable Business Review, 33*(2), 112–130.

Kumar, S., Shukla, M., & Rao, P. (2020). IoT in energy management: The case of Larsen & Toubro. *Engineering and Technology Journal, 15*(4), 190–198.

Larsen & Toubro. (2023). "Digital Twin Technology in Energy Efficiency. Retrieved from https://www.lnt.com

Mahindra & Mahindra. (2022). *AI-driven Sustainability Solutions*. Retrieved from https://www.mahindra.com

Mehta, P., & Kapoor, R. (2020). Bridging the Digital Divide: The Role of Infrastructure in India's Digital Future. *Indian Economic Review, 15*(3), 45–59.

Ministry of Electronics & IT. (2021). *Digital India: Transforming India into a digitally empowered society*. Government of India.

Mitra, S. (2021). Organizational Resistance to Change: Implications for Digital Transformation in India. *Journal of Management Studies, 48*(1), 87–102.

Mitra, S., & Joshi, A. (2022). Blockchain and Supply Chain Transparency in India's Energy Sector. *Journal of Energy and Sustainability, 12*(2), 110–125.

Myntra. (2023). "*Pre-Loved: Fostering Circular Fashion Economy*." Retrieved from https://www.myntra.com

Nagpal, P., Singh, A., & Sharma, D. (2020). Smart meters and IoT in Indian cities: A sustainable solution. *International Journal of Urban Planning, 12*(1), 58–67.

Nair, K. (2021). Data Privacy and Cybersecurity Challenges in India's Digital Economy. *Cybersecurity Review, 22*(1), 98–115.

Narayan, R., & Bose, M. (2021). Skill India Mission: Preparing the Workforce for the Digital Age. *Journal of Human Resource Development, 14*(1), 77–91.

NASSCOM. (2023). *AI and Digital Transformation in the Retail Sector: Flipkart Case Study*. NASSCOM.

Patel, A., & Rathi, M. (2021). Corporate Training for Sustainability Leadership: The Case of Reliance Industries. *Corporate Leadership Review*, *18*(1), 90–105.

Power, T. (2021). Annual [." Tata Power.]. *Sustainability Report*, •••, 2021.

Power, T. (2021). *Smart Grids and Energy Efficiency Initiatives*. Retrieved from https://www.tatapower.com

Power, T. (2022). *Smart Grid and AI-Powered Energy Solutions*. Tata Power.

Ranjan, P., Verma, A., & Sharma, V. (2022). AI-powered energy management: Tata Power's case study. *Journal of Clean Energy*, *9*(2), 85–100.

Reddy, V., ... (2021). "Blockchain Technology in Plastic Waste Management: A Case Study of Hindustan Unilever." *Journal of Circular Economy*, 3(2), 50-68.

Saberi, S., Kouhizadeh, M., Sarkis, J., & Shen, L. (2019). Blockchain technology and its relationships to sustainable supply chain management. *International Journal of Production Research*, *57*(7), 2117–2135. DOI: 10.1080/00207543.2018.1533261

Scott, W. R. (2008). *Institutions and organizations: Ideas and interests*. Sage Publications.

Sen, R., & Gupta, V. (2022). Sustainability and Digital Education in Indian Institutes of Technology. *Journal of Higher Education Studies*, *9*(1), 22–34.

Sharma, A., & Gupta, M. (2022). Green Technologies and Policy Gaps in India: A Comparative Analysis. *Indian Journal of Policy Research*, *11*(2), 34–48.

Sharma, K., & Rao, S. (2022). Eco-packaging solutions in Indian e-commerce: A case study of Flipkart. *Journal of Business and Sustainability*, *14*(2), 143–158.

Sharma, M.. (2020). Indore Smart City: A Model for IoT-Driven Sustainability. *International Journal of Smart Cities*, *6*(2), 112–126.

Singh, A., & Patel, D. (2021). Digital India and Smart Cities: A Pathway to Sustainability. *Indian Journal of Public Policy*, *16*(4), 143–159.

Solutions, Z. (2022). *AI-based Energy Management for Commercial Buildings*. Retrieved from https://www.zenatix.com

Srivastava, R., Mishra, A., & Gupta, N. (2021). Predictive maintenance using AI in Indian manufacturing: Opportunities and challenges. *Journal of Industrial Engineering*, *21*(1), 51–66.

TERI. (2022). *Sustainability and Digital Technologies: A Survey of Indian Corporations*. The Energy and Resources Institute.

Unilever, H. (2022). *Blockchain and Circular Economy in Packaging*.Retrieved from https://www.hul.co.in

Venkatesan, P., & Chakraborty, S. (2023). Blockchain for sustainability in Indian FMCG: The case of Hindustan Unilever. *Journal of Business and Technology*, 19(3), 78-93.

World Bank. (2013). *Diagnostic Assessment of Select Environmental Challenges in India*. Retrieved from https://www.worldbank.org

World Bank (2022). "Digital Technologies for SME Growth: Insights from India." World Bank Group Report.

Zhou, P., Liu, Y., & Huang, Y. (2020). IoT in sustainable manufacturing: Global trends and challenges. *Journal of Sustainable Manufacturing*, *29*(2), 97–110.

Chapter 5
Digital Transformation, Business Model, and Performance in the Context of Digital SMEs: Evidence From France

Taher Alkhalaf
University of Caen Normandy, France

Omar Durrah
College of Commerce and Business Administration, Dhofar University, Oman

Monir Alkhalaf
Rennes School of Business, France

ABSTRACT

The purpose of the study is to evaluate the impact of digital transformation on the performance of innovative small and medium enterprises (SMEs). Despite the broad interest of academics and practitioners in digital transformation, little attention has been paid to the mediating role of business models in the link between digital transformation and SME performance. A survey of 419 innovative SMEs in France was conducted to examine the proposed conceptual model. Structural equation modeling (SEM) was relied upon to detect the correlation and linear regression of the study model. The results indicate that business models had a role in modifying the relationship between digital transformation and performance. The results contribute to deepening knowledge in the field of digital transformation and business models. The findings can form a guide that helps researchers and practitioners

DOI: 10.4018/979-8-3693-4373-9.ch005

manage digital transformation and design performance-enhancing business models in the context of SMEs.

1. INTRODUCTION

New digital technologies, such as artificial intelligence, the Internet of Things, and blockchain technology, among others, have accelerated the pace of digitalization of businesses and heralded a new economic era that relies heavily on creativity and innovation (Merin-Rodrigañez et al., 2024; Zhang et al., 2023). Digital transformation (DT) has received widespread attention from researchers and executive practitioners alike (Bouwman et al., 2019; Singh et al., 2020), due to the role it plays in improving operational and business processes, which enhances value creation for companies (Ritter & Pedersen, 2020). DT initiatives and the new Business Models (BMs) that accompany them are one of the outcomes of the digital revolution (Guo et al., 2022). The transformation process forces managers to modify or completely replace their companies' existing BMs (Downes & Nunes 2013). Therefore, many researchers see DT as objectively related to companies' development of BMs (Bouwman et al., 2019; Merin-Rodrigañez et al., 2024; Vial, 2021). The digital revolution has contributed to the prosperity of some companies and forced managers to modify or completely replace their companies' existing BMs (Guo et al., 2022). However, on the other hand, this was not the case for many companies, as DT may be associated with negative results, companies do not respond in a similar way to the TD process due to their different characteristics, some of them are able to achieve the benefits while other companies struggle to do so (Merin-Rodrigañez et al., 2024).

Based on the evidence that SMEs represent the most common type of corporate organization in EU economies and constitute a crucial source of innovation in those economies (Alkhalaf & Al-Tabbaa, 2024). The European Commission called for a shift to digital technology and to support business owners in achieving this shift (Gay & Szostak, 2019). In this regard, and to support its efforts in this field, the European Commission has developed a system to measure the performance of digital technologies and their impacts on society and the economies of the Union within the framework of the "European Union Strategy 2020" (Kotarba, 2017). This type of company is described as flexible and able to respond to changes in the environment (Alkhalaf & Al-Tabbaa., 2024). Moreover, these companies are distinguished by their ability to deal with modern technology and provide new innovations. Despite the significant contribution to the national product and the provision of job opportunities equivalent to 60-70% of the total jobs in the EU economies, most research focuses more on large companies (Latifi et al., 2021; Hartmann et al., 2013). However, empirical studies on the impact of BMs on performance in digital SMEs remain limited. Therefore, the current study aims to fill this gap by focusing on digitization and BMs and their impact on SMEs.

Reshaping BMs to suit DT requires making many changes, including major business processes, organizational structures, administrative work style, sales channels, and supply chains, as well as opening communication channels and direct interaction with customers, among other issues many (Matt, et al., 2015). DT is defined as the use of digital technologies, "such as mobile, artificial intelligence, cloud, blockchain, and the Internet of things (IoT) technologies" (Warner, & Wäger, 2019, p.326), to enhance performance and change value propositions, operations and customer relationships (Westerman et al., 2014; Zhang et al., 2023). These technologies offer tremendous opportunities for many companies in the physical and/or virtual world (Hoe, 2023). Adopting these innovative technologies can help transform workflow, create new value, and create competitive capabilities that raise the level of performance (Guo et al., 2022).

This research aims to enrich the discussion about the role of DT and its impact on innovating BMs to enhance performance in SMEs in France, from the perspective of resource-based theory (RBT) (Barney, 2001). Resources, especially knowledge constitute effective capabilities to develop competitive advantages for companies (Barney et al., 2021). This perspective assumes that resources, big data, and information can constitute a source of value and sustainable competitive advantage if they meet the VRIN model: valuable, rare, inimitable, not substitutable (Barney, 1991). Furthermore, Moreover, companies' use of new technologies has accelerated the (McCarthy et al., 2023), digital technology revolution, which allows them to create or develop their capabilities or modify their asset base in a way that enhances the acquisition of competitive advantages (Teece, 2007). Accordingly, the research proposes a theoretical framework through which the relationship between DT, BMs innovation and performance in the context of SMEs in France can be shed light. The innovation of digital technology and the accompanying modification of BMs or the creation of new BMs increases the opportunities to benefit from the new value chain and enhance performance (Urbinati et al., 2022; Parida et al., 2019; Teece, 2010). Although, the growing interest by researchers, academics, and consultants in the reality of the impact of DT on BMs in various categories of companies (Guo et al, 2022; Soluk et al., 2021; Wirtz, et al, 2016), there is a lack of empirical research focusing on the mechanism and magnitude of this effect on final performance (Fernández-Portillo et al., 2022; Grover et al, 2022; Clauss et al., 2021), especially in the context of SMEs (Latifi et al., 2021; Verhagen et al., 2023), which justifies conducting research to accompany the development of this phenomenon (Foss & Saebi, 2017). The current study seeks to evaluate the impact of digital transformation on performance and the role of BMs in this relationship, by asking the following question: To what extent do BMs mediate the relationship between DT and performance in the context of SMEs in France?

To validate the proposed conceptual model on the impact of BMs on performance, a survey was conducted on a sample of innovative SMEs in France. This category of companies was chosen due to its innovative nature and its integration of digital technologies into its commercial, financial and marketing procedures and work. Overall, the research contributes to highlighting the ability of digital technologies to shape new BMs for companies. The research results can be useful for practitioners and policy makers in the field of business digitalization to make real-time decisions and generate revenues from the use of digital assets in their companies. Within the framework of the RBT hypotheses and the knowledge-based approach, the research supports managers' strategic perceptions of leading companies towards enhancing performance in the context of French SMEs.

2. THEORETICAL BACKGROUND

2.1. Digital transformation

Chesbrough, (2010) posits that technology alone does not generate economic value until it is commercialized through a BM. Digitization is a state of mind through which tasks are carried out by designing new businesses or new ways of doing business and dealing with customers, it is therefore more than just a technology or the process of using technology (Hancock, 2016). In practice, DT is viewed as a continuous change process that takes advantage of the achievements of the technical revolution accompanied by a change in BMs to create new value (Eklinder-Frick et al., 2023). Matt, et al. (2015) argues that exploiting the technical capabilities of companies does not only affect internal operations in companies, but also extends to suppliers and sales outlets outside the borders of these companies. Therefore, the benefits offered by digitization in the field of productivity, quality improvement, and innovations that help create value are not limited only to owners/managers, but extend beyond that to include customers, suppliers, etc.

McCarthy et al. (2023) argue that companies need a comprehensive strategy to implement DT, and that DT requires a change in mindset and culture so that companies are more flexible and better able to take risks (Kane et al., 2015). Merin-Rodrigañez et al. (2024) suggest a roadmap for initiating the DT process which begins by explaining the goals and reasons for the transformation to employees to reduce resistance to change and support the transformation. Likewise, Cockburn (2024) argues that there is a need to provide appropriate conditions, create the working environment, and prepare employees to use new technologies. However, this transformation remains conditional on the limited resources available to SMEs (Alkhalaf & Al-Tabbaa,. 2024). Hartmann et al. (2016) argue that DT is accompanied by modification of basic components or introduction of new components of BMs. This modification could be the implementation of new operating methods, the result of innovation of a new product or service, or a change in the company's position in the markets (Bouwman et al., 2019). For Zott et al., (2011) it refers to the importance of links between activities, or changes in the company's value chain.

2.2. Business models

According to Latifi et al. (2021) companies are implementing different types of innovations including innovating their BMs. Casadesus-Masanell & Zhu (2013) describe BMs as an organizational innovation that helps develop "new ways to generate revenues and define value propositions for customers, suppliers, and partners" (p.1). The term BM appeared in the literature at the end of the 1990s, (Al-Debei & Avison,. 2010), and alternative, similar, or synonymous expressions have been used to refer to it, such as "business idea," "business concept," and "revenue model," in addition as well as "economic model." (Wirtz et al., 2016, p.1). The multiplicity and difference of terms adds more ambiguity to the concept of business models. According to Casadesus-Masanell & Zhu (2013), this concept is still relatively obscure, at least in the academic field. With the advancement of technology and the emergence of e-business, the BM has gained wide importance (Clauß et al., 2020), in the field of organizing trade exchanges at the industry or company level (Bouwman et al., 2019).

With the rapid development of technology, companies, especially SMEs, are realizing the importance of shifting to digital technology innovations (Gomber, et al., 2018). The acquisition of new technology by companies and its integration into SME activities requires rethinking the formation of existing models (Bouwman et al. 2019), or inventing new models (Hess et al., 2016), based on new digital assets (Singh et al., 2020). It brings about changes in the value chain that differ from those created before the transformation process (Grover et al., 2022). Teece (2010) confirms that the BM implicitly or explicitly describes how activities are organized to meet the needs of its customers, starting from creating value, methods of delivering it to customers, and how to benefit from the revenues and profits achieved by these companies. Therefore, the process of DT forces companies to repeat or change their designs, which will be reflected in their activities in the field of service/product, in the organizational structure, and in the governance system (Hess et al., 2016; Schlecht et al., 2021): Content refers to the activities that companies carry out while dealing with the surrounding environment, while organizational structure refers to the pattern with which the company relates its activities and how it manages its business, which distinguishes it from other companies. As for governance, it refers to the management of these activities with the aim of benefiting from the revenues of those activities. Therefore, BMs represent an important tool for companies to have a clear vision of what they want to achieve and how they will achieve it (Amit, & Zott, 2016).

2.3. Digital transformation and SMEs' performance

Previous literature has revealed that digitalization has an impact on many processes within a company, including business operations, marketing (Nambisan et al., 2017). The DT refers to a company replacing or modifying its BM, which is typically supported by a digital platform that delivers products and services over a technology-based network, allowing the emergence of new capabilities that can be leveraged to enhance the customer experience or enhance competitive advantage (Cockburn, 2024; Zhang et al., 2023), that meet the conditions of the VRIN model: "valuable, rare, inimitable, not substitutable" (Barney, 1991).

For the success of companies, especially SMEs, when embarking on the process of DT, they must spread digital culture (Vial, 2021) to reduce resistance to change (Singh & Hess, 2017). Moreover, companies need to provide resources and professional competencies capable of leading the transformation (Gong & Ribiere, 2021). In practice, previous studies indicate that DT positively affects the performance of innovative SMEs by collecting, classifying and analyzing data and information very quickly, which makes it easier for managers/owners to make decisions in real time, which enhances the performance of companies (Ledro et al 2023; Kumar et al 2023). DT enhances interaction with a large number of customers, which enhances their loyalty and thus their retention (Merin-Rodrigañez et al. (2024). Also, providing product offers through electronic platforms allows customers to learn about new products and their benefits and allows the company to predict demand to meet it in a timely manner, which improves the companies' business results (Matarazzo et al., 2021).

The literature review revealed the impact of BMs on performance in the digital economy through its core components of value creation, value proposition, and value capture (Guo et al., 2022). According to Zott & Ami (2017) the value drivers of BM dimensions interact and integrate with each other so that companies are able to provide products or services that are characterized by higher value. This integration is demonstrated, for example, for example, through the acquisition of PayPal by the online payment services company eBay (Cavallo et al., 2023). The acquisition facilitated trades between sellers and buyers and enhanced the value of the activities carried out by the eBay platform (Zott & Ami 2017). Westerman, et al. (2014), conducted a survey of a sample of 157 managers in various positions in

50 companies adopting DT and spread across 15 countries. The study revealed that companies that have shown maturity in the DT process outperform less mature companies. Pauwels & Weiss (2008) studied the impact of BMs on company performance when changing the way the content is used from a free service to a paid service.

Companies can influence their level of performance by using their material and knowledge resources to innovate new products, or/and through structural adjustments in the methods of presenting value and the mechanism of collecting revenues from customers by encouraging them to pay in exchange for meeting their requests (Zhang et al., 2023). Therefore, some companies increase the value of their resources by satisfying their customers and meeting their requests and thus being able to collect revenues for the value they produced (Priem et al., 2018). Bouwman et al. (2019) conducted an analysis in which they revealed that SMEs can achieve better performance if they decide to implement a DT strategy and allocate sufficient resources to create a BM that suits the nature and size of these companies. Several studies have also confirmed that BMs help create competitive advantages and enhance company performance (Latifi et al., 2021; Zoot & Amit., 2007).

A review of previous studies revealed a mediating role for BMs between DT and performance (Merin-Rodrigañez et al., 2024), while the results of a study (Ferreras-Méndez et al., 2021) revealed mediation between entrepreneurship and performance. Moreover, other research showed mediation of models Business between technology, modern innovations and performance (Al-Debei & Avison., 2010; Zhang et al., 2023; Nasiri et al., 2020). Based on the previous arguments, we propose the following hypotheses:

Hypothesis 1. Digital transformation (DT) positively affects the performance of SMEs.
Hypothesis 2. Digital transformation (DT) positively affects business models (BM).
Hypothesis 3. Business models (BM) positively affect SME performance.
Hypothesis 4: Business model (BM*) plays a mediating role in the relationship between digital transformation (DT) and SME performance.*

3. RESEARCH METHODOLOGY

3.1. Sample and data collection

A sample of companies was selected using the convenience sampling method due to the large number of SMEs. Companies that have websites on the Internet were selected to complete their business transactions and communicate with their customers and suppliers. Companies that use private platforms to display their products without any commercial or financial exchange were excluded. In the current study, data was collected from 419 SMEs French companies that work in the service fields and own social media platforms, so that these companies market various products and collect revenues from their sales of new products or services. A questionnaire was designed and sent to companies to be filled out using a self-administration method, including a letter explaining the aim of the study. The target group was owners/executives of SMEs, or R&D managers for their knowledge of DT strategy, implementation of innovations and BMs. To test the hypotheses, structural equation modeling (SEM) was used, which provides a widely accepted statistical approach in testing the relationship between constructs.

3.2. Measuring instruments

DT was evaluated based on the scale developed by Nasiri et al. (2020). The scale focuses on key DT processes in the context of European SMEs and consists of 5 items. The scale developed by Latifi et al. (2021) was used to examine the BM based, includes 7 items. Regarding the performance of SMEs, the scale of Ferreras-Méndez et al. (2015), was chosen, which consists of 4 items, in addition to specifying the type of industry. Some control variables were used, such as the size of the company, the age of the company, the number of employees, their level of education, and the type of industry.

4. ANALYSIS AND FINDING

4.1. Descriptive statistics

Statistics indicate that the number of employees in companies ranged from 10-160. Participants ranged in age from 25 to 58 years. 51% university educated, 33% professional. Regarding the type of industry, the results revealed that 21% of companies work in the field of medicines, 15% in the field of electronics, 5% in the field of cars, 27% in the field of equipment manufacturing, 13% in the field of producing electrical appliances, and 19% of other companies.

To test the research hypotheses, structural equation modeling was used using Spss-Amos. The stability and validity of the measures were evaluated by examining the reliability values, standard deviation, and correlation between the variables in the research model. The results showed that the values were within recommended limits (O'Brien, 2007; AlKhalaf, 2006). Furthermore, To determine the effect of the most important variables and elements in the model, exploratory factor analysis

(EFA) was used. Table 1 shows that KMO = = 0.878 is above the permissible limit of 0.50. Bartlett's sphericity = 4814.433, with sig = 0.000 less than 0.5 (Reio & Shuck, 2015). The results revealed that there are three influential factors and 14 elements: 5 elements represent DT, 5 elements represent BM, and 4 represent PE. Table 1.

Table 1. Descriptive statistics and CFE

Variable	Items	Loading	Cronbach's alpha	Mean	Std. Deviation	DT	BM	PE
DT	DT1 DT2 DT3 DT4 DT5	0.884 0.930 0.927 0.924 0.880	0.950	3.770	0.826	**1**		
BM	BM1 BM2 BM3 BM4 BM5	0.870 0.889 0.874 0.896 0.815	0.924	3.644	0.980	0.105*	**1**	
PE	PE1 PE2 PE3 PE4	0.857 0.866 0.889 0.855	0.892	3.190	1.175	0.191**	0.244**	**1**

KMO = 0.878; **Df**, 191; **Bartlett's test of sphericity** = 4814.433; **Sig** = 0.000

A CFA test was conducted to ensure that the variables represented the study model (Reio & Shuck, 2015). Ensure the level of trust and honesty. The Cronbach's alpha confidence index and the saturation values of the items were sufficient, and they are among the permissible indicators (Hair et al., 2010). Using the AMOS program, direct linear relationships and mediation between DT and PE were also examined in figure 1.

Figure 1. Test model

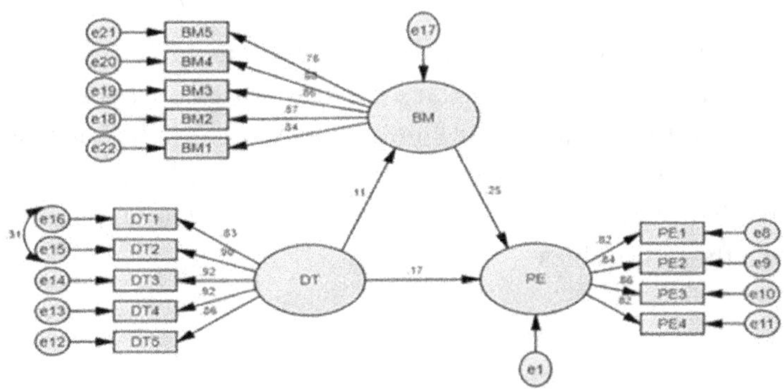

4.2. Structural model and results analysis

Structural equation modeling (SEM) was relied upon to test the interrelationships between the latent variables and to complete the simple and multiple linear regression processes for the research, as in Figure 1. The examination results indicate that they are within the recommended parameters (Gaskin, 2020): CMIN/DF = 2.126 < 5, RMSEA = 0.052 < 0.08. Set of indicators: GFI = 0.952 and CFI = 0.983, higher than 0.90, for PNFI = 0.777 and PGFI = 0.662, higher than 0.50. Based on these results, the model has predictive ability.

4.3. Hypotheses testing

The hypotheses were examined in two stages, Table 3: First, the first hypothesis (H3, H2, H1) was tested, between the variables (DT and PE, DT and BM, BM and PE), respectively, in SMEs. The test results indicate a direct positive effect, as follows (β = .0.068, p-value = .000), (β = .123, p-value = .000) and (β = .290, p-value = .000). Therefore, this result supports hypotheses H1, H2, and H3. Second, the mediation test, the results indicate that BM mediates the relationship between DT and PE in SMEs and that the effect is positive (β = .047, p-value = .000), and this result supports H4.

Table 2. Path analysis results

Hypotheses	Path	(β) Beta	T-Value	F	P-Value	Validation
H1	DT PE	0.068	3.963	15.708	0.000	Supported
H2	DT BM	0.123	12.394	4.644	0.000	Supported
H3	BM PE	0.290	44.729	26.507	0.000	Supported
H4	DT BM PE	0.074	6.501	8.650	0.000	Supported

To examine the size of the mediation effect, the method proposed by Baron & Kenny (1986) was used, which indicates the need for direct hypotheses to be fulfilled and for them to be statistically significant. Table 2 indicates that Baron and Kenny's conditions were met and that the effect of DT on PE increased but did not reach one. In other words, the result indicates partial mediation that moderated the result between those variables

5. DISCUSSION

The motivation for the current study was to examine the impact of DT and BMs on performance in the context of SMEs. The results of the study showed that DT is positively related to performance. The results are consistent with the research of (Merin-Rodrigañez et al., 2024; & Nasiri et al., 2020; Guo et al., 2022), as it has been confirmed that adopting new technology enhances the ability of companies to create competitive advantages or maintain advantages that currently exist in for SMEs, the more companies are able to go digital, it's improve their performance. Companies can create and capture new value by developing new capabilities, technologies and processes, or attracting new partners, which increase their organizational effectiveness.

Likewise, the study provides evidence of an indirect effect of BMs on the relationship between DT and PE. The result is consistent with previous studies that indicated that models are used as a tool that allows revealing the company's activities, strategic objectives, policies and operational programs to achieve the best performance (Merin-Rodrigañez et al., 2024; Ferreras-Méndez et al., 2021). Therefore, BM designs are crucial for companies if they are able to implement DT at the appropriate time and circumstance (Merin-Rodrigañez et al., 2024). The results revealed that BMs provide insight for companies in building broad relationships with customers, understanding their needs, and meeting their demands. These results are consistent with previous studies for example (Priem et al., 2018; Guo et al., 2022; Latifi et al., 2021). Merin-Rodrigañez et al. (2024) argues that a BM can help SMEs develop their business, and at the same time enhance their performance. BM designs are therefore crucial to taking advantage of DT. The results of the study revealed an impact of BMs on performance. This result is consistent with the findings of Verhagen et al (2023) and Latifi et al. (2021) that BMs have a positive impact on performance. Researchers argue that these models help managers translate strategic decisions into executable daily operating plans and programs.

5.1.Theoretical implications

The study presented a verified conceptual framework that allows understanding the mediating mechanisms of BMs and the extent of their impact on company performance. The study provided empirical evidence that investment and adoption of smart technologies in SMEs can provide significant benefits and increase companies' ability to deliver products/services with better performance. The study revealed that integrating BMs as an intermediary variable in the relationship between DT and performance enhances companies' efficiency and increases their productivity. The study contributes to enriching existing knowledge on the impacts of DT on BMs and performance in the context of SMEs. The results contribute to the theoretical literature, especially resource-based theory, specifically cognitive resources and new technologies for this category of firms. New corporate assets can create new advantages based on value creation, presentation and capture. Advantages based on innovations that meet VRIN conditions. The research contributes to answering the research gap on the positive impact of DT on the performance of SMEs mediated by BM.

5.2. Practical implications

The study has positive implications for decision makers if they decide to try digitalization in SMEs. First, the adoption of modern technologies, including communications and the Internet, enables managers/owners to submit offers and communicate via electronic platforms, which increases the chances of success for these companies. Secondly, managers/owners must have high competence to lead DT, create the environment, and explain the benefits and risks resulting from this transformation, in order to accept involvement in adopting modern technology to benefit from its benefits. Third: It is recommended that managers/owners choose an appropriate design for the BM and implement it in a timely manner, with the need to take into account the company's limited resources, size, and competencies, as failure to provide the necessary conditions for DT may result in failure and major losses that companies may not bear.

5.3. Limitations and future research

The results of the study were analyzed in light of some limitations. Data collection was based on the perceptions of managers/owners. Therefore, there is a need for the analysis to be based on real data, which is what qualitative studies cover. The study was conducted in the context of SMEs in France, so the generalizability of the results may not be objective. Therefore, it is possible to conduct research covering different countries. Future studies could investigate the application of DT to startups and entrepreneurial companies. Given the characteristics of SMEs, the impact of DT on performance may be related to many different contexts, such as the size, resources, and technological level of each company. Therefore, these variables can be taken into consideration when conducting future research. These relationships can also be evaluated by introducing mediating variables for a more comprehensive understanding of the role of DT on performance.

6. CONCLUSION

Empirical research has confirmed that new technology, including artificial intelligence, the Internet and the Internet of Things, has affected the performance of companies, including SMEs. BM design is accompanied by the start of using digital technologies (DT), as it can help managers/owners make the necessary changes to various activities, such as the company's relationships with its suppliers and customers, business style, supply chains, etc. Companies can direct their resources based on BMs by creating, displaying and capturing value to create competitive advantages. New BMs help to reformulate the company's strategy and open horizons for partnerships and building alliances to achieve better performance. Some research has indicated that BMs built on new technology assets can save material and cognitive resources, time, and reduce costs, thus creating new advantages. Likewise, the results of the study showed that employee efficiency and creating the appropriate environment are essential elements for the success of DT and the development of companies' BMs.

REFERENCES

Al-Debei, M. M., & Avison, D. (2010). Developing a unified framework of the business model concept. *European Journal of Information Systems*, *19*(3), 359–376. DOI: 10.1057/ejis.2010.21

Alkhalaf, T. (2006). *Les modes de gestion et d'organisation du transport ferroviaire en france et en Grande-Bretagne*. These, Universite de Caen.

Alkhalaf, T., & Al-Tabbaa, O. (2024). The effect of ability, motivation and opportunity (AMO) on SMEs' innovation performance. *Creativity and Innovation Management*, *33*(1), 21–38. DOI: 10.1111/caim.12578

Amit, R., & Zott, C. (2016). Business model design: A dynamic capability perspective. *The Oxford handbook of dynamic capabilities*, Vol. 52, 1-5.

Barney, J. (1991). Firm Resources and Sustained Competitive Advantage. *Journal of Management*, *17*(1), 99–120. DOI: 10.1177/014920639101700108

Barney, J. B. (2001). Resource-Based Theories of Competitive Advantage: A Ten Year Retrospective on the Resource-Based View. *Journal of Management*, *27*(6), 643–650. DOI: 10.1177/014920630102700602

Barney, J. B., Ketchen, D. J.Jr, & Wright, M. (2021). Resource-Based Theory and the Value Creation Framework. *Journal of Management*, *47*(7), 1936–1955. DOI: 10.1177/01492063211021655

Baron, R. M., & Kenny, D. A. (1986). The moderator-mediator variable distinction in social psychological research: Conceptual, strategic, and statistical considerations. *Journal of Personality and Social Psychology*, *51*(6), 1173–1182. DOI: 10.1037/0022-3514.51.6.1173 PMID: 3806354

Bouwman, H., Nikou, S., & de Reuver, M. (2019). Digitalization, business models, and SMEs: How do business model innovation practices improve performance of digitalizing SMEs? *Telecommunications Policy*, *43*(9), 101828. DOI: 10.1016/j.telpol.2019.101828

Casadesus-Masanell, R., & Zhu, F. (2013). Business Model Innovation and Competitive Imitation: The Case of Sponsor-Based Business Models. *Strategic Management Journal*, *34*(4), 464–482. DOI: 10.1002/smj.2022

Cavallo, A., Cosenz, F., & Noto, G. (2023). Business model scaling and growth hacking in digital entrepreneurship. *Journal of Small Business Management*, •••, 1–28.

Chesbrough, H. (2010). Business model innovation: Opportunities and barriers. *Long Range Planning*, *43*(2-3), 354–363. DOI: 10.1016/j.lrp.2009.07.010

Clauss, T., Abebe, M., Tangpong, C., & Hock, M. (2021). Strategic Agility, Business Model Innovation, and Firm Performance: An Empirical Investigation. *IEEE Transactions on Engineering Management*, *68*(3), 767–784. DOI: 10.1109/TEM.2019.2910381

Clauß, T., Bouncken, R. B., Laudien, S., & Sascha, K. (2020). Business model reconfiguration and innovation in smes: A mixed-method analysis from the electronics industry. *International Journal of Innovation Management*, *24*(02), 2050015. DOI: 10.1142/S1363919620500152

Cockburn, T. (2024). Digital Transformation: Strategy, Execution, and Technology. *The Learning Organization*, *31*(3), 458–464. DOI: 10.1108/TLO-04-2024-307

Downes, L., & Nunes, P. F. (2013). Big-Bang Disruption. *Harvard Business Review*, *91*(3), 44–56.

Eklinder-Frick, J., Perna, A., & Fremont, V. H. J. (2023). "Guest editorial": Understanding digital transformation from an inter-organisational network perspective. *Journal of Business and Industrial Marketing*, *38*(6), 1245–1250. DOI: 10.1108/JBIM-06-2023-605

Fernández-Portillo, A., Almodóvar-González, M., Sánchez-Escobedo, M. C., & Coca-Pérez, J. L. (2022). The role of innovation in the relationship between digitalisation and economic and financial performance. A company-level research. *European Research on Management and Business Economics*, *28*(3), 100190. DOI: 10.1016/j.iedeen.2021.100190

Ferreras-Méndez, J. L., Newell, S., Fernández-Mesa, A., & Alegre, J. (2015). Depth and breadth of external knowledge search and performance: The mediating role of absorptive capacity. *Industrial Marketing Management*, *47*, 86–97. DOI: 10.1016/j.indmarman.2015.02.038

Ferreras-Méndez, J. L., Olmos-Peñuela, J., Salas-Vallina, A., & Alegre, J. (2021). Entrepreneurial orientation and new product development performance in SMEs: The mediating role of business model innovation. *Technovation*, *108*, 1–13, 102325. DOI: 10.1016/j.technovation.2021.102325

Foss, N. J., & Saebi, T. (2017). Fifteen Years of Research on Business Model Innovation: How Far Have We Come, and Where Should We Go? *Journal of Management*, *43*(1), 200–227. DOI: 10.1177/0149206316675927

Gaskin, J. E. (2020). *Structural Equation Modeling*. MyEducator.

Gay, C., & Szostak, B. L. (2019). *Innovation and Creativity in SMEs, Challenges, Evolutions and Prospects*. British Library ISTE Ltd and John Wiley & Sons, Inc. DOI: 10.1002/9781119513742

Gomber, P., Kauffman, R. J., Parker, C., & Weber, B. W. (2018). On the Fintech Revolution: Interpreting the forces of innovation, disruption, and transformation in financial services. *Journal of Management Information Systems*, *35*(1), 220–265. DOI: 10.1080/07421222.2018.1440766

Gong, C., & Ribiere, V. (2021). Developing a unified definition of digital transformation. *Technovation*, *102*, 102217. DOI: 10.1016/j.technovation.2020.102217

Grover, P., Kar, A. K., & Dwivedi, Y. K. (2022). Understanding artificial intelligence adoption in operations management: Insights from the review of academic literature and social media discussions. *Annals of Operations Research*, *308*(1-2), 177–213. DOI: 10.1007/s10479-020-03683-9

Guo, H., Guo, A., & Ma, H. (2022). Inside the black box: How business model innovation contributes to digital start-up performance. *Journal of Innovation & Knowledge*, *7*(2), 100188. DOI: 10.1016/j.jik.2022.100188

Guo, H., Tang, J., Su, Z., & Katz, J. A. (2017). Opportunity recognition and SME, performance: The mediating effect of business model innovation. *R & D Management*, *47*(3), 431–442. DOI: 10.1111/radm.12219

Hair, J., Black, W., Babin, B., & Anderson, R. (2010). *Multivariate data analysis* (7th ed.). Prentice-Hall, Inc.

Hancock, A. (2016). *A digital leader – what on earth is that? Retrieved from*https://digileaders.com/adrian-hancock/

Hartmann, M., Oriani, R., & Bateman, H. (2013). The Performance Effect of Business Model Innovation: an Empirical Analysis of Pension Funds. *35th DRUID Celebration Conference*, Barcelona, Spain

Hartmann, P. M., Zaki, M., Feldmann, N., & Neely, A. (2016). Capturing value from big data a taxonomy of data-driven business models used by start-up firms. *International Journal of Operations & Production Management*, *36*(10), 1382–1406. DOI: 10.1108/IJOPM-02-2014-0098

Hess, T., Matt, C., Benlian, A., & Wiesböck, F. (2016). Options for Formulating a Digital Transformation Strategy. *MIS Quarterly Executive*, *15*(2), 103–119.

Hoe, S. L. (2023). Digital transformation strategy, execution, and technology, Taylor & Francis Group, CRC Press.

Kane, G. C., Palmer, D., Phillips, A. N., Kiron, D., & Buckley, N. (2015). *Strategy, not technology, drives digital transformation*. MIT Sloan Management Review and Deloitte University Press.

Kotarba, M. (2017). Measuring digitalization: Key metrics. *Foundations of Management*, *9*(1), 123–138. DOI: 10.1515/fman-2017-0010

Kumar, P., Sharma, S. K., & Dutot, V. (2023). Artificial intelligence (AI)-enabled CRM capability in healthcare: The impact on service innovation. *International Journal of Information Management*, *69*, 102598.

Latifi, M.-A., Nikou, S., & Bouwman, H. (2021). Business model innovation and firm performance: Exploring causal mechanisms in SMEs. *Technovation*, *107*, 102274. DOI: 10.1016/j.technovation.2021.102274

Ledro, C., Nosella, A., & Dalla Pozza, I. (2023). Integration of AI in CRM: Challenges and guidelines. *Journal of Open Innovation*, *9*(4), 100151. DOI: 10.1016/j.joitmc.2023.100151

Matarazzo, M., Penco, L., Profumo, G., & Quaglia, R. (2021). Digital transformation and customer value creation in Made in Italy SMEs: A dynamic capabilities perspective. *Journal of Business Research*, *123*, 642–656. DOI: 10.1016/j.jbusres.2020.10.033

Matt, C., Hess, T., & Benlian, A. (2015). Digital Transformation Strategies, Business and In-formation Systems Engineering. *Business & Information Systems Engineering*, *57*(5), 339–343. DOI: 10.1007/s12599-015-0401-5

McCarthy, A. M., Maor, D., McConney, A., & Cavanaugh, C. (2023). Digital transformation in education: Critical components for leaders of system change. *Social Sciences & Humanities Open*, *8*(1), 100479. DOI: 10.1016/j.ssaho.2023.100479

Merin-Rodrigañez, J., Dasí, A., & Alegre, J. (2024). Digital transformation and firm performance in innovative SMEs: The mediating role of business model innovation. *Technovation*, *134*, 103027. DOI: 10.1016/j.technovation.2024.103027

Nambisan, S., Lyytinen, K., Majchrzak, A., & Song, M. (2017). Digital innovation management: Reinventing innovation management research in a digital world. *Management Information Systems Quarterly*, *41*(1), 223–238. DOI: 10.25300/MISQ/2017/41:1.03

Nasiri, M., Ukko, J., Saunila, M., & Rantala, T. (2020). Managing the digital supply chain: The role of smart technologies. *Technovation*, *96–97*, 102121. DOI: 10.1016/j.technovation.2020.102121

O'brien, R. M. (2007). A caution regarding rules of thumb for variance inflation factors. *Quality & Quantity*, *41*(5), 673–690. DOI: 10.1007/s11135-006-9018-6

Parida, V., Sjödin, D., & Reim, W. (2019). Reviewing Literature on Digitalization, Business Model Innovation, and Sustainable Industry: Past Achievements and Future Promises. *Sustainability (Basel)*, *11*(2), 391. DOI: 10.3390/su11020391

Pauwels, K., & Weiss, A. (2008). Moving from free to fee: How online firms market to change their business model successfully. *Journal of Marketing*, *72*(3), 14–31. DOI: 10.1509/JMKG.72.3.014

Priem, R. L., Wenzel, M., & Koch, J. (2018). Business models and demand-side strategy: Putting value creation for consumers center stage. *Long Range Planning*, *51*(1), 22–31. DOI: 10.1016/j.lrp.2017.07.007

Reio, T. G.Jr, & Shuck, B. (2015). Exploratory factor analysis: Implications for theory, research, and practice. *Advances in Developing Human Resources*, *17*(1), 12–25. DOI: 10.1177/1523422314559804

Ritter, T., & Pedersen, C. L. (2020). Digitization capability and the digitalization of business models in business-to-business firms: Past, present, and future. *Industrial Marketing Management*, *86*, 180–190. DOI: 10.1016/j.indmarman.2019.11.019

Schlecht, L., Schneider, S., & Buchwald, A. (2021). The prospective value creation potential of Blockchain in business models: A Delphi study. *Technological Forecasting and Social Change*, *166*, 120601. DOI: 10.1016/j.techfore.2021.120601

Singh, A., & Hess, T. (2017). How chief digital officers promote the digital transformation of their companies. *MIS Quarterly Executive*, *16*, 1–17.

Singh, A., Klarner, P., & Hess, T. (2020). How do chief digital officers pursue digital transformation activities? The role of organization design parameters. *Long Range Planning*, *53*(3), 101890. DOI: 10.1016/j.lrp.2019.07.001

Soluk, J., Kammerlander, N., & Darwin, S. (2021). Digital entrepreneurship in developing countries: The role of institutional voids. *Technological Forecasting and Social Change*, *170*, 120876. DOI: 10.1016/j.techfore.2021.120876

Teece, D. J. (2007). Explicating dynamic capabilities: The nature and microfoundations of (sustainable) enterprise performance. *Strategic Management Journal*, *28*(13), 1319–1350. DOI: 10.1002/smj.640

Teece, D. J. (2010). Business models, business strategy and innovation. *Long Range Planning*, *43*(2-3), 172–194. DOI: 10.1016/j.lrp.2009.07.003

Urbinati, A., Manelli, L., Frattini, F., & Bogers, M. L. A. M. (2022). The digital transformation of the innovation process: Orchestration mechanisms and future research directions. *Innovation (North Sydney, N.S.W.)*, *24*(1), 65–85. DOI: 10.1080/14479338.2021.1963736

Verhagen, M., de Reuver, M., & Bouwman, H. (2023). Implementing business models into operations: Impact of business model implementation on performance. *IEEE Transactions on Engineering Management*, *70*(1), 173–183. DOI: 10.1109/TEM.2020.3046365

Vial, G. (2021). Understanding digital transformation: a review and a research agenda. In Hinterhuber, A., Vescovi, T., & Checchinato, F. (Eds.), *Managing Digital Transformation: Understanding the Strategic Process* (1st ed.). Routledge. DOI: 10.4324/9781003008637-4

Warner, K. S. R., & Wäger, M. (2019). Building dynamic capabilities for digital transformation: An ongoing process of strategic renewal. *Long Range Planning*, *52*(3), 326–349. Advance online publication. DOI: 10.1016/j.lrp.2018.12.001

Westerman, G., Bonnet, D., & McAfee, A. (2014). The nine elements of digital transformation, available at: https:// sloanreview.mit.edu/article/the-nine-elements -of digital transformation.

Wirtz, B. W., Göttel, V., & Daiser, P. (2016). Business model innovation: Development, concept and future research directions. *Journal of Business Models*, *4*(1), 1–28.

Zhang, Y., Ma, X., Pang, J., Xing, H., & Wang, J. (2023). The impact of digital transformation of manufacturing on corporate performance. The mediating effect of business model innovation and the moderating effect of innovation capability. *Research in International Business and Finance*, *64*, 101890. DOI: 10.1016/j.ribaf.2023.101890

Zott, C., & Ami, R. (2017). Business Model Innovation: How to Create Value in a Digital World. *NIM Marketing Intelligence Review*, *9*(1), 18–23. DOI: 10.1515/gfkmir-2017-0003

Zott, C., Amit, R., & Massa, L. (2011). The Business Model: Recent Developments and Future Research. *Journal of Management*, *37*(4), 1019–1042. DOI: 10.1177/0149206311406265

Chapter 6

Tunisian Fintech's Ecosystem:

To What Extent Can Tunisian Fintech's Be an Engine for Shared Value Creation?

Eya Frioui
South Mediterranean University, Tunisia

Sinda Ben Sedrine Doghri
Higher Institute of Management of Tunis, Tunisia

ABSTRACT

Fintech's have boundless potential, with an increasing need for social inclusion. As new technologies emerge in the market and the boundaries of traditional business models are challenged, financial services can be delivered at a lower cost with greater accountability, efficiency, and accessibility. In Tunisia, 64% of adults are financially excluded or underserved, partly due to the difficulty of accessing physical bank locations and increasing dissatisfaction with the quality of Tunisian banking services. Despite these figures, Fintech's in Africa are expected to be a game changer. Fintechs supplies end-user services and platforms. This paper examines the extent to which Tunisian fintech, supported by the emerging ecosystem, can serve as an engine shared value creation. This paper describes the fintech ecosystem in Tunisia. It illustrates emerging fintech business models. Then, the analysis provides the elements of creating shared value in these Fintech's.

DOI: 10.4018/979-8-3693-4373-9.ch006

INTRODUCTION

Fintech has disrupted the international economy. A 2015 Venture Scanner survey showed that 1,141 fintechs launched new businesses, disrupting existing models in many segments of the finance industry, including individual and financing, payment, asset management, remittance, and insurance, in 53countries. The rise of a new financial offer coupled with the internet's power disrupted old entities. With mutations in customers' preferences, firms are facing new demands. To respond, firms invested in R&D developing new strategies. The pandemic accelerated digital demand. Innovations are the new normal as a cornerstone for competitiveness. The digital transformation accelerated the change too. Historically, traditional financial services used to be the major player in financial systems, seen safe for exchange. This monopoly didn't last after the 2008's financial crisis. These institutions faced many challenges ranging from the brand's deterioration, stakeholders trust, regulatory adjustments and Covid. Web searchers at google about the term Fintech have increased in the last decades demonstrating growing curiosity. It's considered as a global phenomenon not only a temporal bubble. Fintech is driven by innovators, studied by researchers, interesting regulators and leaders. For Saksonova & Kuzmina-Merlino (2017) the growing rise of Fintech's thanks to; first, the customer's unsatisfaction with old banking systems and decreasing performance. Second, the rise of fast technological innovations automating the user experience, responded to the new needs. Old structures failed to satisfy new expectations with others growing number of offer varieties such as Payment, Data analytics, microfinance, venture capital, Crowdfunding, P2P lending, stock exchange and others. In this chapter we introduced fintech's innovation, exploring its evolution. The second section discussed Fintech's key factors and challenges and Fintech's business models. In the third section, we exposed Fintech's ecosystems and international practices. The fourth section studied the Tunisian Fintech's ecosystems.

This chapter entitled " Tunisian Fintech Ecosystem: To which extent Tunisian Fintech's be an engine for shared value creation ? " will mainly illustrate the fintech's innovation, it's different categories generating new business models, how these new innovative entities generate revenue and various values using new technologies ranging from blockchain, Peer-to-Peer lending, Robo-advisers ect.. In Tunisia, 64% of adults are financially excluded or underserved, due in part to the difficulty of reaching a physical bank location and to the increasing dissatisfaction with the quality of Tunisian banking services.

In this chapter our research focus on the Tunisian Fintech's rivalry, in a growing complex ecosystem and context shaping new business model that integrates creating shared value strategies in Tunisian fintech's.

Literature review and theoretical framework

FinTech means the application of technology to finance. For Sahabuddin et al., (2023) there were 1359 publications about FinTech, from 2010 to 2021. When Fintech's papers began there was no clear definition of FinTech. The idiom's first use goes to Citigroup project entitled "Financial Services Technology Consortium", in 1990s. For Gai et al., (2018) FinTech is an emerging technical term that "describes the financial technology sectors in operations for firms or organizations, which addresses the improvement of the service quality by using information technology applications."

Fintech's evolution is categorized into a few key stages, each initiated by technological tools, consumer behavior's shift and changes in the industry. We summarize it as follow:

- Digital Banking emergence (1970s/1990s): Introduction of computers and electronics in the financial sector; ATMs, online banking, and electronic payment systems.
- Internet & Online Transactions (1990/2000): Internet favored the online transactions, such as digital payment. online banking has become the new currency.
- Mobile1 Digital Payments (Late 2000s - Early 2010s): Smartphones expansion developed mobile banking apps and digital wallets. (Apple Pay, Google Wallet)
- P2P Lending & Crowdfunding (Mid 2010s): platforms disrupted old lending models. Crowdfunding initiated the democratization of finance for individuals.
- Blockchain & Cryptocurrencies (Mid 2010s): introducing Bitcoin and open door to decentralized financial systems, digital assets, and more independent transactions.
- Robo-Advisors & AI (Mid 2010s): automated investment platforms, using algorithm-based portfolio management. Facilitated by AI led to more effective risk management.
- Open Banking & API Integration (Late 2010s): application programming interfaces opened possibilities top Open Banking. By sharing financial data easily, a simple cooperation between institutions and third-party services was regulated.
- Digital Identity & RegTech (Late 2010s): addressed regulatory challenges, with regulatory technology, fraud prevention, and risk. Digital identity enhances security.

- Financial Inclusion & Emerging Markets (Ongoing): Fintech's potential to unbanked populations gained attention. Mobile banking is crucial in financial inclusion.
- Advanced Technologies (Ongoing): integration of advanced technologies like AI, machine learning, quantum computing, and biometrics. Fintech is used in applications in sustainable finance, green technology, and decentralized finance (DeFi).

These stages are interconnected and can overlap and still evolve.

Fintech's Strategizing creating shared value to achieve Competitive Advantage

For Mintzberg (1998), strategy is a planned process or an evolving pattern. In CSV, incorporating social issues into a strategy is a choice. Scholars agree that strategy should address competitive advantage, the fintech's external (industry, competition) and internal environments (resources) and optimizing value chain Hofer (1978). Strategy has many levels: corporate, business, and functional Thompson (2022). By creating shared value, Fintech's target business strategy, how Fintech selects which market segments to target with certain offers Akpinar & Saleem, (2019). For Porter (1985) the strategy is selecting the best position against industry competition. A leading Fintech must provide unique value, meeting customer needs differently, by lower costs or distinct offers. According to Porter (2012) creating shared value is built on the three following strategies: First, reconceiving products and markets. Second, redefining productivity in the Value Chain. Third, enabling local cluster development.

Fintech's Reconceiving Products and Markets:

Reconceiving products and markets are rethinking a firm's products about society's needs and the benefit generated. It includes better banking systems adapted to the needs of analphabets in rural sites of developing countries. Meeting needs in underserved markets requires redesigned products or new distribution methods. Fintech's proved a vital role in achieving financial Literacy & financial Inclusion by sustainably providing financial offers such as transactions, payments, savings, credit, and insurance. It deliver needed finance to MSMs. Financial literacy is ability to create informed perceptions and make appropriate choices to money utilization. Financial literacy changes individuals' lives and the quality of markets. Financial inclusion should be integrated with customer education and financial literacy. The obligation of fintech in promoting financial literacy addressed in OJK Regulation of 2018 about the Financial Innovation in the finance Sector. Finansialku.com, geared to millennials, and condenses financial product articles into an accessible investment e-book and provides online courses. Finansialku.com is building the next generation of financial planner facilitating financial education. By reconceiving products, fintech improve social welfare. For McKinsey's report (2022), one of the issues that fintech's solves by reconceiving markets is that firms struggle to secure trade financing from banks, it's a persistent issue causing deeper gaps in the trade finance and the supply and demand's shortfall.

Fintech's Redefining Productivity in the Value Chain:

A firm's value chain offers many opportunities to CSV by enhancing value chain productivity or by finding new ways of collaboration with partnering companies' new ways of collaboration shall be applied, like increasing their access to inputs, sharing technology, or providing financing. The value chain' disadvantages must be considered. The discovery of new distribution channels with less environmental impact is a relevant example. Fintech's enable tackling supply chain risk through AI. Numerous systems help businesses to track consumers engagement, send payments to counterparties, and communicate worldwide. Similar approaches are helping trade finance banks monitor risks in the supply chain more effectively. The answer lies in Fintech's offers adopting AI. For example, if a supplier suffers from cash flow problem, unexpected weather patterns affect supplier's ability to manufacture a product, firms get an early-warning sign and members of trade finance chain and respond quickly. This ensures they are staying ahead of potential risks and systemic events rather than reacting to them. FinTech's it is an example of technology making the global trade and supply chain ecosystem more responsive, agile, and efficient. FinTech's provide AI-powered analytics to assess the riskiness of clients, vendors and individual transactions – all of which can suffer from the knock-on effects of supply chain disruption. Business being client of fintech's, enjoy access to new financing opportunities that were impossible using traditional methods. AI helps by creating more accurate credit scoring models that offer deeper analysis. This include firm's payment history, measurement of the risks of funding a specific transaction when dealing with different counterparties and identification of supply chain risks, then benchmarking them against their peer group. McKinsey's report (2022) titled "Reconceiving the global trade finance ecosystem" spots supply chain issues creating fragility, the insurmountable barriers for business to access funds and lack of interoperability. The solution to the global trade engine is to use new technology incorporating modern infrastructure for more automation, less friction, and reduced costs. This approach is already leading to change by FinTech's but it still at its early stage. The technology needed to solve the trade finance gap. AI tools give firms early warning of supply chain issues.

Fintech's Enabling Local Cluster Development

For Cassar (2004), startup's need a vibrant local business environment to grow. For Ellison (2010) startups rely on external resources called "cluster" geographically. For Cumming (2020) FinTech's use new forms of funding, such as crowdfunding and initial coin offerings (ICOs), that alleviate geographic distance. Fintech are important part of cluster formation. For Block(2018), incubators and accelerators assist FinTech's to build clusters. In finance, location are based on resource availability and the impact of regional economic activities. For Rocha (2004) clusters impact entrepreneurs and regional development. Cluster effects for fintech's is instructive since their market is generally not "local". For Wennberg (2010), economies of scale and network favor concentration, simplifying to get these resources as the fintech's grow. A greater number of startups from the same industry increases competition, reducing the benefits of being in a large cluster. For Beck (2016), innovations drivers banking changes, something that fintech provide to large incumbents who lack innovation's efficiency. For Schwienbacher (2020) fintech are highly concentrated. FinTech's located in larger clusters face lower risks of liquidation but higher probabilities of being acquired thanks to their greater proximity to competitors. Incubated Fintech's face lower risks of failure. Location matters as it affects the survival of fintech's.

The central question of our research is to which extent Tunisian Fintech's, mainly the payment facilitator can be an engine for shared value creation. Consequently, we will focus on the case of the Tunisian Fintech' WeSettle and its derivative Wepay, in ability to create a business value and a social value simultaneously within the complex Tunisian ecosystem.

Methodological framework:

A case study focus on one case, but simultaneously considers the context, and consequently encompass many variables and qualities. Qualitative research produces holistic understandings of rich, contextual, and generally unstructured, non-numeric data (Mason, 2002) by engaging in conversations with the research participants in a natural setting (Creswell, 2009). The defining feature of case study research is its focus on 'how' and 'why' questions (Myers, 2009) and for this reason is appropriate for descriptive and exploratory studies (Mouton, 2001). A case study can focus on describing process(es), individual or group behavior in its total setting, and/or the sequence of events in which the behavior occurs (Stake, 2005).

This research is set in the interpretivist paradigm, through a qualitative methodology, which spots specific situations (Giordano,2033). The object studied is the ability of Tunisian Fintech's (through using a specific innovative business models) through the technique of exploratory and comprehensive research to dive and analyze the experience of the Tunisian Fintech WeSettle and its derivative WePay. First, we will present the context of our analysis by presenting the Tunisian Fintech's and its rivalry through collecting updated data. Second, we will study the different component the Tunisian Fintech's ecosystem. Finally, we will conclude with the legal context and regulation which organize the Fintech's activity.

1. TUNISIAN FINTECH'S AND RIVALRY

1.1. Fintech in Africa

Fintech in Africa is different than other regions. Africa have the large unbanked population. For the World Bank (2022), 60% of adults in Sub-Saharan Africa are unbanked, which is an opportunity for fintech to serve this underserved population. Second, the mobile nature of fintech in Africa. Due to the lack of infrastructure and low penetration of old banking services, mobile technology played a significant role in financial inclusion. For the GSMA, there are over 400 million mobile money accounts in Africa, and fintech used this to provide by mobile platforms. Third, regulation in Africa is different.

For the African Development Bank (2019), Fintech's regulation is in early stages, with an opportunity to shape regulation to favor their growth. By FinTech's, business deliver personalized offers to meet client's needs from payment, credit to investment, savings, and insurances. In a continent with a young population but limited financial infrastructure, African Fintech's are experiencing a boom in demand. Recently, several startups emerged as industry leaders, with some of them becoming unicorns Forbes, (2023).

Africa is expected to have first, the largest market will be Digital Assets with an AUM of US$704.10m in 2024.Second, the average AUM per user in the Digital Assets market is projected to US$16.37 in 2024. Thirds, the Digital Assets market is expected to a revenue growth of 20.03% in 2025. Fourth, in the Digital Payments market, the number of users is expected to 357.00m users by 2028. (Statista 2024). For CHEBILI(2023), Fintech in Africa face serious challenges but still offer green potential. It will grow fast with high value creation. His study showed that Fintech in Africa offer value under 3 themes: Financial inclusion, financial infrastructure, and Convenience.

1.2. Tunisian Fintech's

Globalization favored the intense development of financial markets. Technology, business models, talent, capital, and consumers were all ready to start a FinTech mutation. Governments contributed pressured by the necessity of financial inclusion and higher competition. The financial ecosystem's performance's determinants of financial entities are internal or external, adding macroeconomics. The findings are mixed, since it depends on the period, the context and the country. In our case, Tunisia is facing mutations impacting banking in terms of innovation and competitiveness. The adoption of new technologies was inevitable, but governance issues interrogated the impacts of Fintech. Tunisia is not an exception, politics, liquidity crisis, social challenges all, impacted the financial landscape. 64% of adults are financially excluded or underserved, due to the difficulty of reaching a physical bank location and to the increasing dissatisfaction of banking services' quality . Old financial institutions were challenged. The majority of Tunisian FinTech's operate in the local market only 16 of them in 2022 made breakthroughs internationally.(Fintech's Barometer 2023)Worldwide, Tunisian Fintech's are ranked 68, with advanced classification in the MENA region, ranked 10. In 2018, the Tunisian Professional Association of Banks and Financial Institutions discussed for the first time the rise of FinTech's in Tunisia, spotting the importance to initiate an efficient ecosystem responding to regulatory challenges and stakeholder's expectations, the banking-Fintech's synergies is a must. Fintech's supplies end-user services (in B2C or B2B market) and platforms. Disrupt Tunisia, created a database for Fintech's. According to our investigation, in 2024, the number of Fintech's exceeded 112 firm, but not all of them got the label.

1.2.1 Descriptive analysis of the Tunisian Fintech's context:

Thanks to innovation, financial systems have become interlinked. This new digital architecture launched digital business ecosystems with constant need for updated data. For Lee (2018), understanding the dynamics in Fintech requires analyzing the ecosystem's complexity. The technological developments in infrastructure, big data, data analytics, and mobile devices allow fintech's to disintermediate old financial firms with unique, niche, and personalized services. In Tunisia, the strategic vision of Tunisian Fintech's can summarized as follow:

Table 1. Strategic Vision of Tunisian Fintech's

Finance	Priorities	Collaborators
Series B, Debt Public funding	Extend the offering to several markets particularly internationally.	> 50 employees
Series A, Debt Public funding	Obtain a significant turnover on a critical size market.	10 to 50 employees
Seed money, Debt Public funding	Test a first version of the offer on a market	3 to 9 employees
Family and friends Grants	Create a prototype and set up the business	< 3 employees
By the Founders	Create a concept and analyze the conditions of success in the market	Associates

Source: Barometer Fintech (November 2023)

For Fintech's Barometer (November 2023), Tunisian Fintech's suggest supporting their growth and sustainability in local and international markets in four areas: First, legislation and regulatory framework . Second, financing access and conditions (relationship with banks). Third, Markets: access &prospects: (with incubators). Fourth, Fintech's Talents: availability attractiveness (relationship with Universities R&D).

+ Fintech's Regulatory framework: Limitations and potential solutions

FinTech's demand more commitment from the administration and regulators.

Table 2. Tunisian Fintech's suggestions to regulation

Promotion of the Fintech ecosystem:	Setting up an environment Sustainable & agile sandbox:	Setting up a one-stop shop:
"Strengthen cooperation between administrations, public sector, FinTech's and other players to create a conducive environment to innovation »	"Test their offers in real conditions, fewer constraints, and more freedom… benefit from appropriate support and supervision by authorities… simplify compliance."	"Create a one-stop shop to centralize procedures facilitate access to services. administrative data, regulatory data, finance and contact between FinTech's and authorities."

Source: Barometer Fintech (November 2023)

+ Fintech's Support and Financing: access and conditions

Tunisian FinTech's are calling for better visibility with investors, better understanding of their specificities and the establishment of specific financing mechanisms.

Table 3. Tunisian Fintech's suggestions to finance

Strengthen proximity between FinTech's and volunteers' investors	**Put mechanisms in place and adapted financing products**
Outreach:Organize workshops to raise awareness among Business Angels of Fintech's opportunities.	Set guarantee mechanisms, funds to FinTech's, to reduce the risks perceived by banks, encourage their finance
Connection platforms: Create an online platform to connect FinTech's and Business Angels	Establish financial support mechanisms and tax incentives for FinTech's, by subsidies, research tax credits and dedicated investment funds. This would promote the development and growth of startups in the sector.
Mentoring programs: to help FinTech's develop their entrepreneurial skills, to refine their business models	

Source: Barometer Fintech (November 2023)

+ Markets: Access and prospects:

Access to finance is vital for Fintech's sustainability and growth. Tunisian Fintech's are facing difficulties to fund their activity. They call for practical mechanisms for fundraising.

Table 4. Tunisian Fintech's suggestions to market access

Administrative simplification	**Adaptation of selection criteria:**	**Encouragement of local purchasing & innovation:**
Simplify procedures for Fintech's participation in public markets. Reduce bureaucracy, simplify forms, tender submission process, encourage digital use in administrative. procedures »	"Adapt the public procurement selection criteria considering Fintech's specificities, promote innovation, flexibility, agility rather than size or Fintech's age	"Encourage public actors to favor solutions Local and innovative Fintech in their calls, considering their impact on economy and on the ecosystem digital."

Source: Barometer Fintech (November 2023)

The adoption of specific regulations and banking information to strengthen collaboration with financial institutions, Tunisia fintech's suggested:

Table 5. Tunisian Fintech's suggestions to collaborations with financial institutions

Adapt the regulations	**Openness and interoperability**
"Set an appropriate regulatory framework, recognizing the complementarity of banks and FinTech's, promoting their cooperation. Mainly the sandbox and the simplification compliance. »	Interoperability, Open Banking standards, API standardized and secure could contribute to facilitating collaborations, promoting a more dynamic and inclusive ecosystem with partnerships between old players and

Source: Barometer Fintech (November 2023)

+ Fintech's Talents: availability and attractiveness:

Talent acquisition is a driver of Fintech's competitiveness. Fintech's use innovative business models which require specific needs in talents mastering the last updates and technologies that the local and internal markets demand. Tunisian Fintech's call for favoring international mobility, offering suitable training and education and tax exemptions to assure its mission.

Table 6. Tunisian Fintech's suggestions to talent acquisition

Training and education:	**Tax exemptions:**	**International mobility:**
"Develop specialized Fintech training programs in universities and colleges, in collaboration with industry players. »	"Implement tax exemptions and reductions in social charges for FinTech's that recruit local talent. to face large local firms facing the French market. »	"Facilitate the international mobility of talents work permit procedures for foreign professionals. »

Source: Barometer Fintech (November 2023)

Moreover, to favor a better collaboration with research centers, Tunisian Fintech's call for strengthening the collaboration with these entities to innovate and keep an updated solution.

Table 7. Tunisian Fintech's suggestions in R&D

Strengthening collaboration universities, research & FinTech's:	**Tax & financial incentives for R&D:**	**Creation of a national research network dedicated to FinTech's:**
"Encourage partnerships and joint projects to promote the transfer of knowledge, expertise and innovative solutions. »	"Providing tax benefits and subsidies to FinTech's that invest in R&D and research projects, to stimulate innovation . »	"Establish a national platform that brings together researchers, experts, to exchange of ideas, the dissemination of research results and the promotion innovations in the field of Fintech. »

Source: Barometer Fintech (November 2023)

1.2.2. Tunisian Fintech's Segments

Tunisian FinTech's operate in a B2B model, in payments, financing/investment, and business services. (Fintech's barometer2023). DisrupTunisia[4], directory and aggregation, gathers in an online platform, a database of Fintech's. The major Fintech's segments are:

Figure 1. Fintech segments

+ Payments and Transactions:

Facilitate or make payments, money transfers, transactions exchange, as Money transfer, Mobile Payment, Payment terminals,P2P payment, Online prize pools, Change, such as:

- **Konnect:** integrated payment offering integration process for the developers. It initialize Payment Requests, then the customers accepting those Payment Requests.
- **Sobflous:** is an electronic wallet (web and mobile) that offers users phone recharge, money transfer, merchant payment and invoice payment services.

+ Blockchain & cryptocurrencies

- **SQOIN** a new crypto currency called BASTOJI for Africa. Free crypto, open source, easy use, it's a blockchain providing a secure, free, fast and fluid exchange system.

- **Medcretech** offers a Blockchain app to trace and fluidize the life cycle of real estate.

- **Wealth management:** Facilitate access and/or provide financing and investment products, such as Robo-advisors.

- **CHAKAKA**: online Donations platform allowing associations and individuals to create Donation campaigns, mobilize around /humanitarian causes, projects, or events.
- **Catrim Tech** develops innovative solutions for trading rooms of investment banks.

+ Crowdfunding:

Popular business models are mainly rewards-based, Donation-based and equity-based:

- **Donation-based Crowdfunding**: EffectusCoFundy, boost projects with a social, and environmental impact on society in Africa. Only Tunisians abroad can donate online.
- **Reward- based Crowdfunding**: Coinsence empower people, firms, and communities to collaborate on initiatives that benefit society by blockchain and create impact.

+ Capital market

Fintech's such as VNEURON and DEDALE SOLUTION and more:

- **Finansya.com:** SaaS platform developing of digital solutions for the financial markets.
- **Ilboursa** allows stock market's development and the economic culture contributing to the strengthening of Tunisia Stock Exchange visibility to attract new investors.

+ Fintech's Business Services:

- **Swiver:** an online invoicing and business management software, designed for VSEs and SMEs in Tunisia. It helps small business owners manage the day-to-day operations.
- **WiseBoard:** for IT business for sustainable growth matching with vetted advisors. Advising businesses in: sales, marketing, operations, product, talent and strategy.

+ Others (RegTech)

It is regulatory compliance using technology to automate regulatory processes, to assist financial institutions comply with complex regulatory requirements and reducing the costs associated with compliance. It includes automated reporting, risk management, and identity verification in Tunisia Fintech such as UniQ and FINCONNECT and others.

+ Insurance:

Provide solutions to insurance sector as Integrated digital insurance 2.0, Microinsurance.

- **Dqlick** specializes in digitalization in the insurance sector.
- **AHMINI:** offering digital solutions to improve the quality of life of rural women.

+ Technology, IT & Infrastructure Payments

- **Paypos** leader in the development of innovative electronic payment solutions and the digitalization of banking and financial distribution channels in Tunisia and Africa.
- **Facturation.Tn:** offers an online billing application that complies with Tunisian regulations and which is accessible to several users working on a single interface.

+ Data Analytics: Fintech's such as:

- **Analytix** business intelligence platform offering exploration possibilities on processed, enriched business data presented in Dashboard format using Data Science.
- **YobiTrust:** uses math to analyze data and generate algorithms for AI for (i) secured data storage (ii) solutions to client's data set and problem (iii) optimizing workflow.

Table 8. Most popular FinTech's segments in Tunisia

Fintech	Usage
Crowdfunding	Collect funds worldwide and transmit them (international marketsinvestors).
Wealth	Facilitate access and/or provide financing and investment products, such as Robo-advisors
Mobile Payment	Allow user to make a daily transaction or any banking activities, credit services and transfer money online on any device without going to the bank.
Insuretech	Provide tailored insurance and data security. Update the process by online claims filling, policy management and offer claim service to the client.

Source: Authors Readings

2. TUNISIAN FINTECH'S ECOSYSTEM IN 2024

Tunisia has a rich Fintech ecosystem ; we illustrate its main components:

2.1. Accelerators and Incubators

The Tunisian Fintech's ecosystem is supported by the following entities.

Figure 2. Fintech ecosystem entities

- *Open Startup (OST)*: a non-governmental organization that fosters innovation and capacity building by entrepreneurship across the Middle East and Africa (MEA).
- *Betacube*: Pan-African venture builder, co-creates world class African tech startups.
- *Flat6Labs*: a seed and start-up program seeking to promote the growth of Tunisian startups and provide a source of supply to the industry of Venture Capital in Tunisia.
- *BIATLABS*: incubator of BIAT, NGO that offers free and non-equity.
- *Afkar Incubator* is a free six-month program, incubated entrepreneurs vary on phases.
- *Redstart Tunisia*: strategic partner of startups to ensure the sustainable development.
- *The Founder Institute*: network to turn ideas into startups, and global businesses.
- *CEED Tunisia* (Center for Entrepreneurship and Executive Development) is a Tunisian non-profit organization. It support businesses to develop in emerging markets.

2.2. Promotion and supervision structures

Fintech's needs to demonstrate not only that they are following the growing array of regulatory requirements but that they have considered the various risks posed. Well-managed Fintech's will adopt a proactive response to emerging risks and to evolving regulation and supervision. These supervision structure evolve:

Figure 3. Fintech supervision structure

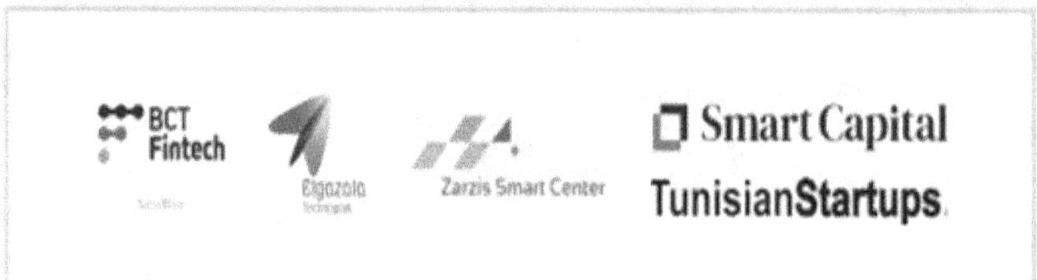

- ***Zarzis Smart Center*:** under the supervision of the Ministry of Industry, Energy and Mines and is governed by a Public-Private Partnership (PPP). Up to 36 firms, in the fields of e-commerce and programming, have an environment to develop their products.
- ***Elgazala Technopark*:** first IT oriented Technopark in Tunisia, suitable for the development of START-UPS, with high technology and high added value. It aims to synergy between research units and firms to facilitate technology transfer process. Its Services are Incubation, Technology Transfer and Business Development.
- ***Smart Capital, the national operator of Startup Tunisia*:** firm approved by the Financial Markets Council, is responsible for the implementation of Startup Tunisia, to make Tunisia a country of Startups at the crossroads of the Mediterranean, the MENA region and Africa. It is mandated by the Tunisian government, structured around:
- *Startup Act:* A unique legal framework dedicated to Startups launching or in Tunisia.
- *Startup Invest*: A new investment framework dedicated to Startups built around the Fund of Funds with a target size of €100 million, supported by a GP incubator.

- *Startup Ecosystem:* A support framework for ecosystem support organizations (OSEs) and Startups, focused on the themes of financing and international connections.
- **BCT Fintech:** Monitor and test the innovative solutions offered by Fintech to assess the inherent risks for the security of the financial services. It's main duties are:
- *Foster financial inclusion*: prioritize Fintech with innovative solutions increasing access to financial offers for targets poorly served by formal financial institutions.
- *Protecting users from financial services*: Require Fintech to provide their innovative solutions with the necessary safeguards to protect users from the inherent risks.
- *Support financial stability:* Monitor and test the innovative solutions offered by Fintech to assess the inherent risks for the security of the financial services.

2.3. Venture capital/Investment structures

Venture capital plays a crucial role in the technological innovation, providing young Fintech's economic support, consultancy, and non-monetary resources. The relationship goes far beyond the simple investment: they actively monitor the Fintech's evolution providing advices to minimize the high information asymmetry widely popular in this industry.

Figure 4. Investment company structures

- **216 Capital**: a venture capital firm focusing on early-stage technology firms. It invests across sectors in creative founders building transformational businesses.
- **Admaius:** independent private equity house experienced in pan-African investment.

- **Carthage Business Angels (NGO)**: network of angel investors, with three pillars: Entrepreneurial, Ecosystem, Enabler, (Univenture- Start'act – Movility- Tasdit)
- **SPE Capital**: private equity firm driving sustainable investments across Africa. SPE is underpinned by leading corporate governance principles.
- **START UP MAXULA SEED FUND**: approved by the Financial Market Council (CMF). It manages assets, by equity to invest in the unlisted sector.
- **MCF:** a corporate finance and investment consulting firm, focuses on changing economies with high growth potential in the Middle East and Africa (or MOA) region.
- **INTILAQ**: Innovation Hub supporting business creation, leading ICT's innovation.
- **Ekuity Capital**, joint venture between Kuwait Investment Authority (KIA), the sovereign wealth fund of Kuwait, the Tunisian government, and the private sector.
- **Impact Partner:** NGO engaged to improve life standards by supporting impact-driven startups. It has developed accelerator programs and offered testing funds.
- **Blue Peak:** Private Capital designs innovative financing solutions to scale in Africa.
- **Africinvest**: investment teams focused on North Africa, Sub-Saharan Africa.
- **CAPSA**: an asset management firm approved by the Financial Markets Council. Investing in Private equity by financing firms with strong growth potential.

2.4. Central Bank of Tunisia: Regulating power

Created in 1985, the central bank is an independent financial entity to manage the economy, to protect the financial stability. It is accountable of monetary policy's sets, currency's management, and controlling the money supply. It has a regulating power in the banking and financial sector and responsible of: First, defining monetary policy. To defend economic stability by currencies value and prices' value, it must set macroeconomic goals and strategies. The central banks have many tools like interest rates regulation, impacting money's cost. Second, the Central Bank is the only authority for creating coins, it regulates the quantity and value of the money in circulation. This money injection assist economic agents to assure regular monetary transactions. The bank assure the stability of the exchange rates, owning and controlling the official reserves. Third role is the stewardship over the market by auditing if the financial laws are respected. The bank is responsible for monitoring the national payment system and its proper functioning. Fourth, it must supply the national banks with liquidity if needed under the loaning liquidity. It is accountable for setting and protecting economic growth stability, it must provide commercial banks with liquidity in the short term and establish price stability by a mediating role for credit fluctuations. Finally, the advisory role, the bank must provide regularly updated research reports relevant for the different stakeholders of the banking sector, for the government and any private firm. The Central bank must exercise all its tasks independently of the political group in power to ensure the stability of the financial system. The decisions of the central bank dependent on the supervisory entity constituting the banking sector and the financial institution. To assist the raise of fintech's, in 2019, Central Bank launched:

- *The Fintech committee*, to link the CBT and the Tunisian ecosystem. The committee collaborates with research centers and universities on innovation initiatives.
- *The "CBT-LAB"*: a platform enabling the CBT to digitize certain internal processes and to watch over financial technological innovations.
- *"Regulatory Sandbox"*: authorize Fintech to test innovative solutions with voluntary for a limited period and under the supervision of the CBT.

In 2019, the CBT had the vision to make Tunisia a regional technological Hub consulting the ecosystem. In 2020, the Fintech committee was created to favor the regulation and the ecosystem's collaboration. It manages the relationship with the old financial institutions. For the central bank the cooperation Fintech's-old financial institutions is a must, as a win-win strategy to generate value and financial inclusion. The ecosystem is composed of: FinTech's, incubators, Professional Association of Banks, finance Institutions, local banks, ministries, telecommunications operators, universities, Consumer Defense Organization, Electronic Certification Agency, the Cyber Security Agency, payment systems' managers.

Discussing FinTech's VS Rivalry: Key players? Mori (2017) questioned who will lead the finance industry using customer data, and CSV? He interrogate if the power of old financial institutions would guarantee their sustainability based on locations' competitiveness, efficient IT systems, and huge capital, providing one type offers using B2C model. But, process changes, using smartphones, these function can be substituted by other channels with lower costs. Bank's business model won't survive.

Table 9. Potential New Success Factors & key players in financial industry

Potential New Success Factors		Key Player & Role ?
Capital	**Branches, IT systems**	**Incumbents source of power but may become legacy assets**
Knowledge	Customer Data	Distributers accumulate data on life activities. Banks know only about total monthly payments
	Technology	Incumbents have experience in house development acquisition of venture & alliances with tech firms
Convenience	Client Access	Banks have more client access than Fintech but less than distributors
	Product range	No unique group covers all offers to unleash Fintech's full potential
Trust	Customers confidence in service providers	Any entity with customer business model, customer strong relationship, high competence will gain customer's trust.

Source: Mori (2017)

2.5. Traditional banking sector and financial institutions

Tunisian banking started with the independence in 1956. The government created a financial system to finance the economy. Until late eighties, the state controlled the banking system, the rates, the credits, and the central bank regulated operations. This strategy slowed savings due to lack of competition. The new structural adjustment plan in 1987 unlocked a new financial system with access to credit. To create a competitive, secure, and stable financial system, new measures were set mobilizing savings and finance investments. In the nineties, government improved banking offer and strengthened the operation's security by electronic banking, favoring the entrance of foreign investors. The financial structure changed thanks liberalization and limited bank's monopolistic position. In 2004, the majority of Tunisian banks were subsidiaries of foreign banks. For innovation, Tunisian banks are in delayed. Any initiative needed the approval of monetary policy. Public innovation's predominance due to rigid regulation. Now, innovation in banking is shaping the banking monopoly with new players. In 2023 the financial sector on the stock exchange, generated a revenue of 1.9 billion dinars, up 11.6% compared over the same period in 2021. The highest increase in revenue came from insurances. The sector is facing deep mutation, explaining new strategic orientation. The banking system faced state's disengagement, foreign investors' entry . Three categories of banks are identified:

- Banks with high state ownership (mainly BNA, STB, and BH).
- Banks with private Tunisian capital (BIAT, BT and Amen Bank).

- Banks with the foreign majority (UIB-SG, UBCI-BNP Paribas, Attijari Bank, ATB).

Currently, there are 25 universal banks, 2 merchant banks, 8 leasing and 3 factoring.

2.5.1. Deposit Institutions: For Saltiel (2009) each bank is specialized:

- ***Public banks:*** five public firms, classified as deposit banks. Offering savings and finance the public and private sector by credits with appropriate rates.
- ***Saving banks:*** government entities managing saving by collecting and paying interest or dividends to savers. It operate under the tutelage of the communication ministry.
- ***Private Deposit Banks:*** constituted of six privates.
- ***Foreign Banks:*** foreign banks collecting deposits called City Bank.
- ***Non-Resident Banks*:** foreign banks manage the international landscape from Tunisia.

2.5.2. Financial Services Institutions:

The stock exchange: The higher council of financial markets created to adjust the vision of the Tunisian stock exchange generating innovation. The stock is centralized gathering firms and gives the opportunity for investors to exchange equities. It collect savings and orient it to the stock investments channels to finance Tunisian investors

2.5.3.Non-Creating Money Financial Institutions:

- ***State Banks:*** supply commercial banking services without creating money. It supports the financial market but not as the central. It impacts the monetary policy.
- ***Development Banks:*** The increase in the financial demand in the economy urged the financial markets to create new institutions to cope with the increasing demand.
- ***Insurances:*** offering direct insurance services and supplying customers with financial protection from potential future risks. (public and private).
- ***Investment companies*:** controlled by three entities: Tunisian Central Bank, ministry of finance and authority of the stock exchange.
- ***Leasing:***They finance the procurement of tangible assets. It is composed of three private capital firms. Their task is to buy equipment and sell it for the consumer.

2.5.4. PARA- Financial Companies:

Social security entity financed from employees and workers' wages participating at firms' capital to benefit from profits. Aims to supply underprivileged customers with credit.

2.6. Financial Customers

The individual or entities who borrow, save, and invest. They make decisions impacting the financial landscape. The analysis of the customers' behavior is mandatory to understand the ecosystem's dynamics . The income consumption, savings volume, assets value and debt fluctuations are important indicators. In Tunisia there are two types of customers. First, individuals with high use of technology. This category doubled from 2013 to 2015 to reach 40% with mobile traffic. Second, firms as banks, insurance, and other financial institutions.

2.7. Technology Developers

Technology entities that creates applications as software's, websites, applications, and support systems. They are based on technical knowledge about coding, debugging source code for applications and software. It uses AI and machine learning, big data, cloud and blockchain. In Tunisia, the technology developers are a major player of the ecosystems. Seen as game changers by offering the technological infrastructure, cloud computing, cryptocurrency, and social media. These technologies enable startup to automatize their processes and offers. FinTech's generate revenue in favor of technology developers.

Consequently, the Tunisian Fintech's ecosystem is impacted by the products, services, and solutions provider by the traditional ecosystem. Moreover, the Tunisian regulation set by the central bank of Tunisia remains evolving according to the evolvement of the dynamics with the Tunisian Financial and technological market. One of the big moves taken by the central bank of Tunisia in January 2024, was setting a regulatory framework to encourage the collaboration between Tunisian Fintech's and Tunisian banks will be explained.

3. REGULATION AND GUIDELINES FOR EXERCISING THE ACTIVITY OF PAYMENT FACILITATOR

The central bank of Tunisia imposed a new procedure. For the financial institutions (Banks, the National Post Office and payment establishments) that in line with the Tunisian central bank's strategy for the development of digital payments, the Central Bank supports the use, in the partnership framework, innovative technological solutions offered by Tunisian FinTech's to allow the financial inclusion of small traders and artisans by the provision of secure and affordable payment gateways facilitating the acceptance of digital payment.

Aware of the legal and operational risks associated with the activity of payment facilitator and their impact on confidence in digital payment, the Central Bank of Tunisia, as part of its general mission of monitoring payment systems and means, insists that the financial institutions must respect the following guidelines when examining any partnership project with payment facilitators. By these new guidelines, the central bank of Tunisia aims activity, to ensure:

- Preserve the interests of sub-merchants.
- Establish platforms that strengthen public confidence in digital payments.
- Guarantee the security of payment transactions and the confidentiality of data,
- Mitigate risks on financial institutions, particularly the risks of money laundering and terrorist financing and reputational risk.

Financial institutions need to:

+ Submit to the Central Bank of Tunisia at least two months before the operationalization of any partnership project with a payment facilitator, a request accompanied by the contractual documents relating to the partnership project and a description of the project.

+ Ensure that the partnership project enshrines the following guiding principles:

- ***Governance:*** the acquiring financial institution pays attention to the governance mode of the payment facilitator and that it has an appropriate internal control system in line with good practices.
- ***Financial base:*** the acquiring financial institution verifies that the payment facilitator has a satisfactory financial structure appropriate to this activity.
- ***Management of "Acquirer/payment facilitator"*** relationships and "payment facilitator/sub-merchant": the acquiring financial institution ensures that the payment facilitator draws up intelligible contracts detailing the obligations and responsibilities of each par-

ty both at the start of the relationship and during the provision of agreed services. The acquiring institution must obtain the express written commitment from the payment facilitator by which the latter undertakes to only contract with sub-merchants engaging in a lawful activity.

-***Risk Management***: the acquiring financial institution verifies that the payment facilitator has a risk management system to prevent fraud and ensure the security of transactions and business continuity.

-***Data protection:*** the acquiring financial institution ensures that the payment facilitator implements robust security measures to protect users' financial and personal data.

-***Meet anti-terrorism financing and anti-money laundering compliance requirements:*** the acquiring financial institution ensures that the payment facilitator identifies and selects sub-merchants following KYC requirements and continuously monitors their activities to detect money laundering and terrorist financing operations.

-**Reporting to sub-merchants:** the financial institution verifies that the payment facilitator can offer reporting functionalities to sub-merchants to monitor their transactions and consult their account balances.

- **Guarantee mechanisms:** to guarantee the interests of the various stakeholders including sub-merchants, the acquiring financial institution ensures:

- **Locate the funds** relating to payments for goods and services from sub-merchants, in a single global account opened in the name of the payment facilitator separately from the account dedicated to its operating or investment needs.
- **Conclude a written agreement** describing the operating methods of the global account and ensure that the debit movements on this account relate only to transfers of amounts to the benefit of sub-merchants and commissions accruing to the facilitator. The agreement must provide that the financial institution undertakes not to be paid in respect of a debt on the amounts held in the payment facilitator's global account.
- **Level the overall account of the payment facilitator** for the benefit of sub-merchants within a period not exceeding 48 hours.

- **Security:** the acquiring financial institution ensures that the payment facilitator secures its platform via a process technological guaranteeing authentication during access, the blocking any unauthorized access to data and prohibiting the abusive use of personal data capable of preserving the traceability of flows.

- **The economic model:** the acquiring financial institution monitors the payment facilitator to apply a viable economic model and incentive for sub-merchants.
- **Claims management:** the acquiring financial institution ensures that the payment facilitator can optimize and formalize a complaints management process capable of preserving trust among users and supervisory authorities.
- **Reporting to the BCT:** the acquiring financial institution ensures carry out quarterly reporting to the Central Bank of Tunisia to the activity of payment facilitator.
- Ensure that the activity of payment facilitator does not extend to activities falling under the banking monopoly (bank, financial institution, and payment establishment).
- Ensure that the payment facilitator does not proceed in a manner of any kind, through advertisements, to create doubt in the minds of users and third parties in general, as to the nature of its activity.

4. RESULTS AND DISCUSSION

4.1. Result: The payment facilitator: the case of We Settle Tunisia and We Pay

We-Settle is a core business startup, created in 2020 and focuses on bill payment and financial management. One of proud achievements, is putting in place We-Settle's platform for the national bill payment aggregator PAYSMART in partnership with the payment processing SMT and in close collaboration with the Central Bank of Tunisia, part of its strategy for deashing and financial inclusion. PAYSMART offers many bills and public service payment and is connected to more than 15 banks and Payment Service Providers. As a strategic move, We-Settle expands its offerings by creating WePay to operate as technology provider and as a payment facilitator enabling payment acceptance solutions in an exclusive partnership with EdfaPay. We Settle play an important role in the implementation of digital payment for municipal services "E-Construction" and "Citizen Space 2.0" through the national aggregation platform PAYSMART in collaboration with "Monétique Tunisie" and the Central Bank of Tunisia. This project allows receiving building permits and municipal services is easier and faster digitally. This project is part of the #Digital4Reforms program implemented by the Deutsche Gesellschaft für Internationale Zusammenarbeit (GIZ) GmbH in partnership with the Tunisian government, the Ministry of the Interior of Tunisia, and the Ministry of Finance. We Settle is a key factor contributing to governmental services digitalization and enabling e-payment of municipal services via the national aggregator Pay smart. ***We-Pay*** offers a One-Stop-Shop platform enabling a range of innovative solutions such as InPerson TapToPay, online multi-payment checkout and cross border services. WePay is born in Tunisia and has already started marking its presence in local and regional markets. In Tunisia, We Pay's Soft POS solution is certified by the authorized authority SMT and is ready to use. It is also closely collaborating with the Central Bank of Tunisia regarding the payment facilitator activity; and we have secured partnerships and customers. On an international scale, we are collaborating with the leading payment networks. We are concluding partnerships in Morocco. Also, We Pay is working on enabling international payment services for Tunisian Diaspora based in Europe.

4.1.1. We Sette & We Pay 's Reconceiving Products and Markets

Within the payment and transaction segment, We Settle & We Pay have been rethinking Fintech's products about society's needs and the benefit generated. It includes better banking systems adapted to the needs of Tunisians looking for better services to assure online payment for We Settle is a key factor contributing to governmental services digitalization and enabling e-payment of municipal services via the national aggregator Paysmart. Analyzing the needs of the Tunisian market, We Settle & We Pay redesigned products or new distribution methods through the collaboration with the Tunisian Bank ATB. These two Fintech's are contributing to financial Literacy & financial Inclusion by sustainably providing financial offers such as transactions, payments, savings, credit, and insurance. It targets both B2B (MSMs) and B2C. Financial literacy is ability to create informed perceptions and make appropriate choices to money utilization. By reconceiving products, fintech improve social welfare.

4.1.2.We Settle & We Pay Redefining Productivity in the Value Chain

Overview of WePay products for local, online, and cross-border payments We Pay Solutions:

- A unified platform offering several innovative solutions for merchants and businesses.
- Proximity payment: with the TAPPY solution, which transforms Android smartphones and devices into soft terminals accepting contactless payment by cards.

- *Online payment:* WePay CHECKOUT An online payment gateway offering several payment methods, such as cards and mobile payment via wallets.
- Cross-border payment: WePay INTERNATIONAL - Integrable payment kit to accept payment with several global solutions, such as PayPal, Google Pay and Apple Pay
- Bill payment aggregator for the private sector: The WeSwitch solution offering the possibility of paying bills from its single Fatourti portal or directly from the solutions of integrated payment service providers, such as the BTNET net banking of the bank of Tunisia, and the application for Very MyEasyTransfer for an international bill payment service which will be available soon
- E-Commerce: The provision of the Shahbandr solution for merchants in Tunisia, allowing the creation of an online and mobile store in a few clicks, and integrating the different WePay payment solutions
- Connection is open for merchants and customers interested in WePay solutions, which will be accessible in June 2024.

4.1.3. We Settle & We Pay Enabling Local Cluster Development

To ensure the activity of payment facilitator, We Settle and We pay, developed many partnerships with strategic members of the Fintech's ecosystem.

First, the PayFac convention with the Tunisian bank ATB, a Tunisian commercial bank, was created in 1982, by the integration of a branch of the Arab Bank Tunis with Tunisian individuals. Its mission was contribution to the economic and financial development of the country. In this partnership the ATB represents a business partner for Tunisian Fintech's We Pay. According to the regulation set by the Tunisian central bank, the bank will ensure the security of the transactions made between the users and the payment facilitator.

Second, the PaySmart convention with "Société monetique Tunisie (SMT), created in 1989 by the Tunisian Banks. Monétique-Tunisie is a company under the Tunisian private law, specializing in the design, integration, operation, and outsourcing. Its strategic vision is investing in new payment methods and creating "customer" value. The company is constantly monitoring developments affecting it. It builds collaborations with strong shareholders: Tunisian Banks and the Post Office are key partners of the company. Their trust and loyalty are guarantees of stability for the development of Monétique Tunisie. It provides benefits and services common to all bank cards (Contactless payment, Mastercard Visa, Mobile Payments, Secure payments). With this partnership, Monétique-Tunisie will be the technological partner of We Pay as payment facilitator.

Third, the convention with Comunik, a new generation software publisher operating in the field of Telecom and IT engineering. Its mission is to optimize the management of business on a technical, economic, and operational level. It offers a smart solution for a better customer relationship with four main services:

- Comunik VoIP: It combines reliability, performance, rich functionality, and integration with business information systems, providing a digital customer relationship.
- Comunik Contact: An innovative high-tech solution to manage all telemarketing and pre-sales service professions with ease of use, speed of handling and unfailing stability, while maintaining a wide range of new features.
- Comunik Sales: to boost business' sales with good organization of business opportunities and careful management of the sales cycles. It provides the ability to take the right decisions.

    -Comunik HelpDesk: it provides business customers with access to express themselves. The business ensures follow-up on users' complaints and communicates with them after-sales service covering the entire customer service process.

Fourth, Soft POS Convention with TOPNET as the first big merchant promoting innovation. TOPNET, is a major player in the ICT sector in Tunisia, operating on the internet market for 20 years. It is the leader in Internet services in Tunisia, both in the residential and professional segments. It has nearly a 62% market share on ADSL, more than 64% market share in Optical Fiber, and a commercial network covering all regions of the country with 15 commercial agencies and more than 140 partners. TOPNET, is part of a digital development approach across the entire value chain, offers a varied catalog of connectivity, managed security and Cloud offers and solutions meeting the needs of each segment of the Tunisian market. (General public, Large account companies, SME/SMI, liberal professions), thus giving its customers a multitude of choices adapted to their specific uses and their budgets. It's main products and solutions are: Pro offers, Univers Data,Security Universe, Cloud Universe, General Public Offers, Connectivity: ADSL, VDSL and GPON, Value-added services: Home Secure (IoT: Video Surveillance), Antivirus Solution, Kid Secure, Topnet Storage (Coud storage space).

Fifth, the Soft POS convention with KAOUN as PayFac partner. Kaoun is a Fintech that fosters financial inclusion through its usage of data science to power payments and credits. It is a startup specializing in Fintech. Its infrastructure allows for better financial inclusion. With this partnership, WePay-Kaoun.users will be able to use a payment solution that offers eKYC, mobile payments and credit solutions built with distributed ledger technology.

Sixth, the Soft POS convention with Konnect Networks as PayFac partner. Konnect Networks is a pioneer in the payment industry in Tunisia. It helps businesses of all sizes and scale grow using different payment methods. With the help of a clear payment solution, it offers multiple payment methods in a simple way. Its mission is to become a reference PSP in Tunisia by simplifying complex financial flows. It currently has nearly 2,000 users in Tunisia.

Seventh, the convention with international partners: Shahbandr convention for E-Commerce promotion with WePay. Shahbandar is an electronic platform that helps merchants in the digital transformation process by helping them start, develop, operate, and grow their e-commerce. It is a fully integrated SaaS e-commerce merchant platform that lets merchants start, grow, and manage a business with a variety of the best tools in the industry. By offering an online store, inventory, secure payments, shipping, and apps.

4.2. Discussion

The findings can serve as data for new research optimizing future actions. This investigation offers few contributions at three levels: theoretical, methodological, and managerial.

- Theoretical Contribution

From an academic view, even though there is increase of research on fintech, when it comes to Fintech's creating shared value, to our best knowledge, there are no studies that investigate this relationship in fintech's in the Tunisian Context. This study can be used as a guide to examine and investigate this phenomenon further.

The theoretical contribution is characterized by the Tunisian business context. The combination of old and recent works in the literature clarified the specificities of Fintech's shared value in the Tunisian context. The exploration study among FinTech's managers identified Fintech's abilities to innovate its business models and achieve optimum performance. The research confirms that business results and social results are two distinct goals but relates to unleash Fintech's competitiveness and sustainability.

- Methodological Contribution: The added value of our study is the empirical validation of the relationships with the arrangement of the qualitative approach based on semi-structured interviews and a quantitative approach . From a methodological point of view, our research attests to the presence of the Fintech's role in creating shared value.

- Managerial Contribution: From an investor's point of view, our findings can orient their investment decisions. With other factors used to determine investment decisions, these results can be used to determine which segment can offer shared value, which segment have a serious potential of growth in the Tunisian context. From a managerial point of view, Fintech's creating shared value, rely on the following:
    - ☐ Introduce or develop new business models based on a deep investigation and analysis of the needs of Tunisian business communities.
    - ☐ Develop an operational approach by improving communication with the target to detect the needs and social issues of the Tunisian community.
    - ☐ Encourage FinTech's to share their knowledge and experiences.
    - ☐ Means and tools promoting data sharing or ideas in Fintech.
    - ☐ The absence of set processes to analyze the needs and issues of Fintech's business communities is an inhibitor for setting CSV within Tunisian Fintech's

Stargazing on CSV will then allow:

- ☐ Improving customer satisfaction to better meet their needs and expectations.
- ☐ Improving operational performance, redefining the productivity within the value chain.
- ☐ Business leaders must understand that CSV's strategies are critical to increase profits, increasing competitive advantages, and succeeding in the future.
- ☐ The innovative business model generated positive impact on the CSV strategies set.

CONCLUSION

First, we examined the emergence of fintech. Second, we studied its main business models. Third, we identified business ecosystems and analyzed Tunisian fintech and market competition. We conclude that fintechs have distinctive characteristics that set them apart from the broader ecosystem. Fintech plays a role in financial inclusion. Research assessed the impact of fintech on poverty reduction. Fintech uses technologies to include marginalized. For Liu (2018) the fall of aggressive P2P lenders in China prove the dangers of fintech unchecked. Interacting with policymakers, scholars are working on frameworks to control the other side of Fintech's.

The theoretical/methodological/empirical limitations of the research

Any investigation has certain limitations. Our work was limited by: First, on the theoretical level, Fintech's is still an on-progress phenomena, there are many controversy within the literature review and it's future is far from being predicted which pressured us to make some choices when it comes to the definition of what is a Fintech's ? Investigating literature, we categorized fintech's definition into three blocks: First technology- oriented identification, Second functional definition, Third Technology-Oriented and Function- Oriented Focus. Second, on the empirical level, we didn't follow advanced models to analyze the data, we selected mainly the case of Wesettle, and We pay based on the data shared and the orientation toward online payment in Tunisia . Finally, many of the fintech's don't figure of the official database. This condition made it extremely difficult for us to collect a large sample of fintech's.

REFERENCES

Aakhus, M., & Bzdak, M. (2012). Revisiting the role of" shared value" in the business-society relationship. *Business & Professional Ethics Journal, 31*(2), 231–246. DOI: 10.5840/bpej201231211

Abbasi, K., Alam, A., Du, M. A., & Huynh, T. L. D. (2021). FinTech, SME efficiency and national culture: Evidence from OECD countries. *Technological Forecasting and Social Change, 163*, 120454. DOI: 10.1016/j.techfore.2020.120454

Acquier, A., Valiorgue, B., & Daudigeos, T. (2017). Sharing the shared value: A transaction cost perspective on strategic CSR policies in global value chains. *Journal of Business Ethics, 144*(1), 139–152. DOI: 10.1007/s10551-015-2820-0

Adams, R. B., & Ferreira, D. (2007). A theory of friendly boards. *The Journal of Finance, 62*(1), 217–250. DOI: 10.1111/j.1540-6261.2007.01206.x

Akpinar, M., & Saleem, S. (2019). Creating shared value in international business: A research agenda.

Al Zubaidi, H. H. A. (2019). Impact of investment decisions on shared value: An analysis of Iraqi tourism companies listed on the Iraqi Stock Exchange for the period 2013-2017.

Alaassar, A. (2021). A phenomenon-driven exploration of regulatory sandboxes in FinTech entrepreneurial ecosystems.

Anshari, M., Almunawar, M. N., Masri, M., & Hamdan, M. (2019). Digital marketplace and FinTech to support agriculture sustainability. *Energy Procedia, 156*, 234–238. DOI: 10.1016/j.egypro.2018.11.134

Arena, M., Azzone, G., & Piantoni, G. (2020). Shared value creation during site decommissioning: A case study from the energy sector. *Journal of Cleaner Production, 251*, 119587. DOI: 10.1016/j.jclepro.2019.119587

Argyres, N., & McGahan, A. M. (2002). An interview with Michael Porter. *The Academy of Management Perspectives, 16*(2), 43–52. DOI: 10.5465/ame.2002.7173495

Arner, D. W., Barberis, J., & Buckley, R. P. (2015). The evolution of Fintech: A new post-crisis paradigm. *SSRN, 47*, 1271. DOI: 10.2139/ssrn.2676553

Arner, D. W., Barberis, J., & Buckley, R. P. (2015). The evolution of Fintech: A new post-crisis paradigm. *SSRN, 47*, 1271. DOI: 10.2139/ssrn.2676553

Arner, D. W., Buckley, R. P., Zetzsche, D. A., & Veidt, R. (2020). Sustainability, FinTech and financial inclusion. *European Business Organization Law Review*, *21*(1), 7–35. DOI: 10.1007/s40804-020-00183-y

Arslanian, H., & Fischer, F. (2019). *The future of finance: The impact of FinTech, AI, and crypto on financial services*. Springer. DOI: 10.1007/978-3-030-14533-0

Ascarya, A. (2009). Lessons learned from repeated financial crises: An Islamic economic perspective. *Bulletin of Monetary Economics and Banking*, *12*(1), 27–74. DOI: 10.21098/bemp.v12i1.466

Ashta, A. (2018). News and trends in Fintech and digital microfinance: Why are European MFIs invisible? *FIIB Business Review*, *7*(4), 232–243. DOI: 10.1177/2319714518805183

Ashta, A., & Herrmann, H. (2021). Artificial intelligence and fintech: An overview of opportunities and risks for banking, investments, and microfinance. *Strategic Change*, *30*(3), 211–222. DOI: 10.1002/jsc.2404

Batunanggar, S. (2019). *Fintech development and regulatory frameworks in Indonesia* (No. 1014). ADBI Working Paper Series.

Beck, T., Chen, T., Lin, C., & Song, F. M. (2016). Financial innovation: The bright and the dark sides. *Journal of Banking & Finance*, *72*, 28–51. DOI: 10.1016/j.jbankfin.2016.06.012

Belfanti, F. *Creating shared value and clusters* (Doctoral dissertation, Università Carlo Cattaneo-LIUC).

Bergquist, A. K., & Eriksson, L. (2019). Sober business: Shared value creation between the insurance industry and the temperance movement. *Business History*, *61*(2), 322–342. DOI: 10.1080/00076791.2017.1380627

Bergquist, A. K., & Lindmark, M. (2016). Sustainability and shared value in the interwar Swedish copper industry. *Business History Review*, *90*(2), 197–225. DOI: 10.1017/S0007680516000374

Beschorner, T. (2014). Creating shared value: The one-trick pony approach. *Business Ethics Journal Review*, *1*(17), 106–112.

Beschorner, T. (2014). Creating shared value: The one-trick pony approach. *Business Ethics Journal Review*, *1*(17), 106–112.

Beschorner, T., & Hajduk, T. (2017). Creating shared value. A fundamental critique. *Creating Shared Value–Concepts, Experience. Criticism*, •••, 27–37.

Bettinger, A. (1972). Fintech: A series of 40 time shared models used at Manufacturers Hanover Trust Company. *Interfaces*, •••, 62–63.

Bill Gates. (2014) Banking is changing. Impatient Optimists. *Bill & Melinda Gates Foundation Web site*.

Blakstad, S., & Allen, R. (2018). FinTech revolution. *Cham, Switzerland: Springer, 121*, 132. https://doi.org/DOI: 10.1007/978-3-319-76014-8

Bockstette, V., Pfitzer, M., & Smith, D. (2015). Banking on shared value. How banks profit by rethinking their purpose. FSG.: http://sharedvalue.org/

Bofondi, M., & Gobbi, G. (2017). The big promise of FinTech. *European economy*, (2), 107-119.

Bollaert, H., Lopez-de-Silanes, F., & Schwienbacher, A. (2021). Fintech and access to finance. *Journal of Corporate Finance*, *68*, 101941. https://doi.org/https://doi.org/10.1016/j.jcorpfin.2021.101941. DOI: 10.1016/j.jcorpfin.2021.101941

BPS. B. P. S. (2018). Statistical yearbook of Indonesia 2018. In BPS-Statistics Indonesia. https://www.bps.go.id/publication/2018/07/03/5a963c1ea9b0fed6497d0845/

Bu, Y., Li, H., & Wu, X. (2022). Effective regulations of FinTech innovations: The case of China. *Economics of Innovation and New Technology*, *31*(8), 751–769. DOI: 10.1080/10438599.2020.1868069

Buchak, G., Matvos, G., Piskorski, T., & Seru, A. (2018). Fintech, regulatory arbitrage, and the rise of shadow banks. *Journal of Financial Economics*, *130*(3), 453–483. DOI: 10.1016/j.jfineco.2018.03.011

Cai, C. W. (2018). Disruption of financial intermediation by FinTech: A review on crowdfunding and blockchain. *Accounting and Finance*, *58*(4), 965–992. DOI: 10.1111/acfi.12405

Camarena-Martinez, J. L., Ochoa-Silva, B., & Wendlandt-Amezaga, T. R. (2016). Exploring the origins of creating shared value in the CSR literature. *International Journal of Business and Management*, *11*(12), 97–109. DOI: 10.5539/ijbm.v11n12p97

Cao, F., Sun, J., & Yuan, R. (2019). Board directors with foreign experience and stock price crash risk: Evidence from China. *Journal of Business Finance & Accounting*, *46*(9-10), 1144–1170. https://corporatefinanceinstitute.com/resources/capital-markets/market-risk/. DOI: 10.1111/jbfa.12400

Castejón Teruel, A. (2018). The rise of FinTech in the global financial markets.

Chakrabarty, S., & Bass, A. E. (2014). Corporate governance in microfinance institutions: Board composition and the ability to face institutional voids. *Corporate Governance, 22*(5), 367–386. DOI: 10.1111/corg.12071

Chen, K. C. (2020). Implications of Fintech developments for traditional banks. *International journal of economics and financial issues, 10*(5), 227.

Chen, Y. R. R., Hung-Baesecke, C. J. F., Bowen, S. A., Zerfass, A., Stacks, D. W., & Boyd, B. (2020). The role of leadership in shared value creation from the public's perspective: A multi-continental study. *Public Relations Review, 46*(1), 101749. DOI: 10.1016/j.pubrev.2018.12.006

Cheng, M., & Qu, Y. (2020). Does bank FinTech reduce credit risk? Evidence from China. *Pacific-Basin Finance Journal, 63*, 101398. DOI: 10.1016/j.pacfin.2020.101398

Chung, K. H., & Zhang, H. (2011). Corporate governance and institutional ownership. *Journal of Financial and Quantitative Analysis, 46*(1), 247–273. DOI: 10.1017/S0022109010000682

Claessens, S., & Laeven, L. (2004). Competition in the financial sector and growth: A cross-country perspective. In *Financial development and economic growth: Explaining the links* (pp. 66–105). Palgrave Macmillan UK. DOI: 10.1057/9780230374270_3

Coase, R. H. (1937). The nature ofthe firm. *Economica, 4*(16), 386–405. DOI: 10.1111/j.1468-0335.1937.tb00002.x

Coles, J. L., Daniel, N. D., & Naveen, L. (2008). Boards: Does one size fit all? *Journal of Financial Economics, 87*(2), 329–356. DOI: 10.1016/j.jfineco.2006.08.008

Corner, P. D., & Pavlovich, K. (2016). Shared value through inner knowledge creation. *Journal of Business Ethics, 135*(3), 543–555. DOI: 10.1007/s10551-014-2488-x

Crane, A., Palazzo, G., Spence, L. J., & Matten, D. (2014). Contesting the value of "creating shared value". *California Management Review, 56*(2), 130–153. DOI: 10.1525/cmr.2014.56.2.130

Cumming, D. J., & Schwienbacher, A. (2021). Fintech venture capital. In *The Routledge Handbook of FinTech* (pp. 11–37). Routledge. DOI: 10.4324/9780429292903-3

Daily, C. M., Dalton, D. R., & Cannella, A. A.Jr. (2003). Corporate governance: Decades of dialogue and data. *Academy of Management Review, 28*(3), 371–382. DOI: 10.2307/30040727

Daood, A., & Menghwar, P. R. E. M. (2017). Understanding" creating shared value". In *EUROMED ACADEMY OF BUSINESS CONFERENCE BOOK OF PROCEEDINGS* (pp. 513-525). EuroMed Press.

Gai, K., Qiu, M., & Sun, X. (2018). A survey on FinTech. *Journal of Network and Computer Applications*, *103*, 262–273.

Malaysia, B. N. (2016). *Financial technology regulatory sandbox framework*. Bank Negara Malaysia., https://www.bnm.gov.my/index.php?ch=57&pg=137&ac=533&bb=file

Menghwar, P. S., & Daood, A. (2021). Creating shared value: A systematic review, synthesis and integrative perspective. *International Journal of Management Reviews*, *23*(4), 466–485. https://www.dawn.com/. DOI: 10.1111/ijmr.12252

Sahabuddin, M., Sakib, M. N., Rahman, M. M., Jibir, A., Fahlevi, M., Aljuaid, M., & Grabowska, S. (2023). The evolution of FinTech in scientific research: A bibliometric analysis. *Sustainability*, *15*(9), 7176.

Saksonova, S., & Kuzmina-Merlino, I. (2017). Fintech as financial innovation–The possibilities and problems of implementation.

Chapter 7
Analyzing the Role of Digitalization in Advancing the Green Economy:
A Systematic Literature Review

Ahsan Riaz
https://orcid.org/0000-0002-8436-3241
Government College University, Faisalabad, Pakistan

Marium Azad Khan
https://orcid.org/0009-0000-9588-650X
National University of Modern Languages, Mirpur, Pakistan

Syeda Fizza Abbas
Kinnaird College for Women, Lahore, Pakistan

Farah Naz
https://orcid.org/0000-0002-4707-5443
Kinnaird College for Women, Lahore, Pakistan

Muhammad Danyal Ahmad
https://orcid.org/0009-0005-4043-1870
Government College University, Faisalabad, Pakistan

ABSTRACT

There is increasing interest in the node of digitalization and green economy due to the recent development of sustainable economic growth. This systematic literature

DOI: 10.4018/979-8-3693-4373-9.ch007

review aims to comprehensively explore and analyze the existing research on the association between digitalization and green economy to discover and highlight the fundamental discoveries and perspectives present in the current body of literature concerning digital currencies and sustainable economic growth. The review adheres to the PRISMA statement, while VOS-Viewer software was utilized to execute the bibliometric analysis. A thorough exploration of academic sources, i.e., Scopus, employed varied keyword combinations. This effort led to the identification of 308 records and subsequent assessment of titles, abstracts, and full texts, including 110 pertinent studies for analysis, covering the period from 2005 to 2023. The findings reveal vital insights into the role of digitalization in contributing to green economy growth and supporting sustainable development goals.

1. INTRODUCTION

Digitalization, the process of introducing and using digital technologies in daily life and commerce, is revolutionizing the world economy. At the same time, the green economy, which focuses on the principles of sustainability, low-carbon development, and resource conservation, is becoming more relevant as countries and companies seek to meet the challenges of climate change and environmental pollution. The integration of these two revolutionary changes is creating new approaches, increasing productivity, and encouraging sustainable development. The widespread adoption of digital technologies and solutions like IoT, AI, big data, blockchain, and cloud defines digitalization. These technologies involve the gathering, management, and analysis of large amounts of data in real-time, supporting better decision-making and process management in different industries. For example, IoT sensors can measure environmental conditions, energy consumption, and equipment usage, which are useful for minimizing wastage, optimizing energy usage, and improving productivity. Through AI and machine learning, equipment failures can be foreseen, supply chain operations can be enhanced, and resources can be managed to minimize emissions and environmental footprint (Endang Sungkawati, 2024).

The green economy, on the other hand, aims at making economic growth less dependent on negative impacts on the environment by supporting sustainable development, renewable energy, and the circular economy. It focuses on resource conservation, reduction of use, and shifting to cleaner energy, including wind, solar, and hydropower. The green economy also promotes sustainable farming, wildlife and habitat protection, and the improvement of air and water quality. Through innovation and sustainability, the green economy seeks to generate employment, stimulate economic development, and improve environmental stability. The link between digitalization and the green economy can be seen in several areas as follows. First, digital technologies are improving energy efficiency and allowing the connection of renewable energy sources to the grid. IoT and AI-enabled smart grids can manage the supply and demand, control the distribution of energy and minimize power loss (Jiayu & Wang, 2024). This enhances the dependability and effectiveness of energy systems and also allows more utilization of renewable energy sources, hence decreasing the use of fossil fuels and emissions of greenhouse gases. Secondly, digitization is transforming the transportation industry, which is one of the largest emitters of greenhouse gases. EVs, connected and autonomous vehicles, and smart transportation systems are revolutionizing how people and goods are transported. Traffic management, traffic congestion, and fuel efficiency can be improved with the help of advanced data analytics and IoT. Moreover, blockchain technology can increase the transparency and effectiveness of supply chains in terms of sourcing, production, and transportation of environmentally friendly products (Lin et al., 2023).

Third, there is evidence showing that digitalization efforts are spurring a circular economy. Automation and interconnectivity of systems and digital technologies make it possible to monitor, reuse, recycle, and repurpose materials and products within the manufacturing process and in other industries. For instance, the digitization of tangible assets means that owners can monitor and manage the physical things from the design, production, use and disposal stages. It also helps minimize the use of resources that would otherwise be used in developing products that are not so relevant in the market, and at the same time, it also adds creativity in the development of products and their assembly. In addition, the enhanced digital environment has empowered consumers to make more sustainable decisions. This involves making the public aware of the environmental impact of various products and services through Mobile apps and other related marketing platforms. E-commerce platforms also have the function of urging consumers to adopt green consumption habits and offering green products to consumers. Social networks and other similar online platforms are also useful in raising awareness about the environment and calling people to unite for a cause of sustainable living (Liu et al., 2023). Thus, it can be concluded that we can observe how the integration of digitalization and the green economy creates more opportunities for sustainable development. In this case, through the use of digital technologies, the performance of an organization, institution, and even its people is enhanced, and new forms of values are created while improving the environment. That change is not only due to the challenges posed by climate change and the depletion of natural resources but also to new opportunities for long and non-renewable economic growth. As the world progresses, everything is shifting towards technology, and it is therefore important that the green economy concepts, as mentioned above, be integrated into the world to make this a better place.

The reasons for understanding the connection between digitalization and the green economy involve some key objectives: sustainable development and climate change. IoT, AI, blockchain, big data, cloud, and 5G are examples of digital technologies that can potentially alter the way more information infrastructure and business is handled. The green economy, which has been formulated to focus on sustainable growth and resource productivity, renewable energy, and circular economy, is therefore aimed at establishing a sustainable economic model that can support growth, as well as the capacity to adapt to shocks and enhance equity. Moreover, it is crucial to identify how these fields are related to introducing innovations in the approach to sustainable development (Luis, 2023).

First, digital technologies facilitate the enhancement of sustainability management by boosting efficiency and efficacy. For instance, IoT devices can assist in the control and proper usage of energy in smart grids, its efficient conservation, and the integration of renewable power systems. Consequently, the utilization of AI in organizations can enable the precise determination of energy requirements, supply, and emissions, thus increasing efficiency and promoting sustainability. It also means that the combination of these areas opens new horizons for the appearance of new technologies and new approaches to the organization of a business that can contribute to the solution of environmental issues. Biosciences, IoT and advanced analytics reflected in such applications as precision agriculture that employs large data in the optimization of crop management and in avoiding adverse impacts on the earth are convincing examples of how traditional techniques can be revamped into sustainable ones by the use of digital tools (Ramón et al., 2023).

Other benefits accrue from integrating digitalization with the green economy include the effect of digitalization on economic growth and employment opportunities. The development of such concepts as smart cities and green technologies produced the concepts of new branches of economy and new vacancies in the sectors related to high technologies and the environment. This is not only beneficial in enhancing economic growth but also opens up the path for innovations. For example, through expenditures in renewable energy technologies and smart technologies, new employment opportunities can also be generated, thus helping to improve the economy moderately. The other important factor is resource utilization efficiency, which refers to the utilization of resources in the shortest time possible in order to minimize wastage. From this perspective, digital technologies can play a significant role in the proper management of natural and physical resources to prevent cases of wastage. For instance, in smart water management systems, leakage could be recognized, and the usage of this water could be regulated and thus considered a vital commodity. Similarly, it can assist in the transition towards renewable energy by providing time series data in order to improve energy availability and reduce demand from the more traditional forms (Ozili, 2023).

Climate change is the biggest problem in the world, and digitalization and green economy solutions are the biggest problems in the world, and that is why it is necessary to use digitalization and green economy solutions. For example, advanced AI and big data are effective in managing and reducing carbon emissions, as well as digital technologies in energy consumption and utilization of green energy. These integrated efforts are important in the context of climate change goals at the global level and when trying to prevent climate change consequences. However, the presented intersection has the following benefits which improve the quality of life: Well-implemented smart and sustainable cities collaboration with the application of sophisticated technologies can reduce the negative impact of pollution, improve the transport infrastructure, and rational and efficient use of resources and services and thus quality life in urban centres. In addition, with this intersection, the world is made equal by eliminating the digital divide, which means that technological and sustainable development is possible for all regions and spaces. It creates a premise that provides a balance between the opportunities given by digital and sustainable innovation (Razzaq et al., 2023).

Moreover, acknowledging this relationship is crucial to the development of corresponding policies and legislation, which will enable the setup of conditions for sustainable development while encouraging the progress of related technologies. It ensures that the drive towards digital innovation is in line with environmental concerns and societal needs as it lays a legal framework for future advancements. In addition, when using a technological approach in combination with a green strategy, the nature of the system is enhanced to respond to different environmental disturbances. For example, the idea of smart infrastructure is useful in disaster issues, and the application of Big data in decision-making also improves disaster management and reconstruction in order to construct sustainable societies. However, it is important to look at the link between digitalization and the green economy, as this paper sheds light on sustainable development, innovation, economic growth, scarce resource utilization, climate change, enhancements in the quality of life, equality, and policy throughout sustainable systems. This approach is essential as far as the development of a balanced and cohesive society is concerned (Sharif et al., 2023).

1.1 Research Problem

As the concept of digitalization and the green economy has gained interest in academic and practice literature, several immense gaps are still evident. First of all, relatively few systematic studies have considered trends in the long-term consequences of digital technologies on the environment. Again, much prior work is typically myopic in its outlook, centres more on strategic gains over the short run and favourable outcomes drawn from specific settings and more frequently fails to adequately consider the negative side effects of their recommendations, for instance, e-waste and high power usage linked to data centres. Second, the literature on the two areas of digitalization and the green economy tends to exist in parallel, and little research has been done on the relationships between the two fields (Sharma et al., 2023).

Generally, there is less research with a focus on the techno-ecological theme, so more studies need to be done to fill the gap between technology and environmental science. Thirdly, the social aspect of digitalization, particularly within the green economy, is an area of study that has received little attention. Concerns on digitalization, including digital dividing line and equity, along with the effects of digital transitions on employment and skills in green industries, are not adequately discussed. The recognition of these social effects is vital in precisely formulating policies that can ensure that both digitalization and the green economy are inclusive. In addition, there is still little information regarding the policy imperatives and the effective regulation of digital technology incorporation with green economy development. Specifically, the involvement of various stakeholders, including governments, international organizations, and the private sector, in the provision of an environment conducive to this fusion is not very clear. Third, there is very limited evidence of the efficacy and viability of green initiatives facilitated by digitalization, although it can be surmised that such schemes are functional on some level, given their continued adoption by organizations.

1.2 Research Question

To address these gaps, the research will focus on the following questions:

- What are the most influential papers and authors in the research domain of digitalization and the green economy?
- Which journals and countries have contributed the most to research on digitalization and the green economy?
- What are the main themes and emerging trends in research linking digitalization with the green economy?
- What are the co-authorship and collaboration patterns in the research domain of digitalization and the green economy?
- What future research directions are suggested by the current literature on digitalization and the green economy?

By addressing these questions, the research aims to fill the existing gaps in the literature and provide actionable insights for policymakers, businesses, and stakeholders involved in promoting sustainable development through digital innovation.

1.3 Research Aim and Objectives

To examine and evaluate the impact of digitalization on the advancement of the green economy through a systematic literature review.

The following are the research objectives of the study.

- To identify and map the most influential studies, authors, and journals contributing to the intersection of digitalization and the green economy.
- To analyze the geographical and institutional distribution of research on digitalization in advancing the green economy.
- To uncover the primary themes and research topics in the literature through keyword analysis.
- To map the collaboration networks of authors, institutions, and countries in the research on digitalization and the green economy.
- To propose future research directions based on gaps identified in the literature.

1.4 Significance of the Study

The importance of the systematic literature review on the impact of digitalization in the promotion of the green economy cuts across disciplinary fields, from academia to policy formulation and implementation, as well as industries in promoting sustainable development and sustainability. This research has immense relevance to many stakeholders because it may help advance sustainable development goals (SDGs) and guide the formulation of policies and business strategies based on empirical evidence. Academically, this study contributes to the body of existing knowledge and research about digitalization and the green economy by presenting a synthesis of the current state of the literature. In this way, scholars are able to pinpoint the existing knowledge deficits, the potential future research directions, and conceptual paradigms that may inform future studies. In addition, it supports cross-disciplinary research by integrating ideas from fragments of environmental science, economics, information technology, and policy studies, enhancing academic discussions and expanding the base of existing knowledge.

From a policy-making perspective, this research provides insights into how digital technologies may be used to support sustainable development goals and respond to environmental issues. Thus, by analyzing the ability of digital solutions to improve resource efficiency, reduce the influence of climate change, and strengthen environmental management, decision-makers can develop policies and legal frameworks for green growth. In addition, it offers insights for overcoming barriers to digitalization and harnessing new technologies to meet challenging sustainability goals outlined in national and international policies and frameworks, including the Paris Agreement and the UN Sustainable Development Goals. To industries, businesses, entrepreneurs, and investors, this study provides a guide to aligning industry digitalization with sustainable business practices and value chains. Thus, focusing on the success stories, examples, and trends associated with the use of digital technologies in various industries helps identify new opportunities for leveraging information technologies for efficiency improvement and competitive advantage. It also highlights the economics of sustainability to argue how digitalization can lead to cost reduction, better brand image, and new business opportunities that respond to consumers' demand for sustainable goods and services.

Concerning its relevance to sustainable development goals (SDGs), this paper falls under the following targets of the 2030 Agenda for Sustainable Development. Concretely, it contributes to the achievement of the following goals: goal 7 (Affordable and Clean Energy), goal 9 (Industry, Innovation and Infrastructure), goal 11 (Sustainable Cities and Communities), goal 12 (Responsible Consumption and Production), and goal 13 (Climate Action). In contributing to the global goals of ensuring that transitioning to renewable energy, sustainable cities and communities, responsible consumption and production, and climate adaptation and resilience are realized, this study encourages the uptake of digital solutions for the delivery of the sustainable development agenda.

2. METHODOLOGY

2.1 Systematic Literature Review (SLR) Framework

A Systematic Literature Review (SLR), therefore, can be described as a systematic and highly structured approach to identifying, evaluating and synthesizing existing research on the researched subject matter or question under review. It entails a process of finding, assessing and integrating information from published and grey literature, such as articles in peer-reviewed journals, conference papers, books, and research reports. Therefore, the use of an SLR approach in this study can be justified by the fact that the method allows the evaluation of the existing state of knowledge of literature without distorting the results by personal views and preferences. An SLR decreases the influence of bias because it adheres to a set of a priori procedures and incorporates all relevant studies, which increases the accuracy and credibility of a study review. This approach makes it easier to look for patterns, lacunae, and contradictions in the relation between empirical research and theoretical frameworks as presented in the scholarly literature. Besides, an SLR allows for the clear identification of such themes, concepts and research methods used in prior research that would serve as a basis for the subsequent analysis and synthesis. In sum, by employing the SLR framework in this study, the researchers are able to follow a comprehensive and critical approach in identifying the current state of knowledge in the field and guide future decision-making as well as contribute to the theoretical development of future research proposals related to the interaction between digitalization and the green economy.

2.2 Search Strategy Criteria

When selecting the databases for this study, Scopus was cited as the most appropriate due to its capacity to provide a wide range of academic publications in different disciplines, which forms a solid ground for accessing appropriate scholarly materials. Since Scopus offers numerous peer-reviewed articles, conferences, proceedings, and other scholarly publications, it is a great source for a full bibliographic search. The literature search involved the application of a search filter that was used systematically to retrieve articles on digitalization and the green economy. The search query included specified words and terms for identifying publications that touched upon digital currencies and blockchains, cryptocurrencies and concepts associated with the circular economy and green economic development. The Boolean operators ("OR" and "AND") included in the search query allowed for the correct linking of keywords and search terms in an effort to maximize the yield of the relevant literature. The selected keywords were digital currency, blockchain, blockchain technology, Cryptocurrency, and novel emerging technologies that may have primary sustainability and green economic growth possibilities (Song et al., 2024).

Furthermore, the following keywords were included to identify studies that provided more general concepts of sustainable economy and environment, 'circular economy,' 'green economy,' 'green economic growth,' and 'economic recovery.' By using this search strategy in Scopus, the study sought to capture a wide cross-section of academic papers, including empirical papers, theoretical papers, case works, and review papers, among others. All the search results were screened and analyzed based on the predetermined criteria for inclusion and exclusion to ensure the high relevance and quality of the systematic literature review conducted. Altogether, employing Scopus as the guide database along with using a set of keywords and respective search terms allowed the study to cover all the important issues concerning digitalization as the driver of the green economy shift, which would be useful for both academia, policymakers and business actors.

2.3 Inclusion and Exclusion Criteria

This systematic literature review's study selection process involved detailed criteria for including and excluding research studies. These criteria were set to make sure that the selected articles would provide a considerable amount of information on the connection between digital currency and the green economy and, at the same time, would meet or exceed all the requirements regarding the quality and relevance of the data. We included studies based on the title of the paper and considered the focus of the piece on digital currency and the green economy. This criterion helped to select only the works that have a direct relationship with these two arenas, thus making the reviewed material more relevant. To support the credibility of the recognized literature, only papers obtained from the Scopus digital database were considered for use. Scopus is well known for its vast coverage of products of scholarly activities in almost all fields of human endeavour, including research articles and conference papers. The review was specifically conducted on Scopus in order to filter out only those quality education studies that can be retrieved from a highly academic database (Ul Haq et al., 2022).

The inclusion criteria also stipulated the publication period of the articles under consideration from 2018 to 2024. This time frame was selected to be sure that only the most recent trends, new developments, and the latest advancements in the area of digital currency and the green economy would be included in the sources. Using only the sources within the six-year time frame thereby ensured that the review reflected the most current and relevant knowledge on the subject matter and eliminated any potentially obsolete research. Language restrictions were another crucial condition by which an article was eligible for analysis, and only articles in English were considered. This criterion made it easy for readers of the selected literature to access them and helped in synthesizing and reporting findings from various studies. However, although there may be good studies in other languages, it was logical to limit the review to articles in English only as this facilitated continuity of approach and ease of comparison.

Policies that guided the exclusion of literature were also developed to ensure that the review only included high-quality publications. These criteria eliminated articles published in non-English languages and various publications that were not peer-reviewed, such as master's or doctorate thesis, conference papers, and editorials. Further, reviews, letters, corrections, imaging studies, brief questionnaires, and other non-original research articles were excluded from confining the study to the highest quality peer-reviewed research. Therefore, through the strict application of the inclusion and exclusion criteria for this systematic review, the authors attempt to identify a large number of high-quality studies that would be helpful in establishing the benefits of digital currency and Green Economy. Such a systematic approach used while selecting the relevant literature helps the study gather literature of high academic value and is useful for analysis and synthesis (Xin et al., 2023).

2.4 Data Extraction and Analysis

The data extraction process included going through the selected papers and extracting all the information and findings concerning the cross-section of the digital currency and the green economy. This process was carried out systematically in a bid to maintain a high level of accuracy and reliability in the extraction of the data. First, we got the information concerning the research questions and objectives of the given study to define the relevant data. Often, these data points covered important ideas, approaches, research findings, theoretical contributions, and conclusions provided in each of the selected works. A data extraction form or template was designed to systematically conduct this process of data extraction so as to make sure that all the pertinent data were extracted coherently in all the selected studies.

After that, the data extraction form was developed, and two researchers independently conducted the process of data extraction for all the identified and included publications. This approach became effective in reducing bias and made sure that all the relevant data were obtained accurately and in the right format. If there were divergences or conflicts in the perceptions of the reviewers, the concerns were deliberated on and settled amicably. After that, these data were summed up and classified into a structured database or spreadsheet for data analysis. This database allowed the accumulation of the data and its comparison across the studies and, consequently, the identification of the common trends and patterns. Based on the type of data that was extracted, several analysis techniques and tools were used to synthesize the results and conclusions from the study (Yadav et al., 2024).

Other data analysis techniques employed for synthesizing the data included qualitative synthesis, which involved reviewing and analyzing textual data to look for patterns such as themes, concepts, and connections. This approach enabled the articulation of the general conclusions as well as the identification of the important findings that could be relevant to the goals of the study. Further, findings may have been subjected to quantitative analysis procedures like descriptive statistics or content analysis. One may have sought to quantify and analyze specific aspects of the data, for instance, the number of times particular issues recurred and their spread. In summary, the process of extracting and analyzing data was deliberately and systematically done to answer the research questions and objectives set in the study. This process of systematically reviewing and synthesizing the findings of the selected papers helped to derive insights into the flow of digital currency to promote the green economy by contributing to knowledge creation, diverse decision-making, and academic discussion in the related field (Ye et al., 2023).

2.5 Prisma Flowchart Diagram

First, there is the process of acquiring necessary records from certain databases, which can be considered as the first stage of data extraction. A total of 308 records were obtained from the above-said databases, and they were screened for study inclusion. In preparation for the screening phase, an initial screen for a total of 7 pairs of duplicate entries was conducted, leading to the removal of these records. After eliminating the duplicates, there were 301 records of the targeted study remaining that had to be screened. In this process, the study reviewed each record to determine if it is relevant to traditional inclusion and exclusion criteria for research studies. Of the above records, 81 were eliminated at this stage, the main reason being that the record did not meet the criteria stipulated in the study. A total of 200 reports were identified as eligible for retrieval following the screening process, with 220 Reports found eligible for retrieval after the screening process. Of these, 60 were not available for various reasons, including restricted access, unavailability, etc. The rest 160 were screened more strictly to ascertain the criteria for inclusion and exclusion, which led to a rejection of 50 reports.

The papers omitted in this phase were conference papers (n = 20), erratum (n = 1), notes (n = 1), and review articles (n = 28). Some of these exclusions were done with a view of largely confining the review to cross-sectional population-based survey research, which formed the criteria for the conduct of this study. Finally, the research team was able to include 110 studies in their systematic review. It is noted that only the studies that met the specified set of criteria for inclusion were considered in order to reveal the potential of the application of digital currency for the further development of the green economy. It was also a strength to gather data at the level of detail and completeness in the present study through the comprehensive process used in the extraction of relevant materials from all the incorporated studies. This entailed the identification of items such as methodologies used, empirical data, and theories, which were helpful in comparing and analyzing the findings from the selected studies. In conclusion, the systematic methodology followed for data collection and analysis has allowed the development of a better understanding of issues concerning the integration of digital currency into a greener economy, together with supporting decision-making processes and advancing the current knowledge in this field.

Figure 1. Prisma Flow Chart

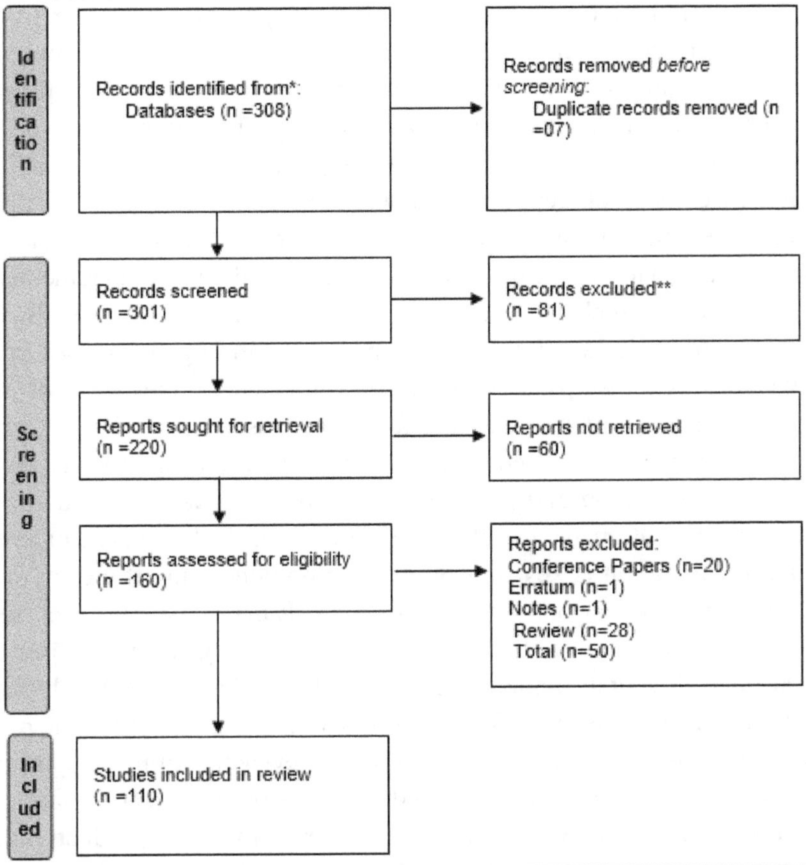

3. THEORETICAL LITERATURE

3.1 Digitalization

Digitalization can be defined as the way of interacting or using digital technologies or assets in society, economy and day-to-day life. It is defined as the process by which information and tasks that would previously have been done on paper or using mechanical means are converted into electronic form to be processed and stored digitally. Some of the most salient aspects of Digitalization are IoT, AI, and Big Data. IoT refers to a network that comprises devices, sensors, and objects that are connected through internet protocols to transmit and receive information. This way,

IoT enables real-time monitoring, automation, and optimization in various domains, including but not limited to healthcare, manufacturing, transport, and smart cities.

AI can be described as technologies that allow computers to mimic human cognitive activities ranging from simple cognitive abilities to more complex functions, such as data acquisition, data analysis, employing logic in searching for solutions, decision-making tasks, etc. AI uses include simple asking or chatbots and more sophisticated machine intelligence that can work for disease diagnosis, car driving, banking and other financial activities. Big Data is defined as an accumulation of very large datasets that have structural organization and can be documented and collected from sources such as social media, sensors and e-transactions. Big Data tools allow data to be gathered, stored, and processed in large quantities in order to identify value, relationships, and trends. Big Data technologies allow data to be collected, stored, processed, and analyzed for the purpose of obtaining information and knowledge. Big Data is used to extract intelligence from various business processes, decision-making and optimization, predictive analytics, and customer experience personalization using tools like Hadoop, Apache Spark, and other tools.

Notably, digitalization is key to growth, development, and efficiency in new-generation industries in various global economies. It drives new product, service and business model innovations because a new idea can only be personalized when resources are available for its implementation. Key technologies like AI, blockchain, and 3D printing have disruptive effects on routine industries and stimulate massive change. It breaks the linear value chain and creates new actors or new opportunities in the digital space. It is in this context that the process of digitalization has become a key factor in supporting economic development by stimulating productivity, efficiency, and new initiatives. Challenges such as improved processes, Reduced cost, and scalability are made easier by the use of 'Digital Technologies.' The result is accelerated economic growth, increased employment opportunities, and increased competitiveness in the international market. In addition, through digitalization, businesses connect with other markets in the world since geographical barriers are non-existent in a digital business environment. Social media platforms and virtual channels are affectionately known for creating proximity to international markets that extend beyond geographical borders. This actually links the various nations of the world in a way that promotes trade, investment and cooperation, thereby enhancing the process of economic globalization.

3.2 Green Economy

A green economy is an approach to economic growth that embraces sustainability, equality, and social justice. It focuses on the preservation of the environment, social well-being, and economic development. It aims to promote sustainable economic growth by including environmental conservation and social justice in the utilization of resources for current and future generations. Essentially, the green economy is the utilization of sustainable resources in an efficient manner with the least harm to the environment and the highest production. It promotes cleaner production, sustainable land management and the use of renewable energy sources to address climate change and pollution. Thus, the green economy focuses on funding social infrastructure and social inclusion as a way to ensure that everyone in the society is provided for once the economy grows. Energy, agriculture, and infrastructure are of the utmost importance in the green economy. Using solar, wind, and hydroelectric power is important for decreasing the usage of fossil fuels and for combating climate change. Organic farming, crop rotation, and the efficient use of water and other natural resources are important to the provision of food, income generation in rural areas, and environmental conservation. The provision of funds for green infrastructure projects improves the ability to cope with the consequences of extreme weather events, reduces greenhouse gas emissions, and improves citizens' quality of life. Thus, societies can achieve more sustainable, fair, and prosperous development by adopting the principles and practices of the green economy. The green economy brings together environmental, social, and economic goals and outlines the way to create sustainable development for people and the earth.

3.3 The intersection of Digitalization and Green Economy

Technology as a whole has merged with the green economy as two advances that bring forth change in modern-day society and the environment. From the theoretical standpoint, it becomes evident that IoT, AI, and Big Data are the enabling technologies for the enhancement of sustainability objectives within the green economy space. These technologies create new possibilities for later detection, control, and improvement of the connection between resource consumption, energy efficiency, and the impact on the environment from different fields. According to this intersectional approach, it is assumed that efficiency gains, evidence-based decisions, and innovation and venture promotion will result. However, the issues that can be seen are technology limitations, the divide between those who have access to technology and those who do not, and the environmental issues tied to the production and recycling of technology. To overcome these challenges, the problems that are the focus of this process are interoperability, cyber security, unequal distribution of digital substances, the environmental consequences of digital activities, and the use of options to design and recycle the devices. Finally, it is notable that the linkage between the digitalization trends and the green economy presents further possibilities for the advancement of sustainable development, provided that the challenges are surmounted through collective actions that will guarantee that benefits will lead to sustainable development without diminishing the resources for future generations.

4. RESULTS AND DISCUSSION

4.1 Year-Wise Analysis

The table listed as "YEAR WISE ANALYSIS" shows the distribution of the papers in terms of publications per year from the year 2020 to 2023, and the total is 110 papers. There is a clear trend of the number of published articles increasing over these years. The papers published in 2020 were the least, with only one paper produced and published. This could be explained by several reasons, such as possible interruptions in the research process and publication process due to the COVID-19 pandemic. In the following year, specifically in 2021, there was a slight improvement; the number of papers published was 6, suggesting that the research activities had slowly picked up or were gradually getting back on track. Forty-eight papers were published in the year 2022, which can be seen as a considerable increase compared to the previous years. This sharp rise might indicate a faster-than-expected recovery or even growth in the research output, possibly due to adjustments made in the post-pandemic world or better funding and focus on research. The upward trend persisted through 2023, and the greatest number of papers published in these periods was 55. This continuous rise in the number of publications year by year may have been occasioned by increased collaboration, improvement in research methods, or enhanced focus on communicating research output. In general, the data indicate an increasing trend in academic output, producing a total of 110 papers over the four years to underscore the vitality of the research culture.

Figure 2. Year Wise Analysis

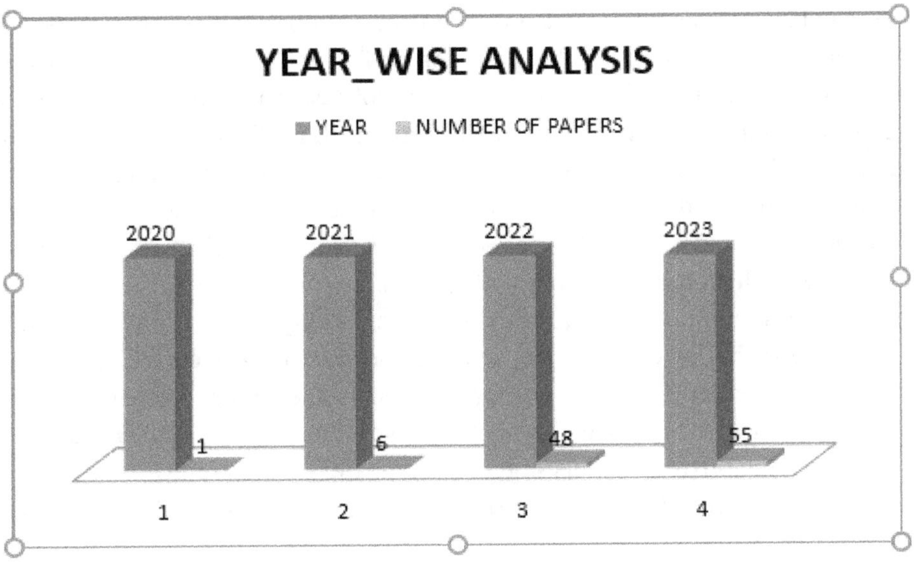

4.2 Journal-Wise Analysis

The table shown below, entitled: "Frequency of Papers Published by Journa," presents the summarization of 43 papers that were distributed across several journals and the respective percentages where every Journal falls. From all the journals identified, the journal "Sustainability (Switzerland)" is the most active, with 9 papers, which is 21% of the total. This suggests that sustainability research is highly valued within the academic community and is in line with the Journal's mission to address global sustainability challenges.

The second category is "Business Strategy and the Environmen," with 7 papers, accounting for 16% of the total. This Journal's emphasis on the ways in which environmental factors can be incorporated into business processes may well be of interest to a large number of scholars, given the growing emphasis on sustainable business practices."Computers and Industrial Engineering" and "Journal of Cleaner Production" each produced 4 papers, accounting for 9% of the total number of publications. These journals probably publish research papers that focus on finding solutions to the conflicts between industry and the environment, as well as the contribution of technology and engineering to sustainable development.

Three journals, specifically "Circular Economy and Sustainability," "Environmental Science and Pollution Research," and "Journal of Business Researc," each submitted 3 papers, which made up 7% of the total papers. This list of journals is about circular economy principles, pollution studies, and business implications, which points to the fact that scholars have a variety of research interests. The remaining journals— "International Journal of Mathematical, Engineering and Management Sciences," "IOP Conference Series: Four journals, namely Earth and Environmental Science," Smart and Sustainable Built Environment," Sustainable Production and Consumption," and "Technological Forecasting and Social Change— produced two papers each which translates to 5% of the total output. These journals are specific interest areas within the general field of sustainability and environmental studies. Thus, the distribution of the papers across these journals reflects the broad scope of sustainability research that comprises papers on business management, engineering, environmental sciences, and policy analysis. The increase in the number of articles and the variety of publishing outlets suggest that the field is both relevant and diverse, as well as multi-disciplinary in its approach to addressing sustainability-related issues.

Table 1. **Frequency of papers published by Journal**

Frequency of papers published by Journal		
Journal	**Number of papers**	**Percentage**
Business Strategy and the Environment	7	16%
Circular Economy and Sustainability	3	7%
Computers and Industrial Engineering	4	9%
Environmental Science and Pollution Research	3	7%
International Journal of Mathematical, Engineering and Management Sciences	2	5%
IOP Conference Series: Earth and Environmental Science	2	5%
Journal of Business Research	3	7%
Journal of Cleaner Production	4	9%
Smart and Sustainable Built Environment	2	5%
Sustainability (Switzerland)	9	21%
Sustainable Production and Consumption	2	5%
Technological Forecasting and Social Change	2	5%
Total	43	100%

5. BIBLIOMETRIC ANALYSIS

5.1 Keywords Analysis

Notably, the circular economy was found to be frequent, with its frequency counting 65 and its total link strength being 110. In this case, the economic model promotes and encourages the use of resources where, after using a particular material or product, it has to be reclaimed, recovered, or repaired and reused in the same way as the initial product without necessarily needing to be changed. Other notable categories include digitalization, with the greatest number (69) and combined link strength (113). This relates to the computerization of various activities in life, resulting in altering how companies work and deal with consumers. Industry 4. 0 On smart manufacturing and automation again, there is some significant interest, with a relevance score of 16 and a total link strength of 33.

Topics of interest include sustainability and sustainable development goals (SDGs), with a total of 32 references and a connection score of 68 for sustainability and 9 references for SDGs, with a connection score of 21. These areas are designed to cover current consumption and production needs without limiting future generations in the same aspect, as they also encompass economic, social, and environmental aspects. A pertinently of significant importance despite appearing three times, environmental sustainability captures the idea of protection of environment and natural resources. Among them, supply chain management is relevant to the theme of efficiency and stability of the flow of goods and services 6(e = 0. 11) times in total. Disposal coming 4 times, with a link strength of 11, is also key to the circular economy, which seeks to minimize waste and properly dispose of the waste produced. A Green Economy with a frequency of 8 and link strength of 4 is defined as a system that takes into account the environmental risks and ecological deficits. Finally, AI can be considered as another disruptive technology mentioned only 3 times, but with the link strength of 8, as it allows for better management of resources in multiple industries and improves sustainability decisions.

Figure 3. Keywords Analysis

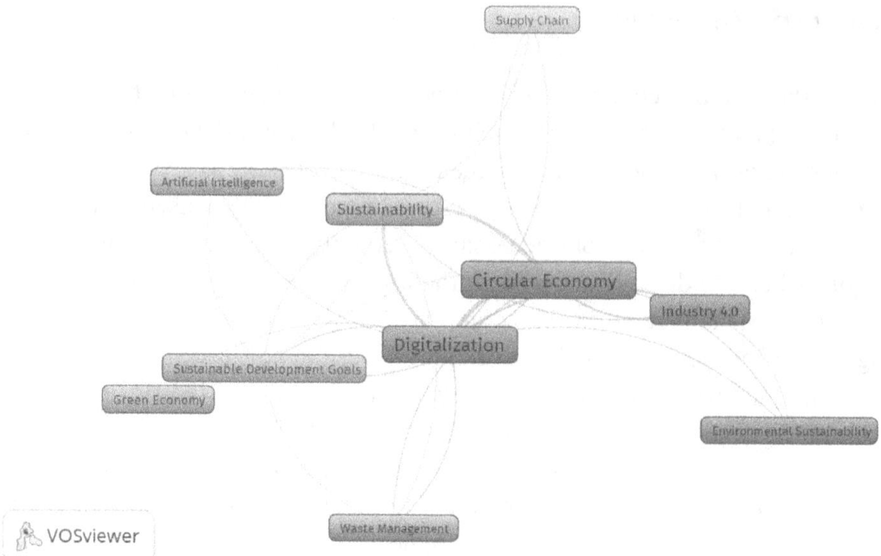

5.2 Countries Analysis

The result of the dataset encompasses the arrangement of the academic contributions of the different countries towards different fields of research with a focus on the documents' count, citation and total link strength. Out of all the countries, the United Kingdom is most noticeable due to the largest total link strength, which is 32, as well as the number of documents – 19, and citations – 384. This shows that there is great influence and presence in scholarly connections. China emerges next, with 22 documents contributing to 232 citations and a link strength of 16, indicating China's increasing presence and engagement in academic work. Likewise, India also shows active participation with 16 papers, 152 citations, and a link strength of 15, showing India is becoming a part of the scholarly research system. Though with fewer documents (10) than China and India, the United States has high citations (281), which means the quality of research done in the United States is very high and impactful. Even though Finland submitted merely nine documents, it has made 171 citations with a total link strength of 11, demonstrating its high research capability and research collaboration.

Another country to be mentioned is Italy, which is represented by 13 documents and 205 citations, which contributes to the assessment of the country's multi-vector development and active participation in science. These two countries, Germany and

Austria, have contributed three and four documents, respectively, but these documents attracted a total of 38 and 59 citations, respectively, and thus significantly impacted certain research fields. There are 4, 8 and 3 documents with total link strengths of 10, 11 and 10, respectively, for Sweden, Malaysia and Tunisia, which shows that these countries are active participants and connected to the world academia field. Among the studied countries, Brazil, Morocco, and Pakistan present fewer documents; however, they remain active in the international research context by obtaining acceptable citation scores and strengthening the combined link. Smaller nations such as South Africa, Turkey and Norway also have considerable documents: 136, 276, and 143 citations, respectively, indicating considerable impact factors. Even those such as Thailand and Hungary, which are represented in the analysis with a smaller number of citations and documents, still have a voice in the research community. However, from the above data, it is clear that academics across the world present scientific production, and the extent of country involvement and outcome may differ significantly. Higher citation indices and even more total link values of some countries demonstrate their key positions and the integration of the global academic environment.

Figure 4. Country Wise Analysis

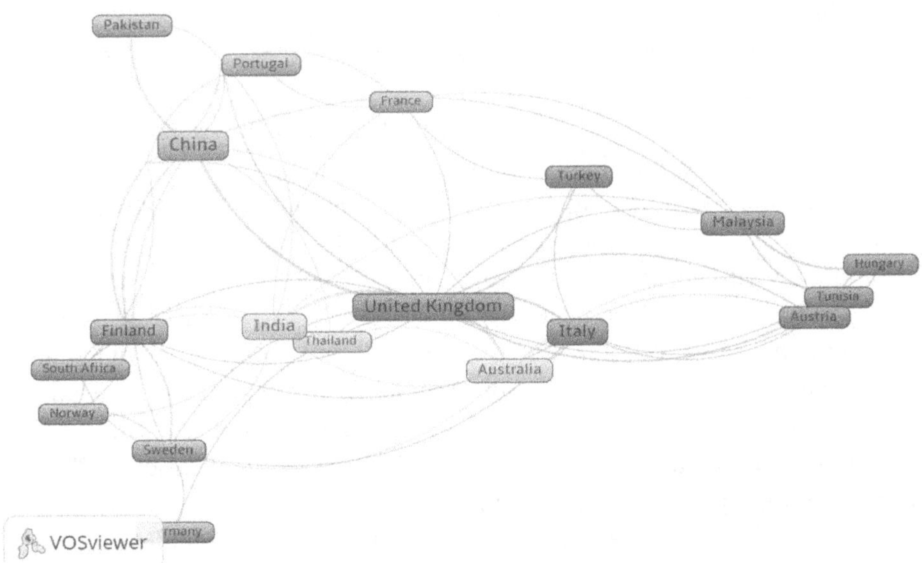

6. CONCLUSION

The data set based on document collection, citation record, and total link strength—demonstrates the production of research articles by nations in the different fields of study. The United Kingdom appears to take the lead of all the countries represented by boasting 32 total link strength – the greatest number of linked documents, 19, and citation count, 384, attesting to its scholarly impact and connections. China comes second and includes 22 documents, 232 citations, and a link strength of 16, as it shows more involvement in research outputs. Another such representation is demonstrated by India, which has 16 papers, 152 citations, and a link strength of 15, indicating that the country is increasingly becoming part of the global academia.

The United States has submitted the lowest number of documents (10), but the citation is high, 281, which gives an idea that American research papers are of high quality and have a high citation rate. Finland, for instance, has only 9 documents, recorded 171 citations, and a total of 11 link strengths, further implying excellent research and cooperation among the scholars. Among all source countries, Italy obtained the largest number of documents and citations, 13 and 205, respectively, which demonstrates the country's great participation and contribution to scientific progress. Countries that supplied few documents, such as Germany (3 documents) and Austria (4 documents), procured citation counts of 38 and 59, respectively. Sweden, Malaysia, and Tunisia, the three medium countries in terms of document counts with medium link strengths, also seem active in the academic field. There are still well-developed countries such as Brazil, Morocco, and Pakistan that have comparatively fewer documents, but they are fairly active in international research, some of them having decent citation scores and link strengths.

South Africa, Turkey, and Norway, with 136 citations, 276 citations, and 143 citations, respectively, are the countries that have smaller populations but are actively contributing towards research. Thus, even countries such as Thailand or Hungary, producing and citing fewer documents than the USA or China, also make considerable efforts within the framework of theoretical research. In total, a variety of countries are involved in academic research to a greater or lesser extent and produce academic works that influence science. Some countries are emphasized as their citation indices and total link strengths are significantly higher than others, which also signifies the importance of their place and incorporation in global academia.

The circular economy appears more often, with a total link strength of 110. This model helps in the reuse of the materials, repair of the equipment, and recycling of the products. The most prominent changes (69 occurrences and 113 link strength) are related to the concept of digitalization, which addresses the dramatic shift in business processes and customer engagement. Industry 4. 0, though mainly related to Manufacturing 4. 0 and automation, demonstrates significant interest with 16 mentions and the link strength of 33 of them. Other topics and concepts include sustainability, with a total of 32 mentions, and the SDGs, with 9 mentions, which relate to the handling of the current needs and the future generations.

Some of the other significant issues are environmental concerns, supply chain, and other disposal systems, all of which are crucial areas keeping efficiency and environmental aspects in view. The green economy is also emphasized for addressing environmental challenges, while artificial intelligence (AI) is also highlighted for its efficiency in the appropriate utilization of resources. The spread of papers across different journals, as illustrated by Table 2, further emphasizes the comprehensive areas of sustainability research. Current journal distribution: Sustainability (Switzerland): 9 papers (21%) Business Strategy and the Environment: 7 papers (16%) This is evidenced by the growing number of articles and the types of publishing sources, which proves that sustainability research is timely, diverse, and interconnected across disciplines.

Distribution of the papers based on the years 2020, 2021, 2022, and 2023 presents 20, 30, 34, and 26 papers, respectively. This trend can be attributed to the growing dynamism of the research tradition, primarily due to advanced cooperation, better research techniques, and a growing focus on the dissemination of obtained research data. The results showcase the worldwide and expanding trend of faculty members' scholarly articles across diversified disciplines, stressing contemporary research concerns of sustainable development and digitization.

6.1 Practical implications

- Identify how factors related to digitalization have effects on different fields of the green economy, including resource handling, energy efficiency and green business strategies in the organization.
- Evaluate the specific technology applications (e.g., IoT, big data, AI) and their ability to contribute to sustainability and decrease the negative effects on the environment.
- Analyze the factors that promote or hinder the further development of the digitalization of the green economy, for example, the issues with the regulation of this process, the supporting infrastructure and the collaboration with other actors.
- Highlight the importance of inclusive approaches while speaking about the green economy's digital switch as a fair for all communities, including minorities.
- Map the existing knowledge in the field and indicate directions for future research to enhance knowledge and apply digitalization to the green economy.

6.2 Societal implications

- Involving different and relevant audiences such as policymakers, industry professionals, and the community to ensure that the effects of changes on society, as pointed out in the review, would have been taken into account.
- In this way, by raising awareness of the social effects of digitalization, the review can aid communities in demanding that the government and other stakeholders embrace more sustainable and equal practices that are beneficial to everyone.
- The review can be useful in determining what specific areas ought to be built to enhance the skills of the workforce in order to achieve the intended goals of the green economy via digitalization.
- Critical analysis of the major digital technologies as a means of outlining the various ethical concerns will assist in preventing abrupt changes that are not in tune with societal values and principles in the shift toward sustainability.
- Evaluating the impact of digitalization on diverse groups indicates that the accessibility and usefulness of Digital Technology should be accepted by all, regardless of demographics, as a means to bridging gaps.
- Such a review can be useful in filling gaps that exist in the current literature by significantly contributing to the understanding of scholars who conduct research on digitalization by pointing them to areas that may present risks to society in the long run, to enable scholars to respond to such issues through their research.

6.3 Research Limitations

- Limiting the review to studies published in a specific language or set of languages may introduce language bias, potentially overlooking relevant research published in other languages.
- Systematic literature reviews typically focus on studies published within a certain timeframe, which may lead to the omission of older studies that could provide valuable insights.
- Limited access to academic databases, journals, or resources may restrict the comprehensiveness of the review and result in the exclusion of relevant studies.
- The choice of search terms and keywords used in the review may influence the breadth and depth of the literature included, potentially overlooking relevant studies that use different terminology.

- Assessing the quality of included studies is essential in systematic reviews, but the subjective nature of quality assessment tools and criteria may introduce bias or inconsistency.
- The perspectives, biases, or assumptions of the researchers conducting the review may influence study selection, data extraction, and interpretation of findings.

6.4 Recommendations

- Investigating the intersection of digitalization and the green economy from multiple disciplinary perspectives, such as environmental science, economics, sociology, and technology studies, could provide a more comprehensive understanding of the topic.
- In-depth case studies of specific digitalization initiatives or green economy projects could offer valuable insights into implementation challenges, success factors, and lessons learned.
- Complementing quantitative analyses with qualitative research methods, such as interviews, focus groups, or participant observations, could provide richer insights into stakeholders' perceptions, experiences, and attitudes toward digitalization in the green economy.
- Evaluating the effectiveness of digitalization policies and strategies in achieving green economy objectives, including their socio-economic impacts, environmental outcomes, and equity considerations, could inform evidence-based policy-making.
- Investigating the potential of emerging digital technologies, such as blockchain, Internet of Things (IoT), and machine learning, in promoting sustainability and resilience within the green economy could be a fruitful area for future research.
- Examining the ethical implications of digitalization in the green economy, such as privacy concerns, data security risks, and power imbalances, could help identify potential pitfalls and inform ethical guidelines for sustainable digitalization practices.

7. REFERENCES

Jiayu, W., & Wang, Z. (2024). Economic integration through renewable energy and digital currency in RCEP. *Economic Change and Restructuring*, *57*(2), 58. Advance online publication. DOI: 10.1007/s10644-024-09646-5

Lin, Y., Wang, Q.-J., & Zheng, M.-Q. (2023). Nexus Among Digital Economy, Green Innovation, and Green Development: Evidence from China. *Emerging Markets Finance & Trade*, 1–20. DOI: 10.1080/1540496X.2023.2258260

Liu, Y., Ma, C., & Huang, Z. (2023). Can the digital economy improve green total factor productivity? An empirical study based on Chinese urban data. *Mathematical Biosciences and Engineering*, *20*(4), 6866–6893. DOI: 10.3934/mbe.2023296 PMID: 37161132

Luis, S. (2023). Can Central Bank Digital Currencies be green and sustainable? *Green Finance*, *5*(4), 603–623. DOI: 10.3934/GF.2023023

Ozili, P. K. (2023). Using Central Bank Digital Currency to Achieve the Sustainable Development Goals. SSRN *Electronic Journal*. DOI: 10.2139/ssrn.4370181

Ramón, J., Campaña, A., Renteria, N., & Intriago, M. (2023). Research of the Development of Green Central Bank Digital Currency, Cbdc. *Social Science Research Network*. DOI: 10.2139/ssrn.4412456

Razzaq, A., Sharif, A., Ozturk, I., & Skare, M. (2023). Asymmetric influence of digital finance and renewable energy technology innovation on green growth in China. *Renewable Energy*, *202*, 310–319. DOI: 10.1016/j.renene.2022.11.082

Sharif, A., Brahim, M., Dogan, E., & Tzeremes, P. (2023). Analysis of the spillover effects between green economy, clean and dirty cryptocurrencies. *Energy Economics*, *120*, 106594. DOI: 10.1016/j.eneco.2023.106594

Sharma, G. D., Shahbaz, M., Singh, S., Chopra, R., & Cifuentes-Faura, J. (2023). Investigating the nexus between green economy, sustainability, bitcoin and oil prices: Contextual evidence from the United States. *Resources Policy*, *80*, 103168. DOI: 10.1016/j.resourpol.2022.103168

Song, Y., Gong, Y., & Song, Y. (2024). The impact of digital financial development on the green economy: An analysis based on a volatility perspective. *Journal of Cleaner Production*, *434*, 140051–140051. DOI: 10.1016/j.jclepro.2023.140051

Sungkawati, E. (2024). Opportunities and challenges: adopting "blue-green economy" terms to achieve SDGs. Revenue Journal: Management and Entrepreneurship, 2(1), 01-13.

Ul Haq, I., Maneengam, A., Chupradit, S., & Huo, C. (2022). Are green bonds and sustainable cryptocurrencies truly sustainable? Evidence from a wavelet coherence analysis. *Economic Research-Ekonomska Istraživanja*, 1–20. DOI: 10.1080/1331677X.2022.2080739

Xin, C., Fan, S., Mbanyele, W., & Shahbaz, M. (2023). Towards inclusive green growth: Does digital economy matter? *Environmental Science and Pollution Research International*, *30*(27), 70348–70370. DOI: 10.1007/s11356-023-27357-8 PMID: 37148510

Yadav, S., Samadhiya, A., Kumar, A., Luthra, S., & Pandey, K. K. (2024). Nexus between fintech, green finance and natural resources management: Transition of BRICS nation industries from resource curse to resource blessed sustainable economies. *Resources Policy*, *91*, 104903–104903. DOI: 10.1016/j.resourpol.2024.104903

Ye, W., Wong, W.-K., Arnone, G., Nassani, A. A., Haffar, M., & Faiz, M. F. (2023). Cryptocurrency and green investment impact on global environment: A time series analysis. *International Review of Economics & Finance*, *86*, 155–169. Advance online publication. DOI: 10.1016/j.iref.2023.01.030

Chapter 8
Assessing Corporate Responsibility in the Digital Age Concerning E-Commerce Entities:
Navigating the Digital Frontier

Yavana Rani Subramanian
https://orcid.org/0000-0001-7870-8007
Jain University, Bengaluru, India

Nishtha Khater
Jain University, Bengaluru, India

K. Kathirvela
Jain University, Bengaluru, India

Govindaraj Muthusamy
https://orcid.org/0000-0001-7563-7776
Jain University, Bengaluru, India

ABSTRACT

The digital age has ushered in unprecedented technological advancements, enabling organizations to leverage powerful tools such as big data analytics, artificial intelligence, and machine learning algorithms. However, this digital transformation has also given rise to critical ethical concerns regarding corporate conduct in the digital realm. Corporate digital responsibility or CDR encompasses a broad spectrum of issues, including data privacy, cybersecurity, algorithmic fairness, digital inclusion, and environmental sustainability. This chapter seeks to delve into the multifaceted

DOI: 10.4018/979-8-3693-4373-9.ch008

dimensions of CDR, examining key drivers, challenges, stakeholder impacts, and best practices across diverse industries and geographical contexts. This chapter aims to provide actionable insights and recommendations for organizations navigating the intersection of technology, ethics, and social responsibility in the digital age, recognizing the interconnectedness of digital activities with broader societal interests.

1.0 INTRODUCTION

In recent years, a rapid evolution of digital technologies has revolutionized how companies operate, communicate, and engage with stakeholders. Organizations have unlocked unprecedented opportunities for efficiency, productivity, and market competitiveness, from using big data analytics to leveraging artificial intelligence and machine learning algorithms. However, amidst this digital transformation, concerns have emerged regarding the ethical implications of corporate actions in the booming yet immature digital environment.

Corporate Digital Responsibility or CDR encompasses a broad spectrum of issues, which include data privacy (Floridi, L. 2016), cybersecurity issues (Lichtenthaler, U. 2020), algorithmic fairness, (Martin, K. E. 2019) digital inclusion, and environmental sustainability. At its core, digital responsibility reflects an organization's commitment to ethical conduct, transparency, and accountability in its digital operations, given the fact that in today's eco-system a majority of an organization's activities happen through online modes. (Jelovac et al.2022). Moreover, it also recognizes the interconnectedness of digital activities with broader societal interests, acknowledging the potential impact on individuals, communities, and the environment.

This chapter seeks to delve into the multifaceted dimensions of corporate digital responsibility, examining key drivers, challenges, impact on stakeholders, and best practices across diverse industries and geographical contexts. By fostering a deeper understanding of this complex landscape, this report aims to provide actionable insights and recommendations for organizations seeking to navigate the intersection of technology, ethics, and social responsibility in the digital age.

2.0 DRIVING ISSUES BEHIND THE NEED FOR CORPORATE DIGITAL RESPONSIBILITY

As technology rapidly progresses, organizations face a myriad of ethical challenges that make Corporate Digital Responsibility (CDR) essential. Addressing critical issues such as data privacy, cybersecurity, algorithmic fairness, digital inclusion, and environmental sustainability has become imperative to uphold ethical standards and maintain public trust. This section delves into these key areas, underscoring their significance in the digital age.

2.1 Data Privacy

Data privacy is a critical component of Corporate Digital Responsibility (CDR) and involves several key challenges that digital entities must address to protect personal information and maintain public trust.

1. Data Breaches and Unauthorized Access: One of the most pressing issues is the risk of data breaches and unauthorized access to sensitive information. Cybercriminals exploit system vulnerabilities or employ techniques such as phishing, malware, or social engineering to infiltrate databases containing customer or employee data. Such incidents can expose financial details, personal identifiers, or health records, leading to privacy violations and potential harm to individuals.
2. Lack of Transparency and Clear Communication: Digital entities often struggle with transparency and effective communication regarding their data practices. (Lipton, 2018) Vague or complex privacy policies, unclear explanations about data collection, usage, and sharing, and inadequate consent mechanisms can erode consumer trust and raise concerns about the misuse of personal data.
3. Inadequate Data Governance and Regulatory Compliance: Robust data governance is essential for the ethical management and protection of personal data. However, many organizations lack comprehensive policies and oversight, leading to insufficient data protection and potential non-compliance with regulations such as GDPR, CCPA, or other regional laws. Non-compliance can result in legal risks, significant fines, and reputational damage. (Holstein et al., 2019).
4. Exploitation of Personal Data: In pursuit of commercial gain, some digital entities may exploit personal data without proper consent or transparency. This includes using data beyond its initial purpose, sharing or selling data to third parties without explicit consent, or failing to provide individuals with control over their information.
5. Balancing Data Privacy and Business Insights: Digital entities rely on big data analytics to drive business decisions and improve services. However, balancing data privacy with the need for business insights can be challenging. Anonymization and de-identification techniques may not always be effective, and there is a risk of re-identifying individuals from anonymized data sets. Colesky *et.al.*, (2016).
6. Cross-Border Data Transfers and Localization Requirements: Navigating different data protection laws and regulations across various jurisdictions poses a significant challenge. Cross-border data transfers and localization requirements

complicate compliance efforts and maintaining consistent data protection standards globally.

Figure 1. The image presents the average cost of a data breach across various industries, according to the IBM Cost of a Data Breach Report 2023. Here's an interpretation based on the data:

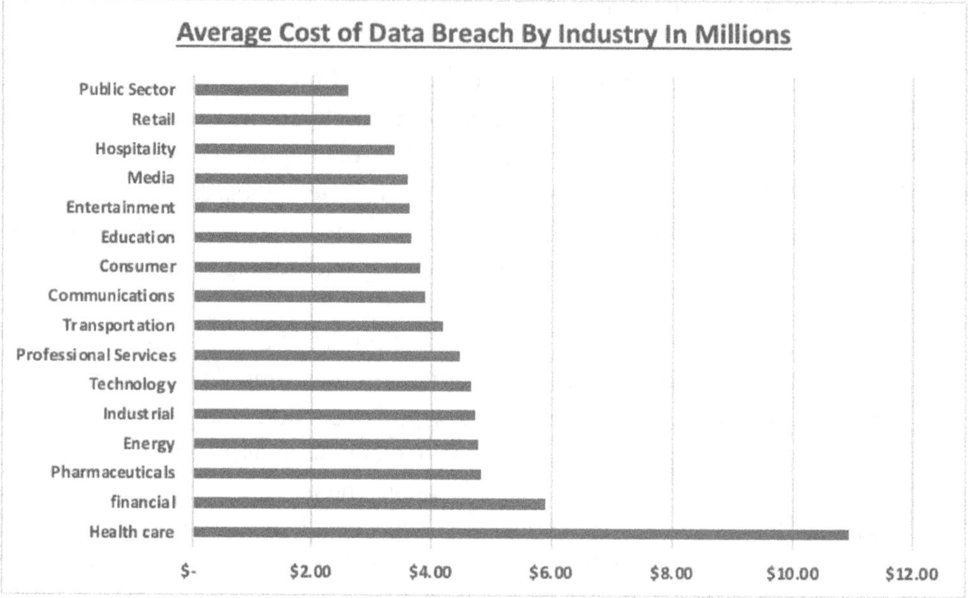

1. The healthcare industry has the highest average cost of a data breach, at $10.93 million. This could be due to the sensitive nature of healthcare data, strict regulations around patient privacy, and the potential for legal and reputational damages in case of a breach.
2. The financial industry has the second-highest average cost of a data breach, at $5.9 million. Financial institutions handle a significant amount of sensitive financial data, and a breach could lead to financial losses, identity theft, and erosion of customer trust.
3. The pharmaceutical industry ranks third, with an average cost of $4.82 million for a data breach. This industry deals with valuable intellectual property, clinical trial data, and sensitive patient information, making data breaches particularly costly.

4. The energy, industrial, and technology sectors follow closely, with average data breach costs ranging from $4.66 million to $4.78 million. These industries rely heavily on operational technology and sensitive data, making them attractive targets for cyber threats.
5. Industries like professional services, transportation, communications, and consumer goods have average data breach costs ranging from $3.9 million to $4.47 million, reflecting the potential financial and reputational impacts of a breach.
6. The education and entertainment industries have relatively lower average data breach costs of $3.65 million and $3.62 million, respectively, which could be due to a lower volume of sensitive data compared to other industries.
7. The media, hospitality, and retail industries have average data breach costs ranging from $2.96 million to $3.58 million, highlighting the importance of data security in these consumer-facing industries.
8. The public sector has the lowest average cost of a data breach at $2.6 million, potentially due to different reporting requirements and lower reputational impacts compared to private sector organizations.

This data underscores the significant financial implications of data breaches across various industries and the critical need for robust cybersecurity measures and data protection strategies. The cost variations among industries likely stem from factors such as the volume and sensitivity of data handled, regulatory requirements, and the potential for reputational and legal consequences in case of a breach.

In today's data-driven world, safeguarding personal information is a fundamental aspect of CDR. Companies must ensure they have robust measures in place to protect data from unauthorized access and misuse. With the proliferation of data analytics and the vast amounts of personal data being collected, it's crucial to implement comprehensive privacy policies and practices that respect individuals' rights and comply with regulatory requirements.

2.2 Cybersecurity

As digital technologies become more pervasive, the frequency and sophistication of cyber threats have surged, posing significant risks to organizations. Digital entities face a constant barrage of attacks, including malware, phishing attempts, DDoS attacks, and advanced persistent threats orchestrated by cybercriminals, nation-states, or hacker groups. These threats can result in data breaches, system disruptions, and financial losses.

Vulnerabilities in software, systems, and networks are common entry points for cyber attackers. These vulnerabilities may arise from coding errors, misconfigurations, outdated software, or design flaws. If not addressed promptly through patching and updates, they can compromise the confidentiality, integrity, and availability of critical systems and data. Insider threats, stemming from negligent or malicious actions by employees, contractors, or privileged users, can be equally damaging. Insider threats may involve intentional data theft, sabotage, or misuse of access privileges, as well as unintentional mistakes, such as falling for phishing scams or using weak passwords.

Figure 2. Estimated cost of cybercrime worldwide.

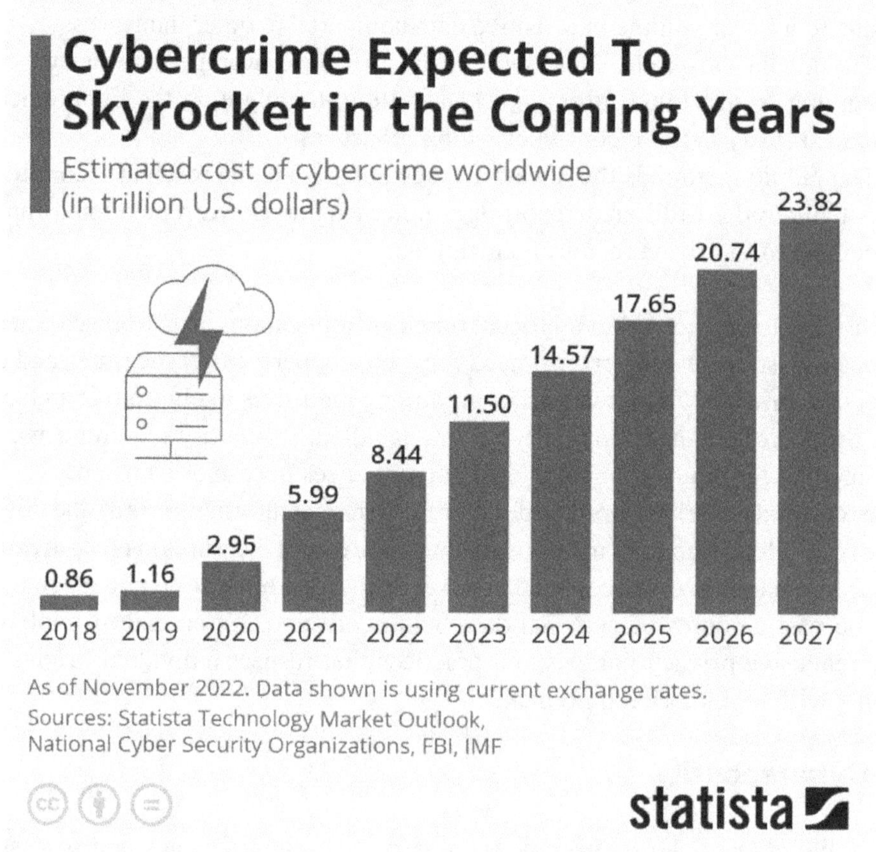

Effective cybersecurity hinges on a strong security culture within the organization, where employees are aware of potential threats and trained in best practices. However, many organizations lack comprehensive cybersecurity awareness and training programs, leaving employees vulnerable to social engineering attacks and poor security practices. Securing complex digital supply chains and third-party ecosystems is another major challenge. Digital entities often rely on third-party vendors, suppliers, and service providers, each introducing potential cybersecurity risks. Managing these risks requires robust vendor risk management processes, contractual agreements, and ongoing monitoring.

Figure 3. Visual representation of security incidents by region from 2020 to 2023 (projected).

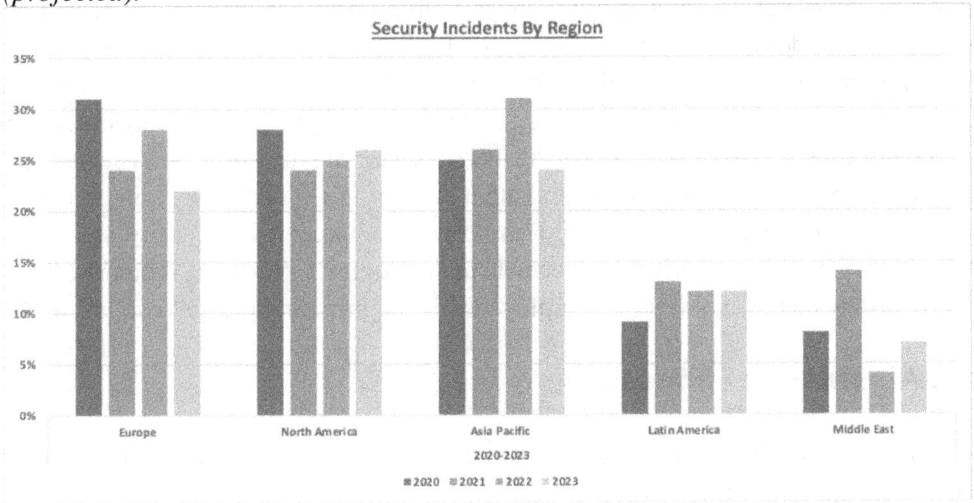

Here's an interpretation based on the data presented:

1. Europe experienced the highest rate of security incidents across all regions during the period shown. The incidents peaked in 2021 but are projected to decline slightly in 2023.
2. North America had the second-highest rate of security incidents, following a similar trend to Europe, with a peak in 2021 and a projected decline in 2023.
3. Asia Pacific region experienced a significant increase in security incidents from 2020 to 2022, surpassing North America in 2022. However, the incidents are projected to decrease in 2023.
4. Latin America maintained a relatively lower rate of security incidents compared to other regions, but a noticeable uptick is observed from 2021 to 2022.
5. The Middle East region had the lowest rate of security incidents across all years, with only a slight increase projected for 2023.
6. Overall, the data suggests a global increase in security incidents from 2020 to 2022, with a projected decline in most regions for 2023, except for the Middle East.

This information can be valuable for organizations and security professionals to understand regional trends and prioritize their cybersecurity efforts accordingly. However, it's important to note that this data represents a projection, and actual incidents may vary based on various factors, such as evolving cyber threats, security measures implemented, and changes in the digital landscape.

Finally, the evolving threat landscape and emerging technologies add another layer of complexity. Digital entities must continuously adapt their cybersecurity strategies to address risks posed by technologies such as IoT, cloud computing, 5G networks, and artificial intelligence. Staying ahead of these threats is crucial to avoid sophisticated cyber-attacks targeting new technologies or exploiting unknown vulnerabilities. Cybersecurity is a critical concern for organizations as cyber threats and data breaches become more prevalent. Protecting sensitive information and maintaining the integrity of digital systems require comprehensive security strategies. This includes deploying advanced security technologies, conducting regular vulnerability assessments, and training employees to recognize and prevent cyber threats.

2.3 Algorithmic Fairness

The key algorithmic fairness issues faced by digital entities in the context of corporate digital responsibility:

1. Perpetuation of Societal Biases and Discrimination: One of the most significant algorithmic fairness issues is the potential for AI systems and algorithmic decision-making processes to perpetuate societal biases and discriminate against individuals or groups based on protected characteristics such as race, gender, age, or disability status. (Mehrabi et al., 2021). These biases can arise from the data used to train the AI models, the algorithms themselves, or the way they are deployed and used in decision-making processes. For example, if an AI system for hiring or lending decisions is trained on historical data that reflects past discrimination or imbalances, it may learn and replicate those biases, leading to unfair treatment of certain groups. Similarly, if the data used to train an AI system is not representative or diverse enough, it may fail to account for the unique characteristics or needs of underrepresented populations.
2. Lack of Transparency and Explainability: Many AI systems and algorithms operate as "black boxes," making it difficult to understand how they arrive at their decisions or recommendations. This lack of transparency and explainability can make it challenging to identify and mitigate potential biases or unfair treatment. It also raises concerns about accountability and the ability to audit these systems for fairness and compliance with anti-discrimination laws and regulations.

3. Inadequate Diversity in AI Development Teams: The teams responsible for developing and deploying AI systems play a crucial role in shaping the algorithms and the data they are trained on. If these teams lack diversity in terms of backgrounds, perspectives, and experiences, there is an increased risk of blind spots and inherent biases being introduced into the AI systems they create. Homogeneous teams may fail to identify potential sources of bias or consider the diverse needs and perspectives of different user groups.
4. Biased or Unrepresentative Training Data: The quality and representativeness of the data used to train AI models are critical factors in determining their fairness and unbiased performance. If the training data itself is biased or lacks diversity, the resulting AI system is likely to reflect and amplify those biases. For example, if facial recognition systems are trained primarily on images of individuals from a particular race or ethnicity, they may perform poorly or exhibit biases when applied to individuals from other backgrounds.
5. Absence of Robust Governance and Accountability Frameworks: Many digital entities may lack robust governance frameworks and accountability mechanisms for the ethical development and deployment of AI systems. Without clear guidelines, principles, and oversight structures in place, there is a risk that algorithmic fairness considerations may be overlooked or given insufficient attention during the AI development lifecycle.

Addressing these algorithmic fairness issues requires a multifaceted approach, involving diverse and inclusive teams, rigorous data auditing and debiasing techniques, transparency and explainability measures, robust governance frameworks, and ongoing monitoring and evaluation of AI systems for fairness and ethical considerations. Digital entities must prioritize algorithmic fairness as a core aspect of their corporate digital responsibility to promote equity, prevent discrimination, and maintain public trust in the use of AI technologies.

2.4 Digital Inclusion

Digital inclusion is a critical aspect of Corporate Digital Responsibility (CDR), ensuring equitable access to digital technologies for all individuals and communities. Addressing digital inclusion involves tackling several key issues:

1. **The Digital Divide**: The digital divide refers to the gap between individuals or communities with access to digital technologies, skills, and resources, and those without. Factors such as socioeconomic status, geographic location, age, disability, and educational background contribute to this divide. Marginalized communities, low-income households, and rural or remote areas often strug-

gle with limited access to digital infrastructure, devices, and reliable internet connectivity. This lack of access perpetuates social and economic inequalities, restricting opportunities for education, employment, healthcare, and civic engagement. Research indicates that a lack of access to digital infrastructure and tools exacerbates social inequalities by restricting educational, employment, and health opportunities (Robinson et al., 2015).

2. **Lack of Digital Literacy and Skills**: Even when digital technologies are available, many individuals lack the necessary digital literacy and skills to effectively use and benefit from them. This skills gap can result from inadequate access to digital education and training programs, language barriers, or limited exposure to digital technologies. Without proper digital literacy, individuals may find it challenging to navigate online resources, leverage digital services, or participate fully in the digital economy, deepening existing social and economic disparities. Digital literacy goes beyond the technical ability to use digital tools and encompasses cognitive, socio-emotional, and ethical skills required for effective and responsible engagement with digital technologies. (Eshet-Alkalai 2012),
3. **Accessibility Barriers in Digital Products and Services**: Many digital products and services are not designed with accessibility in mind, excluding users with disabilities. Websites, applications, and digital platforms that do not comply with accessibility guidelines or incorporate assistive technologies effectively exclude individuals with visual, auditory, cognitive, or physical impairments from fully accessing and benefiting from these offerings. Inclusive design and compliance with accessibility standards are essential for ensuring everyone can participate in the digital world.
4. **Language and Cultural Barriers**: Digital content and services often cater to Western or English-speaking audiences, limiting usability for those with diverse linguistic and cultural backgrounds. The lack of multilingual support or culturally relevant content hinders the adoption and effective use of digital technologies by diverse populations. Providing content that respects linguistic and cultural differences is vital for broader digital inclusion.
5. **Affordability Challenges**: The cost of digital technologies and services can be prohibitive for low-income individuals or communities. Expenses related to device purchases, internet subscriptions, or service fees create financial barriers to digital access. Without affordable options or subsidies, many are excluded from participating in the digital transformation. Ensuring affordability is crucial for bridging the digital divide.

Addressing these digital inclusion challenges requires a comprehensive approach, involving collaboration with government agencies, non-profit organizations, and local communities. Effective strategies include:

- Investing in digital infrastructure to improve access in underserved areas.
- Providing digital literacy programs to enhance skills and knowledge.
- Designing inclusive and accessible products and services.
- Offering multilingual and culturally relevant content.
- Exploring affordable pricing models or subsidies to reduce financial barriers.

By prioritizing digital inclusion, digital entities can foster a more equitable digital ecosystem, empowering marginalized communities to fully participate in and benefit from the opportunities provided by digital technologies. This commitment to inclusivity not only supports social equity but also drives broader economic growth and innovation.

2.5 Environmental Sustainability

Environmental sustainability is a critical element of Corporate Digital Responsibility (CDR). Digital entities must tackle several pressing issues to mitigate their environmental impact.

1. **Energy Consumption and Carbon Footprint**: The growth of digital technologies and increased reliance on digital infrastructure have led to substantial energy usage and a significant carbon footprint. Data centers, which host servers and storage systems for cloud computing and online services, consume vast amounts of electricity for power and cooling. Moreover, the production, use, and disposal of digital devices like computers, smartphones, and networking equipment contribute to greenhouse gas emissions throughout their lifecycle. As the demand for digital services and data storage grows, so does the energy consumption and carbon footprint of digital entities. The shift toward cloud computing and big data analytics has further exacerbated this issue (Masanet et al., 2020).
2. **E-waste and Disposal Challenges**: Rapid technological advancements and frequent device upgrades have resulted in a significant e-waste issue. E-waste includes discarded electronic products such as computers, smartphones, and televisions. These devices often contain hazardous materials like lead, mercury, and cadmium, which can harm human health and the environment if improperly disposed of or recycled. The rapid advancement of technology has led to a surge in e-waste, posing a serious challenge to environmental sustainability (Forti et al., 2020). Incorrect disposal of e-waste can release toxic substances into the soil, water, and air, posing serious environmental and health risks. Additionally, the extraction of raw materials for new digital devices contributes to resource depletion and environmental degradation.

3. **Sustainable Product Design and Lifecycle Management**: Many digital products are designed without considering environmental sustainability, leading to inefficient resource use, short product lifespans, and challenges in repair, reuse, and recycling. The lack of sustainable design principles and circular economy approaches in the development and lifecycle management of digital products can increase waste and resource depletion.
4. **Environmental Impacts of the Digital Supply Chain**: The environmental footprint of digital entities extends beyond their operations to include their entire supply chain. From raw material extraction for manufacturing components to the transportation and distribution of digital products, each stage of the supply chain has its environmental impact.
5. **Awareness and Incentives for Sustainable Practices**: Despite the growing recognition of environmental challenges, many digital entities and their employees may lack awareness or incentives to adopt sustainable practices. Without a strong culture of environmental responsibility and leadership commitment, implementing sustainable initiatives across digital operations and product development can be difficult.

To address these environmental sustainability issues, digital entities should adopt a comprehensive, multi-faceted approach:

- **Investing in Energy-Efficient Technologies**: Investing in energy-efficient technologies and infrastructure can help reduce energy consumption and carbon footprints. Optimizing data centers and implementing energy-saving practices are crucial steps.
- **Adopting Renewable Energy**: Transitioning to renewable energy sources can significantly decrease the environmental impact of digital operations.
- **E-Waste Management Programs**: Implementing effective e-waste management programs is essential to ensure the proper disposal and recycling of electronic products, mitigating the release of toxic substances and promoting responsible e-waste handling.
- **Sustainable Product Design**: Incorporating sustainable design principles and circular economy approaches can lead to more eco-friendly products with longer lifespans, better reparability, and improved recyclability.
- **Cultivating Environmental Responsibility**: Raising awareness and providing training on environmental sustainability can help foster a culture of responsibility within digital entities. Leadership commitment and employee engagement are vital for driving sustainable practices.
- **Collaborating with Stakeholders**: Partnering with suppliers, manufacturers, industry partners, environmental organizations, and regulatory bodies

can help digital entities stay informed about best practices, contribute to the development of sustainability standards, and drive collective action towards a more sustainable digital ecosystem.

By prioritizing these strategies, digital entities can significantly reduce their environmental impact and contribute to a sustainable future.

3.0 CORPORATE RESPONSIBILITY IN THE DIGITAL AGE

The decision to prioritize and enforce digital responsibility within an organization stems from a multitude of factors. Understanding these key drivers is crucial for organizations to align their digital strategies with ethical principles and societal expectations. Some of the primary drivers include:

1. Regulatory Compliance and Legal Obligations
2. Safeguarding Brand Reputation and Consumer Trust
3. Mitigating Cyber Risks and Data Breaches
4. Fostering a Culture of Ethical Innovation
5. Attracting and Retaining Talent

While the benefits of embracing digital responsibility are apparent, organizations often face significant challenges in their pursuit of ethical digital practices. These challenges may arise from various sources, including:

1. Complexity of Digital Ecosystems and Emerging Technologies
2. Lack of Clear Regulatory Frameworks and Industry Standards
3. Balancing Ethical Considerations with Business Objectives
4. Organizational Resistance and Cultural Barriers
5. Resource Constraints and Implementation Costs

By understanding the key drivers and challenges, organizations can better prioritize their digital responsibility initiatives, allocate resources effectively, and develop robust strategies to navigate the complexities of the digital landscape ethically and responsibly.

4.0 KEY DRIVERS AND CHALLENGES IN ENFORCING DIGITAL RESPONSIBILITY

Corporate Digital Responsibility (CDR) is propelled by a multitude of factors that underscore the importance of ethical and responsible practices in the digital landscape:

1. **Increasing Digitalization and Reliance on Digital Technologies**:
   - o The relentless advancement of digital technologies has spurred organizations across industries to heavily rely on them for their operations, products, and services.
   - o Technologies such as cloud computing, big data analytics, artificial intelligence, and the Internet of Things (IoT) have become indispensable tools driving efficiency, innovation, and competitiveness.
2. **Emerging Ethical Concerns and Public Scrutiny**:
   - o The ubiquitous presence of digital technologies has subjected their impact on individuals, communities, and society as a whole to heightened scrutiny.
   - o Concerns over data privacy breaches, algorithmic biases, cybersecurity risks, and the environmental implications of digital infrastructure have captured significant public attention and raised ethical dilemmas.
3. **Regulatory and Legal Requirements**:
   - o Governments and regulatory bodies worldwide are responding to the ethical challenges posed by the digital age by implementing stringent legal frameworks and guidelines.
   - o Regulations such as the General Data Protection Regulation (GDPR), the California Consumer Privacy Act (CCPA), and the emerging AI ethics guidelines mandate organizations to uphold data privacy, transparency, fairness, and accountability in their digital practices.
4. **Consumer Demand for Transparency and Accountability**:
   - o In an era marked by heightened awareness and empowerment, consumers are demanding greater transparency and accountability from organizations regarding their digital activities.
   - o They expect clear communication about data collection practices, algorithmic decision-making processes, and the ethical considerations underlying digital products and services.
5. **Competitive Advantages and Reputational Benefits**:
   - o Embracing corporate digital responsibility can confer significant advantages in today's hypercompetitive business landscape.

- o Organizations that prioritize ethical digital practices differentiate themselves as trustworthy and socially responsible entities, enhancing their brand reputation, attracting loyal customers, and fostering employee pride and engagement.

6. **Interconnectedness of Digital Activities with Societal Interests**:
   - o Digital technologies permeate various facets of society, shaping education, healthcare, employment, and civic engagement.
   - o Organizations acknowledge the profound impact of their digital activities on broader societal well-being, emphasizing the need to align digital practices with stakeholder expectations and societal values.
7. **Global Sustainability Imperatives**:
   - o The escalating environmental challenges and imperatives for sustainability are driving organizations to embed environmental considerations into their digital strategies.
   - o Adopting energy-efficient technologies, minimizing e-waste, and promoting sustainable product design and lifecycle management are integral to corporate digital responsibility efforts.

5.0 KEY CHALLENGES IN ENFORCING DIGITAL RESPONSIBILITY

Despite the imperative for Corporate Digital Responsibility (CDR), organizations encounter various challenges in effectively implementing and enforcing ethical and responsible digital practices. These challenges reflect the complex and dynamic nature of the digital landscape:

1. **Rapid Technological Advancements**:
   - o The rapid pace of technological advancements outpaces regulatory frameworks and organizational policies, creating gaps in addressing emerging ethical concerns.
   - o Novel technologies such as artificial intelligence (AI), blockchain, and quantum computing pose unique ethical dilemmas, requiring continuous adaptation and vigilance from organizations.
2. **Cybersecurity Threats and Vulnerabilities**:
   - o The evolving threat landscape of cyberattacks, data breaches, and security vulnerabilities poses significant challenges to maintaining data integrity, confidentiality, and trust.

- Sophisticated cyber threats, including ransomware, phishing attacks, and insider threats, underscore the need for robust cybersecurity measures and proactive risk management strategies.

3. **Data Privacy and Compliance Complexity**:
   - Navigating the complex regulatory landscape of data privacy laws and compliance requirements presents a daunting challenge for organizations operating across jurisdictions.
   - Compliance with regulations such as GDPR, CCPA, and sector-specific data protection laws demands meticulous data governance frameworks and transparent data management practices.
4. **Ethical Use of AI and Algorithmic Fairness**:
   - Ensuring the ethical use of artificial intelligence (AI) and algorithmic fairness poses significant challenges due to inherent biases, opaque decision-making processes, and potential societal impacts.
   - Addressing algorithmic biases, ensuring transparency and accountability in AI systems, and safeguarding against unintended consequences require interdisciplinary collaboration and ethical AI frameworks.
5. **Cultural and Organizational Change**:
   - Effecting cultural and organizational change to prioritize digital responsibility requires overcoming resistance, fostering awareness, and embedding ethical values into organizational DNA.
   - Shifting from profit-driven metrics to value-based metrics that encompass ethical considerations necessitates leadership commitment, employee empowerment, and stakeholder engagement.
6. **Resource Constraints and Prioritization**:
   - Limited resources, competing priorities, and cost constraints pose challenges to organizations in dedicating adequate resources and investments to implement comprehensive digital responsibility initiatives.
   - Balancing short-term financial objectives with long-term sustainability goals requires strategic prioritization and alignment of digital responsibility efforts with business objectives.
7. **Global Collaboration and Coordination**:
   - Achieving meaningful progress in digital responsibility necessitates global collaboration and coordination among diverse stakeholders, including governments, industry associations, civil society, and academia.
   - Harmonizing standards, sharing best practices, and fostering cross-sector partnerships are essential for addressing shared ethical challenges and advancing responsible digital practices on a global scale.
8. **Mitigating Environmental Impacts**:

- The proliferation of digital infrastructure contributes to significant environmental challenges, including energy consumption, carbon footprint, and electronic waste.
- Organizations must adopt sustainable practices, such as renewable energy sources and responsible e-waste management, to minimize their environmental footprint while meeting the escalating demand for digital services

Addressing these multifaceted challenges requires collaborative efforts among stakeholders, including policymakers, industry leaders, civil society organizations, and academic institutions, to develop robust frameworks, best practices, and innovative solutions for navigating the complexities of Corporate Digital Responsibility (CDR).

6.0 THE IMPACT OF CDR ON THE VARIOUS STAKEHOLDERS INVOLVED

At the heart of CDR lies a profound understanding of the diverse impacts on stakeholders, encompassing concerns related to data privacy, algorithmic fairness, workplace ethics, environmental sustainability, and societal well-being. By recognizing the intricate web of relationships between organizations and their stakeholders, CDR seeks to foster responsible digital practices that uphold ethical standards, mitigate risks, and contribute to the greater societal good.

1. Customers and Consumers:
    - Privacy Protection: Customers expect responsible handling and secure storage of their personal data by organizations to prevent data breaches and identity theft, fostering trust.
    - Fair Treatment: Algorithmic decision-making in targeted advertising or pricing must avoid discrimination, ensuring fair and equitable treatment of all customer groups.
    - Inclusive Access: Organizations must ensure digital products and services are accessible to diverse user groups, including individuals with disabilities or from underserved communities.
2. Employees:
    - Ethical Training: Employees require training on the ethical implications of digital technologies and organizational policies to foster responsible conduct.

   - Workplace Monitoring: Surveillance technologies raise privacy concerns and affect employee well-being and trust, necessitating transparent policies.
   - Algorithmic HR Processes: Algorithms in HR decisions must mitigate biases to ensure fairness in recruitment, performance evaluation, and promotions.
3. Communities:
   - Digital Inclusion: Organizations' digital initiatives should bridge rather than widen the digital divide, ensuring equitable access to information and economic opportunities.
   - Access to Technology: Deployment decisions regarding digital infrastructure impact communities' ability to access and benefit from technology.
   - Environmental Impacts: Organizations' digital operations, including energy consumption and e-waste generation, directly impact local communities and natural environments.
4. Shareholders and Investors:
   - Reputational Risks: Failures in upholding digital responsibility standards can damage organizational reputation, affecting shareholder confidence and investment decisions.
   - Legal Compliance: Non-compliance with regulations can lead to fines and legal battles, impacting shareholder value and business opportunities.
   - Long-term Value Creation: Prioritizing digital responsibility can enhance customer trust and long-term sustainability, contributing to shareholder value.
5. Regulators and Policymakers:
   - Compliance: Regulators ensure organizations adhere to laws and regulations, safeguarding consumer rights and market integrity.
   - Responsible Business Practices: Policymakers promote responsible digital practices to foster a level playing field and protect societal interests.
6. Society at Large:
   - Promoting Digital Equity: Organizations influence digital equity by shaping access to information and economic opportunities for societal groups.
   - Mitigating Negative Impacts: Digital technologies can inadvertently amplify misinformation or contribute to environmental degradation, necessitating ethical use.

- Ethical Technology Use: Society advocates for ethical and responsible technology use, aligning with societal values and minimizing potential harms.

By acknowledging and addressing these stakeholder impacts, organizations can make informed decisions, manage risks, and engage stakeholders effectively, fostering responsible and sustainable digital practices that benefit society at large. In a rapidly evolving digital landscape, Corporate Digital Responsibility serves as a guiding principle for organizations to navigate the ethical, legal, and societal dimensions of digital innovation, ensuring that technological advancements are aligned with the interests of all stakeholders and contribute to the greater social good.

7.0 BEST PRACTICES AND RECOMMENDATIONS

Corporate digital responsibility (CDR) embodies a comprehensive approach to ensuring ethical conduct, transparency, and accountability in digital operations. These encompass a diverse array of best practices aimed at mitigating risks and maximizing benefits across various dimensions of digital activities.

Data governance and privacy protection represent foundational pillars of CDR. Robust data governance frameworks entail the establishment of comprehensive policies and procedures governing the entire lifecycle of personal data—from collection and usage to storage and protection. This framework incorporates principles of privacy by design, integrating privacy considerations into the development and deployment of digital products and services from their inception. Regular privacy impact assessments further aid in identifying and mitigating potential privacy risks associated with data processing activities. Transparent privacy notices and consent mechanisms ensure individuals are informed about the usage of their data and can exercise their rights effectively. Strong data encryption, access controls, and anonymization techniques serve to safeguard sensitive personal data from unauthorized access or misuse.

Cybersecurity measures form another critical component of CDR, given the increasing prevalence of cyber threats. Establishing a robust cybersecurity program involves conducting comprehensive risk assessments, implementing appropriate security controls, and continuously monitoring and testing systems for vulnerabilities. Multi-layered security measures, including firewalls, intrusion detection systems, and endpoint protection solutions, help safeguard digital assets and infrastructure from evolving threats. Regular security awareness training programs equip employees with the knowledge and skills to identify and mitigate potential threats effectively. Moreover, organizations develop and test incident response plans to ensure a prompt and efficient response to cybersecurity incidents, such as data breaches or system compromises. Collaboration with industry partners, government agencies, and cybersecurity experts facilitates staying abreast of emerging threats and adopting best practices.

Algorithmic auditing and bias mitigation techniques address the ethical implications inherent in algorithmic decision-making systems. These systems, powered by machine learning and artificial intelligence, have the potential to perpetuate biases present in training data or algorithms, leading to discriminatory outcomes. Algorithmic auditing frameworks assess the fairness, accountability, and transparency of such systems, while mitigation techniques, including data de-biasing and adversarial training, aim to mitigate discriminatory effects. Involving diverse stakeholders, such as domain experts and ethicists, in the development and evaluation of algorithmic systems enhances transparency and accountability. Additionally, clear governance processes, including mechanisms for human oversight and accountability, ensure responsible algorithmic decision-making.

Inclusive product design and accessible digital services cater to the diverse needs and capabilities of users, promoting digital inclusion. Adopting inclusive design principles involves considering the accessibility needs of users from various backgrounds and abilities during the development process. User research and testing with representative user groups help identify and address potential accessibility barriers, ensuring that digital products and services are usable by individuals with disabilities. Compliance with web accessibility standards, such as the Web Content Accessibility Guidelines (WCAG), further enhances inclusivity. Providing multilingual support and culturally relevant content ensures that digital offerings resonate with diverse user communities, fostering greater engagement and usability.

Sustainable digital infrastructure and operations aim to minimize the environmental footprint of digital activities. Energy-efficient practices, such as virtualization and optimized cooling systems, reduce energy consumption in data centers and digital infrastructure. Leveraging renewable energy sources and exploring opportunities for carbon offsetting further mitigate environmental impact. Adopting circular economy principles in product design and management promotes reuse, repair, and responsible e-waste management. Measuring and reporting on environmental impact, coupled with collaborative initiatives with industry partners and stakeholders, contribute to driving sustainability in digital operations.

Employee training on digital ethics is crucial for fostering a culture of ethical decision-making within organizations. Comprehensive training programs cover ethical principles, organizational policies, and best practices related to digital responsibility. Encouraging open dialogue and providing safe spaces for employees to raise concerns and discuss ethical dilemmas further reinforce ethical behavior. Integrating digital ethics into existing employee development programs ensures that ethical considerations are ingrained in organizational culture and decision-making processes. Recognizing and rewarding employees who exemplify ethical behavior reinforces the importance of digital responsibility.

Stakeholder engagement and transparent reporting practices enhance accountability and promote trust. Establishing regular mechanisms for stakeholder engagement, such as advisory boards or community forums, facilitates gathering diverse perspectives and insights. Developing comprehensive reporting frameworks covering key aspects of digital responsibility, including data privacy, cybersecurity, and environmental sustainability, ensures transparency. Providing accessible and transparent reporting through various channels, such as sustainability reports and corporate websites, fosters trust and accountability. Collaboration with industry associations, civil society organizations, and academic institutions contributes to the development and promotion of best practices in digital responsibility.

In conclusion, by adopting these best practices, organizations demonstrate their commitment to ethical conduct, transparency, and accountability in digital operations. However, it is imperative to recognize that best practices in CDR are continually evolving, necessitating organizations to remain agile and proactive in adapting to new challenges and emerging standards in the dynamic digital landscape.

8.0 CONCLUSION

In the rapidly evolving digital age, corporate digital responsibility (CDR) has emerged as an imperative for organizations navigating the intricate intersection of technology, ethics, and social responsibility. As this comprehensive report has demonstrated, CDR encompasses a wide array of critical issues, ranging from data privacy and cybersecurity to algorithmic fairness, digital inclusion, and environmental sustainability.

Through an in-depth exploration of the key drivers, challenges, stakeholder impacts, and best practices across diverse industries and geographical contexts, this report has underscored the multifaceted nature of CDR and its profound implications for organizations, individuals, communities, and society at large.

By fostering a deeper understanding of this complex landscape, this report aims to provide actionable insights and recommendations for organizations seeking to embrace ethical conduct, transparency, and accountability in their digital operations. Recognizing the interconnectedness of digital activities with broader societal interests, CDR serves as a guiding framework for aligning technological advancements with stakeholder expectations and societal values.

As digital technologies continue to revolutionize every aspect of our lives, it is imperative for organizations to prioritize CDR as a strategic imperative. Implementing robust data governance frameworks, cybersecurity measures, algorithmic auditing techniques, inclusive design practices, and sustainable digital infrastructure is no longer an option but a necessity for maintaining public trust, mitigating risks, and contributing to the greater societal good.

Furthermore, this report emphasizes the importance of collaborative efforts among diverse stakeholders, including policymakers, industry leaders, civil society organizations, and academic institutions. By harmonizing standards, sharing best practices, and fostering cross-sector partnerships, we can collectively address the shared ethical challenges and drive meaningful progress in responsible digital practices on a global scale.

9.0 REFERENCES

Colesky, M., Hoepman, J.-H., & Hillen, C. (2016). *A critical analysis of privacy design strategies.* In 2016 IEEE Security and Privacy Workshops (SPW) (pp. 33-40). IEEE. DOI: 10.1109/SPW.2016.23

Eshet-Alkalai, Y. (2012). Thinking in the digital era: A revised model for digital literacy. *Issues in Informing Science and Information Technology*, *9*, 267–276.

Floridi, L., & Taddeo, M. (2016). What is data ethics? *Philosophical Transactions. Series A, Mathematical, Physical, and Engineering Sciences*, *374*(2083), 20160360. DOI: 10.1098/rsta.2016.0360 PMID: 28336805

Forti, V., Baldé, C. P., Kuehr, R., & Bel, G. (2020). *The Global E-Waste Monitor 2020: Quantities, flows and the circular economy potential.* United Nations University., DOI: 10.1109/SPW.2016.23

Hesselmann, F., & Kallinikos, J. (2022). The responsible organization in the digital age: Corporate digital responsibility and its challenges. *Information Systems Journal*, *32*(2), 213–233. DOI: 10.1111/isj.12342

Holstein, K., Wortman Vaughan, J., Daumé, H.III, Dudik, M., & Wallach, H. (2019). Improving fairness in machine learning systems: What do industry practitioners need? *Proceedings of the 2019 CHI Conference on Human Factors in Computing Systems*, 1-16. https://doi.org/DOI: 10.1145/3290605.3300830

Jelovac, D., Ljubojevic, C., & Ljubojevic, L. (2022). HPC in business: The impact of corporate digital responsibility on building digital trust and responsible corporate digital governance. *Digital Policy, Regulation and Governance*, *24*(6), 485–497. DOI: 10.1108/DPRG-11-2020-0164

Lichtenthaler, U. (2020). Corporate digital responsibility: A framework for success in the digital age. *The Journal of Business Strategy*, *41*(6), 31–37.

Lipton, Z. C. (2018). The mythos of model interpretability. *Communications of the ACM*, *61*(10), 36–43. DOI: 10.1145/3233231

Martin, K. E. (2019). Ethical implications and accountability of algorithms. *Journal of Business Ethics*, *160*(4), 835–850. DOI: 10.1007/s10551-018-3921-3

Masanet, E., Shehabi, A., Lei, N., Smith, S., & Koomey, J. (2020). Recalibrating global data center energy-use estimates. *Science*, *367*(6481), 984–986. DOI: 10.1126/science.aba3758 PMID: 32108103

Mehrabi, N., Morstatter, F., Saxena, N., Lerman, K., & Galstyan, A. (2021). A survey on bias and fairness in machine learning. *ACM Computing Surveys*, *54*(6), 1–35. DOI: 10.1145/3457607

Robinson, L., Cotten, S. R., Ono, H., Quan-Haase, A., Mesch, G., Chen, W., & Stern, M. J. (2015). Digital inequalities and why they matter. *Information Communication and Society*, *18*(5), 569–582. DOI: 10.1080/1369118X.2015.1012532

Chapter 9
Mind the Gap: Exploring Why Socially Responsible Intentions Fall Short of Action

Salma Mahwechi
https://orcid.org/0009-0001-4678-829X
Mediterranean School of Business, Tunisia

ABSTRACT

This study explores the gap between intention and behavior in socially responsible consumption, focusing on personal and contextual factors. Using Social Cognitive Theory, 24 semi-structured interviews with Tunisian consumers (aged 20 to 65) identified key barriers such as financial constraints, social pressures, product availability, and ingrained habits. While consumers are aware of the ethical implications of their choices, these factors often prevent them from acting on their intentions. The research emphasizes the need for affordable sustainable products, better consumer education, and policy interventions to close the intention-behavior gap, providing practical insights for promoting responsible consumption in developing countries.

INTRODUCTION

We are currently witnessing profound changes across all social spheres. Economic challenges, the aftermath of the COVID-19 health crisis, social unrest, and environmental degradation are becoming more pronounced. These developments have led to growing scrutiny of consumption patterns, with a focus on irresponsible behaviors such as overconsumption, impulsive buying, and wastefulness (Ram-Hormozi, 2019). In contrast, the early 2000s marked a rising ecological urgency

DOI: 10.4018/979-8-3693-4373-9.ch009

(Roux and Noûs, 2021), prompting greater consumer awareness of the environmental damage caused by consumption. Many consumers have started shifting their habits, showing increased concern for ethical and social issues like environmental protection, working conditions, and animal welfare (Hosta and Zabkar, 2021; Lecompte and Valette-Florence, 2006). ElHaffar et al. (2020) explored the green attitude-intention-behavior gap, highlighting the need for future research to foster more sustainable behaviors. Yet, despite increased awareness, aligning consumer attitudes, intentions, and actual responsible consumption behavior remains complex (Falcão and Roseira, 2022). Trabelsi (2024) notes that although Tunisia has made strides toward green growth and low-carbon development, significant challenges persist. Since the 1990s, the country has incorporated environmental concerns into public policy, but specific barriers continue to hinder the transition from intention to action. The gaps between attitudes, intentions, and behaviors, particularly within the post-revolutionary context of Tunisia—marked by inequality, unemployment, and financial constraints—have not been sufficiently explored.

This study aims to investigate individual factors influencing socially responsible consumption, with a particular focus on the gap between consumers' intentions and their actual behavior. Using an exploratory qualitative approach, 24 respondents were interviewed in-depth. The ultimate goal is to provide actionable recommendations to encourage more responsible consumption choices across different consumer segments.

LITERATURE REVIEW

Socially responsible consumption can be traced back to Bandura's Social Cognitive Theory (1986), which posits that behavior is regulated by normative influences through two key mechanisms: social sanctions and self-sanctions. Shared social norms enable individuals to anticipate the consequences of their actions within a societal context, acting as a self-regulatory framework. These norms, shaped by the interaction of cognition and external factors, are essential in guiding behavior. However, the concept of socially responsible consumption itself is complex and multifaceted. Shaw (2006) refers to it as a "complex phenomenon," while Cooper-Martin and Holbrook (1993) emphasize the "great diversity of practices" it encompasses.

Webster (1975) was among the first to explore this concept, drawing from sociological insights. He argued that consumers are aware of "the public consequences of private consumption" and often see purchasing as a means to influence societal outcomes. Similarly, Lecompte (2005) defined socially responsible consumption as "the purchase of products and services perceived as having a positive (or less harmful) impact on the environment or society, and/or using purchasing power to express social or environmental concerns." This view highlights the dual role of consumption in addressing both individual values and broader societal issues.

Despite the perceived benefits of socially responsible consumption, there is a notable gap between what consumers claim they believe and their actual behavior. Often, consumers provide socially desirable responses when asked about ethical or social issues, presenting an idealized image of their consumption habits. However, as Lecompte and Valette (2006) found in their qualitative research, there is a significant discrepancy between consumers' verbal support for responsible consumption and their actions in the marketplace. This gap is influenced by social desirability bias, where individuals present themselves in ways they believe will be socially acceptable (Zerbe and Paulhus, 1987).

The divergence between declared intentions and actual behavior, however, is not solely a matter of individual will. It is also shaped by broader societal realities. Several motivations and barriers play a role in socially responsible consumption, which is a multidimensional concept encompassing ecological, social, political, ethical, and individual dimensions. Crane (2001) specifically emphasized the ethical dimension, suggesting that the perceived ability of a product to "do good" or "do no harm" influences consumer decisions and motivates responsible consumption.

Consumers are often driven to make responsible choices by ethical considerations, such as supporting fair trade or purchasing products that align with their values. In addition, factors like corporate social responsibility (CSR), advertising, and the country of origin of a product further influence socially responsible consumption (Crane, 2001). The desire to reduce environmental impact is another common motivator (Piinet, 2004), while ecological concerns have increasingly become a strategic priority for producers and distributors (Zaiem, 2005).

Despite these motivations, significant barriers prevent consumers from fully engaging in socially responsible consumption. Lecompte (2003) identified several obstacles, with the most prominent being financial constraints. The production processes behind fair-trade, local, and environmentally friendly products often result in higher prices, making cost a major deterrent. Lecompte's study showed that most consumers engage in socially responsible consumption only "marginally," citing the price/quality ratio as a key factor influencing their decisions. Additionally, the availability of ecological products, such as seasonal organic fruits and vegetables, poses challenges for some consumers (Dekhili, 2016), further complicating their ability to make responsible choices.

Beyond financial and availability issues, there are other behavioral barriers to socially responsible consumption. Blake (1999) and Ladwein (1999) highlighted that personal resources, including time and money, play a critical role in whether consumers can translate intentions into actions. For many, the desire to purchase responsibly is constrained by their financial capacity.

Habitual behavior also plays a significant role in shaping consumption patterns. Verplanken and Wood (2006) found that when behaviors are new and not yet ingrained, they are guided by conscious decision-making. However, in stable environments where routines dominate, habits become the primary predictor of behavior. This means that even when consumers have intentions to engage in responsible consumption, ingrained habits often override these intentions, especially if the new behavior requires short-term sacrifices or effort.

Social influences are another important factor. Ladwein (1999) pointed out the normative function of reference groups, suggesting that consumers may adjust their behavior to maintain social harmony. Cialdini et al. (1991) further distinguished between descriptive norms (what behavior is commonly observed) and injunctive norms (what behavior is morally expected), both of which can exert pressure on individuals to conform.

Cultural and familial influences also contribute to the gap between consumers' intentions and actions. Childhood experiences, education, and parental role models have a lasting impact on environmental commitment (Chawla, 1998). These factors shape values and attitudes, which may not always align with actual consumption behavior due to external pressures or constraints.

In summary, the gap between intentions and actions in socially responsible consumption is shaped by a complex interplay of personal, social, and environmental factors. While many consumers express a desire to make ethical and responsible choices, barriers such as financial limitations, habits, and social influences often prevent them from acting on these intentions. As a result, despite genuine commitment, the transition to socially responsible consumption remains a challenge for most consumers.

METHODOLOGY

Research Design: To investigate the gap between intention and action in socially responsible consumption, a qualitative exploratory approach was employed. This method was chosen due to its ability to capture in-depth insights into complex behaviors and underlying motivations (Muchielli, 2009). Semi-structured interviews were used as the primary data collection tool, as they provide a flexible yet systematic approach to exploring individual perspectives (Flick, 2007; Sardan, 1995).

Sampling Strategy: A purposive sampling approach (Campbell et al. 2020) was employed to recruit participants likely to provide relevant insights into socially responsible consumption. The sample consisted of 24 Tunisian individuals, aged between 20 and 65 years, with 60% female and 40% male participants. This diverse sample was designed to encompass a broad range of socio-demographic characteristics, allowing for a more nuanced understanding of how different factors, such as age, gender, and socioeconomic status, influence consumption behaviors. The sample size adhered to the principle of theoretical saturation (Glaser & Strauss, 1967), where data collection ceased when additional interviews no longer provided new insights. Saturation was observed during the 24th interview, ensuring the data were sufficiently comprehensive without unnecessary redundancy.

Data Collection Procedure: Semi-structured interviews were chosen for their flexibility in exploring both pre-defined themes and emerging topics relevant to the research. An interview guide was developed based on themes identified in the literature review and the research questions. The main topics covered in the interviews included:

1. Personal understanding of socially responsible consumption.
2. Barriers and motivations affecting the alignment of intentions and actual behavior.
3. The influence of social, cultural, and economic factors on consumption decisions.

The interviews were conducted face-to-face, which allowed for better engagement and more authentic responses. Each interview lasted an average of 45 minutes, providing sufficient time for participants to reflect on their behaviors without leading to fatigue. All interviews were conducted in participants' native language, ensuring clarity and depth in their responses.

Data Recording and Confidentiality: Interviews were audio-recorded with participants' informed consent, ensuring that all responses were captured accurately for analysis. The recordings were transcribed verbatim, and to maintain confidentiality, participants' identities were anonymized, with pseudonyms used throughout the analysis. All data were securely stored in compliance with ethical research standards.

Data Analysis: The transcribed interviews were analyzed using thematic content analysis (Braun & Clarke, 2006). This approach allowed for the systematic identification of recurring themes and patterns within the data. The analysis proceeded in two stages:

1. **Initial coding**: Key themes related to socially responsible consumption and the intention-behavior gap were identified and categorized.
2. **Axial coding**: Relationships between different themes were explored to gain a deeper understanding of the underlying drivers of the intention-behavior gap.

Validity and Reliability: Several measures were implemented to enhance the validity and reliability of the study. First, a pilot test of the interview guide was conducted with a small sample of participants to ensure the clarity and relevance of the questions. Second, member checking was employed, where participants were invited to review summaries of their responses to verify the accuracy of the recorded data. To further enhance the reliability of the analysis, peer debriefing was conducted. Two independent researchers reviewed the coding framework and analysis, providing feedback to ensure that the findings were well-grounded in the data and free from researcher bias.

Ethical Considerations: All participants were provided with a detailed explanation of the study's objectives and their rights as participants. Informed consent was obtained prior to data collection, and participants were informed of their right to withdraw from the study at any time without consequence. Confidentiality and anonymity were maintained throughout the study.

RESULTS ANALYSIS

Personal understanding of socially responsible consumption: When reflecting on socially responsible consumption, the first observation is that although the understanding of socially responsible consumption is often one-dimensional, the Tunisian population is sufficiently aware of the concept, with respondents even providing examples of socially responsible consumption (SRC) from their daily lives. For instance, Ind22 explains that "[... socially responsible consumption is very important... it's about buying organic products without chemical additives and pesticides. I think the fruits and vegetables I buy from the market are organic]." For Ind3, socially responsible consumption means "[primarily saving energy and reducing bills. I try to rationalize water usage at home, and I've been using energy-saving bulbs for years]."

The understanding of the notion of SRC is predominantly one-dimensional among the majority of the sample, as observed in Ind12's response: "[I think I consume very responsibly, especially when it comes to waste. Nothing is thrown away in my house]." However, the respondents did not demonstrate unwavering commitment to socially responsible consumption. Ind19 noted: "[I try to consume better, but it's not always easy]," while Ind4 added, "[consuming responsibly requires time and thought, so I usually give up and make the easiest choice]."

The barriers and motivations influencing the alignment between intentions and actual behavior: were primarily examined to explore the sources of the gap between the intention to consume responsibly and the act of doing so."

The purchasing power of Tunisians does not allow them to consume in a socially responsible way and is revealed to be the main source of this gap. The majority of interviewees agreed that they like the idea of consuming in a socially responsible manner, but since ecological/organic products are expensive, their purchasing power does not allow them to adopt this behavior. Respondents mentioned:

"[... buying ecological products is too expensive compared to the standard of living in Tunisia]," "[... a minority can afford this type of consumption, but the majority of Tunisians are held back by their limited purchasing power...]," "[our budget is usually limited and we can't afford to consume this type of product on a frequent basis…]. Other respondents highlighted the link between the origin of organic products and their prices. For Ind11, [organic products are generally imported, and with inflation, they become too expensive for the average household… they are inaccessible]. Ind6 explained that even when the product is local, it remains costly: [Even locally produced organic products in Tunisia are sold in small quantities and at high prices]. The economic aspect remains undeniable, as explained by Ind12: "[I mostly try to reduce the costs of my consumption]." Disengagement is evident in several responses: "[no, I don't spend much time looking for information on the origins of products]" (Ind17), and "[in a store aisle, my first selection criterion is the price/quality ratio]" (Ind12). These responses reflect a certain desire to consume responsibly, but it is not a behavior deeply ingrained in the daily lives of Tunisian consumers. Other aspects of socially responsible consumption were also discussed. Ind24 raised a very important point: [I care a lot about respecting the environment, but practices like waste sorting require personal effort and a budget]. Ind9 stated: [I like to consume locally and buy Tunisian products. What puzzles me is the high prices of local products—even handicrafts are overrun by "made in China" items, which are much more affordable for the purchasing power of Tunisians].

Indeed, the lack of sufficient material resources and low purchasing power remain the main obstacles to socially responsible consumption. The observation is that while Tunisian consumers are aware of the benefits of socially responsible consumption, the necessary budget blocks the adoption of these good consumer practices.

The Influence of Social, Cultural, and Economic Factors on Consumption Decisions

The Tunisian consumer is inclined to adopt more responsible consumption, but changing habits is difficult. According to the responses, Tunisians have a very positive intention to adopt socially responsible behavior. Ind7 argues that [... we must be aware of the impact of our actions on people and the environment and think about future generations...]. When discussing responsible consumption, Ind3 believes that [it's a form of consumption that allows us to abandon bad habits in favor of practices that are more concerned with general well-being]. However, the general trend of inaction is confirmed once again. For Ind1, [I admit that I don't adopt socially responsible behavior on a daily basis, but I hope to improve and consume better more often...]. Ind23 added, [Even though I make an effort to reduce my expenses, at my age, it's very difficult to change my habits]. In the same context, Ind8 explained, [I'm always in a hurry, and honestly, I don't have time to read labels or recycle… I admit that I choose the comfort of my habits, as it makes my daily life easier].

In conclusion, while Tunisians are aware of the benefits of socially responsible consumption, changing everyday habits remains difficult. As Ind12 expressed, [Currently, we are all aware of the importance of the environment, but the problem is the difficulty of changing habits, especially in terms of food consumption and Ecological practices, I think it's more interesting to educate children to instill good habits in future generations].

The Tunisian consumer is influenced by their social and family environment. Most respondents stated that their behavior is strongly influenced by that of their family and social circle. In this regard, they mentioned: [... we always seek the advice of a family member or friend who has already tried a product and can give us advice...], [... we always trust our family...], [... I think the consumer tends to follow consumption behavior similar to that of their social circle...]. When discussing the influence of social circles on socially responsible consumption practices, Ind10 stated: [I'm the only one in my house who practices recycling, and it puts me in conflict with my family because they don't understand my behavior and don't have the willingness to follow me. My friends also think I recycle because I'm stingy, which bothers me a lot]. Similarly, Ind24 shared: [I really commit to sorting waste, and I try to educate my family members, but they're not interested. The worst part is that they throw the waste carelessly and disrupt my system]. Regarding healthy and organic eating, this practice presents a challenge for several respondents. Ind15 said: [I prefer to eat balanced meals made with fresh and organic products, but my husband and children don't agree; they love traditional dishes, so I end up cooking different meals each time... it's exhausting]. Thus, the family and social circle can be a barrier to adopting socially responsible consumption. The lack of understanding, encouragement, and interest can demotivate even the most enthusiastic individuals.

Socially responsible consumption could become part of Tunisian consumer culture. Culture is a fundamental element in the lives of Tunisians, influencing consumption behavior. Ind1 explained: [Tunisian culture is very rich... when I think about it, our grandparents were responsible consumers... recycling, sorting, homemade meals, and respect for the environment were part of our culture, which has now been abandoned]. Ind5 shared the same view: [My maternal grandmother used to stock up on food for the winter... she made sure of the freshness and availability of the products. This was a big part of our culture that we have lost]. A sense of awareness and guilt is evident among the respondents. They all expressed their intention to adopt socially responsible consumption and integrate it into the broader culture of consumption.

Indeed, the majority mentioned that they had a favorable attitude toward socially responsible consumption (SRC) and that it is necessary to implement various awareness and marketing strategies to see positive results in the long term: [...this behavior will only be observed in Tunisian society if awareness actions are put in place, and a result can then emerge, certainly not in the short term but over future generations], [...We need to promote socially responsible consumption and inform people about it...], [...In the future, yes, but there really needs to be good communication around this topic...]. SRC could become part of Tunisian consumer culture if more focus is placed on it by establishing awareness and advocacy policies directed at Tunisian consumers, while highlighting the advantages and benefits of this type of consumption.

Discussion of Results

The results of this exploratory qualitative study are consistent with the literature review. Socially responsible consumption aligns well with the value system of society, but individual involvement varies depending on primarily personal factors. These factors represent a significant source of the gap between consumers' declarations and their actual, everyday consumption behavior.

First, purchasing power and available resources are identified as the main barriers to socially responsible consumption. Almost all consumers agree that responsible consumption has its benefits, but they also claim that consuming better would be more expensive for them. It is a behavior associated with a sense of "privilege" (Lombardot and Mugel, 2017; Depitre and Havre, 2000). However, when there is a strong awareness of economic, social, and environmental issues, consumers are willing to make trade-offs and concessions in their budgets.

Next, habits are deeply ingrained in behavior, making it difficult for consumers to change their lifestyle overnight. Ouellette and Wood (1998) affirm that in the case of new behaviors, habits are slow to develop and thus constitute a real obstacle to the adoption of socially responsible consumption behavior.

The family and social circle also have an influence on consumer behavior, and in cases of negative influence, this circle can prevent consumers from making the right choices. Ladwein (1999) states that to maintain social conformity, a consumer may temporarily or occasionally give up their opinions, values, or preferences. To evolve within the Tunisian context, socially responsible consumption must be adopted by a larger reference group, such as families and Virtual communities.

In addition, through the interviews conducted, the consumers' conviction towards socially responsible consumption was palpable, but their abstinence is also significant. Despite the enthusiasm and admiration for the benefits of this type of consumption, other variables come into play, such as routine, stress, fatigue, the almost total absence of information on this subject, and a lack of advertising creativity. As a result, consumers opt for a more practical and habitual consumption model.

CONCLUSION AND MANAGERIAL IMPLICATIONS

Despite the countless benefits of socially responsible consumption, many consumers struggle to adopt this behavior, despite a sincere willingness and motivation for social engagement. The qualitative study revealed a behavioral paradox explained mainly by personal factors: resource availability, habits, the influence of surroundings, and culture. Abstractly, consumption is a simple and habitual process; generally, consumers do not dwell on the consequences of their consumption, whereas socially responsible consumption requires reflection that can cost time and money. This is why the majority prefer to stick to their habits despite the benefits of responsible consumption. This suggests that transitioning to this new type of behavior requires a strong personality and great perseverance. Therefore, it is very important at this stage to raise awareness in society to help consumers find their bearings; this is the role of civil organizations.

Addressing the issue of socially responsible consumption is crucial. Companies must recognize the potential of this market by offering products that respect all dimensions of CSR. This behavior will undoubtedly have a significant impact on the functioning of organizations and production methods. In fact, Devinney et al. (2006) assert that ignoring consumers' social and ethical concerns could lead to significant strategic errors. Therefore, it is necessary to detect the real demand for "socially responsible" products and improve communication techniques by promoting awareness campaigns. Companies must maintain a responsible image, which is where research on CSR comes into play. Finally, studies concerning the profiling of socially responsible consumers, particularly their psychological characteristics, need to be developed.

REFERENCES

Ajzen, I. (2001). Nature and Operation of Attitudes. *Annual Review of Psychology*, *52*(1), 27–58. DOI: 10.1146/annurev.psych.52.1.27 PMID: 11148298

Bandura, A. (1986). *Social Foundation of Thought and Action: a social cognitive theory*. Prentice –Hall.

Barnes, W., Gartland, M., & Stack, M. (2004). Old habits die hard: Path dependence and behavioural lock-in. *Journal of Economic Issues*, *38*(2), 371–377. DOI: 10.1080/00213624.2004.11506696

Blake, J. (1999). Overcoming the value-action gap in environmental policy: Tensions between national policy and local experience. *Local Environment*, *4*(3), 257–278. DOI: 10.1080/13549839908725599

Campbell, S., Greenwood, M., Prior, S., Shearer, T., Walkem, K., Young, S., Bywaters, D., & Walker, K. (2020). Purposive sampling: Complex or simple? Research case examples. *Journal of Research in Nursing : JRN*, *25*(8), 652–661. DOI: 10.1177/1744987120927206 PMID: 34394687

Chawla, L. (1998). Significant life experiences revisited: A review of research on sources of pro-environmental sensitivity. *The Journal of Environmental Education*, *29*(3), 3, 11–21. DOI: 10.1080/00958969809599114

Cialdini, R., Kallgren, C., & Reno, R. (1991). A focus theory of normative conduct: A theoretical refinement and re-evaluation of the role of norms in human behaviour. *Advances in Experimental Social Psychology*, *24*, 201–234. DOI: 10.1016/S0065-2601(08)60330-5

Cooper-Martin, E., & Holbrook, M. B. (1993). Ethical consumption experiences and ethical space. In *L.McAlister et M.L. Rothschild (coord.), Advances in Consumer Research, 20* (pp. 113–118). Association for Consumer Research.

Crane, A. (2001). Unpacking the ethical product. *Journal of Business Ethics*, *30*(4), 361–373. DOI: 10.1023/A:1010793013027

De Sardan, J.P.O. (1995). The Politics of the Field, Investigation. Brussels, Belgium: Academia Bruylant, Collection Anthropologie prospective.

Dekhili, S. (2016). Mass retailers: What legitimacy to market ecological products from the point of view of consumers? *Management Avenir*, (5), 55–77. DOI: 10.3917/mav.087.0055

Depitre, B. C., & Havre, L. (2000). Sustainable development and consumer citizenship. 1st International Congess of Marketing Tendencies in Europe.

Devinney, T. M., Auger, P., Eckhardt, G., & Birtchnell, T. (2006). The other CSR: Consumer social responsibility.

ElHaffar, G., Durif, F., & Dubé, L. (2020). Towards closing the attitude-intention-behavior gap in green consumption: A narrative review of the literature and an overview of future research directions. *Journal of Cleaner Production*, *275*, 122556. DOI: 10.1016/j.jclepro.2020.122556

Falcão, D., & Roseira, C. (2022). Mapping the socially responsible consumption gap research: Review and future research agenda. *International Journal of Consumer Studies*, *46*(5), 1718–1760. DOI: 10.1111/ijcs.12803

Flick, U. (2007). The SAGE Qualitative Research Kit (8 cols). London, Angleterre. *Sage (Atlanta, Ga.)*.

François-Lecompte, A. (2003), Towards a better understanding of socially responsible consumption, 19th Congress of the French Marketing Association, Tunis May 2003.

François-Lecompte, A. (2005), Socially Responsible Consumption: Proposal and Validation of an Integrative Conceptual Framework, Thesis for the Doctorate in Management Sciences, Pierre Mendes-France University.

Francois-Lecompte, A., & Roberts, J. A. (2006). Developing a measure of socially responsible consumption in France. *Marketing Management Journal*, *16*(2), 50–66.

François-Lecompte, A., & Valette-Florence, P. (2004) Proposal of a Scale for Measuring Socially Responsible Consumption, *20th Congress of the French Marketing Association*, Saint Malo, May 2004.

Francois-Lecompte, A., & Valette-Florence, P. (2006). Getting to know the socially responsible consumer. *Decisions Marketing*, *41*, 67–79.

Hosta, M., & Zabkar, V. (2021). Antecedents of environmentally and socially responsible sustainable consumer behavior. *Journal of Business Ethics*, *171*(2), 273–293. DOI: 10.1007/s10551-019-04416-0

Kraus, S. J. (1995). Attitudes and the Prediction of Behavior – a Meta-Analysis of the Empirical Literature. *Personality and Social Psychology Bulletin*, *21*(1), 58–75. DOI: 10.1177/0146167295211007

Ladwein, R. (1999). *Consumer and buyer behavior*. Economica.

Lombardot, E., & Mugel, O. (2017). Proposal of an explanatory model of the gap between intention and responsible behaviour in the context of food purchase. Review of the responsible organization, 12(1), 17-33.

Muchielli, A. (2009). *Dictionary of qualitative methods in the humanities and social sciences* (3rd ed.). Armand Colin.

Ouellette, J. A., & Wood, W. (1998). Habit and intention in everyday life: The multiple processes by which past behavior predicts future behavior. *Psychological Bulletin, 124*(1), 54–74. DOI: 10.1037/0033-2909.124.1.54

RamHormozi, H. (2019). *The Anatomy of Consumerism: The Story of Excess, Greed, Self-Indulgence, Wealth Accumulation, Insurmountable Waste, and Environmental Degradation*. FriesenPress.

Roux, N., & Noûs, C. (2021). The choice of common spaces in the inhabited, ecological and solidarity support. Sustainable development and territories. Economics, geography, politics, law, sociology, 12(2).

Shaw, D., Newholm, T., & Dickinson, R. (2006). Consumption as voting: An exploration of consumer empowerment. *European Journal of Marketing, 40*(9/10), 1049–1067. DOI: 10.1108/03090560610681005

Trabelsi, E. (2024). Transition to Sustainable Environment and Economic Growth in Tunisia: An ARDL Approach. *World Development Sustainability*, 100165.

Verplanken, B., & Wood, W. (2006). Interventions to break and create consumer habits. *Journal of Public Policy & Marketing, 25*(1), 90–103. DOI: 10.1509/jppm.25.1.90

Webster, F. E.Jr. (1975). determining the characteristics of socially responsible consumer. *The Journal of Consumer Research, 2*(December), 188–196. DOI: 10.1086/208631

Zaiem, I. (2005). The ecological behaviour of the consumer. La revue des sciences de gestion, (4), 75-88.

Zerbe, W. J., & Paulhus, D. L. (1987). Socially desirable responding in organizational behavior: A reconception. *Academy of Management Review, 12*(2), 250–264. DOI: 10.2307/258533

Chapter 10
The Adverse Consequences of Technostress on Auditors' Strain and Turnover:
The Mitigating Individual Factors

Abir Dhaouadi
https://orcid.org/0009-0009-4604-2808
Institute of High Commercial Studies, Carthage, Tunisia

Anis Khedhaouria
https://orcid.org/0000-0001-8393-3030
Montpellier Business School, France

Neila Boulila
Institute of High Commercial Studies, Carthage, Tunisia

ABSTRACT

While technostress is a wide-spread problem experienced by all professionals irrespective of their area of specialization, most of studies have been related to Information Technology users. The purpose of this study is to explore technostress among auditors and to bring a better understanding of the factors that may alleviate the positive impact of technostress on high turnover rate and increased job burnout noticed within the auditing profession. In this exploratory study, we conducted 17 semi-structured interviews with professional auditors between January and February 2021. The thematic analysis of the telephonic interview evolves from

DOI: 10.4018/979-8-3693-4373-9.ch010

Miles and Huberman (2003) using Nvivo 11. The study's findings emphasize that commonly recognized technostress creators apply to auditors as well. It also highlights new technostress creators that are related to auditors in particular, namely overdependence on ICTs, ICT-enabled work interruption and constant connectivity. Personality traits and segmentation mindset are proven as the main factors that increase/decrease technostress.

INTRODUCTION

Today, information and communication technology (ICT) devices are recognized as being necessary in our daily life. Indeed, smartphones, tablets, PCs are everywhere around us; at home, at work, outside or in the classroom… ICT tools are used to collect, handle, store, or transmit information (Steinmueller, 2000). The use of these devices is omnipresent in an increasing number of occupations. Auditors are no exception. They use these devices for communication, work or search purposes. Almost of public accounting firms have increased the use of IT applications through various audit tasks including; analytical procedures, risk assessment, sampling, internal control evaluation, professional standards research software and electronic work papers (Lowe *et al.,* 2018). Although the use of ICTs promotes efficiency, it results in technostress (Ayyagari *et al.,* 2011; Xie *et al.,* 2018).

Technostress is a partially explored topic since early research has ignored auditors. On the other hand, various populations have examined including engineers, psychologists, IT specialists (Day *et al.,* 2012), managers and professionals in clerical positions (Leung, 2011; Srivastava *et al.,* 2015; Khedhaouria and Cucchi, 2019), institutional business-to-business sales professionals (Tarafdar *et al.,* 2015), employees working at universities (Diaz *et al.,* 2012).

However, the technostress phenomenon is more common in activities that are deadline-driven like the auditing profession. Indeed, the auditor's job is described as highly time-bound, client interaction-oriented, technology intensive, requiring long working hours and heavy work overload.

More precisely, auditors are worth studying, mainly for three reasons. First, auditors are particularly exposed to excessive stress especially during the "busy season". They may spend long hours working during several months to meet tight deadlines (Jones *et al.,* 2010). Second, this stressful situation is exacerbated due to the proliferation of ICT devices (Tarafdar *et al.,* 2010; Boyer-Davis, 2019). Auditors are so immersed in using technologies in the workplace that they can be seen as over-dependent on the technology. These tools erase the boundaries between work and personal life. Accordingly, workload is no more limited to working hours and office boundaries. Auditors are connected all the time to their supervisors and colleagues. They are requested to respond to frequent professional demands. Third, the auditing profession is continuously encountering a serious problem of turnover (Smith *et al.,* 2018). The non-Big 4 American accounting firms with an annual net revenue above $30 million witnessed on average a professional staff turnover of 15.9% (Inside Public Accounting, 2019). Prior studies highlight the determinants of turnover intentions including burnout (Swider and Zimmerman, 2010; Smith *et al.,* 2018), firm commitment and perceived firm fairness (Herda and Lavelle, 2012; Cannon and Herda, 2016), job satisfaction and work-life conflict (Pasewark and Viator, 2006), locus of control, performance and organizational commitment (Donnelly *et al.,* 2003), work exhaustion (Moore, 2001). In a meta-analytic study, Joseph *et al.* (2007) report that more than 30 IS studies over the last 20 years focus on IT personnel turnover while ignoring other groups of employees. However, auditors are encountering a high staff turnover and are concerned by the pervasive technological change as well.

Traditionally, there has been a plethora of valuable research on stress in the audit sector (Hsieh and Wang, 2012; Lopez and Peters, 2012; Smith *et al.,* 2018). Despite this interest and to the best of our knowledge, no one has studied technostress among auditors.

To address this research gap, we rely on an exploratory qualitative study to contextualize the concept of technostress in the Tunisian auditing context according to the professional auditors' viewpoints.

This paper is organized as follows: The first section gives an overview of theoretical foundations. This is followed by a review of prior technostress studies. Then, we describe the qualitative methodology design. Results are reported in the fourth section. We conclude with a discussion of the results, theoretical and practical implications and limitations in the later section.

I. THEORETICAL BACKGROUND

As a special form of stress, technostress is inherent to the use of technologies (Cheung, 2019). It is defined as the 'stress caused by an inability to cope with the demands of organizational computer usage' (Tarafdar *et al.,* 2010, p. 304).

Craig Brod (1984), a clinical psychologist, was the first to use the term Technostress in 1984. The term refers to "the inability of an individual or organization to adapt to the introduction and operation of new technology" (Brod, 1982, p. 754).

In order to provide a better understanding of technostress, we rely on the transactional model of stress and coping of Lazarus and Folkman (1984) and the person-environment (PE) fit model of Edwards and Cooper (1990). According to the transactional model of stress and coping of Lazarus and Folkman (1984), burnout results from the combination of environmental variables and intra-personal traits, which may accelerate or prevent burnout (Hobfoll & Shirom, 1993). The transactional model emphasizes the bidirectional character of the relationship between the person and environment. It is a mutual and dynamic relationship by which person and environment are no longer separately identified as such in the relationship but they are subsumed to generate together stress. Hence, people are affected by external factors but at the same time, they influence their surrounding environments by their personalities and ideas. They contribute to the ever changing nature of the environment by leaving on their mark (Lazarus and Folkman, 1984).

The transactional model of stress and coping suggests that individuals respond mainly in two ways when they are facing a stressful situation and/or a major change in their environment: cognitive appraisal and coping. The cognitive appraisal process implies an assessment of the relevance of the event to the well-being of an individual and how it would be (Folkman *et al.,* 1986). Coping represents cognitive and behavioral attitudes exerted by an individual to deal with a stressful event and/or a change in the environment (Lazarus and Folkman, 1984).

The person-environment (PE) fit model of Edwards and Cooper (1990) suggest that stress results from the congruence between the person's attributes and those of the environment. According to Edwards and Cooper (1990), this model "characterizes stress as a lack of correspondence between characteristics of the person (e.g. abilities, values) and the environment (e.g. demands, supplies). This lack of correspondence is hypothesized to generate deleterious psychological, physiological and behavioral outcomes." (p.293).

Accordingly, stress results from high demands or insufficient supplies to meet the individual's needs (Ayyagari *et al.,* 2011; Cooper *et al.,* 2001). The transactional model of stress and coping represents demand stressors in an ICT-enabled context as technostressors. These stressors increase overall overload. We argue that, with a fit between the person and the environment according to the PE fit theory, the positive impact of technostressors on perceived stress is mitigated. Otherwise, when individual factors are not matching with the demanding environment (primary and secondary appraisal process lead to the conclusion that technostressors are threatening and out of the individual's control), the individual engages in coping process. In our study, we focus on turnover as the ultimate coping mechanism to avoid stress (burnout). Figure 1 illustrates the conceptual model based on the literature review.

Figure 1. Conceptual research model based on the results of the literature review

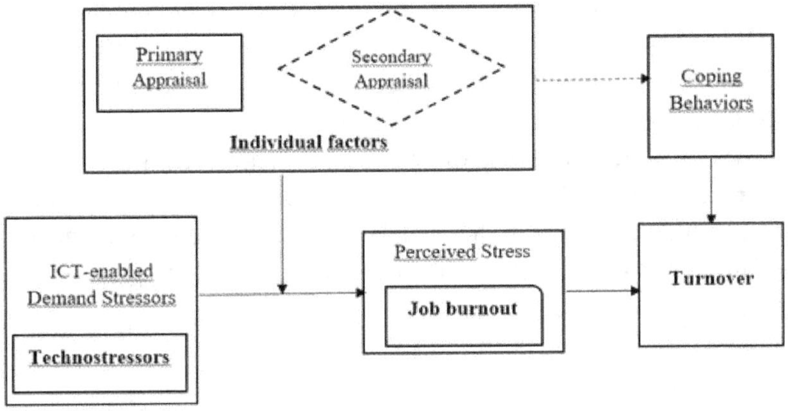

Figure 1. Conceptual Research Model based on the results of the literature review

II. PRIOR STUDIES ON TECHNOSTRESS

A growing body of information systems (IS) literature has examined the antecedents and consequences of technostress (e.g. Tarafdar *et al.,* 2007; Ragu-Nathan *et al.,* 2008; Tarafdar *et al.,* 2010; Ayyagari *et al.,* 2011; Tarafdar *et al.,* 2011; Tarafdar *et al.,* 2014).

However, in the auditing sector, studies have been limited to examine the use extent of information technology in audit companies (Janvrin *et al.,* 2008; Lowe *et al.,* 2018), the productivity of five offices of an international public accounting firm after the implementation of IT like audit software and knowledge-sharing applications (Banker *et al.,* 2002), the benefits of technology use in the audit process (Bierstaker *et al.,* 2001).

Additionally, previous studies have associated technostress creators with many job outcomes such as overall performance (Tarafdar *et al.,* 2014), job commitment (Ragu-Nathan *et al.,* 2008), productivity (Tarafdar *et al.,* 2007), job satisfaction (Tarafdar *et al.,* 2010) and work-to-life conflict (Diaz *et al.,* 2012; Gadeyne *et al.,* 2018).

Despite these recent advancements in technostress research, prior studies have not yet examined the association between technostress and turnover in particular. This relationship is worth studying because the auditing profession is continuously encountering a serious problem of turnover (Hall and Smith, 2009; Nouri and Parker, 2013; Smith *et al.,* 2018). Turnover entails several subsequent costs including separation costs, replacement costs and training costs (Sulu *et al.,* 2010; Herda and Lavelle, 2012; Nouri and Parker, 2020). Indirect costs include the potential loss of corporate memory if knowledgeable and experienced staff leave, decline in staff morale and motivation and an increased workload for the stayers (Smith *et al.,* 2018).

Next to two research gaps that the current paper aims to address (the focus on auditors' population in particular and the association of technostress with turnover), it has remained unknown which technostress creators contribute to job stress in the auditing context.

III. METHOD

In order to provide an overview of the Tunisian auditors' perceptions of technostress, we use a qualitative approach. Qualitative research attempts to neither measure nor quantify, rather it aims at scrutinizing verbal data (interview transcripts) followed by an interpretative approach. More broadly, it helps to answer questions such as « why? » or « how? ». That's why, the sample selection should be compiled for the purpose of understanding a single situation.

In the current study, we rely on the semi-structured interview, listing all the topics to be discussed with all the participants, without imposing the order of discussion. The relative flexibility of this form of interview makes it possible to better understand the logic of the interviewee. Semi structured interviews consist of open ended questions that cover the topic areas of the study. Hence, they enable interviewees to freely express their views, opinions and beliefs, in their own words, and discuss the topic in more detail. In the semi structured interview, initial questions may be followed by more oriented questions or reformulated ones, cues or prompts to incite the interviewee to talk more openly about the unexpected impacts or the contributing factors if he just spoke briefly at the beginning.

Data Collection

The interviews are conducted during the busy season between January and February 2021. Accordingly, these professionals are very busy during this period and have limited time constraints. That's why, all participants are interviewed by telephone. This method represents a viable alternative to face-to-face interviews within the pandemic crisis context. The phone call method enables the interviewee to decide when and where the interview is performed to ensure that he is comfortable in the interview situation. We use the snowballing technique to ask interviewees if they know other potential participants.

Altogether, we interview 17 auditors. Each interview lasts on average 36 minutes. We continue to interview auditors until we reach a reasonable level of saturation whereby there is no new information and the benefit from performing additional interviews seems to be marginal.

Seven of the interviewees are women. The age of the interviewees range from 30 to 39 years. Sixteen interviewees frequently apply their smartphone to access mails, teams,... while only one use the computer only to read mails. All the interviewees log in to the ICTs on a regular basis; several times during the day.

We record each interview to be able to transcribe the whole interview for the purpose of analysis. We follow the recommendation of Miles and Huberman (2003) and transcribe each interview within 24 hours.

The 17 interviews conducted represent more than 10 hours of recording. During the transcription process, we insisted on transcribing as accurately as possible and as comprehensively as it should be the comments of the interviewees. This step, prior to the data analysis phase, allowed us to immerse ourselves in the content of the interviews. At the end of the last one, the corpus obtained is composed of 109 pages (font size 12, line spacing 1.5).

Data Analysis

The analysis of interview transcripts is performed using the qualitative data analytical software Nvivo 11. We read the transcripts and code segments of text using a data-driven coding procedure; open coding wherein no categories are a-priori defined. Codes acting as collection pots for evidence representing distinct thoughts about technostress and turnover are identified. The coding process includes several iterations to obtain a structured and refined code system. During this phase, we constantly move between data collected and literature review to adjust codes and identify emerging codes not mentioned in prior literature.

IV. RESULTS

The interviewees acknowledge that information and communication technologies increase the stress they used to face. Two respondents report that technologies are a source of stress:

« The phone is stressful because you can be reached anytime" / «we can say that the technology increases the stress since others can see you connected or not and if they send you a message on what's up and you saw it but you did not answer, so it is stressful» /"we cannot deny that it is a source of stress since he calls you and he also sends you an email» (Interviewee 12)

« The technologies we have are enough. We do not want any other technology » (Interviewee 15)

Technostressors are either environment-stimulus technostressors that stem from the external environment upon which individuals have no influence. These technostressors identified by Tarafdar *et al.* (2007) involve techno-invasion, techno-overload, techno-complexity, techno-uncertainty and techno-insecurity. Furthermore, they may be individual-stimulus technostressors that are the ICTs criteria against which individuals feel powerless. These employees have uncontrollable routines when using technologies. More precisely, they are slaves of some obsessive behaviors. For instance, the increased dependency and hyperconnectivity are a kind of addiction over which individuals have no control but they are the ones who are acting in such a way.

IV.1. ENVIRONMENT-STIMULUS TECHNOSTRESSORS

- ***Techno-overload***

"Information overload refers to overwhelming volumes of information from different communication channels that ICT users are subject to". (Tarafdar *et al.*, 2010, p. 308).

Many of the interviewed note that audit software, smart phone are drivers of additional workload alongside the workload they are used to endure. So, they think that technology devices increase the demands on the individual.

The financial auditors claim that the pace of work becomes faster with the proliferation of technologies. *"Technologies speed up the work so the pace becomes more intense and then more stressful". (Interviewee 7)*

Auditors also perceive techno-overload through the detailed information they should provide for the documentation of the audit file in the audit software, which makes the audit process very long and boring. "*I spend all my day to finalize the audit engagement and close the steps. All day long on the software, I do not neither correct the tests nor review the work of the staff. After that, I feel so exhausted." (Interviewee 1).*

- ***Techno-insecurity***

Tarafdar *et al.* (2007) claim that: "Techno-insecurity is associated with situations where users feel threatened about losing their jobs, either because of automation from ICTs or to other people who have a better understanding of ICTs" (p.313). Our qualitative analysis reveals sentiments of feeling insecure about losing jobs to other users who are more knowledgeable about ICTs. For example, an auditor reports that his colleagues may have a better understanding of ICT:

« You have to be up to date otherwise your colleagues will know more than you about ICTs. The market is always changing so you have to be always up to date » (Interviewee 8)

Likewise, another auditor underline the role of full job market competition in creating incentives to learn about new technologies: *"It is a must to learn how to use technologies otherwise you cannot work in a very competitive context like consulting and you would be overtaken by competitors. So, you have no choice, either you're up to date with technology or you become useless and you lose your job". (Interviewee 12)*

Auditors feel threatened by the need to update their knowledge and ICT skills, which increase feeling of stress.

- ***Techno-invasion***

Tarafdar *et al.* (2007) assume that "techno-invasion describes the invasive effect of ICTs in situations where employees can be reached anytime and feel the need to be constantly connected, thus blurring work-related and personal contexts" (p.313). In the qualitative study, seven out of 17 interviewees stated that they did not perceive techno-invasion. The reason that auditors provide is that they have the autonomy to decide when to use technology. By doing so, they may set a limit to the invasion of privacy. They can benefit from the use of technologies without being negatively invaded.

"As long as I am the master I have control over the technology, I open my mail whenever I want. Therefore, if you want to check your mailbox from time to time, then the problem is you and not the technology. Technology makes life easier, not the other way around. You need to know how to use it. If I want to close the mailbox, I close or I log out. However, if I have a deadline and I expect someone to send me a file, I check all the time. If not, I see an email I read it quickly and I leave. I do not stick to what it says". (Interviewee 8)

Therefore, it is ultimately the auditors' own decision how to regulate and control the use of these invasive devices. *"It is under my control. When I want to enjoy my free time, I do not use technology, for example, when I want to take care of my children or my family. So, I decide, I control. ...when I want to use it I use it otherwise I do not use it". (Interviewee 15)*

The interviewed auditors claim that they are not willing to use technologies anymore after work because they are already tired. *"With this pace of work, I no longer want to see neither a PC nor a smartphone or anything else. At the limit, I see the TV when I get some rest". (Interviewee 7).* They may also turn off their smartphones after work to avoid to be reached during free time:

"It is rarely where I am reachable after regular working hours unless when there is something urgent. For me, I set a limit. For example, when a client calls me say 19 hours or 19.30 hours I put another chip in my phone so I am no longer reachable. I have the mailbox on my phone but I just check it and I read the emails. I do not respond until the next day unless there is an emergency or a bunch of untreated emails ...." (Interviewee 12)

Other interviewed auditors note that techno-invasion may be perceived in the busy season, particularly. The public accounting profession has long been recognized by ''busy season''. This period is characterized by workload (Lopez and Peters, 2012) and work-family conflicts (Sweeney and Summers, 2002). Almost all of the interviewees, agree that continuous phone calls occur primarily during the busy season. *"I receive emails, messages or calls outside regular working hours mainly during the busy season" (Interviewee 17).* An auditor claims that making phone calls outside regular working hours is very typical during the busy season.

- ***Techno-complexity***

"Techno-complexity describes situations where the complexity associated with ICTs leads users to feel inadequate with regard to their computer skills and forces them to spend time and effort in learning and understanding ICTs" (Tarafdar et al., 2007, p.313). Some auditors explain how they do not have a perfect mastery of technologies. For instance, an auditor says: "the audit software lost us a lot of time because you have to validate too many steps and attach so many templates". (Interviewee 3)

Another one adds that: *"A new audit software fully in place is always accompanied with complexity". (Interviewee 2)*

Auditors feel compelled to update their ICT skills *"We have always to be up-to-date because of the evolving technology". (Interviewee 10).* They add that they should undertake special training every three months to keep up with the rapid change of technologies and overcome security deficiencies.

« I think that we should always have training every 3 months, if necessary because technologies are changing quickly. We have to be trained not only on the technologies usage but also on applying security measures. For example, we need to learn that we have not to connect to any public Wifi network via our profes-

sional computer or smartphone or when we receive an email, we have to check the mail address if it is suspicious or not before opening it». (Interviewee 11)

Auditors compelled to undertake training sessions feel less self-confident which increase their concerns about their professional future and lead to exhaustion.

- ***Techno-uncertainty***

Tarafdar *et al.* (2007) note that: "Techno-uncertainty refers to contexts where continuing ICT changes and upgrades unsettle users and create uncertainty so that they must constantly learn and educate themselves about new ICTs" (p.313). The interviewed auditors struggle to cope with the ever-changing audit software because there are continuous upgrades that unsettle them.

"What bothers me the most is the audit software because even when it is not a new audit engagement and has gone through a quality assessment process, you have to do it all over again because of upgrades » / « Upgrades bother me because this is not the core of the audit and it is not useful to me". (Interviewee 1)

Auditors are uncomfortable with the upgrades, which never end. This ambiguity when using the audit software depletes the energy of employees and becomes a source of stress.

IV.2. Individual-Stimulus Technostressors

- ***Overdependence on ICTs***

The interviews' findings reveal that auditors firmly believe that they are increasingly dependent on ICTs. The interviewed auditors agree that they cannot keep ICTs away from them. *« I am very dependent on technologies, I want always to check my smartphone, and it becomes a reflex. It is impossible for me to turn my phone off or to disable the mailbox function or to leave the smartphone overnight » (Interviewee 16)*

Likewise, auditors seem to be tied to their mobile work phones.

« Most people have their smartphones next to them. When I receive a mail at 10 pm, I read it and I respond if necessary ». / « My smartphone is always next to me. If the phone is off, it is better for me to go home. » (Interviewee 15)

These results are consistent with prior findings of Cavazotte *et al.* (2014) who conclude that employees at a law company are dependent on their smart phones and feel powerless to check them frequently. They add that they feel like slaves to technology.

Being dependent on their mobile devices, auditors are likely to think about professional issues while at home, which may lead to work-family conflict and increase work exhaustion.

- ***ICT-enabled work interruption***

Several interviewees discuss the issue of being interrupted many times during working on their tasks because of incoming mails, phone calls or messages,... which interfere with the work progress. An auditor reports that a task of two hours is performed within four hours because of ICTs interruptions:

« Yes always it is our daily job to get a call from the client and many calls from nearly 20 teams assigned to missions. For example, while you are reviewing an audit engagement, someone may call you to tell you that he has not understood such a point or how he must deal with a blocking case. When I come to work in the morning and I have a job that takes about 2 hours to be done, I know in advance that it will take 4 hours to get the job done because I will be interrupted several times by phone calls or the partner comes to my office and asks me something. So, it's part of the job. You have just to take it into consideration. Sometimes, it gets awkward when you have a deadline and you're in a hurry ». (Interviewee 15)

Comments like this are shared by another auditor who says that he may spend the whole day in responding to mails and phone calls without moving forward on the work he is supposed to do:

"Sometimes, I open the laptop and spend the whole day in managing emails. At the end of the day, I close the laptop without working on any Excel file or completing any audit task. I only respond to phone calls and emails". (Interviewee 1)

These findings corroborate those of Cavazotte *et al.* (2014) who state that lawyers are frequently interrupted because of ICT devices. Similarly, Ter Hoeven *et al.* (2016) conclude that technology use is associated with increased interruptions and unpredictability. Being interrupted several times per day, auditors lose concentration and become concerned about the work progress, which may increase pressure on them. Hence, they are more likely to exhibit burnout.

- ***Constant connectivity***

The majority of the interviewed auditors agree that they are embarrassed by the constant connectivity they are exposed to. Given that they are equipped with smartphones and laptops, work becomes nearly a 24-hour activity.

« I am always connected 24 / 24 » (Interviewee 12).

« You no longer have a normal daily life, you work all the time, you are always on call » (Interviewee 14)

Constant connectivity is accompanied by boundary less working habits as work can be done from any place and at any time. An auditor considers constant connectivity as a way to be reachable and always available for work demands:

> *« When you become a senior auditor the firm offers you a smartphone that involves mail, time sheet, tools and all. So, even when you are in vacation, you are always available and they tell you keep your phone on so that in case we need you, we can call you to come or work remotely» (Interviewee 5)*

In this vein, constant connectivity is a source of stress for another auditor: *« I feel stressed because work is no longer bounded by scheduled timetables from 8 am to 6 pm. Now, you have your smartphone with full access to corporate mail, so, you check each time. You feel like you are available all the time 24 hours and 7/7. » (Interviewee 3)*

Similarly, Cavazotte *et al.* (2014) claim that being continuously connected implies an implicit requirement. Indeed, Middleton (2007) adds that the always-connected nature entails being accessible even outside normal business hours.

IV.3. Personal Factors Alleviating Technostress

The findings of this qualitative study illustrate how individuals with some personality traits are able to manage technostress better than other ones.

- ***Conviction of how our job is***

The interviewed individuals who are convinced that this is the nature of the profession to make phone calls all the time, to work after regular hours,...appear to be less technostressed than others. This falls within the awareness of the jobs' duties, which refers to the conscientiousness trait (Costa and McCrae, 1985; Saucier and Ostendorf, 1999).

> *"We are like that. It's an inherent thing to our business to call your superior or your superior to call you after hours, it's the nature of our business, and we can't do otherwise". (Interviewee 16)*
>
> *"Over time, I've learned that stress is part of the job. You've chosen this job; you have to accept it including its disadvantages". (Interviewee 3)*
>
> *"That's our job. We deal with it. When I say after all that is our job, it reduces a lot of stress. So you either accept or you change the job". (Interviewee 13)*

- ***Sense of organization***

The interviews reveal that auditors who tend to be well organized are less likely to face technostress because they have an orderly mind. This supports the idea that personality traits and especially conscientiousness have an impact on technostress management. The following quotations show how the sense of organization is useful to reduce the stress.

"I try to rest, to get away a little bit, to concentrate because concentration is the most important thing because when you think about several things together you waste a lot of time but when you think about what you're going to do exactly you can do it. The most important thing is to have a sense of organization". (Interviewee 16)

"Over time, I manage to organize myself well. I plan what I have to do for these 2 hours and the next 2 hours. It is clear to me. I can estimate how much time my work takes .... Our job requires organization. If a mission is well organized and the files and emails are classified, it can be done quickly. If we do not make an effort in this regard, we will be in trouble". (Interviewee 7)

"Finally, it's a matter of organization. If you handle things well, technology is not going to be an obstacle". (Interviewee 9)

- ***Sense of responsibility***

The interviewees discuss the trait of being responsible. This point falls within the personality trait of conscientiousness. As mentioned below, responsible people are aware of the need for efforts devoted in order to comply with the requirements of the audit profession.

"For me, since I have a sense of responsibility I cannot take a leave of absence when I know in advance that there is a board of directors or a general assembly" (Interviewee 13)

"That's what I tell the team members. We work based on sense of responsibility. There is no obligation." (Interviewee 13)

The study's results show that conscious people are able to perceive technostress creators as challenges rather than threats. Conscientious individuals are aware of their jobs' duties and struggle to maintain perseverance (Costa and McCrae, 1985).

As highly conscientious individuals are goal oriented, technology may be perceived as a mean to improve job performance (Srivastava *et al.,* 2015). Consequently, they are willing to show their acceptance of the associated technostress creators and are less likely to exhibit job burnout or have turnover intentions due to technostress.

- ***Passion of work***

The qualitative study reveals thoughts about passion of work. The interviewed auditors explain how passion of work alleviates the feeling of stress:

"I work with pleasure because I like my job. If I don't like it, I can't work like this. The fact that I'm passionate about my job diminishes the stress of the job". (Interviewee 13)

"I work in a field I like" (Interviewee 17)

From a personality traits' perspective, extraverts are optimistic, enthusiastic and cheerful individuals who are more likely to experience positive emotions, compared to introverts (Clark and Watson, 1999). They are energetic and talkative (McCrae and John, 1992). Extravert people are also hopeful about their professional future work performance, which may reduce levels of emotional exhaustion and influence their current work evaluations. This feeling of work passion may be considered within extraversion personality trait.

- ***Segmentation mindset***

The qualitative study reveals that auditors who can separate work domain from private domain can manage stress more efficiently:

"It's now over time I've learned how to leave work stress behind me once I get home. There are people like staff who may have a blockage; they may have insomnia due to stress". (Interviewee 3)

"I make 100% of separation between work and private life but considering 100% is very difficult to do, I say 70% of separation. Once I go home, I don't think about any work problems whatever they are". (Interviewee 8)

"I try not to check my smartphone and my laptop during the days off because it stresses me. During the vacation, I try to keep my distance" (Interviewee 3)

For example, an auditor decides to not be connected to any device in his day off: "*When I have a day off, it is a day off. I do not open the email at all. I delete the email application from my phone. Therefore, I do not have neither mail nor Lync in order to not open the emails. If there is something, they call me by phone. Before, I had the mail application on my phone but when I bought a new phone, I did not install the application again to not be bothered by an email and stay with my son". (Interviewee 7)*

It appears that auditors who have a segmentation mindset are empowered with mental abilities to prevent the work tensions from spilling over into the private domain. Hence, they set clear boundaries between professional and personal domains. In other words, they leave work issues at work once they go back home and home tensions at home once they go to work. This spirit seems to dampen the intrusiveness of ICTs.

This findings corroborates those of Powell and Greenhaus (2010) who show that role segmentation is negatively associated with work-family conflict.

Figure 2. Conceptual model based on the results of the qualitative study.

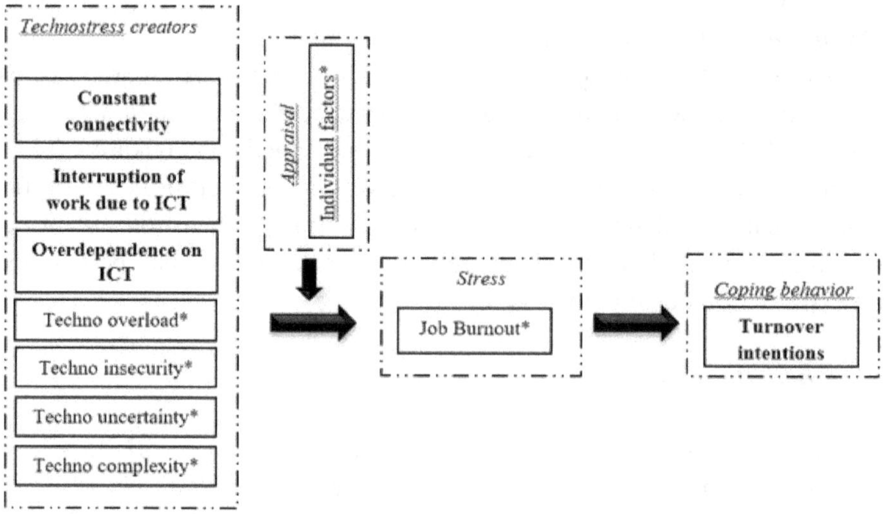

Figure 2. Conceptual model based on the results of the qualitative study.

Bold text: New finding-not found by prior literature

**: Known from prior literature (Maier et al., 2019; Srivastava et al., 2015; Khedhaouria and Cucchi, 2019)*

V. DISCUSSION

Despite the growing number of technostress studies (Maier *et al.,* 2019; Srivastava *et al.,* 2015; Khedhaouria and Cucchi, 2019; Ayyagari *et al.,* 2011; Tarafdar *et al.,* 2007, 2010, 2014, 2017; Ragu-Nathan, 2008), few researchers have addressed the issue of technostress in the auditing context in particular. More specifically, the kinds of technostress creators that trigger burnout and ultimately turnover intentions in the auditing context have been unknown until now.

Prior studies also have valuably associated technostress creators with several job outcomes including job burnout (Maier *et al.,* 2019). To extend this knowledge, this study links technostress creators with turnover intentions known as a widespread problem in the auditing sector. Reviewing the technostress literature, we could not identify any study that indicates constant connectivity, interruption of work due to ICT and overdependence on ICT as technostress creators. This new set of findings suggest that stressors in the auditing context differ from those that are common in all occupations. So, we can offer a solution to a key problem in audit firms, namely, that "For decades, accounting practitioners and academics have noted that employee turnover is an important issue in public accounting firms" (Nouri and Parker, 2020, p.2494). In addition, Califf *et al.* (2020) suggest that future research may identify moderators of the relationship between technostressors and job outcomes. More specifically, in their review of turnover in public accounting firms, Nouri and Parker (2020) question the need for investigating the moderators of the relationship between person–organization fit and turnover.

The findings of the present study have considerable managerial implications. First, by identifying personality traits that may buffer the job stress, it becomes possible for audit companies to draw the profile of persons likely to be at burnout risk. Therefore, they may take corrective actions if necessary by transferring these profiles to less demanding departments.

An additional important implication is that this study could be a useful aid for recruiters who may take preventive actions during job interviews to have the right person at the right place. Accordingly, questions asked during interviews should focus on personality traits on equal footing with technical questions. By this way, audit firms can increase retention of high performers and ensure firm effectiveness.

Finally, as voluntary turnover has long been a serious issue for companies (Lee and Mitchell, 1994) as it entails several subsequent costs including separation costs, this study might help to solve the turnover problem. Nouri and Parker (2020) confirm that the firm loses substantial costs incurred for recruiting and training an employee when the employee leaves. The study's focus on technostress can provide an appropriate novel explanation for turnover next to common reasons (e.g., burnout (Swider and Zimmerman, 2010; Smith *et al.*, 2018), firm commitment and perceived firm fairness (Herda and Lavelle, 2012; Cannon and Herda, 2016), job satisfaction and work-life conflict (Pasewark and Viator, 2006)). Hence, audit companies can try to alleviate technostress by allowing to employees to turn off their laptops or smartphones outside regular working hours.

Although the present study contributes significantly to the technostress literature, we are aware that our research may have some limitations. First, this study uses ICTs as a group of many technologies. Further work needs to be performed to focus on a specific type of technology because auditors' perception of technostress may depend on the technology used. Second, interviews are conducted in the Tunisian context. So, the findings may be relevant to this context in particular because results can be influenced by workplace culture. Third, the study relies on cross-sectional data as auditors' perceptions are measured at a single point in time. Therefore, it is recommended that longitudinal research should be undertaken to examine how the exposure to technostressors may affect the psychological responses across time is strongly needed. Given the small sample size, the findings might not be generalized to the whole population of auditors.

CONCLUSION

This study attempts to provide a better understanding of technostress in the auditing context. Through a qualitative exploratory study based on semi-structured interviews conducted with professional auditors, the study identifies several contextually relevant technostressors that are associated with turnover intentions and investigates how individual factors buffer the relationship between technostressors, job burnout and turnover intentions.

REFERENCES

Ayyagari, R., Grover, V., & Purvis, R. (2011). Technostress: Technological Antecedents and Implications. *Management Information Systems Quarterly*, *35*(4), 831–858. DOI: 10.2307/41409963

Banker, R. D., Chang, H., & Kao, Y. (2002). Impact of Information Technology on Public Accounting Firm Productivity. *Journal of Information Systems*, *16*(2), 209–222. DOI: 10.2308/jis.2002.16.2.209

Bierstaker, J. L., Burnaby, P., & Thibodeau, J. (2001). The impact of information technology on the audit process: An assessment of the state of the art and implications for the future. *Managerial Auditing Journal*, *16*(3), 159–164. DOI: 10.1108/02686900110385489

Boyer-Davis, S. (2019). Technostress in Accounting Professionals: A Quantitative Examination of the Differences Between Managers and Non-Managers. *Journal of Accounting and Finance*, *19*(2), 25–41.

Brod, C. (1982). Managing technostress: Optimizing the use of computer technology. *The Personnel Journal*, *61*(10), 753–757. PMID: 10258012

Brod, C. (1984). *Technostress: The Human Cost of Computer Revolution*. Addison-Wesley.

Califf, C., Sarker, S., & Sarker, S. (2020). The Bright and Dark Sides of Technostress: A Mixed-Methods Study Involving Healthcare IT. *Management Information Systems Quarterly*, *44*(2), 809–856. DOI: 10.25300/MISQ/2020/14818

Cannon, N. H., & Herda, D. N. (2016). Auditors' Organizational Commitment, Burnout and Turnover Intention: A Replication. *Behavioral Research in Accounting*, *28*(2), 69–74. DOI: 10.2308/bria-51455

Cavazotte, F., Lemos, A. H., & Villadsen, K. (2014). Corporate smart phones: Professionals' conscious engagement in escalating work connectivity. *New Technology, Work and Employment*, *29*, 72–87.

Cheung, C. M. (2019). Panel report: The dark side of the digitization of the individual. *Internet Research*, *29*(2), 274–288. DOI: 10.1108/INTR-04-2019-541

Clark, L. A., & Watson, D. (1999). Temperament: A new paradigm for trait psychology. Dans L. A. (Eds.), *Handbook of personality: Theory and research* (pp. 399–423). Guilford Press.

Cooper, C. L. (1998). *Job stress*. Oxford University Press.

Cooper, C. L., Dewe, P., & O'Driscoll, M. (2001). *Organizational Stress: A review and critique of theory, research, and applications*. Sage. DOI: 10.4135/9781452231235

Costa, P. T., & McCrae, R. R. (1985). *NEO personality inventory professional manual*. Psychological Assessment Resources, Inc.

Day, A., Paquet, S., Scott, N., & Hambley, L. (2012). Perceived information and communication technology (ICT) demands on employee outcomes: The moderating effect of organizational ICT support. *Journal of Occupational Health Psychology*, *17*(4), 473–491. DOI: 10.1037/a0029837 PMID: 23066697

Diaz, I., Chiaburu, D. S., Zimmerman, R. D., & Boswell, W. R. (2012). Communication technology: Pros and cons of constant connection to work. *Journal of Vocational Behavior*, *80*(2), 500–508. DOI: 10.1016/j.jvb.2011.08.007

Donnelly, D. P., Quirin, J. J., & O'Bryan, D. (2003). Auditor acceptance of dysfunctional audit behavior: An explanatory model using auditors' personal characteristics. *Behavioral Research in Accounting*, *15*(1), 87–110. DOI: 10.2308/bria.2003.15.1.87

Edwards, J. R., & Cooper, C. L. (1990). The person€nvironment fit approach to stress: Recurring problems and some suggested solutions. *Journal of Organizational Behavior*, *11*(4), 293–307. DOI: 10.1002/job.4030110405

Folkman, S., Lazarus, R., Dunkel-Schetter, D., Delongis, A., & Gruen, R. (1986). Dynamics of a stressful encounter: Cognitive appraisal, coping and encounter outcomes. *Journal of Personality and Social Psychology*, *50*(5), 992–1003. DOI: 10.1037/0022-3514.50.5.992 PMID: 3712234

Gadeyne, N., Verbruggen, M., Delanoeije, J., & De Cooman, R. (2018). All wired, all tired? Work-related ICT-use outside work hours and work-to-home conflict: The role of integration preference, integration norms and work demands. *Journal of Vocational Behavior*, *107*, 86–99. DOI: 10.1016/j.jvb.2018.03.008

Hall, M., & Smith, D. (2009). Mentoring and turnover intentions in public accounting firms: A research note. *Accounting, Organizations and Society*, *34*(6-7), 695–704. DOI: 10.1016/j.aos.2008.11.003

Herda, D. N., & Lavelle, J. J. (2012). The Auditor-Audit Firm Relationship and Its effect on Burnout and Turnover Intention. *Accounting Horizons*, *26*(4), 707–723. DOI: 10.2308/acch-50181

Hobfoll, S. E., & Shirom, A. (1993). Stress and burnout in work organizations. Dans R. G. (Ed.) (Éd.), *Handbook of organization behavior* (pp. 41-61). New York: Dekker.

Hsieh, Y., & Wang, M. (2012). The moderating role of personality in HRM from the influence of job stress on job burnout perspective. *International Management Review*, *8*(2), 5–18.

Janvrin, D., Bierstaker, J., & Jordan, D. (2008, March). An Examination of Audit Information Technology Use and Perceived Importance. *Accounting Horizons*, *22*(1), 1–21. DOI: 10.2308/acch.2008.22.1.1

Jones, A.III, Norman, C. S., & Wier, B. (2010). Healthy Lifestyle as a Coping Mechanism for Role Stress in Public Accounting. *Behavioral Research in Accounting*, *22*(1), 21–41. DOI: 10.2308/bria.2010.22.1.21

Joseph, D., Ng, K.-Y., Koh, C., & Ang, S. (2007). Turnover of information technology professionals: A narrative review, meta-analytic structural equation modeling, and model development. *Management Information Systems Quarterly*, *31*(3), 3. DOI: 10.2307/25148807

Khedhaouria, A., & Cucchi, A. (2019). Technostress creators, personality traits, and job burnout: A fuzzy-set configurational analysis. *Journal of Business Research*, *101*, 349–361. DOI: 10.1016/j.jbusres.2019.04.029

Lazarus, R., & Folkman, S. (1984). *Stress, Appraisal, and Coping*. Springer.

Lee, T., & Mitchell, T. (1994). An alternative approach: The unfolding model of voluntary employee turnover. . *Academy of Management Review*, 19(1), 51–89. Récupéré sur http://dx.doi.org/DOI: 10.5465/amr.1994.9410122008

Leung, L. (2011). Effects of ICT connectedness, permeability, flexibility, and negative spillovers on burnout and job and family satisfaction. *Human Technology*, *7*(3), 250–267. DOI: 10.17011/ht/urn.2011112211714

Lopez, D., & Peters, G. (2012). The Effect of Workload Compression on Audit Quality. *Auditing*, *31*(4), 139–165. DOI: 10.2308/ajpt-10305

Lowe, D. J., Bierstaker, J. L., Janvrin, D. J., & Jenkins, J. G. (2017). Information Technology in an Audit Context: Have the Big 4 Lost Their Advantage? *Accounting Publications*, 32(1), 87-107. doi:https://lib.dr.iastate.edu/acct_pubs/19

Maier, C., Laumer, S., Wirth, J., & Weitzel, T. (2019). Technostress and the hierarchical levels of personality: A two-wave study with multiple data samples. *European Journal of Information Systems*, *28*(5), 496–522. DOI: 10.1080/0960085X.2019.1614739

Miles, M. B., & Huberman, M. A. (2003). *Analyse des données qualitatives*. De Boeck Supérieur.

Moore, J. E. (2001). One Road to Turnover: An Examination of Work Exhaustion in Technology Professionals. *Management Information Systems Quarterly*, *24*(1), 141–168. DOI: 10.2307/3250982

Nouri, H., & Parker, R. (2013, June). Career growth opportunities and employee turnover intentions in public accounting firms. *The British Accounting Review*, *45*(2), 138–148. DOI: 10.1016/j.bar.2013.03.002

Nouri, H., & Parker, R. J. (2020). Turnover in public accounting firms: A literature review. *Managerial Auditing Journal*, *35*(2), 294–321. DOI: 10.1108/MAJ-03-2018-1823

Pasewark, W., & Viator, R. (2006). Sources of work-family conflict in the accounting profession. *Behavioral Research in Accounting*, *18*(1), 147–165. DOI: 10.2308/bria.2006.18.1.147

Ragu-nathan, T. S., Tarafdar, M., Ragu-nathan, B. S., & Tu, Q. (2008). The consequences of technostress for end users in organizations: Conceptual development and empirical validation. *Information Systems Research*, *19*(4), 417–433. DOI: 10.1287/isre.1070.0165

Saucier, G., & Ostendorf, F. (1999). Hierarchical subcomponents of the Big Five personality factors: A cross-languagereplication. *Journal of Personality and Social Psychology*, *76*(4), 613–627. DOI: 10.1037/0022-3514.76.4.613 PMID: 10234848

Smith, K. J., Emerson, D. J., & Boster, C. R. (2018, September). An examination of reduced audit quality practices within the beyond the role stress model. *Managerial Auditing Journal*, *33*(8/9), 736–759. DOI: 10.1108/MAJ-07-2017-1611

Srivastava, S. C., Chandra, S., & Shirish, A. (2015). Technostress creators and job outcomes: Theorising the moderating influence of personality traits. *Information Systems Journal*, *25*(4), 355–401. DOI: 10.1111/isj.12067

Sulu, S., Ceylan, A., & Kaynak, R. (2010, July). Work Alienation as a Mediator of the Relationship between Organizational Injustice and Organizational Commitment: Implications for Healthcare Professionals. *International Journal of Business and Management*, *5*(8), 27–38. DOI: 10.5539/ijbm.v5n8p27

Sweeney, J., & Summers, S. (2002). The Effect of the Busy Season Workload on Public Accountants' Job Burnout. *Behavioral Research in Accounting*, *14*(1), 223–245. DOI: 10.2308/bria.2002.14.1.223

Swider, B. W., & Zimmerman, R. D. (2010). Born to burnout: A meta-analytic path model of personality, job burnout, and work outcomes. *Journal of Vocational Behavior*, *76*(3), 487–506. DOI: 10.1016/j.jvb.2010.01.003

Tarafdar, M., Gupta, A., & Turel, O. (2015). Editorial: Special Issue on "dark side of information technology use": An Introduction and a framework for research. *Information Systems Journal, 25*(3), 161–170. DOI: 10.1111/isj.12070

Tarafdar, M., Pullins, E. B., & Ragu-Nathan, T. S. (2015). Technostress: Negative effect on performance and possible mitigations. *Information Systems Journal, 25*(2), 103–132. DOI: 10.1111/isj.12042

Tarafdar, M., Tu, Q., Ragu-Nathan, B. S., & Ragu-Nathan, T. S. (2007). The Impact of Technostress on Role Stress and Productivity. *Journal of Management Information Systems, 24*(1), 301–328. DOI: 10.2753/MIS0742-1222240109

Tarafdar, M., Tu, Q., & Ragu-Nathan, T. S. (2010). Impact of Technostress on End-User Satisfaction and Performance. *Journal of Management Information Systems, 27*(3), 303334. DOI: 10.2753/MIS0742-1222270311

Tarafdar, M., Tu, Q., Ragu-Nathan, T. S., & Ragu-Nathan, B. S. (2011). Crossing to the Dark Side: Examining Creators, Outcomes, and Inhibitors of Technostress. *Communications of the ACM, 54*(9), 113–120. DOI: 10.1145/1995376.1995403

Ter Hoeven, C. L., van Zoonen, W., & Fonner, K. L. (2016). The practical paradox of technology: The influence of communication technology use on employee burnout and engagement. *Communication Monographs, 83*(2), 239–263. DOI: 10.1080/03637751.2015.1133920 PMID: 27226694

Xie, J., Ma, H., Zhou, Z., & Hanying, T. (2017). Work-Related Use of Information and Communication Technologies after Hours (W_ICTs) and Emotional Exhaustion: A Mediated Moderation Model. *Computers in Human Behavior*. Advance online publication. DOI: 10.1016/j.chb.2017.10.023

Chapter 11
Spatial Data Management Strategies to Improve Green Innovation

Jan Vrba
https://orcid.org/0000-0002-8404-5091
Akademia Jagiellońska w Toruniu, Poland

Muhammad Akbar
https://orcid.org/0009-0005-1762-042X
Centre of Excellence in Water Resources Engineering, University of Engineering and Technology, Lahore, Pakistan

Emmanuel Emmanuel Eze
https://orcid.org/0009-0002-3385-4697
First Moscow State University, Russia

Munir Ahmad
https://orcid.org/0000-0003-4836-6151
Survey of Pakistan, Pakistan

ABSTRACT

Effective management of spatial data can drive green innovation by identifying environmental challenges such as air and water quality, deforestation, soil health, and climate vulnerability. Spatial data supports pollution detection and forest cover analysis, along with soil sampling for erosion assessment. It can also guide targeted initiatives like clean air efforts and sustainable forestry. Moreover, it can optimize resource allocation by pinpointing renewable energy sources and sustainable materials. Spatial data can tailor innovations to local contexts, inform urban planning, enhance waste and agriculture practices, and monitor environmental impact. Key

DOI: 10.4018/979-8-3693-4373-9.ch011

strategies of spatial data management involve collecting high-quality data from diverse sources, integrating it into accessible platforms, and ensuring data quality. Collaboration and knowledge sharing can enhance spatial data's role in green innovation. Challenges such as data access, ownership, and privacy concerns necessitate solutions like open data policies, clear agreements, and capacity-building programs.

INTRODUCTION

Spatial Data Management may be defined as undertaking activities, methods, tools, and procedures of capturing, storing, processing, analyzing, administering, and visualizing spatial or geographical data. This type of data characterizes the properties of the geometric nature of objects and is related to spatial position and arrangement. Spatial data management is a core element of Geographic Information System (GIS) and is important for applications like mapping, planning, monitoring, and services that are based on locations. Spatial data management is characterized by various data elements which can contain spatial qualities, these include the geometries, coordinates, and topology of the data. Such data can come in several types including vector – points, lines, polygons, and raster – grids and pixels. Some of the characteristics are the ability to index the spatial data for fast retrieval of data, spatial properties such as proximity, spatial operators such as adjacency or inclusion, and performing geometric operations on the geometric data including overlay, buffering, and proximity analysis. Also, proper management of spatial data involves manipulating and storing quality data free from errors to improve its integration with other platforms and uses.

Spatial data management also has the following essential goals: Spatial data must be accessible, accurate, and usable to different users within the intended applications. It is intended to offer a sound solution for dealing with vast amounts of spatial information and its application in planning, monitoring, and organizing society spaces. Another aim is to support ways through which spatial data is combined with other varieties of data to support subsequent analysis and visualization to improve comprehension and insights into spatial occurrences. Also, spatial data management emphasizes data integrity and confidentiality where spatial information is kept secure and produces accurate results that are up to date to the user. Spatial data management encompasses the collection, analysis, and utilization of geographical information to inform decision-making processes regarding green initiatives. This includes mapping environmental conditions, identifying areas susceptible to pollution or climate-related risks, and optimizing resource allocation for sustainable development projects (Bakirci, 2024; Hinsby et al., 2024; Kopp et al., 2024; Külling et al., 2024; D. Sharma et al., 2024; N. Sharma et al., 2024; Shinde et al.,

2024). By leveraging spatial data, policymakers, businesses, and researchers can gain valuable insights into the spatial distribution of environmental challenges and opportunities, facilitating targeted interventions and maximizing the impact of green innovations. Effective spatial data management not only enhances the efficiency and effectiveness of green initiatives but also ensures that limited resources are allocated to areas where they are most needed, ultimately advancing environmental sustainability goals.

The fight against climate change demands constant innovation in sustainable practices. Nikolaou et al. (2020) argued that to address climate change-affected water scarcity issues, methods such as deficit irrigation and the use of alternative water sources like wastewater and brackish groundwater are being employed. They further asserted that sustainable water productivity can be achieved through protected cultivation systems like greenhouses and screenhouses, especially when integrated with artificial intelligence technology. George et al. (2021) noted that integration of digital sustainability fosters growth and innovation in entrepreneurship and business strategy and contributes to the well-being of society by addressing environmental and social challenges. Similarly, Habib-ur-Rahman et al. (2022) argued that adapting agricultural methods like modifying sowing schedules and crop densities, rotating crops with legumes, practicing agroforestry, integrating mixed livestock systems, cultivating climate-resistant species, raising single-stomach livestock, using early warning and decision support tools, increasing carbon capture, and implementing advanced technologies for climate, water, energy, and soil management, along with fostering biodiversity, can lessen the harmful effects of climate change. Moreover, Balogun et al. (2020) asserted that high-tech digital devices and platforms demonstrate the power of digitalization to support sustainable development in urban centers by improving early warning and emergency response systems, bolstering food and water security, optimizing power infrastructure, facilitating citizen involvement in adaptation efforts, and reducing the effects of climatic hazards.

Green innovation, often referred to as eco-innovation, pertains to the process of creating novel production techniques and technologies aimed at mitigating environmental risks, such as pollution and the adverse impacts of resource depletion (Castellacci & Lie, 2017). Green innovation, encompassing technological advancements and process optimizations geared towards environmental well-being, plays a crucial role in achieving sustainability goals. This type of innovation involves developing new technologies and improving existing processes to reduce environmental impact, enhance resource efficiency, and promote the use of renewable energy sources. By fostering eco-friendly practices and solutions, green innovation helps mitigate climate change, reduce pollution, and conserve natural resources (Umar & Safi, 2023; K. Q. Zhang et al., 2022). Moreover, green innovation supports regulatory compliance and enhances corporate reputation, company performance (Huong et al.,

2021), overseeing organizational knowledge (Shahzad et al., 2021), and encouraging businesses to adopt more sustainable practices.

While the importance of green innovations is widely recognized, their successful implementation relies significantly on an often-underestimated factor: spatial data management. Existing literature on green innovation primarily focuses on technological advancements and policy frameworks (Afeltra et al., 2023; Silvestre & Ţîrcă, 2019). While these areas are undoubtedly crucial, there is a gap in understanding how effectively managing spatial data can significantly enhance green innovation efforts. Spatial data, comprising geographic details on resources, infrastructure, and environmental parameters, offers essential context for devising and executing sustainable strategies. By understanding the spatial distribution of resources and environmental challenges, stakeholders can tailor interventions to specific regions, optimizing their effectiveness and minimizing negative impacts.

This chapter explores the significance of spatial data management in fostering green innovation. We argue that effectively managing spatial data empowers us to identify areas most in need of sustainable solutions, tailor innovations to specific contexts, and monitor their environmental impact. By bridging this knowledge gap, this chapter aims to equip stakeholders with the tools necessary to leverage spatial data for impactful green innovation. To achieve this aim of the chapter, the main questions are. (1) How spatial data management can empower green innovation; (2) what are the strategies for managing spatial data effectively; (3) what are the potential challenges associated with implementing spatial data management strategies in green innovation?

METHODOLOGY

To address the above-mentioned questions, a literature review methodology is adopted. This approach involves evaluating the existing research and scholarly articles related to the topic at hand. By conducting a review of the literature, the methodology aims to gather relevant insights, theoretical perspectives, and empirical evidence that can help in understanding the research problem more thoroughly.

SPATIAL DATA MANAGEMENT FOR GREEN INNOVATION

This section explores the various methods through which effective spatial data management can empower sustainable development initiatives.

Identifying Environmental Challenges

Spatial data can be used to pinpoint areas with high levels of pollution, resource depletion, or vulnerability to climate change impacts. Spatial data can be a powerful tool for targeted green innovation efforts directed at the most pressing environmental issues such as: -

Air and Water Quality

Satellite imagery can detect changes in water clarity, identifying areas with potential pollution sources. Air quality monitoring networks combined with spatial analysis can pinpoint areas with high concentrations of pollutants, informing targeted clean air initiatives or the development of localized air filtration systems. For example, transitioning to electric vehicles (EVs) is a key strategy to reduce greenhouse gas emissions, but its effects on air quality are complex and region-specific. Mousavinezhad et al. (2024) analyzed changes in PM2.5, ozone, and their precursors in major US urban areas under various EV adoption scenarios. The results showed that the Full Electrification (FullE) scenario displayed significant PM2.5 reductions, except in some areas like eastern Los Angeles, where PM2.5 increased due to shifts in atmospheric chemistry. Health benefits included substantial reductions in premature deaths in cities such as New York, Chicago, and Houston, while Los Angeles faced potential increases in mortality due to higher PM2.5 and ozone levels. Economically, the FullE scenario provided significant health-related savings for several cities, though Los Angeles might experience economic losses.

Deforestation Rates

Spatial data analysis allows for tracking changes in forest cover over time. This information can be used to identify areas experiencing rapid deforestation and guide the development of targeted conservation efforts, such as sustainable forestry practices or REDD+ (Reducing Emissions from Deforestation and Forest Degradation) programs. For example, Niknam et al. (2024) evaluated the potential GHG emission reductions from implementing a REDD project aimed at combating deforestation and forest degradation. Using Landsat imagery and sophisticated algorithms, changes in forest cover from 1985 to 2020 were analyzed, revealing significant increases in forest cover since 2000. Projections indicate that without REDD, 199,569 hectares would be deforested by 2050, resulting in 1,995,695 tCO2e emissions. However, with REDD implementation, emissions would drop to 405,512 tCO2e, preventing 1,590,183 tCO2e emissions.

Soil Health

Soil sampling data combined with satellite imagery can be used to assess soil health and identify areas with erosion or degradation. Soil erosion, a major global problem, can lead to land degradation, lower agricultural productivity, and more landslides, exacerbated by global warming and drought. This information can inform the development of sustainable agricultural practices, such as cover cropping or precision agriculture techniques. Weslati & Serbaji (2024) examined soil erosion in the Mellegue catchment, shared by Tunisia and Algeria, using the Revised Universal Soil Loss Equation (RUSLE) and GIS tools. The analysis revealed a significant increase in erosion risk from 2002 to 2018, with many new areas becoming vulnerable and total soil loss rising sharply. These results also underscored the importance of effective land management and conservation strategies to mitigate erosion's impact. Similarly, Shekar & Mathew (2024) assessed soil erosion in India's Murredu watershed using GIS and the RUSLE model, and found a high mean annual soil loss of 14.06 t/ha/year. Sub-watersheds 2 and 14 had the highest and lowest soil losses, respectively. The sediment delivery ratio was 0.227, with an annual sediment yield of 3.19 t/ha/year at the watershed outlet. These insights are crucial for stakeholders and policymakers to manage the watershed sustainably. Whereas, Pandey et al. (2024) utilized the RUSLE and SDR models with GIS to assess annual sedimentation and soil organic carbon (SOC) control services of Indian forests. The highest soil loss rates were found in Tropical Thorn Forests and the Ganga River basin, while Tropical Dry Deciduous Forests excelled in sediment control and SOC conservation, with annual values of 33,056,560 tonnes and 331,115.06 tonnes, respectively.

Climate Change Vulnerability

Spatial data analysis can be used to assess a region's vulnerability to climate change impacts, such as sea level rise, extreme weather events, or changes in precipitation patterns. This information can guide the development of adaptation strategies, such as building sea walls or flood defenses or developing drought-resistant crops. Ahmed (2024) evaluated the vulnerability of urban union councils in Rawalpindi-Pakistan to climate change and pandemics such as COVID-19 through a composite index using 20 physical, economic, social, and institutional indicators. A survey of 440 households indicated that some areas were the least vulnerable, and some were the most vulnerable. Factors like high population density, inadequate healthcare, and low income contributed to the higher vulnerability and chronic disease outbreaks in urban areas. Similarly, Salim et al. (2024) conducted a vulnerability assessment for climate-related disasters, such as coastal flooding and sea-level rise, in the coastal districts of Indramayu, Subang, and Cirebon, Indonesia. Using georeferenced data and GIS, the study produced a spatial vulnerability index, revealing that 9 out of 16 districts are highly vulnerable. Indramayu and Subang face high vulnerability due to intense rainfall, rising sea levels, and crucial infrastructure, while Cirebon's vulnerability is primarily due to poor socio-economic conditions.

Optimizing Resource Allocation

Spatial data analysis can reveal the location and availability of renewable energy resources, sustainable materials, and existing green infrastructure. This information can be used to optimize the allocation of resources for green innovation projects.

Renewable Energy Resources

Analyzing wind and solar potential maps can guide the optimal placement of wind turbines and solar panels, maximizing energy generation. With a growing emphasis on sustainable development, the utilization of renewable energy sources is crucial, and wind wave generation holds significant promise. Upadhyaya et al. (2024) evaluated the potential of the Indian coastline for substantial renewable energy using hindcast data from Global Climate Models and a numerical wave model developed with the MIKE 21 SW module. The study specifically examined the offshore wind energy potential along the Indian coast and identified locations off Goa, Karnataka, Kerala, Tamil Nadu, and Andhra Pradesh as favorable for offshore wind turbine installations, based on validated numerical simulations. Similarly, Ren et al. (2024) evaluated wind energy resources in the coastal regions of Guangdong, China, focusing on spatial and seasonal variations. Findings revealed that wind speeds are highest offshore, indicating favorable conditions for wind energy development. Coastal areas in eastern Guangdong exhibited greater wind energy density and development potential compared to the west. Seasonal differences in wind energy variability are observed, with stability higher in winter and spring, suggesting potential for consistent wind energy production.

Geothermal Resources

Geospatial data analysis can identify areas with geothermal potential, informing the development of geothermal power plants as a clean and reliable energy source. Wang et al. (2024) evaluated geothermal feasibility within Yangmingshan National Park, Taiwan by considering geological and social factors. Employing play fairway methodology and geological susceptibility and landslide maps, three viable development sites—Matsao, Leng-shui-keng, and Long-feng-ku—are identified. Matsao emerged as the most promising prospect, offering significant geothermal potential while minimizing environmental impact, subject to moderate regulatory adjustments. Similarly, S. Wang et al. (2024) analyzed data from numerous wells and temperature measurements, using ArcGIS to map the shallow to medium-deep geothermal field and predict temperatures at depths of 4,000 meters. Through stochastic modeling and numerical simulation, they developed a reservoir attribute parameter database, identifying favorable deep, high-temperature geothermal areas within a 139.5 km^2 play fairway. The study highlighted the Fan 54 wellblock in the Boxing-Jijia region as crucial for developing deep geothermal resources. Cap layers from the Cenozoic to Upper Paleozoic are deemed effective reservoirs, with the Lower Paleozoic offering significant exploitable resource volumes, estimated at up to 127 million tons of standard coal.

Sustainable Materials Deposits

Spatial data can reveal the location of deposits of critical materials for green technologies, such as lithium for batteries or rare earth elements for wind turbines. This information can help streamline supply chains and promote responsible sourcing practices. By analyzing critical minerals and socio-economic data spatially, Burton et al. (2024) uncovered that several of Australia's most marginalized regions are home to a significant number of critical minerals mines and deposits.

Existing Green Infrastructure

Spatial data can map existing recycling facilities, composting plants, or renewable energy generation facilities. This knowledge allows for the strategic placement of new green innovations to leverage existing infrastructure and maximize their impact. Graham (2024) employed GIS analysis to assess Costa Rica's plastic waste recycling capacity, focusing on facility availability and public access. The results showed that despite progressive regulations, insufficient recycling facilities, and limited public access pose hurdles to achieving a plastics-free status. Similarly, Khan et al. (2024) proposed an optimized solution employing mathematical modeling and GIS to enhance waste collection efficiency, transportation, and resource recovery in Peshawar, Pakistan. Through linear mathematical modeling and ArcGIS Network Analyst, the study achieved a 13% route optimization in one area of the city, indicating the potential for a more sustainable waste collection system in urban Peshawar. Various scenarios, including improving collection efficiency and adopting waste-to-energy technologies, were explored, demonstrating enhanced economic viability and reduced payback periods. Borase et al. (2024) utilized GIS to investigate solutions for solid waste management, enhancing system efficiency, reducing workload, saving time and costs, and aiding decision-making in the Thane district of India.

Tailoring Innovations to Local Contexts

Spatial data provides insights into local environmental conditions, infrastructure, and community needs. This allows for the development and implementation of green innovations that are most effective within a specific geographic context.

Urban Planning

Analyzing data on traffic patterns, building density, and energy consumption can inform the development of sustainable urban planning strategies, such as promoting walkable cities, public transportation networks, or energy-efficient buildings. Poggi & Amado (2024) investigated how energy consumption in urban areas is influenced by physical and functional parameters, aiming to create a model to inform energy efficiency policies. It viewed energy consumption as a spatial process and employed a GIS to analyze urban morphologies, densities, and land uses. The proposed "morpho-energetic analysis" helped to classify urban areas based on energy consumption zones, offering valuable insights for policymakers and planners. Li et al. (2024) investigated how urban morphology influences building energy consumption by presenting a framework for analysis. It defined and measured urban morphological factors (UMFs) using spatial proximity analysis, developed an urban building energy model, and used explainable artificial intelligence (AI) methods to assess each factor's impact on energy usage. The study identified 26 UMFs related to urban buildings and road networks, highlighting significant factors and offering planning recommendations. It found that these factors affect energy consumption consistently across different building types, although their contributions vary. Y. Wang et al. (2024) explored how population density influences per capita energy consumption (PCEC) in urban areas of Chinarch. Through spatial regression analysis and examination of 9 years of balanced panel data from 276 cities, the study revealed a significant negative relationship and heterogeneity between population density and PCEC. Specifically, it found that a 1% increase in population density correlates with a 0.074% increase in PCEC. Abulibdeh (2024) examined the carbon footprint (CF) of residential buildings in Doha City, Qatar, with a focus on water and electricity consumption in villas and flats from 2017 to 2020. Using the Multi-Regional Input-Output Life Cycle Assessment (MRIO-LCA) model, the research calculated CF emissions and employed statistical and spatial analyses to assess their distribution. Results showed that villas contribute significantly more to CF emissions as compared to flats, with annual electricity emissions totaling around 7 MtCO2 equivalent. Seasonal variations, particularly during summer, and spatial clustering patterns are identified, indicating areas with elevated CF emissions.

Water Management

Understanding local water availability and usage patterns through spatial data analysis can guide the development of targeted water conservation initiatives, such as rainwater harvesting systems or drip irrigation techniques. Kamyab et al. (2023) investigated how Artificial Intelligence (AI) and Big Data Analytics (BDA) can transform water resource management (WRM) by overcoming traditional challenges such as real-time data acquisition, effective analysis, and informed decision-making. Smith & Boers (2023) explored the resilience of vegetated ecosystems worldwide by analyzing remotely sensed vegetation data through empirical and theoretical resilience metrics with the aim of understanding how water availability and variability influence vegetation resilience on a global scale. The research uncovered a strong correlation between higher water availability and increased vegetation resilience across regions. Moreover, it identified that regions experiencing greater inter-annual precipitation variability tend to exhibit lower resilience.

Waste Management

Spatial data can reveal the location and capacity of landfills, composting facilities, and recycling centers. This information can inform the development of efficient waste management systems, such as waste-to-energy plants or improved recycling programs. Z. Zhang et al. (2024) delved into the evolution and determinants of waste disposal facilities in China over the period from 2003 to 2020, utilizing a comprehensive dataset that merges municipal-level socioeconomic indicators with establishment-level data on waste disposal facilities. Findings revealed a notable shift in the composition of waste disposal infrastructure, characterized by a decline in landfill sites and a concurrent rise in incineration and composting plants. The spatial analysis uncovered a geographical disparity in facility distribution, with landfills predominantly situated in central regions, incineration plants clustered in the east, and composting facilities dispersed across various areas. Results from a dynamic spatial Durbin model highlighted consumption levels and land area as primary drivers behind the overall increase in waste disposal facilities, with specific magnitudes of increase associated with each 1% rise in these factors. Durlević et al. (2023) utilized a multi-criteria analysis, supported by GIS, to identify suitable landfill site locations in urban areas of Serbia. Fifteen environmental and socioeconomic factors are assessed using the fuzzy analytic-hierarchy process method. The analysis involved visually selecting the ten most suitable locations from a synthetic convenience map, followed by final site ranking using fuzzy multi-objective analysis by ratio and the full multiplicative form method, considering additional criteria. The study identified sanitary landfill candidate site A4 as the most suitable option, given its expansive area (569 ha) and proximity to the urban zone (8 km).

Climate-Smart Agriculture

Spatial data analysis can identify areas with specific climate challenges, such as drought or flooding. This information can be used to develop targeted agricultural innovations, such as drought-resistant crop varieties or flood-resistant agricultural practices. Fabian et al. (2023) emphasized the need for collaborative efforts to grasp the connections between climate extremes (floods and droughts) and water quality, crucial for preserving aquatic ecosystems. Tanir et al. (2024) presented a comprehensive method to assess combined flood and drought risks for agricultural areas across the United States. By integrating social vulnerability indicators with flood and drought exposure data, it identified the most at-risk regions. By merging geospatial techniques with a fuzzy logic algorithm, Islam et al. (2024) considered various meteorological, physical, and social factors to offer a comprehensive view of drought impacts. Focusing on Iowa's Corn Belt region from 2015 to 2021, the study produced maps depicting drought vulnerability and risk. Notably, the methodology incorporates weights assigned to parameters based on previous research, enhancing precision. Results highlighted a worrying increase in the proportion of Iowa's land area classified as 'very high' drought risk, signaling heightened vulnerability. Mid-Iowa and the western region emerged as particularly at risk.

Monitoring and Evaluating Environmental Impact

By tracking changes in environmental parameters over time and space, spatial data allows us to monitor the effectiveness of green innovations and identify areas for further improvement.

Air Quality Monitoring

Tracking changes in air quality data after the implementation of clean air initiatives, such as electric vehicle adoption or low-emission zones, provides evidence for their effectiveness. With increasing concerns about air quality stemming from industrial and transportation activities, conventional monitoring systems struggle to deliver real-time data at adequate spatial and temporal resolutions without incurring high costs. To tackle this challenge, Paithankar et al. (2023) introduced an innovative approach to harness Internet-of-things (IoT) technology for air quality monitoring. Employing portable sensors connected to a low-power wide area network, the system facilitates real-time data transmission. Through IoT, collected data undergo analysis and assessment. Though air pollution's impact on public health is globally recognized, less attention is given to the intricate relationship between atmospheric environmental policy (AEP), air pollution, and public health outcomes. Z. Zhang et al. (2023), utilizing panel data from 30 Chinese provinces, delved into this connection. Through spatial econometric models, it investigated how AEP shapes air pollution levels, how air pollution influences public health, and how air pollution acts as a mediator between AEP and public health outcomes. Findings revealed a significant positive spatial spillover effect of soot and dust emissions and overall air pollution levels.

Sustainable Forestry Practices

Monitoring changes in deforestation rates after the introduction of sustainable logging practices or conservation programs allows for evaluating their impact on forest health and biodiversity. Dryland forests play a vital role in the ecological and socioeconomic landscape of sub-Saharan Africa, particularly in Sudan, however, H.E. Yasin et al. (2023) noted that various ecological, human, socio-economic, and policy factors have led to their degradation, resulting in adverse consequences such as food shortages, land and water resource degradation, biodiversity loss, and contribution to global warming.

Renewable Energy Projects

Analyzing the power generation data from wind farms or solar panels allows for assessing their efficiency and identifying potential areas for improvement, such as optimizing turbine placement or panel orientation for maximum sun exposure. Chen et al. (2023) argued that Earth observation data offers a promising avenue for estimating PV energy potential and assessing the status of PV system development, crucial for informed and cost-effective planning strategies. Terés-Zubiaga et al. (2023) presented a straightforward methodology for identifying and monitoring energy-vulnerable areas using publicly available databases. By leveraging existing data, the methodology allows for the assessment of energy vulnerability levels and the evaluation of potential interventions' effectiveness. The approach maps and diagnoses energy vulnerability at the census section level, utilizing a three-dimensional index incorporating building characteristics, energy expenses, and socio-economic indicators. The methodology is applied to assess energy vulnerability in the Greater Bilbao region of northern Spain, identifying 13% of census sections, accounting for 93,000 inhabitants, as experiencing varying degrees of energy vulnerability. A distinct geographical pattern of vulnerability is observed in the region.

Biodiversity Conservation

Spatial data analysis can be used to track changes in animal populations and habitat health. Monitoring wildlife corridors and protected areas allows for evaluating the effectiveness of conservation efforts and identifying areas in need of further protection. TSchwartz-Belkin & Portman (2023) introduced various Geospatial technology tools for developing, implementing, and monitoring marine spatial plans. These tools include satellites, water-based platforms with sensors for ocean data collection, vessel tracking, and animal telemetry using multispectral, acoustic, radar, and other technologies.

Effective spatial data management can unlock several additional benefits that contribute to successful green innovation:

- Spatial data can be used to create interactive platforms that visualize environmental challenges and the impact of green innovations. This fosters transparency, facilitates communication between stakeholders, and encourages public participation in environmental decision-making.
- Spatial data analysis can inform the development of targeted environmental policies at local, regional, and national levels. By pinpointing areas with the most pressing environmental issues, policymakers can design effective regulations and incentives to promote green innovation.
- Spatial data can expedite environmental permitting processes for green innovation projects. By providing clear information about potential environmental impacts and proposed mitigation strategies, spatial data analysis can streamline approvals and reduce project delays.

STRATEGIES FOR EFFECTIVE SPATIAL DATA MANAGEMENT

Building on the identified benefits, this section will delve into specific strategies for managing spatial data effectively to support green innovation. Here are some potential areas of exploration:

Data Collection and Integration

This section presents strategies for collecting high-quality spatial data from diverse sources like sensors, satellite imagery, and citizen science initiatives as well as integrating this data from various sources into a unified and accessible platform. High-quality spatial data is the foundation for successful green innovation efforts. Here are some strategies for collecting data from diverse sources:

- Deploying sensor networks across various environments allows for real-time monitoring of environmental parameters like air quality, soil moisture, or water quality. This data provides valuable insights into environmental conditions and can be used to identify areas requiring green innovation solutions.
- Moreover, remote sensing platforms like satellites can gather data on a large scale. Satellite imagery can be used to track changes in land cover, monitor deforestation rates, or assess the potential for renewable energy sources like solar or wind (Bauer, 2020; J. Chen et al., 2022; Khelifi & Mignotte, 2020; J. Li et al., 2022; S. Zhang et al., 2023; Zhao et al., 2023).
- Furthermore, engaging citizens in data collection through apps or online platforms can provide valuable information on local environmental conditions, such as invasive species sightings or pollution hotspots (Adamantopoulou et al., 2023; Santos et al., 2023). Citizen science initiatives can also be used to collect data in areas where deploying traditional sensor networks might be impractical.

Integrating data from these diverse sources requires robust strategies such as:

- Developing and adhering to standardized data formats, such as those promoted by organizations like the Open Geospatial Consortium (OGC), ensures data compatibility and facilitates seamless integration from various sources.
- Building central data repositories (data warehouses) allows for storing, organizing, and managing spatial data from various sources in a unified and accessible platform. This facilitates data analysis and dissemination to stakeholders involved in green innovation efforts.

Data Standardization and Quality Control

Establishing standardized data formats and robust quality control measures to ensure data accuracy and consistency is important. Implementing data validation protocols helps identify and rectify errors or inconsistencies in the collected data. This may involve checking for outliers, ensuring proper geospatial referencing, and verifying data against established standards. Moreover, techniques like data imputation or outlier removal can address missing values or inconsistencies within datasets, ensuring the integrity of the data used for green innovation analysis. Furthermore, detailed metadata documentation for each data set is crucial. Metadata describes the content, origin, format, and quality of the data, allowing for proper interpretation and facilitating future analysis.

Spatial Data Analysis Tools and Techniques

A range of powerful tools and techniques can be applied to analyze spatial data and extract meaningful insights for green innovation projects. For example, GIS software platforms are widely used to visualize, analyze, and manage spatial data (Tu & Hoang, 2023). GIS allows for overlaying different data sets on a map, identifying spatial patterns, and performing spatial queries to inform green innovation initiatives. Moreover, advanced statistical techniques designed for spatial data analysis can be employed to identify spatial relationships, assess trends, and model environmental phenomena. Spatial statistics can be used to identify areas with high concentrations of pollution, model the spread of invasive species, or predict the impact of climate change on different regions. In addition, machine Learning: Machine learning algorithms can be utilized for spatial data analysis tasks such as image classification (e.g., identifying deforestation areas from satellite imagery) or anomaly detection (e.g., pinpointing potential environmental hazards) (Bauer, 2020; J. Chen et al., 2022; S. Zhang et al., 2023).

Knowledge Sharing and Collaboration

Facilitating collaboration and knowledge sharing among stakeholders is critical for maximizing the impact of spatial data in green innovation. Establishing open-access platforms for sharing spatial data can empower diverse stakeholders, including researchers, policymakers, and entrepreneurs, to access and utilize data for developing green innovations. Additionally, encouraging collaborative research projects that bring together scientists, engineers, and policymakers with expertise in spatial data management and green innovation can foster the development of cutting-edge solutions. Furthermore, providing training and capacity-building programs on spatial data management tools and techniques equips various stakeholders with the necessary skills to effectively utilize spatial data in green innovation initiatives.

CHALLENGES AND SOLUTIONS

While spatial data management offers immense potential for green innovation, some challenges need to be addressed to fully harness its power.

Data Access and Ownership

Obtaining and utilizing spatial data for green innovation efforts can be hindered by issues related to data access and ownership. Certain spatial datasets might be restricted due to national security concerns, privacy limitations, or commercial interests. This can limit the availability of valuable data for green innovation initiatives. To address these challenges of restricted access, open data policies should be promoted to encourage government agencies and private organizations to share spatial data publicly, following appropriate anonymization and security protocols. This can increase data accessibility for green innovation projects.

Moreover, data ownership rights might be unclear, particularly for data collected from multiple sources or through citizen science initiatives. This creates uncertainty regarding data usage permissions and can hinder data-sharing efforts. Establishing clear data-sharing agreements between data owners and users can address ownership concerns. These agreements can outline usage permissions, attribution requirements, and data security measures. Furthermore, the establishment of Spatial Data Infrastructures should be encouraged to facilitate data sharing among different stakeholders.

Data Privacy Concerns

Utilizing spatial data for green innovation raises concerns regarding data privacy, particularly when dealing with personal information. Spatial data linked to individuals, such as location data collected through mobile phones, requires careful handling to ensure privacy protection. To address these challenges, anonymizing spatial data by removing personally identifiable information can allow for data utilization while protecting individual privacy.

Moreover, data aggregation practices might inadvertently reveal sensitive information about specific communities. Techniques like differential privacy can help mitigate this risk. Implementing privacy-preserving techniques like differential privacy or federated learning can allow for collaborative data analysis without compromising individual or community privacy.

Technical Expertise and Infrastructure

Effective spatial data management for green innovation requires overcoming challenges related to technical expertise and infrastructure. A skilled workforce with expertise in spatial data analysis, GIS tools, and data science methodologies is crucial for maximizing the value of spatial data in green innovation initiatives. Developing capacity-building programs and training initiatives can equip stakeholders with the necessary technical skills for spatial data management and analysis.

Moreover, building and maintaining robust data infrastructure, including storage solutions, processing capabilities, and data visualization tools, is essential for effective spatial data management. Leveraging cloud-based platforms for data storage, processing, and analysis can provide cost-effective and scalable solutions, particularly for smaller organizations or resource-constrained projects.

CONCLUSION

Effective spatial data management empowers green innovation by utilizing spatial data to identify environmental challenges such as air and water quality, deforestation rates, soil health, and climate change vulnerability. For instance, satellite imagery aids in detecting pollution sources and changes in forest cover, while soil sampling combined with satellite data assesses soil erosion and degradation. Spatial data analysis also guides the development of targeted initiatives like clean air efforts and sustainable forestry practices. Additionally, it optimizes resource allocation by identifying renewable energy resources, sustainable materials deposits, and existing green infrastructure. Furthermore, spatial data tailors innovations to local contexts, informs urban planning for energy efficiency and water management, enhances waste and climate-smart agriculture, and monitors environmental impact post-implementation. Beyond these benefits, effective spatial data management fosters transparency, aids policymaking, and expedites permitting processes for green projects.

Effective spatial data management for green innovation involves several key strategies. Firstly, collecting high-quality spatial data from diverse sources such as sensors, satellites, and citizen science initiatives is crucial. This data can be integrated into unified platforms for accessibility and analysis, facilitated by standardized formats and central repositories. Ensuring data quality through validation protocols and metadata documentation is essential. Secondly, utilizing spatial data analysis tools like GIS and advanced statistical techniques allows for meaningful insights extraction. Machine learning algorithms further enhance analysis capabilities. Thirdly, fostering collaboration and knowledge sharing among stakeholders maximizes spatial data's impact in green innovation. However, challenges like data access, ownership, privacy concerns, and technical expertise need addressing. Open data policies, clear data-sharing agreements, and privacy-preserving techniques are vital solutions, alongside capacity-building programs and cloud-based infrastructure development.

REFERENCES

Abulibdeh, A. (2024). Geospatial assessment of the carbon footprint of water and electricity consumption in residential buildings in Doha, Qatar. *Journal of Cleaner Production, 445*, 141262. Advance online publication. DOI: 10.1016/j.jclepro.2024.141262

Adamantopoulou, S., Karamanlidis, A. A., Dendrinos, P., & Gimenez, O. (2023). Citizen science indicates significant range recovery and defines new conservation priorities for Earth's most endangered pinniped in Greece. *Animal Conservation, 26*(1), 115–125. Advance online publication. DOI: 10.1111/acv.12806

Afeltra, G., Alerasoul, S. A., & Strozzi, F. (2023). The evolution of sustainable innovation: from the past to the future. In *European Journal of Innovation Management* (Vol. 26, Issue 2). DOI: 10.1108/EJIM-02-2021-0113

Ahmed, N. (2024). Spatial vulnerability assessment of urbanites of Rawalpindi to the combined effects of climate change and pandemics using GIS mapping. *Local Environment, 29*(8), 1–19. DOI: 10.1080/13549839.2024.2353048

Bakirci, M. (2024). Enhancing air pollution mapping with autonomous UAV networks for extended coverage and consistency. *Atmospheric Research, 306*, 107480. https://doi.org/https://doi.org/10.1016/j.atmosres.2024.107480. DOI: 10.1016/j.atmosres.2024.107480

Balogun, A. L., Marks, D., Sharma, R., Shekhar, H., Balmes, C., Maheng, D., Arshad, A., & Salehi, P. (2020). Assessing the Potentials of Digitalization as a Tool for Climate Change Adaptation and Sustainable Development in Urban Centres. *Sustainable Cities and Society, 53*, 101888. Advance online publication. DOI: 10.1016/j.scs.2019.101888

Bauer, M. E. (2020). Remote Sensing of Environment: History, Philosophy, Approach and Contributions, 1969 –2019. *Remote Sensing of Environment, 237*, 111522. Advance online publication. DOI: 10.1016/j.rse.2019.111522

Borase, A. A., Bokil, S., & Sakhare, V. (2024). Geospatial solution for sustainable waste management: A case study. *Innovative Infrastructure Solutions, 9*(6), 218. DOI: 10.1007/s41062-024-01539-w

Burton, J., Kemp, D., Barnes, R., & Parmenter, J. (2024). A socio-spatial analysis of Australia's critical minerals endowment and policy implications. *Resources Policy, 88*, 104448. Advance online publication. DOI: 10.1016/j.resourpol.2023.104448

Castellacci, F., & Lie, C. M. (2017). A taxonomy of green innovators: Empirical evidence from South Korea. *Journal of Cleaner Production, 143*, 1036–1047. Advance online publication. DOI: 10.1016/j.jclepro.2016.12.016

Chen, J., Chen, S., Fu, R., Li, D., Jiang, H., Wang, C., Peng, Y., Jia, K., & Hicks, B. J. (2022). Remote Sensing Big Data for Water Environment Monitoring: Current Status, Challenges, and Future Prospects. In *Earth's Future* (Vol. 10, Issue 2). DOI: 10.1029/2021EF002289

Chen, Q., Li, X., Zhang, Z., Zhou, C., Guo, Z., Liu, Z., & Zhang, H. (2023). Remote sensing of photovoltaic scenarios: Techniques, applications and future directions. *Applied Energy, 333*, 120579. Advance online publication. DOI: 10.1016/j.apenergy.2022.120579

Durlević, U., Novković, I., Carević, I., Valjarević, D., Marjanović, A., Batoćanin, N., Krstić, F., Stojanović, L., & Valjarević, A. (2023). Sanitary landfill site selection using GIS-based on a fuzzy multi-criteria evaluation technique: A case study of the City of Kraljevo, Serbia. *Environmental Science and Pollution Research International, 30*(13), 37961–37980. Advance online publication. DOI: 10.1007/s11356-022-24884-8 PMID: 36576628

Fabian, P. S., Kwon, H. H., Vithanage, M., & Lee, J. H. (2023). Modeling, challenges, and strategies for understanding impacts of climate extremes (droughts and floods) on water quality in Asia: A review. In *Environmental Research* (Vol. 225). DOI: 10.1016/j.envres.2023.115617

George, G., Merrill, R. K., & Schillebeeckx, S. J. D. (2021). Digital Sustainability and Entrepreneurship: How Digital Innovations Are Helping Tackle Climate Change and Sustainable Development. *Entrepreneurship Theory and Practice, 45*(5), 999–1027. Advance online publication. DOI: 10.1177/1042258719899425

Graham, C. C. (2024). The role of Geographic Information Systems in mitigating plastics pollution in the Global South—A spatial analysis of recycling facilities in Costa Rica. *The Science of the Total Environment, 937*, 173396. https://doi.org/https://doi.org/10.1016/j.scitotenv.2024.173396. DOI: 10.1016/j.scitotenv.2024.173396 PMID: 38796014

Habib-ur-Rahman, M., Ahmad, A., Raza, A., Hasnain, M. U., Alharby, H. F., Alzahrani, Y. M., ... & El Sabagh, A. (2022). Impact of climate change on agricultural production; Issues, challenges, and opportunities in Asia. *Frontiers in Plant Science, 13*, 925548.

Hinsby, K., Négrel, P., de Oliveira, D., Barros, R., Venvik, G., Ladenberger, A., Griffioen, J., Piessens, K., Calcagno, P., Götzl, G., Broers, H. P., Gourcy, L., van Heteren, S., Hollis, J., Poyiadji, E., Čápová, D., & Tulstrup, J. (2024). Mapping and understanding Earth: Open access to digital geoscience data and knowledge supports societal needs and UN sustainable development goals. *International Journal of Applied Earth Observation and Geoinformation*, *130*, 103835. https://doi.org/https://doi.org/10.1016/j.jag.2024.103835. DOI: 10.1016/j.jag.2024.103835

Huong, P. T., Cherian, J., Hien, N. T., Sial, M. S., Samad, S., & Tuan, B. A. (2021). Environmental management, green innovation, and social–open innovation. *Journal of Open Innovation*, *7*(1), 89. Advance online publication. DOI: 10.3390/joitmc7010089

Islam, S. M. S., Yeşilköy, S., Baydaroğlu, Ö., Yıldırım, E., & Demir, I. (2024). State-level multidimensional agricultural drought susceptibility and risk assessment for agriculturally prominent areas. *International Journal of River Basin Management*, 1–18. Advance online publication. DOI: 10.1080/15715124.2024.2304546

Kamyab, H., Khademi, T., Chelliapan, S., SaberiKamarposhti, M., Rezania, S., Yusuf, M., Farajnezhad, M., Abbas, M., Hun Jeon, B., & Ahn, Y. (2023). The latest innovative avenues for the utilization of artificial Intelligence and big data analytics in water resource management. *Results in Engineering*, *20*, 101566. Advance online publication. DOI: 10.1016/j.rineng.2023.101566

Khan, M. A., Khan, R., Al-Zghoul, T. M., Khan, A., Hussain, A., Baarimah, A. O., & Arshad, M. A. (2024). Optimizing municipal solid waste management in urban Peshawar: A linear mathematical modeling and GIS approach for efficiency and sustainability. *Case Studies in Chemical and Environmental Engineering*, *9*, 100704. https://doi.org/https://doi.org/10.1016/j.cscee.2024.100704. DOI: 10.1016/j.cscee.2024.100704

Khelifi, L., & Mignotte, M. (2020). Deep Learning for Change Detection in Remote Sensing Images: Comprehensive Review and Meta-Analysis. *IEEE Access : Practical Innovations, Open Solutions*, *8*, 126385–126400. Advance online publication. DOI: 10.1109/ACCESS.2020.3008036

Kopp, J., Preis, J., Žák, P., & Vogt, D. (2024). Mapping the Environmental Quality of University Campus Areas for the Needs of Blue-Green Infrastructure Planning. In *The Contribution of Universities Towards Education for Sustainable Development* (pp. 211–231). Springer. DOI: 10.1007/978-3-031-49853-4_13

Külling, N., Adde, A., Lambiel, A., Wicki, S., Guisan, A., Grêt-Regamey, A., & Lehmann, A. (2024). Nature's contributions to people and biodiversity mapping in switzerland: Spatial patterns and environmental drivers. *Ecological Indicators, 163*, 112079. DOI: 10.1016/j.ecolind.2024.112079

Li, J., Huang, X., Tu, L., Zhang, T., & Wang, L. (2022). A review of building detection from very high resolution optical remote sensing images. In *GIScience and Remote Sensing* (Vol. 59, Issue 1). DOI: 10.1080/15481603.2022.2101727

Li, Z., Ma, J., Jiang, F., Zhang, S., & Tan, Y. (2024). Assessing the impacts of urban morphological factors on urban building energy modeling based on spatial proximity analysis and explainable machine learning. *Journal of Building Engineering, 85*, 108675. Advance online publication. DOI: 10.1016/j.jobe.2024.108675

Mousavinezhad, S., Choi, Y., Khorshidian, N., Ghahremanloo, M., & Momeni, M. (2024). Air quality and health co-benefits of vehicle electrification and emission controls in the most populated United States urban hubs: Insights from New York, Los Angeles, Chicago, and Houston. *The Science of the Total Environment, 912*, 169577. Advance online publication. DOI: 10.1016/j.scitotenv.2023.169577 PMID: 38154628

Niknam, A., Sarli, R., Taherizadeh, M., Attarroshan, S., & Pourmansouri, F. (2024). REDD implementation for greenhouse gas reduction and climate change mitigation in Hyrcanian forests: A case study of the Kojoor Watershed, Northern Iran. *Environmental Monitoring and Assessment, 196*(5), 474. DOI: 10.1007/s10661-024-12616-z PMID: 38662125

Nikolaou, G., Neocleous, D., Christou, A., Kitta, E., & Katsoulas, N. (2020). Implementing sustainable irrigation in water-scarce regions under the impact of climate change. In *Agronomy* (Vol. 10, Issue 8). DOI: 10.3390/agronomy10081120

Paithankar, D. N., Pabale, A. R., Kolhe, R. V., William, P., & Yawalkar, P. M. (2023). Framework for implementing air quality monitoring system using LPWA-based IoT technique. *Measurement. Sensors, 26*, 100709. Advance online publication. DOI: 10.1016/j.measen.2023.100709

Pandey, R., Mehta, D., Kumar, V., & Prakash Pradhan, R. (2024). Quantifying soil erosion and soil organic carbon conservation services in indian forests: A RUSLE-SDR and GIS-based assessment. *Ecological Indicators, 163*, 112086. https://doi.org/https://doi.org/10.1016/j.ecolind.2024.112086. DOI: 10.1016/j.ecolind.2024.112086

Poggi, F., & Amado, M. (2024). The spatial dimension of energy consumption in cities. *Energy Policy, 187*, 114023. Advance online publication. DOI: 10.1016/j.enpol.2024.114023

Ren, L., Zhang, W., Wang, Y., Wang, H., Yang, H., Yao, P., & Zhu, Z. (2024). Distribution characteristics and assessment of wind energy resources in the coastal areas of Guangdong. *Sustainable Horizons*, *9*, 100081. Advance online publication. DOI: 10.1016/j.horiz.2023.100081

Salim, W., Wijaya, N., Ramadhan, F., & Iman, H. K. (2024). Spatial vulnerability assessment of climate-related disasters in the Rebana Metropolitan Coastal Area, West Java Province. *IOP Conference Series. Earth and Environmental Science*, *1318*(1), 12008. DOI: 10.1088/1755-1315/1318/1/012008

Santos, E. G., Wiederhecker, H. C., Lopes, L. E., & Marini, M. Â. (2023). Equivalence of citizen science and scientific data for modelling species distribution of birds from a tropical savanna. *Austral Ecology*, *48*(8), 2171–2184. Advance online publication. DOI: 10.1111/aec.13454

Schwartz-Belkin, I., & Portman, M. E. (2023). A review of geospatial technologies for improving Marine Spatial Planning: Challenges and opportunities. In *Ocean and Coastal Management* (Vol. 231). DOI: 10.1016/j.ocecoaman.2022.106280

Shahzad, M., Qu, Y., Zafar, A. U., & Appolloni, A. (2021). Does the interaction between the knowledge management process and sustainable development practices boost corporate green innovation? *Business Strategy and the Environment*, *30*(8), 4206–4222. Advance online publication. DOI: 10.1002/bse.2865

Sharma, D., Thapar, S., Jain, D., & Sachdeva, K. (2024). Mapping the Spatiotemporal Variability of Particulate Matter Pollution in Delhi: Insights from Land Use Regression Modelling. *Photonirvachak (Dehra Dun)*, *52*(6), 1329–1346. Advance online publication. DOI: 10.1007/s12524-024-01879-1

Sharma, N., Saharia, M., & Ramana, G. V. (2024). High resolution landslide susceptibility mapping using ensemble machine learning and geospatial big data. *Catena*, *235*, 107653. Advance online publication. DOI: 10.1016/j.catena.2023.107653

Shekar, P. R., & Mathew, A. (2024). GIS-based assessment of soil erosion and sediment yield using the revised universal soil loss equation (RUSLE) model in the Murredu Watershed, Telangana, India. *HydroResearch*, *7*, 315–325. https://doi.org/ https://doi.org/10.1016/j.hydres.2024.05.003

Shinde, S. P., Barai, V. N., Gavit, B. K., Kadam, S. A., Atre, A. A., Pande, C. B., Pal, S. C., Radwan, N., Tolche, A. D., & Elkhrachy, I. (2024). Assessment of groundwater potential zone mapping for semi-arid environment areas using AHP and MIF techniques. *Environmental Sciences Europe*, *36*(1), 87. DOI: 10.1186/ s12302-024-00906-9

Silvestre, B. S., & Ţîrcă, D. M. (2019). Innovations for sustainable development: Moving toward a sustainable future. In *Journal of Cleaner Production* (Vol. 208). DOI: 10.1016/j.jclepro.2018.09.244

Smith, T., & Boers, N. (2023). Global vegetation resilience linked to water availability and variability. *Nature Communications*, *14*(1), 498. Advance online publication. DOI: 10.1038/s41467-023-36207-7 PMID: 36717585

Tanir, T., Yildirim, E., Ferreira, C. M., & Demir, I. (2024). Social vulnerability and climate risk assessment for agricultural communities in the United States. *The Science of the Total Environment*, *908*, 168346. Advance online publication. DOI: 10.1016/j.scitotenv.2023.168346 PMID: 37939966

Terés-Zubiaga, J., González-Pino, I., Álvarez-González, I., & Campos-Celador, Á. (2023). Multidimensional procedure for mapping and monitoring urban energy vulnerability at regional level using public data: Proposal and implementation into a case study in Spain. *Sustainable Cities and Society*, *89*, 104301. Advance online publication. DOI: 10.1016/j.scs.2022.104301

Tu, T. T., & Hoang, H. Y. (2023). Applications of Geographic Information System (GIS) in Environmental Management. *Scientific Collection «InterConf»*.

Umar, M., & Safi, A. (2023). Do green finance and innovation matter for environmental protection? A case of OECD economies. *Energy Economics*, *119*, 106560. Advance online publication. DOI: 10.1016/j.eneco.2023.106560

Upadhyaya, S., Rao, S., & Rao, M. (2024). Assessment of wind and wave energy potential along the Indian coast. *Cogent Engineering*, *11*(1), 2316950. Advance online publication. DOI: 10.1080/23311916.2024.2316950

Wang, C., Lu, Y. C., & Song, S. R. (2024). Geothermal feasibility analysis inside Yangmingshan National Park, Taiwan. *Geothermics*, *116*, 102834. Advance online publication. DOI: 10.1016/j.geothermics.2023.102834

Wang, S., Zhou, Y., Zhang, X., Wang, Y., Yang, Y., Shang, Y., Chen, Y., & Shi, X. (2024). Mapping and resource evaluation of deep high-temperature geothermal resources in the Jiyang Depression, China. *Energy Geoscience*, 100320. https://doi.org/https://doi.org/10.1016/j.engeos.2024.100320

Wang, Y., Sun, G., Wu, Y., Wang, S., Yue, X., & Zhang, H. (2024). Urban population density and energy conservation: Empirical evidence from 276 cities in China. *Heliyon*, *10*(5), e26882. Advance online publication. DOI: 10.1016/j.heliyon.2024.e26882 PMID: 38434365

Weslati, O., & Serbaji, M. M. (2024). Spatial assessment of soil erosion by water using RUSLE model, remote sensing and GIS: A case study of Mellegue Watershed, Algeria–Tunisia. *Environmental Monitoring and Assessment*, *196*(1), 14. Advance online publication. DOI: 10.1007/s10661-023-12163-z PMID: 38055082

Yasin, E. H., Siddig, A. A., Deiab, E. E., Kornel, C., Hasoba, A., & Osman, A. (2023). *Forest Degradation in Dryland Ecosystems of Sudan: Review of the Causes, Consequences, Assessment Methods, and Potential Solutions*. Mitigating Global Climate Change-Enhancing Adaptation, Evaluation, and Restoration of Mountain Ecosystems.

Zhang, K. Q., Chen, H. H., Tang, L. Z., & Qiao, S. (2022). Green Finance, Innovation and the Energy-Environment-Climate Nexus. *Frontiers in Environmental Science*, *10*, 879681. Advance online publication. DOI: 10.3389/fenvs.2022.879681

Zhang, S., Bai, M., Wang, X., Peng, X., Chen, A., & Peng, P. (2023). Remote sensing technology for rapid extraction of burned areas and ecosystem environmental assessment. *PeerJ*, *11*, e14557. Advance online publication. DOI: 10.7717/peerj.14557 PMID: 36778148

Zhang, Z., Liu, N., & Zhao, L. (2024). Spatio-temporal evolution and driving factors of waste disposal facilities in China. *Journal of Environmental Planning and Management*, *67*(8), 1805–1829. Advance online publication. DOI: 10.1080/09640568.2023.2182187

Zhang, Z., Zhang, G., & Li, L. (2023). The spatial impact of atmospheric environmental policy on public health based on the mediation effect of air pollution in China. *Environmental Science and Pollution Research International*, *30*(55), 116584–116600. Advance online publication. DOI: 10.1007/s11356-022-21501-6 PMID: 35779217

Zhao, S., Tu, K., Ye, S., Tang, H., Hu, Y., & Xie, C. (2023). Land Use and Land Cover Classification Meets Deep Learning: A Review. In *Sensors (Basel, Switzerland)* (Vol. 23, Issue 21). DOI: 10.3390/s23218966

KEY TERMS AND DEFINITIONS

Data Integration: The process of combining data from different sources into a unified and coherent view. This process involves merging data from disparate systems, databases, or formats to create a comprehensive dataset that can be easily accessed and analyzed. Data integration is crucial for enabling organizations to leverage the full potential of their data, facilitating more informed decision-making, and ensuring that all relevant information is available in a consistent and usable format.

Geographic Information System (GIS): A framework for gathering, managing, analyzing, and visualizing spatial and geographic data. GIS integrates various types of data, such as maps, satellite imagery, and statistical data, to provide a comprehensive view of geographic areas. It allows users to create layered maps, perform spatial analysis, and generate detailed reports to support decision-making in fields like urban planning, environmental management, transportation, and disaster response.

Green Innovation: Refers to the development and implementation of new products, processes, services, or business models that reduce environmental impact and promote sustainability. This innovation can occur in various sectors, including energy, transportation, agriculture, and manufacturing, and often involves the use of renewable resources, energy efficiency, waste reduction, and pollution control.

Spatial Data: Also known as geospatial data, refers to information that identifies the geographic location of features and boundaries on Earth. This data is typically represented by coordinates, such as latitude and longitude, or other spatial descriptors like addresses or regions. Spatial data can include various types of information, such as the physical characteristics of the land, infrastructure, population distribution, and environmental conditions.

Spatial Data Management: Refers to the processes and technologies used to efficiently capture, store, manipulate, analyze, and present spatial data. This involves organizing and maintaining spatial data in databases, ensuring its accuracy, consistency, and accessibility for various applications. Spatial data management is essential for supporting geographic information systems (GIS), enabling users to perform complex spatial analyses, make informed decisions, and generate visual representations of geographic information.

Chapter 12
Developing the Volunteer Spatial Information Using OpenStreetMap for Countryside Sustainable Development in UVA Province, Sri Lanka

Ibra Lebbe Mohamed Zahir
https://orcid.org/0000-0001-6553-1986
South Eastern University of Sri Lanka, Sri Lanka

Sundaralingam Suthakaran
Eastern University, Sri Lanka

Zarouk Mohamed Zihan
UNDP, Sri Lanka

Atham Lebbe Iyoob
South Eastern University of Sri Lanka, Sri Lanka

Vijayachandran Thanujan
Uva Wellassa University of Sri Lanka, Sri Lanka

Subeenthiran Naksala
Uva Wellassa University of Sri Lanka, Sri Lanka

ABSTRACT

The OpenStreetMap (OSM) platform aids SDGs by fostering global geospatial data exchange. It's vital in regions lacking commercial incentives, promoting public collaboration. Initiatives like Open Mapping Hub - Asia Pacific support SDGs through participatory mapping. Case studies, like in Sri Lanka's Uva Province, showcase OSM's impact on infrastructure planning, disaster risk reduction, and citizen engagement. Training methods, tools, and outcomes emphasize improved decision-

DOI: 10.4018/979-8-3693-4373-9.ch012

making and stakeholder engagement through data visualization. This underscores the importance of digital technologies for sustainability and quality control.

INTRODUCTION

Volunteer Geographic Information (VGI) emphasizes the volunteer nature of data contribution with active and actual public participation for global digital transformation (Goodchild, 2007; Neis and Zielstra, 2014). The VGI gathers spatial information from the community participating in mapping, along with the most detailed information. This information can be achieved either by tracing georeferenced aerial imagery or by actively collecting Global Position System) GPS tracks using a designated device (Neis and Zielstra, 2014). In addition, a broadband internet connection and extra hardware, such as a smartphone or personal computer, are required. While these prerequisites may appear trivial in most modern societies, we will advanced discuss how they help explain certain patterns in the global distribution of VGI projects.

OpenStreetMap (OSM) is a worldwide digitalizing system that can be user-created content on the web platform to develop free and open-source map data through the efforts of volunteers, which approach is a participatory mapping platform for user-generated geospatial data (Degrossi et al., 2018). A study by Bertolotto et al. (2020) OSM is widely regarded as a leading example of VGI. This reputation stems from its extensive volunteer base (exceeding six million as of May 2020), the substantial volume of spatial data it produces, the high frequency of data updates, the diversity of data formats, its permissive licensing, and the wide range of projects that incorporate OSM data. Goodchild (2008) pointed out that VGI is a general web phenomenon of user-generated content on web-based applications and has supported the prospect of rural information. However, the OSM has recognized the digital platform of the community-based map with natural and man-made features (Albrecht, 2020), as a web-based Geographic Information System (GIS) product that can also be used to access through the smartphone. Sehra et al. (2019) emphasize that the mobile GIS mapping process strengthens the editing, downloading, and uploading of geographic-based information within administrative domains. This process utilizes popular data sources and finds increasing utility in applications such as Wikipedia, Map Box, CartoDB, Field Papers, Maps.me, Java OpenStreetMap (JOSM), Humanitarian OpenStreetMap Team (HOT) Task Manager, and Foursquare. These platform has been used by almost 4.7 million users, contributing almost 6.2 billion GPS points and 514 million lines, which are partially based on 4.6 billion notes and 5.9 million relations that have been uploaded (OSM stats, 2018).

Recently, advanced technology of VGI uses with a public contribution to attaining the SD goal for various applications such as to support several studies including village administrative boundary mapping by public contribution with local knowledge (Kanthi & Purwanto, 2016), urban studies (Goodchild, 2008), environmental monitoring of landscapes and ecologies of the tropical world (Yan et al., 2022; Zhang et al., 2021; Albuquerque et al, 2021), land and land cover map validation (Yan et al., 2020), street networks (Arsanjani et al., 2015; Natera Orozco et al., 2020; Liu, C., & Duan., 2020), community policing and crime analysis (Jelokhani-Niaraki et al., 2020), location-based services (Tan et al., 2020), public health (Goranson et al., 2012), mitigating disaster risk in the novel scope of risk assessment (Suthakaran et al., 2020), sharing spatial data regarding business reviews (Rahimi et al., 2018). It also emerges to promise information sources through VGI from the collaborative (Zook et al., 2010; Herfort et al., 2015; Yagoub, 2015; Mirbabaie et al., 2016), community mapping for urban planning (Suthakaran et al., 2020; Grinberger et al., 2022) and assisting to plan the administrative boundary mapping (Kanthi & Purwanto, 2016). Similarly, spatial data is an essential part of Disaster Risk Reduction (DRR) and allows preparedness. In minimizing DRR, one of the main challenges is the lack of sufficient spatial data. Suthakaran et al. (2022) describes the degree of hazard estimates by constructed elements such as buildings and roads. Therefore, spatial data collection plays a significant role in early warning systems, emergency response services, and the design of DRR to attain for united nation SD goals.

Countryside Sustainable Development (CSD) involves the management of natural resources, the promotion of economic and social development in rural areas. It is a holistic approach to development that takes into consideration the interdependence of social, economic, and environmental factors. For instance, Haklay (2010) emphasized the importance of participatory mapping and the potential of OSM as a collaborative platform for data collection and community engagement. The OSM platform can empower local communities to actively contribute to mapping efforts, fostering a sense of ownership and promoting inclusive decision-making processes. The participation of volunteers in community mapping initiatives is critical for the success of SD, and the use of OSM provides an opportunity for volunteers to contribute towards the development of sustainable communities (Haklay et al., 2010). Moreover, Budhathoki and Haythornthwaite (2013) highlighted the significance of VGI platforms, such as OSM, in enhancing spatial data infrastructure and promoting citizen participation in development processes. The geospatial technologies, including OSM, support urban planning and governance by providing valuable information on population distribution, infrastructure networks, and land use patterns. However, the potential of OSM to bridge data gaps and enhance evidence-based decision-making, particularly in data-scarce environments.

Consequently, the research focused on developing volunteer-generated spatial information through OSM platform for community spatial development in Uva Province, Sri Lanka, is highly valuable for both academic inquiry and practical implementation. In rural regions, access to accurate and current spatial data is limited, which hinders effective planning, infrastructure development, and disaster preparedness. By leveraging OSM, this study highlights a community-driven, cost-effective approach to map and address the unique needs of Uva's rural areas. Through participatory mapping, local residents contribute valuable insights that enhance the accuracy of geographic data, thus empowering communities and creating a sense of ownership over development processes. Additionally, this research provides a model for integrating VGI into SD frameworks, particularly in areas with limited resources. The findings can inform policymakers, local Non-government Organizations (NGOs), and other stakeholders on the potential of VGI to support rural resilience, environmental conservation, and equitable access to services. Furthermore, the study also contributes to the growing body of literature on VGI by exploring its application in Sri Lanka's unique context, helping to bridge gaps in geographic information and laying the groundwork for future community-based initiatives in rural development and environmental management. The study aims to investigate how volunteer spatial information via OSM can support SD in Uva Province, Sri Lanka. In order to addresses the following research questions:

1. How can volunteer-generated spatial information through OSM enhance SD efforts in Uva Province, Sri Lanka?
2. What are the most effective strategies for involving local communities in mapping and data collection processes using OSM?
3. In what ways does OSM-based mapping contribute to specific SD goals, such as infrastructure improvement, environmental conservation, and disaster resilience, in rural contexts?
4. What challenges and limitations exist in implementing community-driven mapping in Uva Province, and how can these be mitigated?

LITERATURE REVIEW

Role of Volunteers in Countryside Sustainable Development

CSD involves the management of natural resources, the promotion of economic and social development in rural areas. It is a holistic approach to development that takes into consideration the interdependence of social, economic, and environmental factors. For instance, Haklay (2010) emphasized the importance of participatory mapping and the potential of OSM as a collaborative platform for data collection and community engagement. The OSM platform can empower local communities to actively contribute to mapping efforts, fostering a sense of ownership and promoting inclusive decision-making processes. Moreover, Budhathoki and Haythornthwaite (2013) highlighted the significance of VGI platforms, such as OSM, in enhancing spatial data infrastructure and promoting citizen participation in development processes. In the specific context of capacity development for local governments, various studies have emphasized the importance of leveraging geospatial data and tools. The geospatial technologies, including OSM, support urban planning and governance by providing valuable information on population distribution, infrastructure networks, and land use patterns. However, the potential of OSM to bridge data gaps and enhance evidence-based decision-making, particularly in data-scarce environments. Furthermore, the use of OSM in disaster risk management has been extensively explored. For example, Neis & Zipf (2008) discussed how OSM can support disaster response and recovery efforts by providing real-time data on infrastructure damage, evacuation routes, and affected areas.

Theoretical frameworks such as the concept of data-driven governance have also been applied to understand the potential of geospatial data and OSM in supporting SD. The source of open and freely available geospatial data, it can contribute to data-driven decision-making and governance processes. However, achieving CSD requires the participation of various stakeholders, including government agencies, private organizations, and local communities. Volunteers are also important stakeholders in CSD as they contribute their time and skills towards various initiatives that promote SD. The use of OSM in community mapping initiatives can provide valuable information on the rural infrastructure and natural resources that can be used for planning and development initiatives (Goodchild, 2008). The participation of volunteers in community mapping initiatives is critical for the success of SD, and the use of OSM provides an opportunity for volunteers to contribute towards the development of sustainable communities (Haklay et al., 2010).

Application of OSM in Community Mapping

Community mapping is a participatory approach to mapping that involves the active participation of community members in the mapping process. These mapping initiatives have been widely used to map the rural infrastructure and to identify areas that require development (Haklay et al., 2010). However, the OSM provides an opportunity for volunteers to contribute towards the creation of spatial information that can be used for planning and development initiatives. Because it is an open-source, mapping platform that allows users to create and edit maps using satellite imagery and GPS data. A study by Goodchild (2008) the OSM platform is widely used in community mapping initiatives as it provides a free and open-source platform that can be used by anyone with an internet connection. The study highlighted that the use of OSM in community mapping initiatives improved the accuracy and completeness of map data and provided valuable information for rural development initiatives. A study conducted by Haklay et al. (2010) expressed that the application of OSM in community mapping initiatives improved the quality of map data and provided valuable information for urban planning. However, the use of OSM in community mapping initiatives has also been explored in the context of disaster management. A study conducted by Zook et al. (2010) explored the use of OSM in community mapping, improved the accuracy and completeness of map data and provided valuable information for disaster management initiatives in Haiti after the earthquake in 2010. Therefore, the use of OSM in community mapping initiatives has the potential to improve the accuracy and completeness of map data and to provide valuable information for rural development initiatives.

Fostering a Collaborative Tactic

The basic principle of open mapping is a care of strong connections for implantation, uptake and sustainability with the range of communities and institutions. It leads to increased legitimacy and stability to share investment of resources and technical expertise and innovation for open data. In a global phenomenon, the open mapping environment is a pre-existing group of activities of individuals and organizations in the target area (Massung et al., 2013). It is a design phase and increases their sense of enhancement of fruitful collaboration. Open mapping provides valuable resources, expertise and authority to map making to contribute to natural resource management, transportation, public health, DRR and urban planning (Cadag & Gaillard, 2012). Globally, the OSM community is dynamic and will, in quite, have a local presence with the familiar map-making process, technical knowledge about mapping work and a mechanism of a group of volunteer participants.

Individual Mappers

Individual mappers are the backbone of the OSM community (Schröder-Bergen et al., 2022). These are people who contribute to the platform on their own, often motivated by a desire to improve maps in their local area or to contribute to a global community. Individual mappers use a range of mapping techniques, including GPS, satellite imagery, and field surveys, to add data to the map. They also use a range of tools, including OSM's web-based editor ID and desktop editing software like JOSM (Suthakaran et al., 2022). Individual mappers contribute to the project in a variety of ways. Some focus on adding roads and other infrastructure to the map, while others focus on adding points of interest like shops, restaurants, and tourist attractions. Some mappers also specialize in adding more complex features like building footprints and land use information. Individual mappers are critical to the success of OSM, as they provide the bulk of the data that makes up the map.

Mapping Communities

Mapping communities are groups of individuals who come together to contribute to OSM in a coordinated way. Such communities can be formed around a shared interest in a particular region or theme, or they can be organized around a specific event or project. Mapping communities are often focused on improving maps in a specific area. For example, the HOT is a mapping community that focuses on improving maps in disaster-prone areas. HOT volunteers work to create detailed maps of these areas before a disaster strikes (Herfort et al., 2021), so that aid organizations have the information they need to respond quickly and effectively when a disaster does occur. Similarly, other mapping communities focus on specific themes. For example, the Missing Maps is a collaboration between several organizations that aims to create detailed maps of areas that are at risk of humanitarian crises, such as areas with high rates of health related issues (Schröder-Bergen et al., 2022). The Missing Maps project relies on volunteers from around the world to create these maps, and has already made a significant impact in improving the ability of aid organizations to respond to crises.

Corporate and Institutional Contributors

Corporate and institutional contributors are organizations that support OSM by contributing data, funding, or technical expertise. These organizations may include technology companies, government agencies, or non-profit organizations. An example of a corporate contributor to OSM is Mapbox, a mapping technology company that provides tools and services that facilitate the creation of maps using OSM data (Mooney & Minghini, 2017). Mapbox further enhances the OSM project by improving the quality of OSM data, particularly in areas that are less well mapped. However, government agencies can also be contributors to the OSM project. For example, the United State of America (USA) has supported the creation of detailed maps of areas that are important for national security reasons, such as the Middle East and Afghanistan. These maps are used by USA Government agencies and aid organizations to support their work in these areas.

Furthermore, nonprofits can also be contributors to the OSM project. For example, the World Bank has supported the creation of detailed maps of developing countries (Panek & Netek, 2019), which are used to support development programs in these areas. The World Bank also provides funding and technical support to local mapping communities, helping them to improve maps in their areas.

Academic and Research Communities

The academic and research communities also play an important role in the OSM project. Researchers use OSM data to study a range of topics, from urban development, land use planning, environment and bio diversity studies to transportation planning to disaster response. The researchers often contribute to the project by creating new tools and techniques for working with OSM data, and by contributing data to the map. Academic institutions also support OSM by providing resources and expertise to the project (Mobasheri et al., 2018). For example, the University of Heidelberg in Germany hosts the OSM database and provides technical support to the project. The university also conducts research on OSM and contributes to the development of new mapping tools and techniques.

Developing Map Literacy for Volunteers Through the OSM Platform

Maps have been used for centuries as tools for navigation, exploration, and communication of spatial information. In recent years, digital maps have become increasingly popular due to their accessibility, ease of use, and the ability to collect and share data in real-time. OSM has made it a popular tool for humanitarian organizations, researchers, and individuals looking to access and contribute to spatial data by open sources. While the availability of open-source maps has increased, the ability to read and interpret these maps, known as map literacy, has not necessarily kept up. Many people lack the necessary skills to effectively use digital maps, particularly in developing countries where access to technology and training may be limited. This can limit the potential benefits that open-source maps can provide in terms of improving disaster response, urban planning, and community development.

Map literacy refers to the ability to read and interpret maps, understand spatial relationships, and use maps effectively in decision-making. It is important for a variety of reasons, including disaster response, urban planning, and community development. However, while digital maps have become more widely available, many people lack the necessary skills to use them effectively (Budhathoki et al., 2008). In the context of volunteer mapping using OSM, map literacy is particularly important. OSM relies on volunteers to collect and contribute data, which is used to create and update maps. However, volunteers may not have the necessary map literacy skills to effectively contribute to OSM (Budhathoki et al., 2008). Several studies have examined map literacy in the context of volunteer mapping using OSM.

Budhathoki et al. (2008) conducted a study in Nepal to examine the map literacy skills of local volunteers. The study highlighted that while many of the volunteers had basic map literacy skills, such as the ability to read a map and understand symbols, they lacked more advanced skills, such as the ability to interpret satellite imagery and understand spatial relationships.

Similarly, Johnson & Sieber (2017) conducted a study in Haiti to examine the map literacy skills of local volunteers. However, several strategies have been identified for improving map literacy in the context of volunteer mapping using OSM. Budhathoki et al. (2008) suggest that training programs should focus on developing advanced map literacy skills, such as the ability to interpret satellite imagery and understand spatial relationships. Johnson & Sieber (2017) suggest that training programs should also focus on developing technical skills, such as the ability to use GPS devices and map editing software. Similarly, other strategies for improving map literacy include the use of interactive and participatory training methods (Budhathoki et al., 2008; Johnson & Sieber, 2017), the creation of user-friendly map editing software (Kumar et al., 2018), and the development of mobile mapping applications that can be used in the field. In addition to the strategies mentioned above, research has also suggested that incorporating local knowledge and cultural context into map literacy training can be beneficial. For example, AlZoubi & Ali (2024) conducted a study in Jordan where they developed a culturally-sensitive map literacy training program for Syrian refugees. They found that incorporating local cultural norms and using language that was familiar to the refugees helped to increase their map literacy skills and their ability to effectively use maps for decision-making.

Furthermore, it is important to consider the accessibility of map literacy training programs. In many developing countries, access to technology and internet connectivity may be limited, which can make it difficult for individuals to access online training resources (Johnson & Sieber, 2017). Strategies such as providing offline training materials and conducting in-person training sessions can help to increase the accessibility of map literacy training programs. Lastly, the importance of promoting the value of map literacy and the potential benefits of open-source maps cannot be overstated. By highlighting the potential applications of maps, including disaster response, urban planning, and community development, individuals may be more motivated to improve their map literacy skills and contribute to volunteer mapping efforts (Budhathoki et al., 2008).

Crowd-Source Spatial Information Beneath an Umbrella for Achieving SDGs

OSM is a widely recognized community-driven open platform to crowd-source geospatial data from around the world through the VGI (Minghini et al., 2017). This platform contributes to publicly owning, modifying and sharing data policy because users can be free and easy to access compared to other GIS applications, whereas building a geodatabase of survey data for various purposes of mapping exercises. Suthakaran et al. (2022) pointed out that most free internet map applications have legal and technical restrictions preventing users from using the data freely. But, the OSM platform both the maps and underlying data can highly be for a user-friendly environment without restrictions. Moreover, in many places of the world where there is no commercial motivation to develop this geospatial data, OSM is often the best available resource both the online and offline modes for public collaborative contribution and freedom of mapping content.

United Nations (UN) agenda for 2030, the Sustainable Development Goals (SDGs) represents the availability of spatial data (Štampach et al., 2021). The OSM platform contributes to achieving the SDGs through open mapping for reducing disaster risk (Clark, et al, 2016). According to the description of Štampach et al. (2021) collaborative community participation is contributed to critical data sources from the context of open data policy of the fundamentals, details, and times for monitoring SDGs. Therefore, the OSM might support reaching the SDGs through the crowd-sourced mapping including buildings, roads, and places example: in UN agenda the Goal 1 - No Poverty, using household footprint maps for land rights which are enhanced to government use, citizen accountability and development planning, Goal 3 - Good Health and Well-being, in 2018, preventing for the malaria campaign in Guatemala and Botswana using HOT, and protect public health in Kenya and Mozambique (Kgoroebutswe et al., 2020), Goal 4 - Quality Education, providing technical and vocational skills to distributing for educational facilities by GIS survey, Goal 5 - Gender Equality, since 2015, the Crowd2Map is established to access the development of services such as schools, hospitals, roads, buildings, and villages for protecting girls at risk of female genital mutilation in Tanzania (UNFPA, 2020), Gola 7 - Affordable and Clean Energy, the large-scale digital household survey and mapping for settlements, electricity and renewable energy in Tanzania (McCray, 2018), Goal 9 - Industry, Innovation, and Infrastructure, the characteristics of information can be visible in the OSM spatial platform of building, road and place such as types, condition and surface quality, etc., Goal 16 - Peace, Justice, and Strong Institution, VGI promotes the collaborative works for enhancing community development with OSM humanitarian agencies in decision-making.

To achieve the SDGs, the spatial data have to be standardized beneath an umbrella. Solís et al. (2018); Štampach et al. (2021) denoted that public participatory mapping helps a greater understanding of connections among places, the people, and the phenomenon of global change and grasps from scholars, youth, and policymakers. However, in Sri Lanka, the OSM is a new terminology for spatial applications that open-source substitutions for uses while helping communities in an organized way to collect geospatial data which becomes value-added products (Suthakaran et al. (2020). It provides adequate methods and skills for contributors through community involvement and empowerment (Herfort et al. 2021). However, modern technology is needed to develop spatial information in developing countries (Kaleel & Zahir, 2016). As described by Suthakaran et al. (2020) the spatial maps are insufficient to create a detailed map with updated information at village levels and are essential for many areas for SD in Sri Lanka. The spatial information should be standardized at the village level because the administrative system emphasizes distributing the resources in convenient ways for community development. In addition, government organizations can utilize the OSM platform to improve village information free of charge with community collaboration to the needs of reliable native information for SD.

The community collaborative SD integrated with the dashboard on OSM is a web-based tool in the study area, which has been increasingly used as a tool for SD planning, as it provides users with a comprehensive view of the data collected on the platform. The dashboard on OSM provides users with a high-resolution map of rural areas, enabling them to identify key features such as roads, waterways, buildings, and other infrastructure. However, the dashboard on OSM to map rural roads that provided a more accurate and up-to-date representation of the road network than existing data sources, and improved rural infrastructure planning for SD. The dashboard on OSM assists to engage local communities, promoting community engagement, improving the accuracy and completeness of the map in mapping informal settlements. In overall, the decision making mapping dashboard with the interface of the OSM is a powerful tool that can help to promote SD, improve disaster response, and engage local communities in the mapping process. Its versatility, user-friendliness, and ability to integrate with other tools and platforms make it an essential tool for policymakers, researchers, and practitioners working in rural areas. Therefore, this study focuses on the development of VGI using OSM for CSD, the role of volunteers in promoting SD, the possible method of collecting geospatial data to achieve SD and model in the OSM platform nationally through community-based participation in Uva province, Sri Lanka.

MATERIALS AND METHODS

Study Area

The Uva Province, once part of the nine provinces of Sri Lanka, is situated in the southeastern regions of the country. Bordered by the Central Province to the north, the Eastern Province to the northeast, the Southern Province to the south, and the Sabaragamuwa Province to the west, Uva boasts a rich tapestry of geography and culture (Figure 1). The provincial capital is the charming city of Badulla, and Uva is administratively divided into two main districts: Badulla and Monaragala. Distinguished by diverse landscapes encompassing mountainous terrains, expansive plains, and verdant valleys, Uva Province is renowned for its breathtaking scenery, expansive tea plantations, and vibrant agricultural activities.

Figure 1. Study area

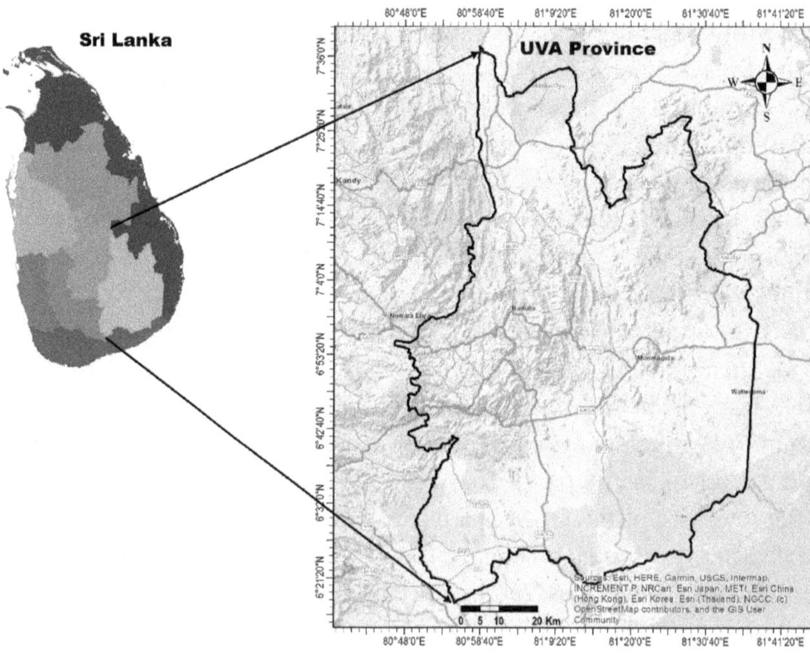

Collecting Data

Establishing a mapping team in Sri Lanka marked the initiation of a comprehensive strategy for collecting geospatial data. The first crucial step involved providing OSM training to 50 local authority technical officers in Uva Province, with the valuable support of the United Nations Development Programme (UNDP). The training process employed the HOT task manager for task, leveraging its capabilities to trace essential elements such as buildings, footprints, road networks, and land uses. Utilizing tools and applications like JOSM editor and OSM (Figure 2).

Figure 2. JOSM interface for the digitizing

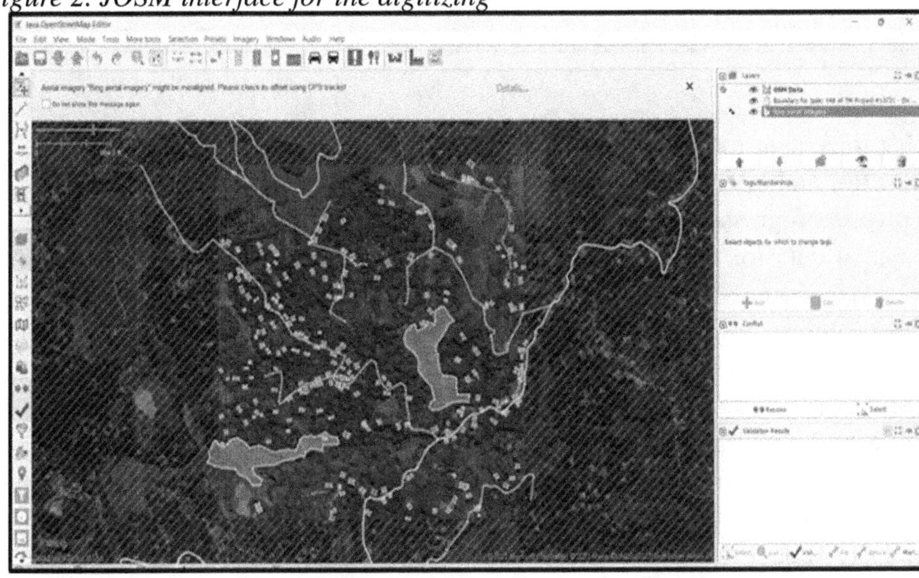

This training not only equipped the local authority technical officers with essential mapping skills but also laid the foundation for robust geospatial data collection, contributing to the broader mapping objectives of the initiative.

Figure 3. Task manager for the Uva province road connectivity project

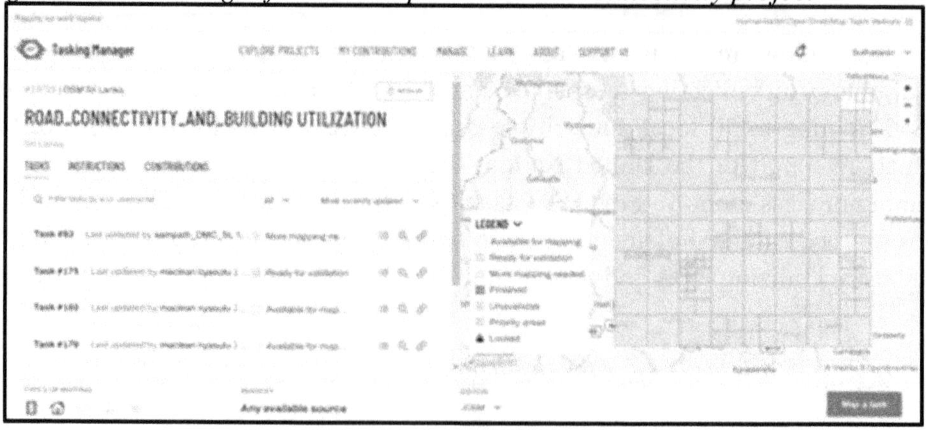

It's important to note that ongoing collaboration and coordination with local authorities and UNDP, were integral to the success of this mapping endeavor. As the project progressed, these efforts aimed to enhance the quality and accuracy of geospatial data for the Uva Province, fostering a collaborative approach toward effective mapping and data utilization by Task Manager (Figure 3).

The volunteer training played a pivotal role in bolstering the sustainability of local authority. Following the training initiative, the number of mappers in the province experienced a remarkable surge, growing from 25 participants to an impressive 52 (Figure 4). This notable increase stands as a significant achievement, underscoring the success of the mapping training program and emphasizing the enduring sustainability of open mapping practices within the community. The expanded pool of mappers not only signifies the effectiveness of the training but also contributes to the ongoing success and resilience of local mapping efforts.

Figure 4. Mappers participants and contribution in task manager

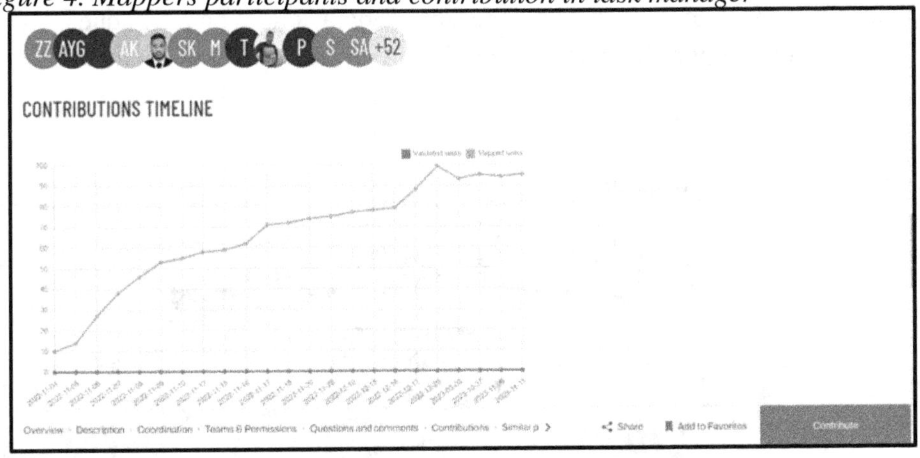

Tools for on the Ground Data Collection

In order to gather data for the road inventory, we created a specialized road inventory sheet. Subsequently, we provided essential training to local authority officers involved in collecting road information, points of interest, and road inventory details. The training covered the utilization of GPS essential, Maps.me, Field Paper, Mapillary, OpenMapkit and GPS tools. Officers were instructed on capturing various road-related data, including road width, bridges, causeways, culverts, road surface characteristics, types of roads, and overall road conditions. This comprehensive approach ensures the accurate and detailed documentation of essential information for effective road management and planning.

Collecting data on the ground is an integral part of editing OSM which typically richer in detail and more accurate than map data that is generated solely by remote tracing. Mappers can choose from a number of free and open tools that facilitate on-the-ground data collection in both online and offline settings.

Method

The flowchart illustrates (Figure 5), the systematic approach of developing VGI for SD in Uva Province, Sri Lanka.

- **Project Setup and Planning** initiates the study by defining objectives, identifying stakeholders, and securing resources and funding.

- **Training and Capacity Building** follows, where volunteers and local authorities are trained in OSM and geospatial data collection techniques, laying the foundation for effective community involvement.

Figure 5. Graphical flowchart

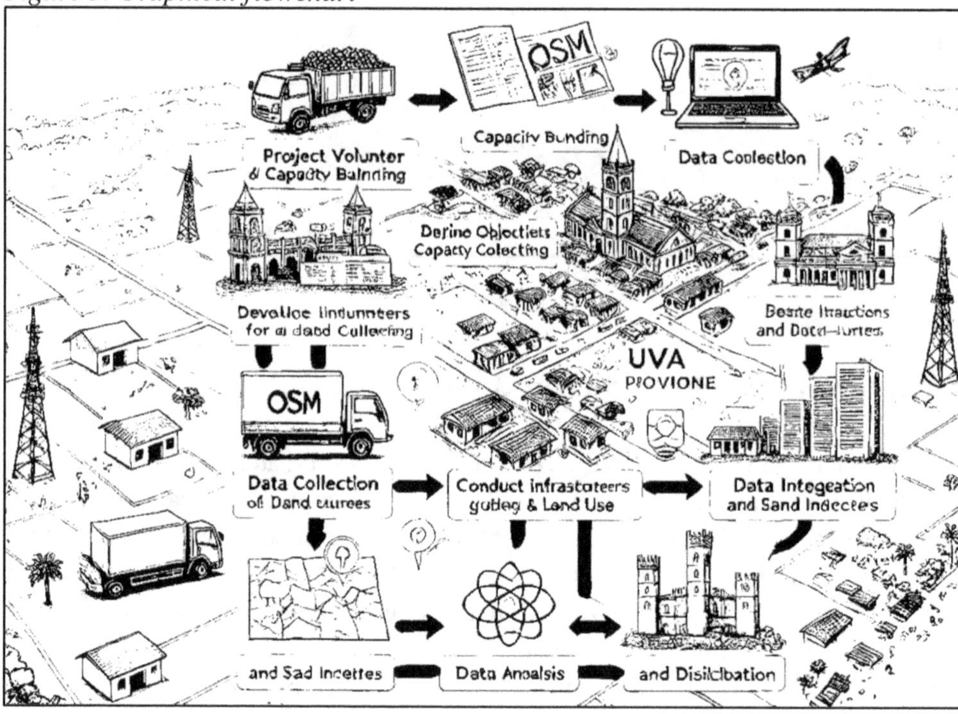

- **Data Collection** involves aerial and GPS-based tracing of features like roads and land use, enhanced by ground data collection for accuracy.
- **Data Integration and Visualization** focuses on exporting the collected data in GeoJSON format, building an interactive map dashboard with MapTiler and ReactJS for visualizing maps and SD indicators.
- **Analysis and Application** identifies gaps in infrastructure, disaster-prone areas, and community needs, using findings to support SDGs and rural development strategies.
- **Monitoring and Evaluation** compares pre- and post-project data, incorporating feedback to enhance project impact.

- **Reporting and Dissemination** concludes the cycle by sharing results with stakeholders, publishing findings, and promoting OSM use for further SD initiatives.

RESULTS

Contributing the Strengthening Transformation, Reconciliation and Inclusive Democratic Engagement (STRIDE)

The UNDP STRIDE Capacity Development of Local Governments project played a crucial role in supporting the achievement of the SDGs through the use of OSM in the Uva Province. This project aimed to enhance the capacity of local governments to effectively plan and implement SD initiatives, with a specific focus on leveraging geospatial data and tools for decision-making. By utilizing OSM, the project empowered local governments to address various development challenges and contribute to the realization of the SDGs. The STRIDE project recognized the potential of OSM in supporting SD efforts by enabling local governments to harness the power of geospatial data.

Use of OSM for the improvement of citizen centric service delivery and digitalization of local authority has been identified in the Uva Province. The project focused on capacity development, knowledge sharing, and technical support to enhance data availability and quality the utilization of OSM in the local government. It organized mapping activities, engaging local government officers, university students, and volunteers to contribute to OSM. By crowdsourcing data, which is crucial for evidence-based decision-making and planning processes.

Figure 6. OSM for local DRR

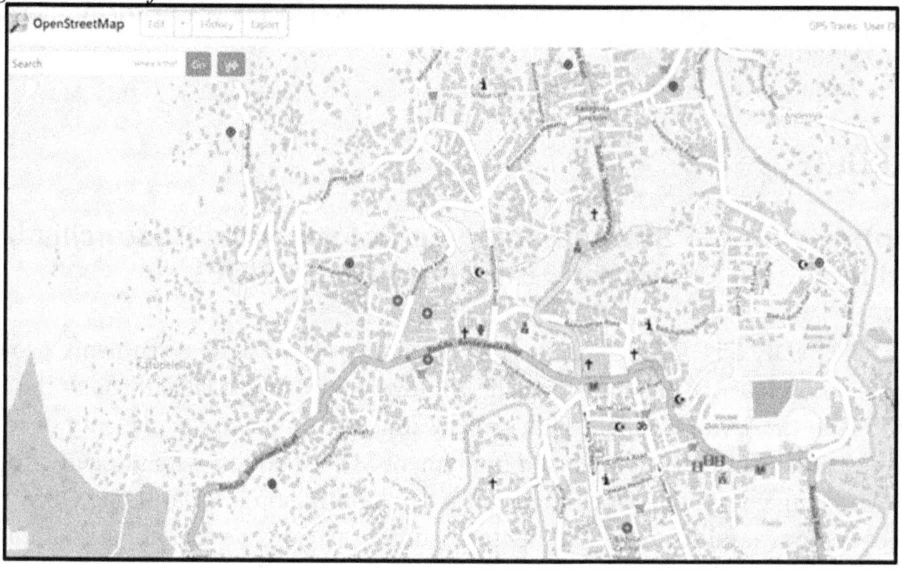

The use of OSM enabled local governments in the Uva Province to improve their planning and decision-making processes. By leveraging accurate and up-to-date geospatial data, they could better understand the needs and priorities of their communities. This information was used to develop development plans and strategies aligned with the SDGs, ensuring that resources were allocated effectively to address pressing challenges. The initiative also contributed to building in-house capacity on OSM, thereby supporting the mapping of local authority road networks in selected areas, a crucial step in gazetting the road networks. Additionally, it enhances services related to providing street lines and building construction permits for citizens when requested for construction works.

The UNDP STRIDE project recognized the importance of citizen engagement and participation in SD initiatives. OSM provided a platform for citizens to actively contribute to the mapping process, giving them a sense of ownership and empowerment. This participatory approach fostered transparency, accountability, and inclusivity in decision-making processes, promoting the achievement of the SDGs. For example, some local authorities have utilized OSM to mark streetlights and have engaged with communities to report any needs for repair or replacement works.

The Uva Province is prone to various natural hazards, including floods and landslides. The project utilized OSM to support DRR efforts by mapping vulnerable areas, infrastructure, and evacuation routes. This information was used to develop comprehensive disaster response plans, ensuring the safety and well-being of communities in times of emergencies (Figure 6). For example, some local authorities have used OSM to mark and identify Dengue breeding hotspots.

OSM played a vital role in supporting infrastructure development in the Uva Province. By mapping existing infrastructure, such as roads, buildings, and utilities, local governments could identify gaps and prioritize investments accordingly. This contributed to the improvement of essential services, such as transportation, healthcare, and education, which are crucial for achieving the SDGs. For example, local authorities are in the process of demarcating landslide-prone areas in their respective jurisdictions, which will enable them to enhance services related to the approval of building permits.

The UNDP STRIDE project facilitated cross-sector collaboration among local governments, civil society organizations, academia, and the private sector. By utilizing OSM as a common platform, stakeholders were able to share data, knowledge, and best practices, fostering a multi-stakeholder approach to sustainable development. This collaboration enhanced the effectiveness and efficiency of development efforts in the Uva Province. Additionally, the project emphasized capacity development at the local level by organizing training programs and workshops to enhance the technical skills of local government officials and other stakeholders in utilizing OSM for SD. By building local capacity, the project ensured the sustainability and long-term impact of its interventions, empowering local governments.

Furthermore, the project recognized the importance of environmental conservation for SD. OSM was used to map and monitor natural resources, protected areas, and biodiversity hotspots in the Uva Province. This information helped local governments formulate policies and strategies for effective environmental management, contributing to SDG 15 (Life on Land). The project also engaged with policymakers and stakeholders to advocate for policies promoting the use of geospatial data and OSM for SD. It raised awareness about OSM's potential in achieving the SDGs and demonstrated its impact through successful case studies and pilot projects, creating an enabling environment for utilizing OSM in development planning and implementation.

OSM played a crucial role in improving access to basic services for marginalized communities in the Uva Province. By mapping schools, healthcare facilities, water sources, and sanitation infrastructure, local governments identified areas with inadequate service coverage. This information enabled targeted interventions to ensure equitable access to essential services, supporting SDG 3 (Good Health and Well-being) and SDG 6 (Clean Water and Sanitation). The project also used OSM to map agricultural areas, irrigation systems, and marketplaces, aiding local governments in designing agricultural development plans, promoting sustainable farming practices, and improving market linkages. These efforts contributed to SDG 2 (Zero Hunger) and SDG 8 (Decent Work and Economic Growth).

Additionally, OSM was utilized to map tourist attractions, heritage sites, and recreational areas. By promoting sustainable tourism practices and improving infrastructure in these areas, local governments contributed to SDG 8 (Decent Work and Economic Growth) and SDG 11 (Sustainable Cities and Communities). OSM also provided a valuable tool for monitoring and evaluating the impact of development projects in the Uva Province. By comparing pre- and post-project maps, local governments could assess the effectiveness of interventions and identify areas for improvement, facilitating evidence-based decision-making and accountability, contributing to SDG 17 (Partnerships for the Goals).

Moreover, the project facilitated knowledge sharing and replication of best practices beyond the Uva Province. Lessons learned, methodologies, and data collected through the use of OSM were shared with other provinces, fostering a culture of innovation and collaboration, supporting the achievement of the SDGs at the national level. The Uva Province, being vulnerable to climate change impacts such as erratic rainfall patterns and increased temperatures, used OSM to map climate-related risks like flood-prone areas and drought-susceptible regions. This information facilitated the development of climate change adaptation and mitigation strategies, supporting SDG 13 (Climate Action).

Developed Dashboard for Visualizing Data

To transform complex data into meaningful and understandable forms, data visualization is very important. For Visualizing the data as easy, understandable and accessible for any kind of audience this dashboard gave a space for the graphical representation maps. With its powerful filtering capabilities, which allow users to analyze certain information selectively, this visualization boosted decision-making capacity. This system capacity is far more useful in the context of SD for presenting complicated information, finding patterns and trends, and guiding decision-making processes.

Figure 7.Developed dashboard for data visualization: Boundary map.

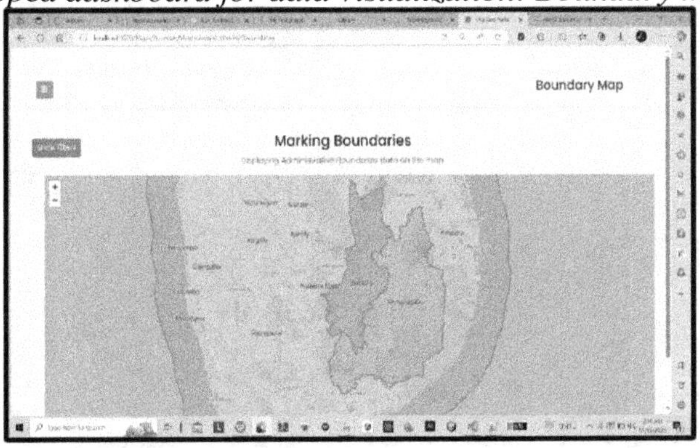

Figure 8. Building

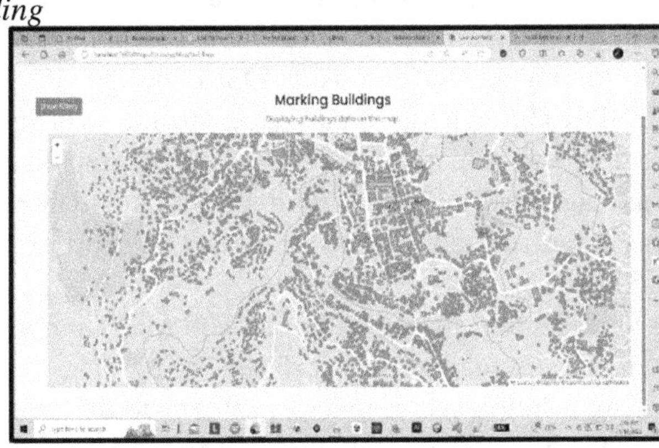

Figure 9. Road

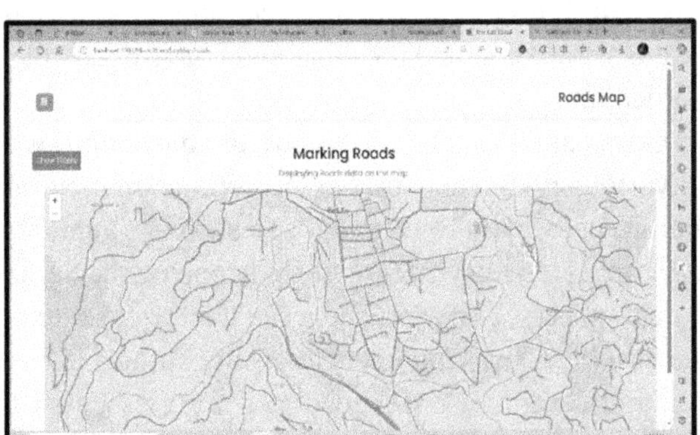

Figure 10. Filter

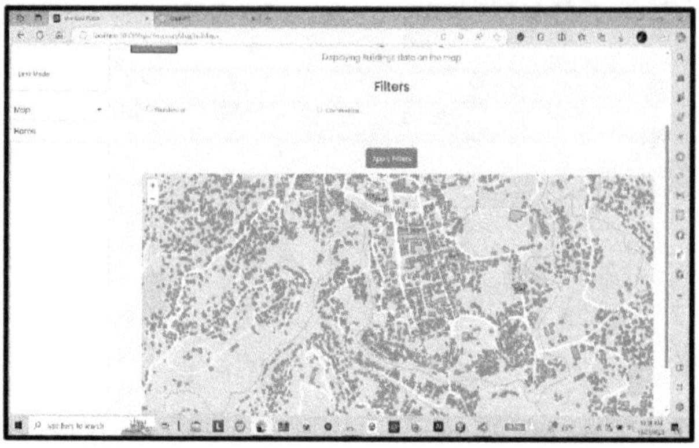

The study initiative utilized pre-existing geospatial data that had been meticulously gathered and mapped as part of an ongoing project. This data originated from a comprehensive strategy initiated by forming a mapping team in Sri Lanka. The team received training sessions on using OSM and the HOT Task Manager, supported by the UNDP. Through this training, local residents in the Uva Province's local authority were able to map and trace important geographic features, such as land use, buildings, and road networks. Following this collaborative effort, the geospatial data was organized and exported from HOT Export to create GeoJSON files aligned with SD goals.

As part of the visualization strategy, ReactJS and MapTiler were combined to create a comprehensive and interactive interface (Figure 7, 8, 9 & 10). MapTiler provided the mapping solution and seamlessly integrated the extracted GeoJSON data, while ReactJS facilitated the development of user-friendly interfaces. These GeoJSON datasets, sourced from Hot Export, formed the basis for different layers representing various aspects of SD. During the development phase, top priority was given to applying state-of-the-art visualization methods to accurately depict the pre-existing GeoJSON data. Integrating graphical components such as graphs, charts, and maps into the dashboard enabled the clear and comprehensible communication of complex SD indicators.

Consequently, extra care was taken to ensure the dashboard was accessible and adjustable across various platforms and devices. It was meticulously crafted with JavaScript programming to adapt to different screen sizes, guaranteeing an optimal user experience. Rigorous testing was conducted to ensure the dashboard functioned correctly, loaded data quickly, and provided a satisfactory user experience. Following these tests, the dashboard was deployed to ensure authorized users could access it. Iterative testing and continuous user feedback were essential in enhancing the dashboard's functionality and performance.

DISCUSSION

The UNDP STRIDE CDLG project effectively utilized OSM to support the achievement of the SDGs in the Uva Province. Through the project's focus on capacity development, knowledge sharing, and technical support, local governments were empowered to leverage geospatial data and tools for decision-making, planning, and implementation of SD initiatives. This studies have emphasized the potential of OSM in enhancing data availability, improving planning processes, promoting citizen engagement, supporting disaster risk management, and fostering collaboration across sectors. The use of OSM has proven beneficial in areas such as environmental conservation, access to basic services, agricultural development, climate change adaptation and mitigation, tourism promotion, and monitoring and evaluation of development. By enhancing data quality and availability, local governments were better equipped to understand community needs and prioritize resources accordingly. The participatory nature of OSM enabled citizens to actively contribute to mapping efforts, fostering transparency, accountability, and inclusivity in decision-making processes.

Furthermore, OSM supported disaster risk management efforts by providing critical information on vulnerable areas, infrastructure, and evacuation routes. It facilitated infrastructure development planning, improved access to basic services, and promoted sustainable agricultural practices. OSM also played a crucial role in monitoring and evaluating development projects, ensuring their impact and supporting evidence-based decision-making.

The process of developing a data visualization dashboard, as discussed earlier, involves key steps for creating an effective tool to communicate complex data. Initially, data visualization dashboards are crucial in enhancing data comprehension and supporting evidence-based decision-making. By visually representing data in a clear and intuitive manner, dashboards allow users to quickly understand underlying patterns, trends, and relationships within the data. This empowers decision-makers to make informed choices and develop strategies to address sustainability challenges effectively.

Additionally, data visualization dashboards promote stakeholder engagement and transparency in SD initiatives. When data is presented visually and made accessible to a broad range of stakeholders, it fosters transparency and accountability. Visualizations enable stakeholders to explore and interact with the data, encouraging active participation and involvement in decision-making processes. This inclusiveness and transparency build trust and credibility among stakeholders.

Furthermore, data visualization dashboards help overcome data complexity and information overload. By presenting data in a visually appealing and interactive manner, dashboards simplify the understanding of complex information. Users can explore specific aspects of the data, filter information based on their needs, and gain valuable insights without being overwhelmed by excessive data.

Moreover, data visualization dashboards address challenges in sustainable development by providing real-time data updates, tracking progress toward goals, and identifying areas for intervention. Dashboards can monitor key performance indicators (KPIs) related to specific SDGs, allowing decision-makers to evaluate the impact of interventions and take timely actions to address gaps or challenges.

In the context of SD, data often originates from diverse sources, including government agencies, research institutions, and citizen-generated data. Developing a data visualization dashboard requires integrating data from these disparate sources to provide a comprehensive view of the situation. This integration can be challenging due to variations in data formats, quality, and compatibility. However, by implementing data integration strategies and ensuring data interoperability, dashboards can effectively consolidate and visualize data from multiple sources.

Finally, the field of data visualization is continuously evolving, with future advancements offering promising opportunities for supporting SD. Advances in technologies, such as machine learning and artificial intelligence, can enable automated data analysis and dynamic visualizations. The integration of real-time data streams, Internet of Things (IoT) devices, and spatial data can further enhance the capabilities of data visualization dashboards in monitoring and managing SD initiatives.

CONCLUSIONS

Finally, the UNDP STRIDE CDLG project's utilization of OSM effectively supported the achievement of the SDGs in the Uva Province. It demonstrated the value of geospatial data and OSM in enhancing planning processes, promoting citizen engagement, supporting disaster risk management, and fostering collaboration across sectors. The project's success serves as a valuable example for future initiatives aiming to leverage geospatial data for SD at the local level. Similarly, the development of data visualization dashboards is a valuable approach to support SD initiatives. These dashboards enhance data understanding, facilitate evidence-based decision-making, promote stakeholder engagement and transparency, and address the challenges of data complexity and information overload. By leveraging the power of data visualization, organizations and decision-makers can effectively communicate insights, monitor progress, and drive SD efforts.

REFERENCES

Albrecht, C. M., Zhang, R., Cui, X., Freitag, M., Hamann, H. F., Klein, L. J., & Lu, S. (2020). Change detection from remote sensing to guide OpenStreetMap labeling. *ISPRS International Journal of Geo-Information*, *9*(7), 427. DOI: 10.3390/ijgi9070427

Albuquerque, U. P., Ludwig, D., Feitosa, I. S., de Moura, J. M. B., Gonçalves, P. H. S., da Silva, R. H., & Ferreira, W. S.Junior. (2021). Integrating traditional ecological knowledge into academic research at local and global scales. *Regional Environmental Change*, *21*(2), 1–11. DOI: 10.1007/s10113-021-01774-2

Alzoubi, F. A., & Ali, R. A. (2024). Breaking Silence: Women and Men's Experiences of Preventing IPV. *The Qualitative Report*, *29*(3). Advance online publication. DOI: 10.46743/2160-3715/2024.6535

Arsanjani, J. J., Mooney, P., Helbich, M., & Zipf, A. (2015). An exploration of future patterns of the contributions to OpenStreetMap and development of a Contribution Index. *Transactions in GIS*, *19*(6), 896–914. DOI: 10.1111/tgis.12139

Bertolotto, M., McArdle, G., & Schoen-Phelan, B. (2020). Volunteered and crowdsourced geographic information: The OpenStreetMap project. *Journal of Spatial Information Science*, *20*(20), 65–70. DOI: 10.5311/JOSIS.2020.20.659

Boss, D., Nelson, T., Winters, M., & Ferster, C. J. (2018). Using crowdsourced data to monitor change in spatial patterns of bicycle ridership. *Journal of Transport & Health*, *9*, 226–233. DOI: 10.1016/j.jth.2018.02.008

Budhathoki, N. R., Bruce, B., & Nedovic-Budic, Z. (2008). Reconceptualizing the role of the user of spatial data infrastructure. *GeoJournal*, *72*(3-4), 149–160. DOI: 10.1007/s10708-008-9189-x

Budhathoki, N. R., & Haythornthwaite, C. (2013). Motivation for open collaboration: Crowd and community models and the case of OpenStreetMap. *The American Behavioral Scientist*, *57*(5), 548–575. DOI: 10.1177/0002764212469364

Cadag, J. R. D., & Gaillard, J. C. (2012). Integrating knowledge and actions in disaster risk reduction: The contribution of participatory mapping. *Area*, *44*(1), 100–109. DOI: 10.1111/j.1475-4762.2011.01065.x

Clark, C., Maron, M., Patel, D., Radford, T., Soden, R. J., & Uithol, P. (2016). *Open mapping for the SDGs: a practical guide to launching and growing open mapping initiatives at the national and local levels* (No. 139458, pp. 1-27). The World Bank.

Degrossi, L. C., Porto de Albuquerque, J., Santos Rocha, R. D., & Zipf, A. (2018). A taxonomy of quality assessment methods for volunteered and crowdsourced geographic information. *Transactions in GIS*, *22*(2), 542–560. DOI: 10.1111/tgis.12329 PMID: 29937686

Elwood, S. (2010). Geographic information science: Emerging research on the societal implications of the geospatial web. *Progress in Human Geography*, *34*(3), 349–357. DOI: 10.1177/0309132509340711

Goodchild, M. F. (2007). Citizens as sensors: The world of volunteered geography. *GeoJournal*, *69*(4), 211–221. DOI: 10.1007/s10708-007-9111-y

Goodchild, M. F. (2008). The use cases of digital earth. *International Journal of Digital Earth*, *1*(1), 31–42. DOI: 10.1080/17538940701782528

Goodchild, M. F., & Glennon, J. A. (2010). Crowdsourcing geographic information for disaster response: A research frontier. *International Journal of Digital Earth*, *3*(3), 231–241. DOI: 10.1080/17538941003759255

Goodchild, M. F., & Glennon, J. A. (2010). Crowdsourcing geographic information for disaster response: A research frontier. *International Journal of Digital Earth*, *3*(3), 231–241. DOI: 10.1080/17538941003759255

Goranson, C., Thihalolipavan, S., & di Tada, N. (2012). VGI and Public Health: Possibilities and Pitfalls. Crowdsourcing Geographic Knowledge: Volunteered Geographic Information (VGI). *Theory into Practice*, 329–340.

Grinberger, A. Y., Minghini, M., Yeboah, G., Juhász, L., & Mooney, P. (2022). Bridges and barriers: An exploration of engagements of the research community with the OpenStreetMap community. *ISPRS International Journal of Geo-Information*, *11*(1), 54.

Hagen, E. (2020). Sustainability in OpenStreetMap Building a More Stable Ecosystem in OSM for Development and Humanitarianism.

Haklay, M. (2010). How good is volunteered geographical information? A comparative study of OpenStreetMap and Ordnance Survey datasets. *Environment and Planning. B, Planning & Design*, *37*(4), 682–703. DOI: 10.1068/b35097

Haklay, M., Basiouka, S., Antoniou, V., & Ather, A. (2010). How many volunteers does it take to map an area well? The validity of Linus' law to volunteered geographic information. *The Cartographic Journal*, *47*(4), 315–322. DOI: 10.1179/000870410X12911304958827

Herfort, B., Eckle, M., de Albuquerque, J. P., & Zipf, A. (2015, May). Towards assessing the quality of volunteered geographic information from OpenStreetMap for identifying critical infrastructures. In *ISCRAM*.

Herfort, B., Lautenbach, S., Porto de Albuquerque, J., Anderson, J., & Zipf, A. (2021). The evolution of humanitarian mapping within the OpenStreetMap community. *Scientific reports, 11*(1), 3037. https://doi.org/DOI: 10.1038/s41598-021-82404-z

Jelokhani-Niaraki, M., Bastami Mofrad, R., Yazdanpanah Dero, Q., Hajiloo, F., & Sadeghi-Niaraki, A. (2020). A volunteered geographic information system for monitoring and managing urban crimes: A case study of Tehran, Iran. *Police Practice and Research, 21*(6), 547–561. DOI: 10.1080/15614263.2019.1644175

Johnson, P. A., & Sieber, R. E. (2017). The Geoweb for community-based organizations: Tool development, implementation, and sustainability in an era of Google Maps. *The Journal of Community Informatics, 13*(1). Advance online publication. DOI: 10.15353/joci.v13i1.3295

Kaleel, M., & Zahir, I. (2016). Web Based Land Information System for Nintavur Divisional Secretariat Division (DSD), Sri Lanka. *Journal of Geography. Environment and Earth Science International, 5*(4), 1–6.

Kanthi, N. S., & Purwanto, T. H. (2016, November). Application of OpenStreetMap (OSM) to support the mapping village in Indonesia. In *IOP Conference Series: Earth and Environmental Science* (Vol. 47, No. 1, p. 012003). IOP Publishing. DOI: 10.1088/1755-1315/47/1/012003

Kgoroebutswe, T. K., Makate, N., Fillinger, U., Mpho, M., Segoea, G., Sangoro, P. O., Mutero, C. M., Chanda, E., Ntebela, D., Mogopa, M., Mosweunyane, T., & Nkya, T. E. (2020). Vector control for malaria elimination in Botswana: Progress, gaps and opportunities. *Malaria Journal, 19*(1), 1–12. DOI: 10.1186/s12936-020-03375-6 PMID: 32843037

Kgoroebutswe, T. K., Makate, N., Fillinger, U., Mpho, M., Segoea, G., Sangoro, P. O., Mutero, C. M., Chanda, E., Ntebela, D., Mogopa, M., Mosweunyane, T., & Nkya, T. E. (2020). Vector control for malaria elimination in Botswana: Progress, gaps and opportunities. *Malaria Journal, 19*(1), 1–12. DOI: 10.1186/s12936-020-03375-6 PMID: 32843037

Kumar, N., Singh, S. K., Mishra, V. N., Reddy, G. O., & Bajpai, R. K. (2018). Open-source satellite data and GIS for land resource mapping. Geospatial Technologies in Land Resources Mapping, *Monitoring and Management*, 185-200.

Liu, C., & Duan, D. (2020). Spatial inequality of bus transit dependence on urban streets and its relationships with socioeconomic intensities: A tale of two megacities in China. *Journal of Transport Geography*, *86*, 102768. DOI: 10.1016/j.jtrangeo.2020.102768

Liu, X., Zeng, X., & Chen, H. (2018). Exploring the determinants of citizen participation in voluntary geographic information initiatives. *International Journal of Geographical Information Science*, *32*, 1423–1440.

Massung, E., Coyle, D., Cater, K. F., Jay, M., & Preist, C. (2013, April). Using crowdsourcing to support pro-environmental community activism. In *Proceedings of the SIGCHI Conference on human factors in Computing systems* (pp. 371-380). DOI: 10.1145/2470654.2470708

McCray, N. (2018). Mapping Energy Access in Rural Tanzania: 2017 Summer Internship with the World Resources Institute. https://commons.clarku.edu/idce_masters_papers/203

McCray, N. (2018). Mapping Energy Access in Rural Tanzania: 2017 Summer Internship with the World Resources Institute.

McLafferty, S. L., & Wang, F. (2012). Spatial disparities in access to nursing home facilities in Illinois: Implications for long-term care policy. *The Gerontologist*, *52*, 219–230.

Minghini, M., Antoniou, V., Fonte, C. C., Estima, J., Olteanu-Raimond, A. M., See, L., & Lupia, F. (2017). The relevance of protocols for VGI collection. In *Mapping and the citizen sensor* (pp. 223–247). Ubiquity Press.

Mirbabaie, M., Stieglitz, S., & Volkeri, S. (2016, January). Volunteered geographic information and its implications for disaster management. In *2016 49th Hawaii International Conference on System Sciences (HICSS)* (pp. 207-216). IEEE. DOI: 10.1109/HICSS.2016.33

Mobasheri, A., Zipf, A., & Francis, L. (2018). OpenStreetMap data quality enrichment through awareness raising and collective action tools—Experiences from a European project. *Geo-Spatial Information Science*, *21*(3), 234–246. DOI: 10.1080/10095020.2018.1493817

Mobasheri, A., Zipf, A., & Francis, L. (2018). OpenStreetMap data quality enrichment through awareness raising and collective action tools—Experiences from a European project. *Geo-Spatial Information Science*, *21*(3), 234–246. DOI: 10.1080/10095020.2018.1493817

Mooney, P., & Minghini, M. (2017). A Review of OpenStreetMap Data. In Foody, G., See, L., Fritz, S., Mooney, P., Olteanu-Raimond, A.-M., Fonte, C. C., & Antoniou, V. (Eds.), *Mapping and the Citizen Sensor* (pp. 37–59). Ubiquity Press., DOI: 10.5334/bbf

Mooney, P., Minghini, M., Foody, G. M., See, L., Fritz, S., Mooney, P., & Antoniou, V. (2017). *A review of OpenStreetMap data*. Mapping and the Citizen Sensor.

Natera Orozco, L. G., Deritei, D., Vancso, A., & Vasarhelyi, O. (2020). Quantifying life quality as walkability on urban networks: The case of Budapest. In *Complex Networks and Their Applications VIII: Volume 2 Proceedings of the Eighth International Conference on Complex Networks and Their Applications COMPLEX NETWORKS 2019 8* (pp. 905-918). Springer International Publishing.

Neis, P., & Zielstra, D. (2014). Recent Developments and Future Trends in Volunteered Geographic Information Research: The Case of OpenStreetMap. *Future Internet*, *6*(1), 76–106. DOI: 10.3390/fi6010076

Neis, P., Zielstra, D., & Zipf, A. (2011). The street network evolution of crowdsourced maps: OpenStreetMap in Germany 2007–2011. *Future Internet*, *4*(1), 1–21. DOI: 10.3390/fi4010001

Panek, J., & Netek, R. (2019). Collaborative mapping and digital participation: A tool for local empowerment in developing countries. *Information (Basel)*, *10*(8), 255. DOI: 10.3390/info10080255

Paudel, B., & Thapa, R. B. (2018). Community mapping for disaster risk reduction and management: A review. *International Journal of Disaster Risk Reduction*, *31*, 1099–1112.

Rahimi, F. B., Levy, R. M., Boyd, J. E., & Dadkhahfard, S. (2018). Human behaviour and cognition of spatial experience; a model for enhancing the quality of spatial experiences in the built environment. *International Journal of Industrial Ergonomics*, *68*, 245–255. DOI: 10.1016/j.ergon.2018.08.002

Schröder-Bergen, S., Glasze, G., Michel, B., & Dammann, F. (2022). De/colonizing OpenStreetMap? Local mappers, humanitarian and commercial actors and the changing modes of collaborative mapping. *GeoJournal*, *2022*(87), 5051–5066. DOI: 10.1007/s10708-021-10547-7

Sehra, S. S., Singh, J., Rai, H. S., & Anand, S. S. (2020). Extending processing toolbox for assessing the logical consistency of OpenStreetMap data. *Transactions in GIS*, *24*(1), 44–71. DOI: 10.1111/tgis.12587

Solís, P., McCusker, B., Menkiti, N., Cowan, N., & Blevins, C. (2018). Engaging global youth in participatory spatial data creation for the UN sustainable development goals: The case of open mapping for malaria prevention. *Applied Geography (Sevenoaks, England)*, *98*, 143–155. DOI: 10.1016/j.apgeog.2018.07.013

Štampach, R., Herman, L., Trojan, J., Tajovská, K., & Řezník, T. (2021). Humanitarian mapping as a contribution to achieving sustainable development goals: Research into the motivation of volunteers and the ideal setting of mapathons. *Sustainability (Basel)*, *13*(24), 13991. DOI: 10.3390/su132413991

Suthakaran, S., Jayakody, S., Subasinghe, S., Seneviratne, N., & Alahakoon, R. (2022). Mapping the Flood Risk Exposure Using Open-Source Geospatial Tools and Techniques: A Case of Gampaha Divisional Secretariat Division, Sri Lanka. *Journal of Geoscience and Environment Protection*, *10*(10), 18–31. DOI: 10.4236/gep.2022.1010002

Suthakaran, S., Withanage, A., Gunawardhane, M., & Gunatilake, J. (2018, December). A flood risk assessment based on an OpenStreetMap application: a case study in Manmunai North Divisional Secretariat of Batticaloa, Sri Lanka. In *FOSS4G Asia 2018 conference. Department of Town and Country Planning, University of MoratuwaMorawa. Sri Lanka* (pp. 02-05).

Tan, Z., Wang, C., Yan, C., Zhou, M., & Jiang, C. (2020). Protecting privacy of location-based services in road networks. *IEEE Transactions on Intelligent Transportation Systems*, *22*(10), 6435–6448. DOI: 10.1109/TITS.2020.2992232

Tanzania, N. F. P. A., & Tanzania, U. N. F. P. A. (2020). *Fact Sheet: FGM in the United Republic of Tanzania*. UNFPA., Available from https://tanzania.unfpa.org/en/publications/fact-sheet-fgm-united-republic-tanzania

UNFPA. (2018). Crowdsourced maps, East and Southern Africa, *Tanzania*. 2018. https://esaro.unfpa.org/en/news/girls-escaping-fgm-rural-tanzania-crowdsourced-maps-show-way-safety

Wesolowski, A., Eagle, N., Noor, A. M., Snow, R. W., Buckee, C. O., & Simeone, A. (2014). The impact of biases in mobile phone ownership on estimates of human mobility. *Journal of the Royal Society, Interface*, *2014*(11), 20120986. PMID: 23389897

Yagoub, M. M. (2015). Public perception on disaster management using volunteered geographic information (VGI): Case of UAE. *ISPRS Annals of the Photogrammetry, Remote Sensing and Spatial Information Sciences*, *2*(W2), 241–246. DOI: 10.5194/isprsannals-II-2-W2-241-2015

Yan, J., Chen, X., Chen, Y., & Liang, D. (2020). Multistep prediction of land cover from dense time series remote sensing images with temporal convolutional networks. *IEEE Journal of Selected Topics in Applied Earth Observations and Remote Sensing*, *13*, 5149–5161. DOI: 10.1109/JSTARS.2020.3020839

Yan, J., Li, G., Qi, G., Qiao, H., Nie, Z., Huang, C., & Yao, X. (2021). Landscape ecological risk assessment of farming-pastoral ecotone in China based on terrain gradients. *Human and Ecological Risk Assessment*, *27*(8), 2124–2141. DOI: 10.1080/10807039.2021.1956300

Zhang, X., Estoque, R. C., Murayama, Y., & Ranagalage, M. (2021). Capturing urban heat island formation in a subtropical city of China based on Landsat images: Implications for sustainable urban development. *Environmental Monitoring and Assessment*, *193*(3), 1–13. DOI: 10.1007/s10661-021-08890-w PMID: 33587190

Zook, M., Graham, M., Shelton, T., & Gorman, S. (2010). Volunteered geographic information and crowdsourcing disaster relief: A case study of the Haitian earthquake. *World Medical & Health Policy*, *2*(2), 7–33. DOI: 10.2202/1948-4682.1069

Chapter 13
Spatial Data Governance for Healthcare Metaverse

Bimol Chandra Das
https://orcid.org/0009-0007-8388-8883
Trine University, USA

Rida Zahid
https://orcid.org/0000-0002-4738-6938
International School, Capital Medical University, China

Pujita Roy
https://orcid.org/0009-0007-7693-9232
North South University, Bangladesh

Munir Ahmad
https://orcid.org/0000-0003-4836-6151
Survey of Pakistan, Pakistan

ABSTRACT

The healthcare metaverse, leveraging VR and AR, revolutionizes medical services, education, and research by creating immersive, interactive environments. However, integrating spatial health data poses challenges in data accuracy, security, privacy, and ethical considerations, necessitating frameworks. The chapter proposes a framework for spatial data governance in the healthcare metaverse, focusing on patient control over health information. It includes rigorous data security and privacy protocols, ensures transparency and accountability, addresses ethical concerns, and encourages collaboration among stakeholders. This framework aims to uphold responsible data practices, protect patient privacy, and improve the effectiveness of healthcare services within the metaverse.

DOI: 10.4018/979-8-3693-4373-9.ch013

INTRODUCTION

Metaverse world can be technically described as a virtual reality and it enrages traditional 2D UI and offers true 3D immersion, including the lifelike replication of people and things people do in real life (Ahmad & Ali, 2023; Lippert et al., 2021; Weinberger, 2022). The journey of Metaverse in general depends on six fundamentals namely; AI, VR, AR, digital twin, Internetworking/telecommunication, and Blockchain among others as postulated by (Hulsen, 2023). The existence of a healthcare metaverse, an environment created for the management, governance, and utilization specifically for healthcare needs, has been gaining increasing attention over the last five years. This virtual environment has the potential to create a radical change in the field of healthcare solutions by allowing remote consultations, realistic medical training, and virtual rehabilitation (Bansal et al., 2022; Chengoden et al., 2023). Today, the representatives of the healthcare sphere are considering the various possibilities of its application, such as the creation of an exact three-dimensional model of the patient's body in the Metaverse that is useful for surgeons before and during operations. In addition, the use of VR environments in the domain of psychiatric therapy is aimed at achieving the benefits of the virtual environment in which doctors and patients can have therapeutic conversations and treat the patients.

In the context of a high rate of constant changes to deliver the best regarding the concepts of the contemporary healthcare system, the Metaverse integration is aimed at enhancing the effectiveness of healthcare services. For instance, the Department of Health-Abu Dhabi (DoH) recently launched the Abu Dhabi Life Science Hub using its metaverse application (Zeina et al., 2023). In the same manner, Medcare, a new hospital in Dubai, started the first metaverse hospital and enabled the patients to virtually see the hospital services and the interaction of doctors with the patients (Zeina et al., 2023). Besides, the Seha Virtual Hospital was established in Saudi Arabia to build extensive meaningful and revolutionary developments in the virtual care sector(MOH, 2024; Zeina et al., 2023). The metaverse in the healthcare market is anticipated to expand significantly at 52.9% from 2023 to 2028, growing from USD 9.5 billion to USD 79.6 billion, driven by the increased adoption of mixed reality (MR) for minimally invasive surgeries and enhancing patient experiences, and the use of digital twins to create models for simulations and insights. But the extension is moderated by the issues related to the protection of data and its security along with the high rate of implementation cost (MarketsandMarkets, 2023).

However, integrating spatial data which is information attached to individual geographical locations in the metaverse remains a significant concern that needs strong governance measures (Ahmad & Ali, 2023; Mobo & Ahmad, 2024). The following are some of the reasons that make it important to instill effective spatial data governance in the healthcare metaverse: First, it preserves patient confidentiality since it allows only authorized personnel to retrieve the hidden and encrypted healthcare information integrated into the spatial context. Secondly, evidenced and effective governance practices enhance data protection mechanisms that give control over the access, manipulation, or breach inside the metaverse. Lastly, established governing bodies promote the concepts of ethics on how spatial data can be incorporated into healthcare solutions when implemented in the metaverse.

Specifically, this chapter seek to identify the approach to effective management of spatial data in the framework of healthcare metaverse. This chapter focuses on the key issues concerning space data management in this virtual setting and provides recommendations for the proper and ethical use of data. The chapter can be divided into the following sections. First, we explain the ever-evolving idea of the healthcare metaverse and how spatial data fits into the picture. Following that, the paper determines the major issues regarding spatial data governance in this line. Next, a coherent conceptual framework for the management of spatial data in the healthcare metaverse environment is outlined. Finally, we outline how the advancement of this framework might influence future research and development in this area.

HEALTHCARE METAVERSE AND SPATIAL DATA

The healthcare metaverse offers more than just a digital environment for appointments. This gives concepts of an enhanced and highly complex multi-sensory environment for creating new healthcare models and processes in terms of education, learning, and research. These include characteristics, potential applications, and the role that spatial data can play in this virtual environment.

Characteristics of the Healthcare Metaverse

This section lists a few characteristics of the healthcare metaverse.

Immersion and Presence

The metaverse incorporates both VR and AR to foster a very engaging environment, particularly for patient treatment as well as to healthcare providers. Virtual and augmented reality technologies enable patient-centered approaches that improve engagement and compliance. Consider the case of a patient put on a VR headset, and virtually transported into a hospital ward than to have him get a feel of being in a healthcare facility, let alone, the examination room with a digital doctor. An engaging environment can help the medical personnel maintain a more patient-oriented approach to the treatment procedure, which can help with anxiety and enhance communication (Liang et al., 2023; Shin et al., 2023; Yoon & Nam, 2024).

Interactivity and Collaboration

The metaverse is not some kind of a background in which the activities of players take place. This makes it convenient to meet patients' needs, communicate with them, and share information with other doctors and caregivers. For instance, one can have a team of surgeons who are from different geographical regions, but who can work in a virtual operating room, and can perform a complicated surgery using virtual models which mirror the physical anatomy of the patient that they are operating on in actual time. It can help improve surgical results and play a big role in ways that officers and medical teams interact within a healthcare organization (Alpala et al., 2022; Land et al., 2011; Purdy, 2022).

Personalization and Customization

AI and big data analytics drive personalized treatments and interventions. The metaverse for health care is versatile in that it can be made specific to users' wants and demands. One way in which patients can manage aspects of their treatment is that they are allowed to choose the appearance of their avatars, thus easing their psychological transition to virtual environments. Furthermore, the blueprint of treatment may also be adaptable within the metaverse such that, one could design unique virtual rehabilitation programs or equally unique teaching sessions for patients with certain ailments (Liu & Siau, 2023; Ribeiro et al., 2024; Warden et al., 2024).

Accessibility and Scalability

In the environment of the metaverse, geographical limitations may no longer be a significant factor and improved accessibility may be realized in the sphere of healthcare. The metaverse has the potential to bridge gaps in healthcare access, especially for underserved populations. Some of the possible advantages include the ability to provide sophisticated healthcare services remotely wherein patients with physical disabilities or residents of rural areas could consult doctors virtually in the metaverse. At the same time, the use of the metaverse potentially introduces the ability for a high number of users to engage within the set virtual environment to access healthcare resources, which may further enhance the utilization rate (Abilkaiyrkyzy et al., 2023; Yang et al., 2023; Zhe et al., 2023).

Data Integration and Analytics

For the metaverse to be viable, it must be scalable and compatible with current healthcare systems. The healthcare metaverse can integrate real-time patient data with virtual environments. This allows healthcare professionals to analyze data within the context of a virtual consultation or treatment session, leading to more informed clinical decision-making. Additionally, the metaverse can facilitate the aggregation and analysis of vast amounts of healthcare data, potentially leading to groundbreaking discoveries in medical research (Qu et al., 2024; Sarwatt et al., 2024).

Potential Applications of the Healthcare Metaverse

This section provides some examples of possible applications of the healthcare metaverse.

Remote Patient Monitoring and Management

One of the potential benefits that have been identified with the use of the metaverse is in telemonitoring where a patient's health information is linked to his/her avatar in the virtual world (Cerda et al., 2024; Robert, 2022). It is also conceivable that physicians, nurses, and other healthcare workers could subsequently check patients' vital signs, record therapy outcomes, and even perform telehealth assessments in this virtually rendered environment. Thus, this approach might be of particular relevance for chronic disease patients or people living in rural areas.

Virtual Mental Health Support

Metaverse has the potential to become a source of fresh approaches to presenting digital mental health services (Ezawa et al., 2023; Rahi et al., 2023). For example, a patient with anxiety can enter a virtual relaxation room in the metaverse environment, and listen to music that makes the patient feel comfortable. Further, the metaverse can be used by therapists to simulate exposure therapy—people would be treating phobia or any anxiety disorder in a simulated environment to make them comfortable.

Medical Education and Training

The metaverse presents an opportunity for reinvention and improvement of medical education and training methodologies (Kala, 2022; Hulsen, 2023; S.-J. Wang & Park, 2023). In the same way that physicians can perform intricate surgical operations on virtual patients within an impressive 3D environment that has been developed to look like actual life practice, medical students can also use similar procedures to sharpen their skills without causing any harm to real patients. In addition, in the context of the metaverse, it can be enhanced by making collaborative learning and practice possible through the simultaneous participation of students from different universities in a virtual healthcare system.

Sources of Data in Healthcare Metaverse

This section listed different types of health-related information that can be generated within the metaverse.

Physiological Data

Physiological data can be collected through various types of sensor types. Biometric wearables can monitor heart rate, blood pressure, oxygen saturation level, and other aspects that relate to physical health and possibly stress. Also, the motion capture suits can be used within the controlled environment of the metaverse for the purposes measuring range of motion, gait analysis, and other features of motor control that might be important in physical therapy or rehabilitation. Similarly, brain-computer interfaces (BCIs) can enable monitoring of the brain activity and possibly even subjective data concerning mood or some other values (Dagher et al., 2020; Dietrick, 2021; Kačerová et al., 2022; Kadirvelu et al., 2023; Somani et al., 2022; Sun & Ye, 2023; Willis & Cross, 2022).

Behavioral Data

Analyzing movement designs seems to offer assistance in evaluating mobility, recognizing potential risks of falls in elderly people, or indeed screening adherence to workout schedules within the metaverse. How people connect with virtual objects, such as workout gear or recovery instruments, may give important information on their execution, engagement, and potential regions for enhancement. Information on how people utilize virtual meetings, take an interest in treatment sessions, or follow directions within the metaverse can offer important bits of knowledge into their healthcare journey and treatment viability (Horak et al., 2023; Hwang et al., 2023).

Cognitive Data

Virtual recreations outlined to imitate real-world scenarios can be utilized to evaluate cognitive processes like decision-making, problem-solving, and memory, possibly supporting the early discovery of cognitive decline. Coordination of cognitive assignments into engaging diversions inside the metaverse can provide a more common and engaging way to gather information on consideration, focus, and cognitive adaptability, possibly valuable for observing mental health or cognitive work (Bratu & Sabău, 2022; Zvarikova et al., 2022).

Sources of Spatial Health Data

Biometric Wearables

Smart peripherals connected to wearable devices such as a watch, a band, or even clothing can monitor one's physiological response in real-time, including heart and respiration rates, as well as muscle activity. It reacts to body features and capabilities to facilitate constant tracking of a user's health status during virtual exercises (Dagher et al., 2020; Dietrick, 2021; Somani et al., 2022; Willis & Cross, 2022; Wu et al., 2022).

Environmental Sensors

These sensors can maintain data on the presence of environmental conditions like light, humidity, and temperature in the context of VR environments. Such correlations can provide more information to care to providers about how the environment impacts members' health, which can help specify causes for specific ailments or improve therapeutic settings (Joe et al., 2018; Mena et al., 2022; Reis et al., 2015).

Avatar-Based Data

Users in virtual environments are assigned avatars that control movement in the virtual space to record information from motion, position, and object engagement. It may indicate health characteristics such as physical strengths, dexterity, and coordination, and may even give hints about a user's emotional status, which is all valuable data for understanding a user's health (Guillaudeux et al., 2023; Horne et al., 2020; Zheng et al., 2023).

Augmented Reality (AR) Overlays

Mobile technologies such as AR which enables the superimposition of digital information on the physical world can be fitted with sensors to provide data on physical exercises, positions, and regimes at which medication is taken. For instance, AR applications can track the movements of the user and provide feedback regarding exercises or check whether the patient has taken his/her prescribed medicines on time, thereby helping the user to follow a correct prescribed plan of action.

Role of Spatial Data

Spatial data can be defined as the healthcare metaverse's foundation, as it offers the necessary locational information in this virtual space. Some of the roles of spatial data are defined below.

Creating Realistic Virtual Environments

Spatial data refers to the coordinates that determine the placement and position of the items in the metaverse. It can offer the implementation of lifelike facilities such as hospitals, clinics, and treatment rooms and even the positions of the equipment and furniture in the rooms. This added attention to spatial or territorial dimensions can help contribute positively to values of interaction for user experience within the realm of the healthcare metaverse.

Tracking Movement and Interaction

Interaction data covers the presence and cooperation of avatars as objects in space derived from messages. This can enable healthcare professionals to watch the avatar of a particular patient when doing exercises for physical therapy or during the Virtual Rehabilitation Programme. In other words, spatial data analysis can provide therapists with an opportunity to get indispensable information about the given patient's progress, as well as to take appropriate measures to modify the further therapy plan.

Facilitating Data Visualization

Healthcare data can be incorporated into the metaverse for visualization and analysis of spatial data. For example, think of a surgeon who intervenes in a virtual environment operating theatre to control a digital image of a patient and parts of his body that need surgery, with spatial indication of areas of interest. Therefore, such maps can be helpful to various healthcare workers as they plan and decide on processes such as surgeries.

CHALLENGES IN SPATIAL HEALTH DATA GOVERNANCE

Integrating spatial health data into the metaverse raises several challenges that are listed as follows: -

Accuracy and Validity

Wearable devices in the metaverse can be less accurate and reliable as compared to traditional medical tools and equipment whereby there is a possibility of a compromise on the data being collected (Bayoumy et al., 2021; Pardamean et al., 2020; Veerubhotla et al., 2022). Moreover, one limitation of virtual reality research involves real-world inconsistency, and therefore, the generalizability of data and information collected in the metaverse for actual healthcare research is doubtful. The merging of the metaverse data with the regular healthcare data sources can be difficult since the data can be formatted, collected, and potentially have different assumptions from the rest of the healthcare data collected through standard methods. Effective calibration and validation methods of wearable sensors and virtual environments will be paramount in enhancing the reliability of spatial health information.

Security and Privacy Concerns

The metaverse fosters new ways of exploiting computer systems, so there is a risk of healthcare data leakage. Collecting spatial health data on various platforms and their re-use elsewhere can be a problematic issue of privacy and should be accompanied by specific measures for data control (Bayoumy et al., 2021; Boumpa et al., 2022; Suhluli & Ali Khan, 2022). Appropriate controls and security measures may be implemented on metaverse platforms and healthcare systems to minimize the risk of data breaches by users with the potential to compromise organizational security. Another issue relates to the privacy and protection of the personal data of individuals using metaverse services. Health data may be exposed to unauthorized parties, and attackers can use it for negative purposes such as stealing individuals' identities, discriminating against them, or harming physical wellbeing. Lack of sufficient control over the data in the metaverse may be concerning since users can barely control the accumulation, storage, and availability of their information. Given that there might be malicious intent users who formulate and exploit the weaknesses to gain illicit access to user data, it becomes an efficient solution to form a "clone cloud" and "private copy", starting right from the sensory level up to the behavioral level (Falchuk et al., 2018).

Ethical Considerations

The act of obtaining genuinely informed consent in the metaverse is especially complicated. While the data is collected and used through user interactions and other features of the environment of the information space, the users may not fully understand the consequences of having their data collected and used in a perpetually changing virtual space. Identifying who is responsible for owning and governing spatial health data in the metaverse is not an easy task. While using these platforms, several entities may gather user data, such as platforms themselves, healthcare facilities, and even other users within exceptional social encounters. Determining the specific entity that takes full responsibility for the space and where its health data is stored, given multiple entities may be involved (for example, metaverse owners, healthcare providers, and patients) is vital. One potential concern of bias is that the algorithms applied to spatial health data may themselves be contributing to bias due to factors such as user demographics, virtual environment design, or even the data itself that is used by the algorithms. Algorithms' bias reduction and means to promote fairness across data analysis and decision-making processes are still a concern and need attention (Canali et al., 2022, 2024; Ford et al., 2023; Gavette et al., 2023; Heikkilä et al., 2018; Tang et al., 2024).

Regulatory Landscape and Enforcement

Current data protection laws may not be sufficient to capture the intricacies of space-based health data within the realm of the metaverse and, therefore, may need to be updated and compared continually (Bayoumy et al., 2021). The metaverse is a global platform that requires the coordination of efforts and legal frameworks with the different countries to ensure correct recognition of data-related crimes as well as their subsequent enforcement. Regulating data governance frameworks in the decentralized virtual reality environment presents major challenges where new measures have to be applied constantly in an organization to ensure compliance or penalize defaulters. That means the legal and ethical rules regarding the process of data acquisition and utilization in and around the metaverse are not very well developed yet. These issues yet unregulated bring ambiguity to the users and the developers of such sites and, therefore cannot guarantee good data handling. Since the metaverse extends beyond physical national limits, questions related to data jurisdiction and adherence to various regional laws emerge. This is achievable if the metaverse data governance will need collective effort toward the formulation of a universal approach to data in the global society.

FRAMEWORK FOR SPATIAL DATA GOVERNANCE IN THE HEALTHCARE METAVERSE

Health Data Governance Frameworks

HIPAA (Health Insurance Portability and Accountability Act) in the US sets the national level to safeguard the privacy of the identity of individual health information (Lutkevich, 2019). Hitherto it only suits the conventional healthcare environment, nevertheless, principles such as informed consent, personally identifiable information, and safeguards for the control to personal information could be easily transversal to the metaverse.

GDPR (General Data Protection Regulation) in the EU focuses on each person and their right to privacy and to decide what should or should not happen to his/ her data (Meszaros et al., 2022). It puts certain requirements for the accountability and operation of organizations that process personal data, such as the requirement of consent, data protection, and providing copies to the data subjects. These principles for governing spatial health data can be useful for metaverse data, especially regarding EU users.

HIPAA in the United States and GDPR in the EU are well-articulated frameworks as they set clear principles for patient data privacy and security. These frameworks stress on elegance of consent, the least possible collection of data, and responsibility among the providers of health care. However, as these frameworks are made with traditional health facilities in mind, they may not capture all the features of data acquisition within the metaverse environment. Regarding data stored in databases: although some of the metaverse challenges, such as real-time data processing and analysis, may be of a different level, the fundamental question of how to protect the data is still paramount.

Spatial Data Governance Frameworks

Open Geospatial Consortium (OGC) Standards provide recommendations on how location-based information should be handled and utilized (Kemp, 2014). They stress data quality, compatibility of formats to ensure data interchangeability, and ease of use, which are cardinal aspects when it comes to health data that involves spatial location and movement in the scope of the metaverse.

SensorML (Sensor Model Language) aims to offer a specification for characterizing sensor capacity and sensor data structure (Botts & Robin, 2007; T. Wang et al., 2022). It can be useful for works related to harmonizing the integration and sharing of data from worn-down sensors applied to the metaverse for health outcomes.

Guidelines offered by OGC are valuable for solving the problem of handling these location-based data responsibly. They emphasize the quality of the data, its normalization, and the ability to cross-reference data between two different metaverse platforms which can be important once spatial health data is being integrated. However, these mostly concentrated on the integrity and uniformity of the data for uses that are not strictly related to health. These regulations may not capture several aspects of privacy and ethical use of health information in its management.

Metaverse Governance Frameworks

Metaverse Standards Forum is formed to devise best practices for building and managing the metaverse and its associated datasets (Havele et al., 2023; Hemphill, 2023). Although their work keeps on continuing, it can be invaluable in the creation of guidelines about the collection, use, and protection of data in the metaverse in general and spatial health data in particular.

Gaming industry guidelines are relatively limited existing guidance on how to effectively manage user data in virtual environments from the gaming industry, however, guidelines such as the Entertainment Software Rating Board (ESRB) do offer some useful information (Budziszewski, 2021). Nevertheless, such standards may require some customization and extension to meet the requirements of properly dealing with delicate health information in the context of the metaverse.

Newer guiding principles, which are based on the works of the Metaverse Standards Forum, are attempting to set the standard for how data can be used responsibly in virtual spaces. These frameworks advocate for user engagement and ownership, and the provision of timely as well as accurate information which are some of the most essential components that should characterize the governing of spatial health data. These frameworks are still emerging and have not developed the complete legal and regulatory support that current models such as HIPAA or GDPR provide. Possibly does not capture all aspects of the unique characteristics present in spatial health data, and may need further development in this respect.

Proposed Data Governance Framework for Spatial Health Data

To meet these requirements, a detailed framework for regulating spatial information in the healthcare metaverse is required. Here are some key elements that such a framework should encompass:

Data Ownership and Access Control

The incorporation of spatial healthcare data needs to be backed up by distinct ownership requirements. Such a framework may further advance a patient-oriented model which would mean that patients themselves own data and are free to control its use in the context of metaverse. However, the question remains how to protect privacy; there is a need for better security control to restrict access to the data owned by the respective patient who may be a health professional with certain authorization to access the spatial environment. The patient should retain control of their own spatial health information which means that the patients should be able to grant, revoke, and modify consent. Users should be able to define what data is harvested and for what purpose as well as select who has access to the harvested data. Users must have a clear and easily assessable way of obtaining their data as well as downloading the data in an easily understandable format. It should also be possible to anonymize data with certain conditions and restrictions, for example, to delete data that does not meet legal requirements for storage. There is also a need to regulate those organizations involved in the collection and use of spatial health data in that they must be made to organizations must clearly explain how they collect, use, and store data, along with the potential risks and benefits involved. Ensure individuals can easily transfer their spatial health data between different metaverse platforms or healthcare providers. This fosters user agency and facilitates the integration of data from various sources for holistic health assessments.

Data Security and Privacy

Ideally, the framework should outline some of the best practices and some of the technical standards that need to be put in place to protect the spatial data in the metaverse. This may include protection of data both when stored and when transmitted, strict user authentication, annual reviews for the metaverse structure security among others. Also, integration of a secure data transfer protocol should be enhanced within the framework for protecting health information through a secure communication protocol for the exchange of sensitive health care information in virtual world. Using software tools that can effectively scan for security flaws and ensure proper handling of spatial health is crucial as well as performing security check ups and penetration tests on systems used to store and process spatial health data are important in ensuring that these are done efficiently and at the right time. Techniques like differential privacy add noise to datasets to hinder identification while retaining their statistical properties which is quite useful as it hinders identification of particular users while still being useful statistically. It is recommended to use secure encryption methods, access control, and deep packet inspection for spatial health data security while at rest as well as in transit. This hinders the occurrence of cases of privacy infringement and unauthorized access to the data. Investigate and leverage anonymization methods for analyzing spatial health data with preserving the identity of individuals.

Transparency and Accountability

Clear and transparent data use policies are paramount to fostering trust within the healthcare metaverse. Sound agreements outlining the specific data collection and use practices should be presented to users in a way that is easy to understand before obtaining consent. Exploring and implementing privacy-enhancing technologies like anonymization, pseudonymization, and federated learning can minimize the risk of identifying individuals while still allowing for valuable data analysis. Regular independent audits and reviews of data governance practices can help ensure compliance with established frameworks and identify areas for improvement. Providing users with comprehensive and readily understandable summaries of data collection practices, storage methods, and potential uses of their data can foster trust and allow informed decision-making. Tracking the origin, usage history and any modifications made to spatial health data is crucial to allows for accountability and ensure responsible data handling practices by organizations. Establishing mechanisms for independent audits of data governance practices within the metaverse provides safeguards against potential misuse and helps maintain the integrity of the data ecosystem.

Ethical Considerations

Conducting ethical impact assessments before deploying new spatial health data collection initiatives can help identify potential risks and develop mitigation strategies. Including individuals with expertise in ethics, privacy, healthcare, and technology in developing and refining the ethical framework for spatial health data governance. Regularly reviewing and adapting the ethical framework to ensure it remains relevant and addresses the evolving nature of the metaverse and its impact on health data practices. Ensuring metaverse platforms and healthcare applications are designed and developed with inclusivity and accessibility in mind can prevent potential biases and ensures equitable access to healthcare services for all users. Developing and implementing mechanisms to audit and ensure the fairness of algorithms used to analyze spatial health data can prevent discriminatory outcomes and promote responsible AI development in the healthcare context.

Multi-Stakeholder Collaboration

Collaboration between metaverse platform developers, healthcare providers, and technology companies is crucial for developing and implementing consistent and effective data governance practices across different virtual spaces. Governments can play a vital role by Defining clear legal frameworks that address data privacy, security, and ownership in the context of spatial health data. Supporting research initiatives exploring technical solutions and ethical considerations related to spatial health data governance is also important. Moreover, it is required to foster dialogue and collaboration among stakeholders to develop and implement comprehensive data governance frameworks for the metaverse. Furthermore, actively engaging users in the development and implementation of data governance frameworks can ensures that their perspectives and concerns are considered, leading to more user-centric and ethical data practices.

By implementing these elements, the framework can promote responsible data practices and empower patients to make informed decisions about how their information is used within the healthcare metaverse. The proposed framework is described in Figure 1.

Figure 1. Proposed spatial data governance framework in healthcare metaverse

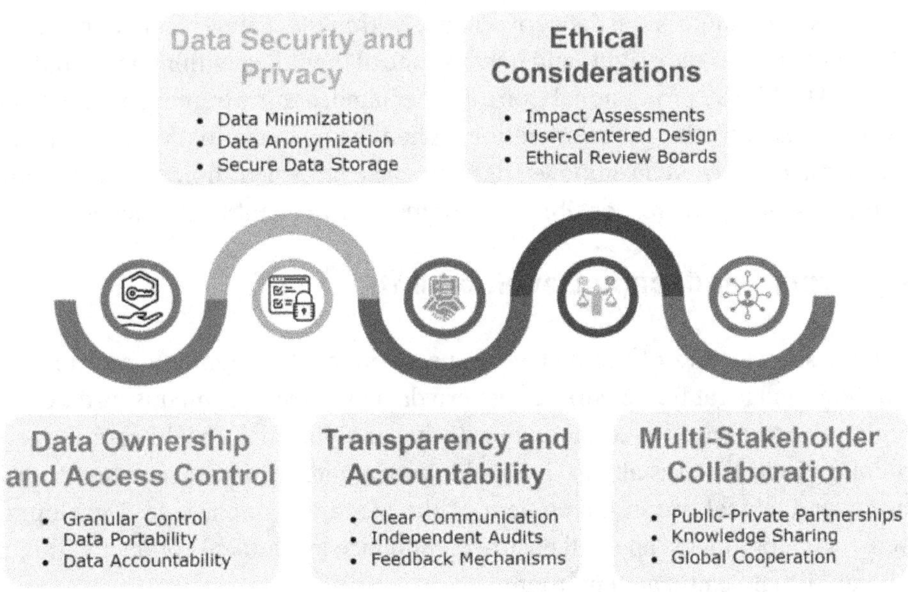

IMPLICATIONS FOR FUTURE RESEARCH AND DEVELOPMENT

The proposed framework for spatial data governance lays the groundwork for the responsible development and utilization of the healthcare metaverse. However, further research and development efforts are necessary to address emerging challenges and ensure the continued success of this virtual healthcare platform. Here are some key areas for future exploration:

Standardization and Interoperability

The current metaverse landscape is fragmented, with various platforms emerging with potentially incompatible data formats and protocols. Future research should focus on developing standardized data formats and interoperability protocols specifically designed for healthcare applications within the metaverse. This would enable seamless data exchange between different metaverse platforms, facilitating collaboration between healthcare providers and fostering innovation in the development of spatial healthcare applications.

User Education and Awareness

Both patients and healthcare professionals require education and awareness campaigns regarding spatial data governance within the metaverse. Patients need to understand their privacy rights and how to control their data within the virtual environment. Healthcare professionals, on the other hand, require training on responsible data practices and ethical considerations when using spatial data for patient care. Educational initiatives can empower users to make informed choices and participate actively in shaping the responsible development of the healthcare metaverse.

Regulatory Landscape Development

The nascent nature of the metaverse necessitates the ongoing development of regulations and legal frameworks to govern data practices within this virtual space. Regulatory bodies need to collaborate with stakeholders in the healthcare sector and technology industry to establish clear guidelines regarding data ownership, security, privacy, and ethical use in the context of the healthcare metaverse. Developing a robust regulatory landscape will ensure compliance and ethical conduct within this evolving virtual healthcare environment.

By addressing these future research and development areas, we can solidify the foundation for a secure, ethical, and patient-centric healthcare metaverse. This virtual platform holds immense potential to transform healthcare delivery, education, and research, and by prioritizing responsible spatial data governance, we can ensure its positive impact on patients and healthcare professionals alike.

CONCLUSION

The healthcare metaverse represents a transformative leap in how medical services, education, and research can be conducted. By integrating virtual reality (VR) and augmented reality (AR), the metaverse creates a highly immersive, interactive, and personalized environment that extends the reach and capabilities of traditional healthcare systems. This digital landscape offers unique advantages, such as remote patient monitoring, virtual mental health support, and innovative medical education and training platforms. These applications have the potential to revolutionize patient care, enhance healthcare accessibility, and foster global collaboration among medical professionals. However, the integration of spatial health data within the metaverse introduces significant challenges. Ensuring the accuracy and validity of data collected from wearable devices and virtual interactions is critical, as is addressing security and privacy concerns. The ethical implications of data collection and usage in a virtual environment must be carefully managed to protect user rights and maintain trust. Furthermore, the regulatory landscape must evolve to encompass the complexities of metaverse-based healthcare, necessitating updates to existing frameworks like HIPAA and GDPR.

A robust framework for spatial data governance in the healthcare metaverse is essential. To this end, a framework for spatial data governance for the healthcare metaverse is proposed in the chapter. The framework emphasizes data ownership and access control, ensuring that patients have control over their health information. It incorporates stringent data security and privacy measures, maintains transparency and accountability, addresses ethical considerations, and promotes multi-stakeholder collaboration. By adhering to these principles, the framework can support responsible data practices, safeguard patient privacy, and enhance the overall efficacy of healthcare services in the metaverse.

REFERENCES

Abilkaiyrkyzy, A., Elhagry, A., Laamarti, F., & El Saddik, A. (2023). Metaverse Key Requirements and Platforms Survey. *IEEE Access : Practical Innovations, Open Solutions*, *11*, 117765–117787. Advance online publication. DOI: 10.1109/ACCESS.2023.3325844

Ahmad, M., & Ali, A. (2023). Integrated Geospatial Information Management in the World of Metaverse: Challenges and Opportunities. In Lekhi, P., & Kaur, G. (Eds.), *Concepts, Technologies, Challenges, and the Future of Web 3* (pp. 248–270). IGI Global., DOI: 10.4018/978-1-6684-9919-1.ch013

Alpala, L. O., Quiroga-Parra, D. J., Torres, J. C., & Peluffo-Ordóñez, D. H. (2022). Smart Factory Using Virtual Reality and Online Multi-User: Towards a Metaverse for Experimental Frameworks. *Applied Sciences (Basel, Switzerland)*, *12*(12), 6258. Advance online publication. DOI: 10.3390/app12126258

Bansal, G., Rajgopal, K., Chamola, V., Xiong, Z., & Niyato, D. (2022). Healthcare in Metaverse: A Survey on Current Metaverse Applications in Healthcare. *IEEE Access : Practical Innovations, Open Solutions*, *10*, 119914–119946. Advance online publication. DOI: 10.1109/ACCESS.2022.3219845

Bayoumy, K., Gaber, M., Elshafeey, A., Mhaimeed, O., Dineen, E. H., Marvel, F. A., Martin, S. S., Muse, E. D., Turakhia, M. P., Tarakji, K. G., & Elshazly, M. B. (2021). Smart wearable devices in cardiovascular care: where we are and how to move forward. In *Nature Reviews Cardiology* (Vol. 18, Issue 8). DOI: 10.1038/s41569-021-00522-7

Botts, M., & Robin, A. (2007). *OpenGIS ® Sensor Model Language (SensorML) Implementation Specification*. Design.

Boumpa, E., Tsoukas, V., Gkogkidis, A., Spathoulas, G., & Kakarountas, A. (2022). Security and Privacy Concerns for Healthcare Wearable Devices and Emerging Alternative Approaches. *Lecture Notes of the Institute for Computer Sciences, Social-Informatics and Telecommunications Engineering, LNICST, 440 LNICST*. DOI: 10.1007/978-3-031-06368-8_2

Bratu, S., & Sabău, R. I. (2022). Digital Commerce in the Immersive Metaverse Environment: Cognitive Analytics Management, Real-Time Purchasing Data, and Seamless Connected Shopping Experiences. *Linguistic and Philosophical Investigations*, *21*(0), 170. Advance online publication. DOI: 10.22381/lpi21202211

Budziszewski, P. K. (2021). Entertainment Software Rating Board (ESRB). In *Encyclopedia of Video Games: The Culture, Technology, and Art of Gaming: 3 Volumes, Second Edition* (Vol. 1).

Canali, S., Ferretti, A., Schiaffonati, V., & Blasimme, A. (2024). Wearable Technologies for Healthy Ageing: Prospects, Challenges, and Ethical Considerations. In *Journal of Frailty and Aging* (Vol. 13, Issue 2). DOI: 10.14283/jfa.2024.19

Canali, S., Schiaffonati, V., & Aliverti, A. (2022). Challenges and recommendations for wearable devices in digital health: Data quality, interoperability, health equity, fairness. *PLOS Digital Health*, *1*(10), e0000104. Advance online publication. DOI: 10.1371/journal.pdig.0000104 PMID: 36812619

Cerda, I. H., Therond, A., Moreau, S., Studer, K., Donjow, A. R., Crowther, J. E., Mazzolenis, M. E., Lang, M., Tolba, R., Gilligan, C., Ashina, S., Kaye, A. D., Yong, R. J., Schatman, M. E., & Robinson, C. L. (2024). Telehealth and Virtual Reality Technologies in Chronic Pain Management: A Narrative Review. In *Current Pain and Headache Reports* (Vol. 28, Issue 3). DOI: 10.1007/s11916-023-01205-3

Chengoden, R., Victor, N., Huynh-The, T., Yenduri, G., Jhaveri, R. H., Alazab, M., Bhattacharya, S., Hegde, P., Maddikunta, P. K. R., & Gadekallu, T. R. (2023). Metaverse for Healthcare: A Survey on Potential Applications, Challenges and Future Directions. *IEEE Access : Practical Innovations, Open Solutions*, *11*, 12765–12795. Advance online publication. DOI: 10.1109/ACCESS.2023.3241628

Dagher, L., Shi, H., Zhao, Y., & Marrouche, N. F. (2020). Wearables in cardiology: Here to stay. *Heart Rhythm*, *17*(5), 889–895. Advance online publication. DOI: 10.1016/j.hrthm.2020.02.023 PMID: 32354455

Dietrick, T. A. (2021). Biometric Monitoring Devices: Modern Solutions to Protecting Athletes' Data Privacy. *Pittsburgh Journal of Technology Law & Policy*, *21*(1). Advance online publication. DOI: 10.5195/tlp.2021.245

Ezawa, I. D., Hollon, S. D., & Robinson, N. (2023). Examining Predictors of Depression and Anxiety Symptom Change in Cognitive Behavioral Immersion: Observational Study. *JMIR Mental Health*, *10*, e42377. Advance online publication. DOI: 10.2196/42377 PMID: 37450322

Falchuk, B., Loeb, S., & Neff, R. (2018). The Social Metaverse: Battle for Privacy. *IEEE Technology and Society Magazine*, *37*(2), 52–61. Advance online publication. DOI: 10.1109/MTS.2018.2826060

Ford, E., Milne, R., & Curlewis, K. (2023). Ethical issues when using digital biomarkers and artificial intelligence for the early detection of dementia. In *Wiley Interdisciplinary Reviews*. Data Mining and Knowledge Discovery., DOI: 10.1002/widm.1492

Gavette, H., McDonald, C. L., Kostick-Quenet, K., Mullen, A., Najafi, B., & Finco, M. G. (2023). Advances in prosthetic technology: A perspective on ethical considerations for development and clinical translation. *Frontiers in Rehabilitation Sciences*, *4*, 1335966. Advance online publication. DOI: 10.3389/fresc.2023.1335966 PMID: 38293290

Guillaudeux, M., Rousseau, O., Petot, J., Bennis, Z., Dein, C. A., Goronflot, T., Vince, N., Limou, S., Karakachoff, M., Wargny, M., & Gourraud, P. A. (2023). Patient-centric synthetic data generation, no reason to risk re-identification in biomedical data analysis. *NPJ Digital Medicine*, *6*(1), 37. Advance online publication. DOI: 10.1038/s41746-023-00771-5 PMID: 36899082

Havele, A., Polys, N., & Behr, J. (2023). Building 3D Web Interoperability for the Metaverse. *Proceedings - Web3D 2023: 28th International Conference on Web3D Technology*. DOI: 10.1145/3611314.3623584

Heikkilä, P., Schmalfuß, F., Honka, A., Kaasinen, E., Mach, S., & Väänänen, K. (2018). Quantified Factory Worker - Expert Evaluation and Ethical Considerations of Wearable Self-tracking Devices. *ACM International Conference Proceeding Series*. DOI: 10.1145/3275116.3275119

Hemphill, T. A. (2023). The 'Metaverse' and the challenge of responsible standards development. *Journal of Responsible Innovation*, *10*(1), 2243121. Advance online publication. DOI: 10.1080/23299460.2023.2243121

Horak, J., Voumik, L. C., & Popescu, G. H. (2023). Remote Sensing Data Fusion Techniques, Multimodal Behavioral Predictive and Mobile Location Analytics, and Spatial Cognition and Context Awareness Algorithms in the Metaverse Economy. *Linguistic and Philosophical Investigations*, *22*(0), 77. Advance online publication. DOI: 10.22381/lpi2220235

Horne, M., Hill, A., Murells, T., & Ugail, H. Irving, Chinnadorai, R., & Hardy, M. (2020). Using avatars in weight management settings: A systematic review. In *Internet Interventions* (Vol. 19). DOI: 10.1016/j.invent.2019.100295

Hulsen, T. (2023). Applications of the metaverse in medicine and healthcare. *Advances in Laboratory Medicine/Avances En Medicina de Laboratorio, 0*.

Hwang, Y., Shin, D., & Lee, H. (2023). Students' perception on immersive learning through 2D and 3D metaverse platforms. *Educational Technology Research and Development*, *71*(4), 1687–1708. Advance online publication. DOI: 10.1007/s11423-023-10238-9 PMID: 37359489

Joe, H. E., Yun, H., Jo, S. H., Jun, M. B. G., & Min, B. K. (2018). A review on optical fiber sensors for environmental monitoring. In *International Journal of Precision Engineering and Manufacturing - Green Technology* (Vol. 5, Issue 1). DOI: 10.1007/s40684-018-0017-6

Kačerová, I., Kubr, J., Hořejší, P., & Kleinová, J. (2022). Ergonomic Design of a Workplace Using Virtual Reality and a Motion Capture Suit. *Applied Sciences (Basel, Switzerland)*, *12*(4), 2150. Advance online publication. DOI: 10.3390/app12042150

Kadirvelu, B., Gavriel, C., Nageshwaran, S., Chan, J. P. K., Nethisinghe, S., Athanasopoulos, S., Ricotti, V., Voit, T., Giunti, P., Festenstein, R., & Faisal, A. A. (2023). A wearable motion capture suit and machine learning predict disease progression in Friedreich's ataxia. *Nature Medicine*, *29*(1), 86–94. Advance online publication. DOI: 10.1038/s41591-022-02159-6 PMID: 36658420

Kala, N. (2022). Revolutionizing medical education with metaverse. International Journal of Scientific Research in Computer Science. *Engineering and Information Technology*, *8*(4), 26–32.

Kemp, K. (2014). Open Geospatial Consortium (OGC). In *Encyclopedia of Geographic Information Science*. DOI: 10.4135/9781412953962.n152

Land, S., van der, , Land, S., van der, , & Schouten, A., Hooff, van den, & Feldberg, F. (2011). Modeling the Metaverse: A Theoretical Model of Effective Team Collaboration.... *Journal of Virtual Worlds Research*, *4*(3).

Liang, J., Li, G., Zhang, F., Fan, D., & Luo, H. (2023). Benefits and challenges of the educational metaverse: Evidence from quantitative and qualitative data. *Journal of Educational Technology Development and Exchange*, *16*(1), 71–91. Advance online publication. DOI: 10.18785/jetde.1601.04

Lippert, K., Khan, M. N. R., Rabbi, M. M., Dutta, A., & Cloutier, R. (2021). A Framework of Metaverse for Systems Engineering. *Proceedings of 2021 IEEE International Conference on Signal Processing, Information, Communication and Systems, SPICSCON 2021*. DOI: 10.1109/SPICSCON54707.2021.9885722

Liu, Y., & Siau, K. L. (2023). Human-AI Interaction and AI Avatars. *Lecture Notes in Computer Science (Including Subseries Lecture Notes in Artificial Intelligence and Lecture Notes in Bioinformatics), 14059 LNCS*. DOI: 10.1007/978-3-031-48057-7_8

Lutkevich, B. (2019). What is HIPAA (Health Insurance Portability and Accountability Act)? In *WhatIs.com.*

MarketsandMarkets. (2023). *Metaverse in Healthcare Market.* https://www.marketsandmarkets.com/Market-Reports/metaverse-in-healthcare-market-225839181.html

Mena, A. R., Ceballos, H. G., & Alvarado-Uribe, J. (2022). Measuring Indoor Occupancy through Environmental Sensors: A Systematic Review on Sensor Deployment. In *Sensors* (Vol. 22, Issue 10). DOI: 10.3390/s22103770

Meszaros, J., Minari, J., & Huys, I. (2022). The future regulation of artificial intelligence systems in healthcare services and medical research in the European Union. *Frontiers in Genetics, 13*, 927721. Advance online publication. DOI: 10.3389/fgene.2022.927721 PMID: 36267404

Mobo, F. D., & Ahmad, M. (2024). Spatial Data-Driven Citizen Engagement in the Metaverse. In Guo, Y. (Ed.), *Emerging Developments and Technologies in Digital Government* (pp. 181–203). IGI Global., DOI: 10.4018/979-8-3693-2363-2.ch010

MOH. (2024). *Seha Virtual Hospital.* https://www.moh.gov.sa/en/Ministry/Projects/Pages/Seha-Virtual-Hospital.aspx

Pardamean, B., Soeparno, H., Budiarto, A., Mahesworo, B., & Baurley, J. (2020). Quantified self-using consumer wearable device: Predicting physical and mental health. *Healthcare Informatics Research, 26*(2), 83–92. Advance online publication. DOI: 10.4258/hir.2020.26.2.83 PMID: 32547805

Purdy, M. (2022). How the Metaverse Could Change Work. In *Harvard Business Review.*

Qu, J., Kizil, M. S., Yahyaei, M., & Knights, P. F. (2024). Developing a digital twin for a laboratory ball mill operation – a step towards mining metaverse. *Mining Technology, 133*(1), 3–16. Advance online publication. DOI: 10.1177/25726668231222990

Rahi, P., Sood, S. P., Kalhotra, S. K., Khan, I. R., & Dandotiya, M. (2023). Artificial Intelligence of Things (AIoT) and metaverse technology for brain health, mental health, and wellbeing. In *Contemporary Applications of Data Fusion for Advanced Healthcare Informatics.* DOI: 10.4018/978-1-6684-8913-0.ch019

Reis, S., Seto, E., Northcross, A., Quinn, N. W. T., Convertino, M., Jones, R. L., Maier, H. R., Schlink, U., Steinle, S., Vieno, M., & Wimberly, M. C. (2015). Integrating modelling and smart sensors for environmental and human health. *Environmental Modelling & Software, 74*, 238–246. Advance online publication. DOI: 10.1016/j.envsoft.2015.06.003 PMID: 26644778

Ribeiro, A., Vieira, V., Alves, L., & Maciel, C. (2024). VISHnu: An approach to support the personalization of self-expressive avatars using context-awareness. *International Journal of Human-Computer Studies*, *185*, 103243. Advance online publication. DOI: 10.1016/j.ijhcs.2024.103243

Robert, B. (2022). Healthcare Diagnosis and Treatment in the Metaverse: Remote Sensing Algorithms, Networked Wearable Devices, and Virtual Patient Data. *American Journal of Medical Research (New York, N.Y.)*, *9*(2), 41. Advance online publication. DOI: 10.22381/ajmr9220223

Sarwatt, D. S., Lin, Y., Ding, J., Sun, Y., & Ning, H. (2024). Metaverse for Intelligent Transportation Systems (ITS): A Comprehensive Review of Technologies, Applications, Implications, Challenges and Future Directions. *IEEE Transactions on Intelligent Transportation Systems*, *25*(7), 6290–6308. Advance online publication. DOI: 10.1109/TITS.2023.3347280

Shin, S., Kim, H., Yoo, J., & Park, M. (2023). The Effects of Metaverse Avatar Identification on Immersion, Vicarious Pleasure, and Fashion Brand Item Sharing Intention. *Journal of the Korean Society of Clothing and Textiles*, *47*(3). Advance online publication. DOI: 10.5850/JKSCT.2023.47.3.492

Somani, S. N., Yu, K. M., Chiu, A. G., Sykes, K. J., & Villwock, J. A. (2022). Consumer Wearables for Patient Monitoring in Otolaryngology: A State of the Art Review. In *Otolaryngology - Head and Neck Surgery (United States)* (Vol. 167, Issue 4). DOI: 10.1177/01945998211061681

Suhluli, S. A., & Ali Khan, S. M. F. (2022). Determinants of user acceptance of wearable IoT devices. *Cogent Engineering*, *9*(1), 2087456. Advance online publication. DOI: 10.1080/23311916.2022.2087456

Sun, X., & Ye, B. (2023). The functional differentiation of brain–computer interfaces (BCIs) and its ethical implications. *Humanities & Social Sciences Communications*, *10*(1), 878. Advance online publication. DOI: 10.1057/s41599-023-02419-x

Tang, C., Yi, W., Occhipinti, E., Dai, Y., Gao, S., & Occhipinti, L. G. (2024). A roadmap for the development of human body digital twins. *Nature Reviews Electrical Engineering*, *1*(3), 199–207. Advance online publication. DOI: 10.1038/s44287-024-00025-w

Veerubhotla, A., Krantz, A., Ibironke, O., & Pilkar, R. (2022). Wearable devices for tracking physical activity in the community after an acquired brain injury: A systematic review. In *PM and R* (Vol. 14, Issue 10). DOI: 10.1002/pmrj.12725

Wang, S.-J., & Park, S. Y. (2023). Disaster Education in Hospitals using Metaverse: Focusing on COVID-19. *Prehospital and Disaster Medicine*, *38*(S1), s85. Advance online publication. DOI: 10.1017/S1049023X23002431

Wang, T., Gan, V. J. L., Hu, D., & Liu, H. (2022). Digital twin-enabled built environment sensing and monitoring through semantic enrichment of BIM with SensorML. *Automation in Construction*, *144*, 104625. Advance online publication. DOI: 10.1016/j.autcon.2022.104625

Warden, C. A., Chen, J. F., & Yen, W. H. (2024). Metaverse Servicescape: Emotional Response to Virtual Retail Design. *International Journal of Human-Computer Interaction*. Advance online publication. DOI: 10.1080/10447318.2024.2322200

Weinberger, M. (2022). What Is Metaverse?—A Definition Based on Qualitative Meta-Synthesis. *Future Internet*, *14*(11), 310. Advance online publication. DOI: 10.3390/fi14110310

Willis, K. S., & Cross, E. (2022). Investigating the potential of EDA data from biometric wearables to inform inclusive design of the built environment. *Emotion, Space and Society*, *45*, 100906. Advance online publication. DOI: 10.1016/j.emospa.2022.100906

Wu, J. Y., Ching, C. T. S., Wang, H. M. D., & De Liao, L. (2022). Emerging Wearable Biosensor Technologies for Stress Monitoring and Their Real-World Applications. In *Biosensors* (Vol. 12, Issue 12). DOI: 10.3390/bios12121097

Yang, X., Huang, M., Luo, L., Guo, H., & Zhu, C. (2023). Efficient Panoramic Video Coding for Immersive Metaverse Experience. *IEEE Network*, *37*(6), 58–66. Advance online publication. DOI: 10.1109/MNET.2023.3319958

Yoon, S., & Nam, Y. (2024). Metaverse engagement and Korea travel intentions: Understanding affordances, presence, and place attachment among Brazilian ZEPETO users. *Journal of Destination Marketing & Management*, *31*, 100865. Advance online publication. DOI: 10.1016/j.jdmm.2024.100865

Zeina, K., Eyad, A.-M., Janahan, T., Richard, J., & Guy, P. (2023). *The Future of Healthcare in the Metaverse*. PWC. https://www.pwc.com/m1/en/industries/healthcare/the-future-of-healthcare-in-the-metaverse.html

Zhe, C., Huilan, G., Jiang, W., & Zhongyi, H. (2023). The Ideal and Reality of Metaverse: User Perception of VR Products Based on Review Mining. *Data Analysis and Knowledge Discovery*, *7*(1). Advance online publication. DOI: 10.11925/infotech.2096-3467.2022.0371

Zheng, Z., Zhao, X., Zhang, H., Liu, B., & Liu, Y. (2023). AvatarReX: Real-Time Expressive Full-body Avatars. *ACM Transactions on Graphics*, *42*(4), 1–19. Advance online publication. DOI: 10.1145/3592101

Zvarikova, K., Michalikova, K. F., & Rowland, M. (2022). Retail Data Measurement Tools, Cognitive Artificial Intelligence Algorithms, and Metaverse Live Shopping Analytics in Immersive Hyper-Connected Virtual Spaces. *Linguistic and Philosophical Investigations*, *21*(0), 9. Advance online publication. DOI: 10.22381/lpi2120221

Chapter 14
Strategies for Implementing Education 5.0

Mahesh Singh
ATMS-SBS Swiss Business School, Ras Al Khaimah, UAE

Manoj Kumar Rao
https://orcid.org/0000-0001-8105-1130
J.D. College of Engineering and Management, Nagpur, India

Manoj B Pandey
https://orcid.org/0000-0002-5112-2054
Jhulelal Institute of Technology, Nagpur, India

Abdul Ahad
Central India College of Business Management and Studies, Nagpur, India

Shashi Kant Gupta
https://orcid.org/0000-0001-6587-5607
Eudoxia Research University, New Castle, USA

ABSTRACT

An essential component of a nation's infrastructure development is education, which has evolved through standards from Education 1.0 to the present Education 5.0. A study evaluates the historical development of education and its applicability to contemporary requirements. The assessment of the literature, we examine the use of Education 5.0 in both industrialized and advancing nations in this research. Saudi Arabia and Malaysia have been chosen for examination as examples of industrialized nations that have effectively implemented Education 5.0, using the PRISMA

DOI: 10.4018/979-8-3693-4373-9.ch014

technique based on research conducted over the previous six years. Furthermore, two poor nations Sri Lanka and Zimbabwe are selected to assess the Education 5.0 deployment gap. The study emphasizes the urgent need to reassess Education 5.0 implementation in developing countries, notwithstanding successful implementation in wealthier ones. The results of this research should be conducted to examine hidden implementation issues with Education 5.0 by employing a variety of approaches.

1. INTRODUCTION

The desire for academic learning has been essential to cultures from the dawn of humankind. Using the most recent materials and methods, the process of developing students' adept practical academic knowledge in line with the demands of a competitive market is continuous (Samiha, 2022). World society's habits and lives are impacted by the technological advancements of the industrial revolution. To facilitate regeneration, scientific and technological advancements set off the revolutionary paradigm that is developing today. It is necessary for the education sector to enhance its system in light of the revolution's progress. Schooling is one of the investments that helps human civilization advance (Rusman, 2023). Education is one way to prepare excellent human beings. When it comes to being competitive and overcoming obstacles in the 5.0 era, education is crucial. Since educated and competent people are essential to a nation's success, education is highly valued in emerging nations like Indonesia (Rakhmawati, 2023). Within the educational context, it strongly emphasizes on helping students acquire high order thinking skills HOTS to adequately equip them for life's opportunities and obstacles in a technologically sophisticated world (Astriana, 2024). The education 5.0 is displayed in Figure 1.1 below as follows.

Figure 1. Education 5.0. Source: Author

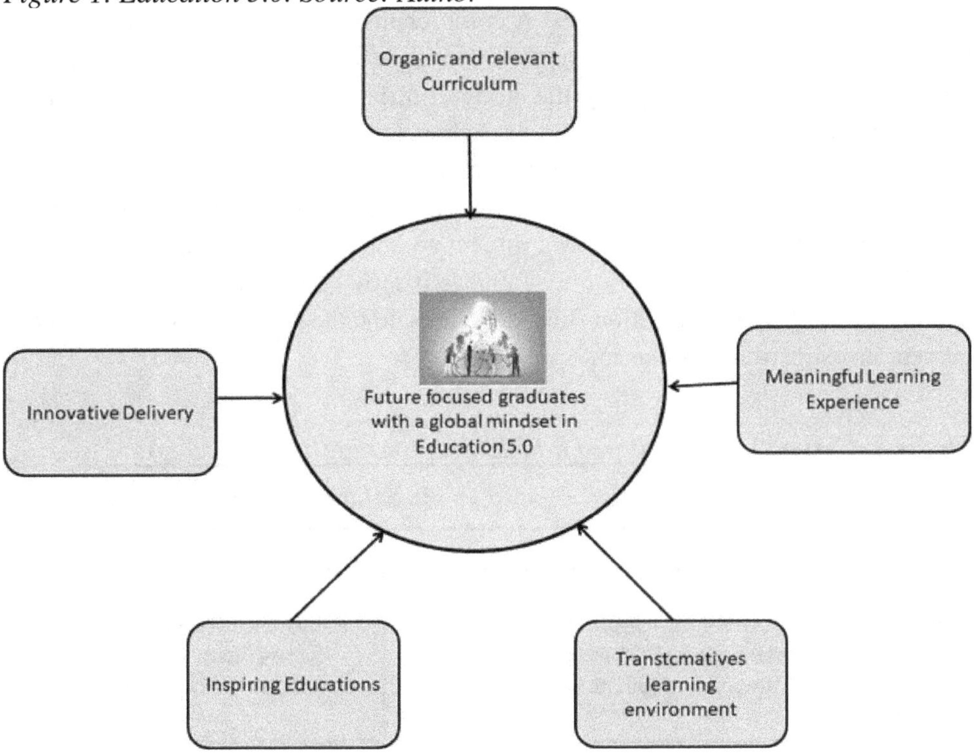

Higher education institutions are crucial to the creation of a sophisticated learning environment that uses advanced technologies to nurture the next generation. Two of the numerous countries that have implemented the newest technology in the field of education are Saudi Arabia and Malaysia, which are highly regarded in the ranking of the world's most developed nations (Khaimovich, 2020). In this research, we evaluate the literature and look at how Education 5.0 is used and developed with industrialized nations.

2. METHOD FOR SELECTING RESEARCH PAPERS AND ARTICLES

The majority of the research that was found focused on education standards, IT and Information & Communication Technology ICT. It was imperative that the research be published in journals with peer review and a promise of full text availability in English, with the study emphasizes every interplay between education and technology (Togo, 2021). Similar reasons for rejection included the use of

ICT, the article's non-English language, an unclear research methodology, and the fact study was published as a review. A comprehensive method was used to search web databases for the necessary articles to mitigate bias in the selection process. After using a filter procedure by the study criteria, a total of 69 research papers were located. These articles support the education sector's digitalization efforts, upgrade the academic process, and systematize operations in line with Education 5.0 (Asmirajanti, 2023). Following the process outlined, a total of 30 research articles were deemed pertinent to the study's subject and chosen to be utilized as a source of reference. The detailed literature synthesis is provided Figure 1.2 below, which depicts the PRISMAinformation flow, describes how the pertinent literature for the current investigation was chosen.

Figure 2. Current study employed a PRISMA flow diagram. Source: Author

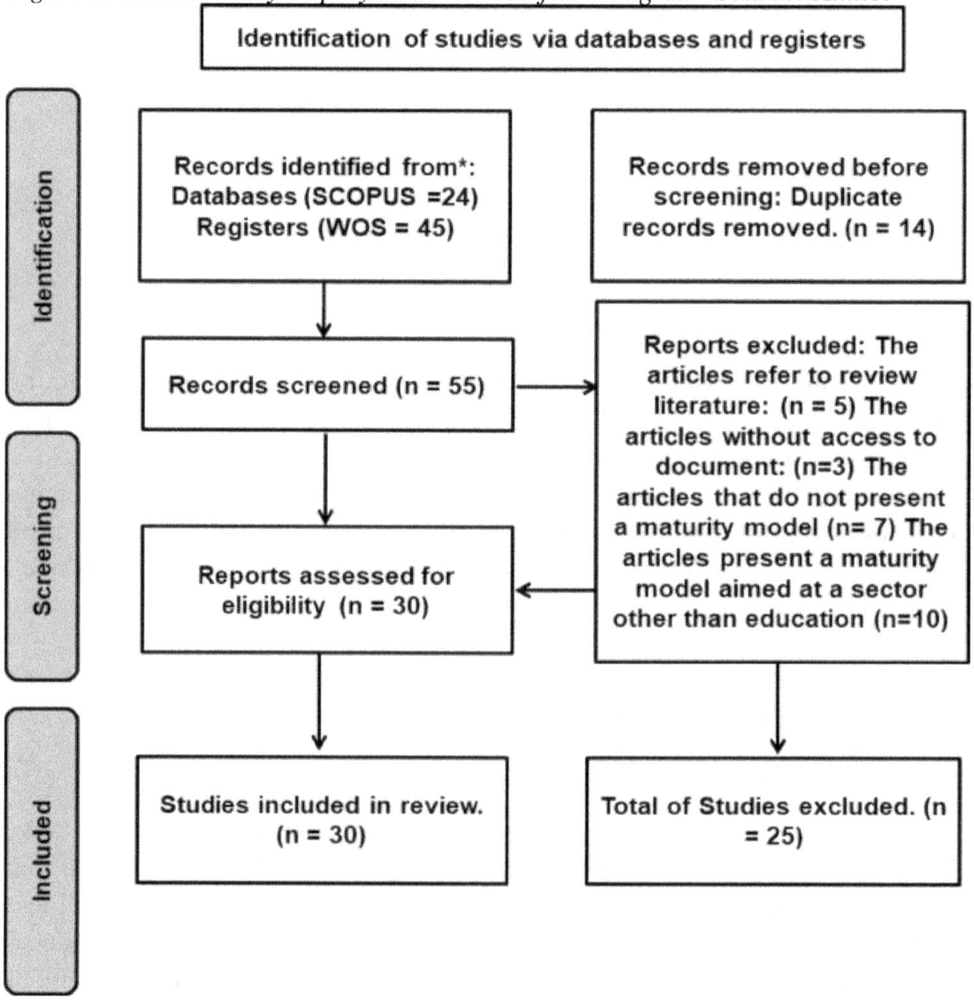

3. MALAYSIA'S IMPLEMENTATION OF EDUCATION 5.0 IN THE DEVELOPED WORLD

The most prosperous nations are offering sufficient funding for higher learning industry toward expand and satisfy consumer expectations. They think that, this is the foundation for the nation's prospects for economic and industrial progress in the future. The majority of academic institutions in the modern world rate highly indicating that they are abiding by market demands and utilizing advanced technologies to deliver creative instruction as shown in Table 1.1 for Industry 5.0 require skill.

Table 1. Production 5.0 requires skill (Awang, 2020)

Era	Skill	Reference
5.0	• Language skill • IT Literacy • writing skill • Leadership	(Darmaji, 2019)
5.0	• Information literacy • Technological • Literacy • Human Literacy	(Hikmat, 2022)

In recent times, Malaysia and other nations have demonstrated remarkable progress in developing and modernizing their educational systems, drawing attention across the globe. In addition to meeting the needs of their citizens, they have been welcoming students from the surrounding area that wish to pursue higher education. Their main goal is to change students' aptitude for traditional instruction to experience-based learning by introducing fresh, creative concepts, raising important issues, and creating a adaptable, appealing learning environment. To determine the effects of contemporary approaches used in the higher education sector on learning outcomes (Maria, 2018).

4. SAUDI ARABIA'S PERFORMANCE OF EDUCATION 5.0 IN THE INDUSTRIAL WORLD

To expand the education sector and fulfill market expectations and needs that are in line with worldwide standards, Saudi Arabia is investing a significant amount of money and human resources in this area (Mirghani, 2020). This demonstrates how the nation is raising the young of the Kingdom to assist and develop them to gather international standards.

4.1 Development of Education

The government's top objective is to concentrate on developing educational development, including curricular goals, policies, and philosophies, as shown in Table 1.2. The second step is creating a framework for integrating philosophy and policy to create a professional academic environment and accomplish the goals. Connecting the school environment with integrated and supportive services will enable the learner to experience a comfortable learning environment while developing their skills, personality, and confidence (Sart, 2022). It will also foster a creative spirit in the classroom.

Table 2. Education 5.0 and Education 4.0 classifications aspects of the fifth society (Laura, 2023)

Categories	Explanation		Reference
Competencies	Transversal competencies	• Critical thinking • Co-operation • Collaboration • Communication • Creativity	(Miranda, 2021)
	Disciplinary proficiencies	• Instruction and the development of knowledge in the areas of function, technology, and effective workplace performance. • The ability to investigate, plan, develop, with use novel systems. • Provide guidance on tech-related issues and best practices.	
Learning methods	Learning delivery modalities	• Online remote education • Mobile learning • Blended or hybrid learning • Face to face learning	(Ramírez, 2020)
	Learning techniques	• Educational strategies including solving problems	
Level of infrastructure	Internet space	• Disruptive technologies are among the scientific enablers of 4.0, smart technologies, open technologies, and models of technological innovation.	(Pérez, 2022)
	Physical space	• Infrastructure and Buildings: internet access, robotics, Gesell rooms, immersive rooms, infrastructure for communications, multimedia production labs, protection, and cozy areas	

continued on following page

Table 2. Continued

Categories	Explanation		Reference
Organization dimensions	Platforms for cooperation and organizations	• Culture and leadership, Digitalization of markets, logistics, financial viability, as well as dynamic and digital capabilities	(Rodríguez, 2021)
	Liaison	• Relationships and other industries, cooperation between institutions, lifelong learning, and I+D initiatives	

The establishment of private educational institutions alongside the state sector was supported by the Saudi government. This is a cost-effective educational system with competitive and healthy growth. Teachers and students can receive advanced resources for knowledge transfer from intelligent schools. The majority of Saudi Arabia's institutions, universities, and schools are connected to these innovative educational settings because of the government's encouragement of smart schools. The Saudi government offers scholarships to deserving individuals to pursue further education at respectable foreign colleges (Aljabri, 2020).

4.2 Zimbabwe's Application of Education 5.0 in Developing Nation

Underdeveloped nations are dealing with several challenges, including financial and economic ones that have a significant impact on the health and education sectors in particular. Zimbabwe is a growing nation dealing with a variety of problems, including both economic and political. In the public university of Zimbabwe, a recent study was done to investigate how students felt about contemporary teaching approaches like Education 5.0 (Kangara, 2022). Table 1.3 summarizes few of the studies that stress the importance of several core elements of Education 5.0.

Table 3. Selected investigations and tutorials that address education-related attributes (Ahmad, 2023)

Reference	Contribution	Mobile learning	Digital technology	Data analysis	Personalized learning	Collaborative learning
(Quadir, 2022)	The application of data analytics can enhance student results and facilitate individualized learning.		✓	✓	✓	✓
(Green, 2020)	To make better use of online learning management systems, they can be redesigned		✓			
(Raj, 2022)	Personalized learning can be supported by recommender systems.		✓	✓	✓	
(Li, 2021)	Individualized learning can be facilitated by mobile learning in a mixed-learning setting	✓	✓		✓	
(Major, 2021)	The use of digital technology can facilitate individualized learning and increase educational access.		✓			

A study revealed that several shortcomings in the education system as a whole prevent from meeting market expectations and aligning with them. To close the gap between the level of knowledge in academia provided by institutions and the needs of the domestic market, for public higher learning, Education 5.0 was recommended (Keche, 2021). The goal of Education 5.0 is to build an educational environment that is more focused on exploring, therefore the main objective was to turn the old education system into a learning-based academic environment that is in line with market demands. It offers social services and creative integration of the industry and education sectors.

5. SRI LANKA IS AN EXAMPLE OF THE USE OF EDUCATION IN THE DEVELOPING WORLD

The majority of developing nations have seen severe economic declines after the COVID-19 epidemic occurred, which also affected the education industry. Sri Lanka was among the nations most impacted and it found itself in a precarious financial default scenario. Previous research indicates that the economic downturn began before the COVID-19 outbreak and pandemic, which further exacerbated the situation and led to default (Gunasekera, 2020). The authors advise that to achieve the nation's industrial and economic growth, the academic environment for long-term, sustainable education models must be prepared via significant efforts at the early childhood and higher education levels. An overview of the obstacles that may arise during table 1.4 provides information on Education 5.0 system installation.

Table 4. Review of difficulties in making open questions and the realities of education 5.0

Reference	Possible solutions	Obstacles	Open Questions
(Kumar, 2022)	Financing innovative technology	Rate of implementation	How can limited funding be used to achieve Education 5.0? How can the technologies be updated and maintained throughout time?
(Hyun, 2023)	Provide instruction for teachers	Insufficient training for educators	How can limited-resource developing nations offer teacher training? How do we get past teachers' aversion to change?
(Lin, 2022)	Granting all pupils equal access to resources and technology	Internet lag	What steps may be taken to close the educational digital gap? What steps can be taken to guarantee that every student has access to the tools and resources they require?
(Gan, 2022)	Creating individualized and engaging educational resources	Restricted resources for producing content	How might resource exchange and sharing be facilitated? With little funding, how can interactive and customized learning materials be created?
(Corbett, 2020)	Making technological investments	High cost of implementation	How can limited funding be used to achieve Education 5.0? How can the technologies be upgraded and maintained throughout time?

To ensure long-term and sustained academic progress, researchers advocated setting up high-quality education centers with well-trained personnel, a robust curriculum focused on the market, and state of the art classroom facilities. The recommendation was made after extensive investigation, and it was backed by solid evidence for use in elementary and secondary education. An investigation that looked at the issues with the educational system generally in terms of providing high-quality academic instruction and other elements that might impact the nation's overall circumstances (Rajaguru, 2021). They addressed every facet of the education sector, including the majority of crucial elements for improved observation, evaluation and outcomes. The primary aim of the research was to offer education to individuals of all abilities utilizing top-notch instruction, highly qualified faculty, and advanced learning environments (Mutanga, 2018). A robust foundation for robust and sustained academic progress at all levels was found to be provided by a framework for results-oriented learning should serve as the basis for a control and monitoring system for the assessment of academic activities. The following is a list of recommendations for improving Sri Lanka's educational standards.

6. CONCLUSION

Reviewing pertinent literature on technology and education in industrialized and emerging nations was the initial goal of the project. Using the literature to inform the study's composition and address the problems and concerns that both developed and developing nations face in the actual world were other considerations. Given that modernizing education is one of the fundamental tenets of a nation's development. The findings of the study indicate that implementing Education 5.0 may greatly enhance the quality of education by using modern technology. Education 5.0 is undergoing updates to a body of information; it is highly recommended that further study to be done to solve the issues as well as worries and present workable answers for improving the general academic environment. Due to its conceptual research design, which limited its scope, the study might be further broadened to use a quantitative approach to qualitative research technique for improved observation and evaluation.

REFERENCES

Ahmad, S., Umirzakova, S., Mujtaba, G., Amin, M. S., & Whangbo, T. (2023). "Education 5.0: requirements, enabling technologies, and future directions." arXiv preprint arXiv:2307.15846 https://doi.org//arXiv.2307.15846DOI: 10.48550

Aljabri, N., & Bhutoria, A. (2020). Access to educational technology and its implications on learning outcomes of 15-year olds in Saudi Arabia empirical evidence from OECD PISA 2018 in the context of COVID-19. *Journal of Educational Science*, *6*(1), 367–400.

Asmirajanti, M., Antia, A., & Dewi, R. (2023). "Implementation of Nursing Center in improving the quality of Nursing Higher Education in the era of Society 5.0: Systematic review." Jurnal Aisyah. *Jurnal Ilmu Kesehatan*, *8*(2). Advance online publication. DOI: 10.30604/jika.v8i2.1814

Astriana, L., Regina, R., & Yohanes, G. S. Y. (2024). THE IMPLEMENTATION OF SOCIETY 5.0 IN POLICY AND EDUCATIONAL STRATEGIES IN THE 21st CENTURY. In *PROSIDING SEMINAR NASIONAL PENELITIAN DAN PENGABDIAN KEPADA MASYARAKAT* (Vol. 3, pp. 115–130). SNPP.

Awang, Y., Taib, A., & Muda, N. (2020). Perceived challenges towards Education 4.0 implementation among academicians: A preliminary analysis. e-Academia Journal, 9(2).

Corbett, F., & Spinello, E. (2020). Connectivism and leadership: Harnessing a learning theory for the digital age to redefine leadership in the twenty-first century. *Heliyon*, *6*(1), e03250. Advance online publication. DOI: 10.1016/j.heliyon.2020.e03250 PMID: 31993523

Darmaji, D., Mustiningsih, M., & Arifin, I. "Quality management education in the industrial revolution era 4.0 and society 5.0." In *5th International Conference on Education and Technology (ICET 2019)*, pp. 565-570. Atlantis Press, 2019. https://doi.org/DOI: 10.2991/icet-19.2019.141

Gan, W., Dao, M. S., Zettsu, K., & Sun, Y. "Iot-based multimodal analysis for smart education: Current status, challenges and opportunities." In *Proceedings of the 3rd ACM Workshop on Intelligent Cross-Data Analysis and Retrieval*, pp. 32-40. 2022. https://doi.org/DOI: 10.1145/3512731.3534208

Green, K. R., & Chewning, H. L. (2020). The fault in our systems: LMS as a vehicle for critical pedagogy. *TechTrends*, *64*(3), 423–431. DOI: 10.1007/s11528-020-00480-w

Gunasekera, C., & Balasubramani, R. (2020). *Use of Information Communication Technology by School Teachers in Information Provision: An analysis of Sri Lankan perspective*. Library Philosophy & Practice.

Hikmat, H. (2022). The Readiness of Education in Indonesia in Facing The Society Era 5.0. *Jurnal Basicedu*, *6*(2), 2953–2961. DOI: 10.31004/basicedu.v6i2.2526 10

Hyun, W. (2023, February). Study on standardization for interoperable metaverse. In 2023 25th International Conference on Advanced Communication Technology (ICACT) (pp. 319-322). IEEE.

Icela, L., González-Pérez, R.-M. M. S., & Antonio, E.-G. J. (2023). Education 4.0 Maturity Models for Society 5.0: Systematic literature review. *Cogent Business & Management*, *10*(3), 2256095. DOI: 10.1080/23311975.2023.2256095

Kangara, C. T. C., Gocha, M., Tsokota, T., & Marovah, T. "Assessing Readiness for Teaching and Learning Using Icts in Zimbabwean Secondary Schools in Gweru Distrct, Zimbabwe." (2022).https://doi.org/DOI: 10.21203/rs.3.rs-1652431/v1

Keche, K. (2021). *Relevancy of new higher education approaches in 'Second Republic Zimbabwe*. Higher Education-New Approaches to Accreditation, Digitalization, and Globalization in the Age of Covid.

Khaimovich, I., Ramzaev, V., & Chumak, V. (2020). Data modelling for analysis of readness of municipal education in industry 5.0. *CEUR Workshop Proceedings*, *2667*, 1–4.

Kumar, K., & Al-Besher, A. (2022). IoT enabled e-learning system for higher education. *Measurement. Sensors*, *24*, 100480. DOI: 10.1016/j.measen.2022.100480

Li, X., & Heng, Q. (2021, June). Design of mobile learning resources based on new blended learning: a case study of superstar learning app. In 2021 IEEE 3rd International Conference on Computer Science and Educational Informatization (CSEI) (pp. 333-338). IEEE.

Lin, H., Wan, S., Gan, W., Chen, J., & Chao, H. C. (2022, December). Metaverse in education: Vision, opportunities, and challenges. In 2022 IEEE International Conference on Big Data (Big Data) (pp. 2857-2866). IEEE.

Major, L., Francis, G. A., & Tsapali, M. (2021). The effectiveness of technology-supported personalised learning in low-and middle-income countries: A meta-analysis. *British Journal of Educational Technology*, *52*(5), 1935–1964. DOI: 10.1111/bjet.13116

Maria, M., Shahbodin, F., & Pee, N. C. (2018). "Malaysian higher education system towards industry 4.0–current trends overview." In AIP Conference Proceedings, vol. 2016, no. 1. AIP Publishing, https://doi.org/DOI: 10.1063/1.5055483

Miranda, J., Navarrete, C., Noguez, J., Molina-Espinosa, J.-M., Ramírez-Montoya, M.-S., Navarro-Tuch, S. A., Bustamante-Bello, M.-R., Rosas-Fernández, J.-B., & Molina, A. (2021). The core components of education 4.0 in higher education: Three case studies in engineering education. *Computers & Electrical Engineering*, *93*, 107278. DOI: 10.1016/j.compeleceng.2021.107278

Mirghani, T. (2020). The Growing Demand for Education in Saudi Arabia: How Effective Is Borrowing Educational Models from the West? *Journal of Education and Learning*, *9*(6), 59. Advance online publication. DOI: 10.5539/jel.v9n6p59

Mutanga, P., Nezandonyi, J., & Bhukuvhani, C. (2018). Enhancing Engineering Education through Technological Pedagogical and Content Knowledge (TPACK): A Case Study. *International Journal of Education and Development Using Information and Communication Technology*, *14*(3), 38–49.

Pérez, L. I. G., María, S. R. M., & Francisco, J. G. P. (2022). Habilitadores tecnológicos 4.0 para impulsar la educación abierta: Aportaciones para las recomendaciones de la UNESCO. *RIED-Revista Iberoamericana de Educación a Distancia*, *25*(2), 23–43. DOI: 10.5944/ried.25.2.33088

Quadir, B., Chen, N.-S., & Isaias, P. (2022). Analyzing the educational goals, problems and techniques used in educational big data research from 2010 to 2018. *Interactive Learning Environments*, *30*(8), 1539–1555. DOI: 10.1080/10494820.2020.1712427

Raj, N. S., & Renumol, V. G. (2022). A systematic literature review on adaptive content recommenders in personalized learning environments from 2015 to 2020. *Journal of Computers in Education*, *9*(1), 113–148. DOI: 10.1007/s40692-021-00199-4

Rajaguru, S. (2021). Forced and Unplanned Digital Transformation of Education in Sri Lanka during [Crisis: A Case Study.]. *COVID*, •••, 19.

Rakhmawati, D., & Sartono, K. E. (2023). Implementation Of Character Education At Civic Education In 5.0 Era On Fifth Grade State Elementary EDUCATION VIDYA QASANA. *PROGRES PENDIDIKAN*, *4*(1), 32–37. DOI: 10.29303/prospek.v4i1.315

Ramírez-Montoya, M.-S., & Lugo-Ocando, J. (2020). Systematic review of mixed methods in the framework of educational innovation. *Comunicar*, *28*(65), 9–20. DOI: 10.3916/C65-2020-01

Rodríguez-Abitia, G., & Bribiesca-Correa, G. (2021). Assessing digital transformation in universities. *Future Internet, 13*(2), 52. DOI: 10.3390/fi13020052

Rusman, A., Mas'udi, M. M., Hermoyo, R. P., Yarno, Y., Yunianti, S., & Rafsanjani, H. (2023, June). Education transformation in 5.0 society development era. In AIP Conference Proceedings (Vol. 2727, No. 1). AIP Publishing.

Samiha, Y. T., Handayani, T., Razaq, A., Fithriyah, M., Fitri, A., & Anshari, M. (2022, March). Implementation of Education 4.0 as sustainable decisions for a sustainable development. In 2022 International conference on decision aid sciences and applications (DASA) (pp. 846-850). IEEE.

Sart, G. (2022). Impact of Higher Education and Globalization on Sustainable Development in the New EU Member States. *Sustainability (Basel), 14*(19), 11916. DOI: 10.3390/su141911916

Togo, M., & Gandidzanwa, C. P. (2021). The role of Education 5.0 in accelerating the implementation of SDGs and challenges encountered at the University of Zimbabwe. *International Journal of Sustainability in Higher Education, 22*(7), 1520–1535. DOI: 10.1108/IJSHE-05-2020-0158

Compilation of References

Aakhus, M., & Bzdak, M. (2012). Revisiting the role of" shared value" in the business-society relationship. *Business & Professional Ethics Journal*, *31*(2), 231–246. DOI: 10.5840/bpej201231211

Abbasi, K., Alam, A., Du, M. A., & Huynh, T. L. D. (2021). FinTech, SME efficiency and national culture: Evidence from OECD countries. *Technological Forecasting and Social Change*, *163*, 120454. DOI: 10.1016/j.techfore.2020.120454

Abilkaiyrkyzy, A., Elhagry, A., Laamarti, F., & El Saddik, A. (2023). Metaverse Key Requirements and Platforms Survey. *IEEE Access : Practical Innovations, Open Solutions*, *11*, 117765–117787. Advance online publication. DOI: 10.1109/ACCESS.2023.3325844

Abulibdeh, A. (2024). Geospatial assessment of the carbon footprint of water and electricity consumption in residential buildings in Doha, Qatar. *Journal of Cleaner Production*, *445*, 141262. Advance online publication. DOI: 10.1016/j.jclepro.2024.141262

Achibane, M., & Elhamma, A. (2016). Balanced Scorecard Et Incertitude Environnementale: Cas Des Entreprises Au Maroc. *European Scientific Journal*, *12*(7), 459–469. DOI: 10.19044/esj.2016.v12n7p459

Acquier, A., Valiorgue, B., & Daudigeos, T. (2017). Sharing the shared value: A transaction cost perspective on strategic CSR policies in global value chains. *Journal of Business Ethics*, *144*(1), 139–152. DOI: 10.1007/s10551-015-2820-0

Adamantopoulou, S., Karamanlidis, A. A., Dendrinos, P., & Gimenez, O. (2023). Citizen science indicates significant range recovery and defines new conservation priorities for Earth's most endangered pinniped in Greece. *Animal Conservation*, *26*(1), 115–125. Advance online publication. DOI: 10.1111/acv.12806

Adams, R. B., & Ferreira, D. (2007). A theory of friendly boards. *The Journal of Finance*, *62*(1), 217–250. DOI: 10.1111/j.1540-6261.2007.01206.x

Afeltra, G., Alerasoul, S. A., & Strozzi, F. (2023). The evolution of sustainable innovation: from the past to the future. In *European Journal of Innovation Management* (Vol. 26, Issue 2). DOI: 10.1108/EJIM-02-2021-0113

Agyabeng-Mensah, Y., Tang, L., Afum, E., Baah, C., & Dacosta, E. (2021). Organisational identity and circular economy: Are inter and intra organisational learning, lean management and zero waste practices worth pursuing? *Sustainable Production and Consumption*, *28*, 648–662. Advance online publication. DOI: 10.1016/j.spc.2021.06.018

Agyapong, M., Maaledidong, P. D., & Mensah, H. K. (2021). Performance outcome of entrepreneurial behavior of SMEs in a developing economy: The role of international mindset. *Journal of Strategy and Management*, *14*(2), 227–245. DOI: 10.1108/JSMA-07-2020-0173

Ahmad, S., Umirzakova, S., Mujtaba, G., Amin, M. S., & Whangbo, T. (2023). "Education 5.0: requirements, enabling technologies, and future directions." arXiv preprint arXiv:2307.15846 https://doi.org//arXiv.2307.15846DOI: 10.48550

Ahmad, M., & Ali, A. (2023). Integrated Geospatial Information Management in the World of Metaverse: Challenges and Opportunities. In Lekhi, P., & Kaur, G. (Eds.), *Concepts, Technologies, Challenges, and the Future of Web 3* (pp. 248–270). IGI Global., DOI: 10.4018/978-1-6684-9919-1.ch013

Ahmad, S. Z., Abu Bakar, A. R., & Ahmad, N. (2019). Social media adoption and its impact on firm performance: The case of the UAE. *International Journal of Entrepreneurial Behaviour & Research*, *25*(1), 84–111. DOI: 10.1108/IJEBR-08-2017-0299

Ahmed, N. (2024). Spatial vulnerability assessment of urbanites of Rawalpindi to the combined effects of climate change and pandemics using GIS mapping. *Local Environment*, *29*(8), 1–19. DOI: 10.1080/13549839.2024.2353048

Ahmed, W. A. H., & MacCarthy, B. L. (2023). Blockchain-enabled supply chain traceability – How wide? How deep? *International Journal of Production Economics*, *263*, 108963. Advance online publication. DOI: 10.1016/j.ijpe.2023.108963

Ajzen, I. (2001). Nature and Operation of Attitudes. *Annual Review of Psychology*, *52*(1), 27–58. DOI: 10.1146/annurev.psych.52.1.27 PMID: 11148298

Akhtar, S., Tian, H., Alsedrah, I. T., Anwar, A., & Bashir, S. (2024). Green mining in China: Fintech's contribution to enhancing innovation performance aimed at sustainable and digital transformation in the mining sector. *Resources Policy*, *92*, 104968. Advance online publication. DOI: 10.1016/j.resourpol.2024.104968

Akpinar, M., & Saleem, S. (2019). Creating shared value in international business: A research agenda.

Al Zubaidi, H. H. A. (2019). Impact of investment decisions on shared value: An analysis of Iraqi tourism companies listed on the Iraqi Stock Exchange for the period 2013-2017.

Alaassar, A. (2021). A phenomenon-driven exploration of regulatory sandboxes in FinTech entrepreneurial ecosystems.

Alazard, C. and Sépari, S. (2001). Contrôle de gestion DECF. 5ème édition, édition Dunod.

Al-Bakri, A. A., & Katsioloudes, M. I. (2015). The factors affecting e-commerce adoption by Jordanian SMEs. *Management Research Review*, *38*(7), 726–749. DOI: 10.1108/MRR-12-2013-0291

Albrecht, C. M., Zhang, R., Cui, X., Freitag, M., Hamann, H. F., Klein, L. J., & Lu, S. (2020). Change detection from remote sensing to guide OpenStreetMap labeling. *ISPRS International Journal of Geo-Information*, *9*(7), 427. DOI: 10.3390/ijgi9070427

Albuquerque, U. P., Ludwig, D., Feitosa, I. S., de Moura, J. M. B., Gonçalves, P. H. S., da Silva, R. H., & Ferreira, W. S.Junior. (2021). Integrating traditional ecological knowledge into academic research at local and global scales. *Regional Environmental Change*, *21*(2), 1–11. DOI: 10.1007/s10113-021-01774-2

Al-Debei, M. M., & Avison, D. (2010). Developing a unified framework of the business model concept. *European Journal of Information Systems*, *19*(3), 359–376. DOI: 10.1057/ejis.2010.21

Al-Emran, M., & Griffy-Brown, C. (2023). The role of technology adoption in sustainable development: Overview, opportunities, challenges, and future research agendas. *Technology in Society*, *73*, 102240. Advance online publication. DOI: 10.1016/j.techsoc.2023.102240

Al-Htaybat, K., & von Alberti-Alhtaybat, L. (2017). Big data and corporate reporting: Impacts and paradoxes. *Accounting, Auditing & Accountability Journal*, *30*(4), 850–873. DOI: 10.1108/AAAJ-07-2015-2139

Aljabri, N., & Bhutoria, A. (2020). Access to educational technology and its implications on learning outcomes of 15-year olds in Saudi Arabia empirical evidence from OECD PISA 2018 in the context of COVID-19. *Journal of Educational Science*, *6*(1), 367–400.

Alkhalaf, T. (2006). *Les modes de gestion et d'organisation du transport ferroviaire en france et en Grande-Bretagne*. These, Universite de Caen.

Alkhalaf, T., & Al-Tabbaa, O. (2024). The effect of ability, motivation and opportunity (AMO) on SMEs' innovation performance. *Creativity and Innovation Management*, *33*(1), 21–38. DOI: 10.1111/caim.12578

Alpala, L. O., Quiroga-Parra, D. J., Torres, J. C., & Peluffo-Ordóñez, D. H. (2022). Smart Factory Using Virtual Reality and Online Multi-User: Towards a Metaverse for Experimental Frameworks. *Applied Sciences (Basel, Switzerland)*, *12*(12), 6258. Advance online publication. DOI: 10.3390/app12126258

Al-Qirim, N. (2007). The adoption of eCommerce communications and applications technologies in small businesses in New Zealand. *Electronic Commerce Research and Applications*, *6*(4), 462–473. DOI: 10.1016/j.elerap.2007.02.012

Alrammal, M., Abu-Amara, F., Ismail, Z., & Nadeem, M. (2023). Blockchain technology for sustainable management of electricity and water consumption. *Engineering Proceedings*. Advance online publication. DOI: 10.3390/engproc2023059223

Alzoubi, F. A., & Ali, R. A. (2024). Breaking Silence: Women and Men's Experiences of Preventing IPV. *The Qualitative Report*, *29*(3). Advance online publication. DOI: 10.46743/2160-3715/2024.6535

Amit, R., & Zott, C. (2016). Business model design: A dynamic capability perspective. *The Oxford handbook of dynamic capabilities*, Vol. 52, 1-5.

Amoo, O. M., Fagbenle, R. O., & Oyewola, M. O. (2022). *Benchmark assessment of performance indices of a selection of hybrid nanofluids in a hybrid photovoltaic/thermal system*. Clean Energy., DOI: 10.1093/ce/zkac008

Ancín, M., Pindado, E., & Sánchez, M. (2022). New trends in the global digital transformation process of the agri-food sector: An exploratory study based on Twitter. *Agricultural Systems*, *209*, 103520. DOI: 10.1016/j.agsy.2022.103520

Anshari, M., Almunawar, M. N., Masri, M., & Hamdan, M. (2019). Digital marketplace and FinTech to support agriculture sustainability. *Energy Procedia*, *156*, 234–238. DOI: 10.1016/j.egypro.2018.11.134

Anthony, R. N. (1965). *Planning and Control Systems, A Framework for Analysis, Division of Research*. Harvard University.

Anthony, R. N. (1988). *The management Control function*. Harvard Business School Press.

Anttila, H., Anttila, M., & Luoma, M.-L. (2022). A governmental programme to support well-being, ageing and care at home with new technologies. *Gerontechnology (Valkenswaard), 21*(s), 1. Advance online publication. DOI: 10.4017/gt.2022.21.s.725.opp7

Anwar, S., Lindgren, P., & Prasad, R. (2021). Collaborative strategies and socio-dynamic cues (SDC) insights for Assistive Healthcare Technology Applications. *Journal of Mobile Multimedia*. DOI: 10.13052/jmm1550-4646.171311

Appelbaum, D., Kogan, A., Vasarhelyi, M., & Yan, Z. (2015). Impact of business analytics and enterprise systems on managerial accounting. *International Journal of Accounting Information Systems, 25*, 29–44. DOI: 10.1016/j.accinf.2017.03.003

Arena, M., Azzone, G., & Piantoni, G. (2020). Shared value creation during site decommissioning: A case study from the energy sector. *Journal of Cleaner Production, 251*, 119587. DOI: 10.1016/j.jclepro.2019.119587

Argente García, J. E., Yazici, B., Richa, A., Touil, S., Richart Díaz, V. J., Ramallo-González, A. P., & Skarmeta Gómez, A. F. (2024). Digitalising governance processes and water resources management to foster sustainability strategies in the Mediterranean agriculture. *Environmental Science & Policy, 158*, 103805. Advance online publication. DOI: 10.1016/j.envsci.2024.103805

Argyres, N., & McGahan, A. M. (2002). An interview with Michael Porter. *The Academy of Management Perspectives, 16*(2), 43–52. DOI: 10.5465/ame.2002.7173495

Arner, D. W., Barberis, J., & Buckley, R. P. (2015). The evolution of Fintech: A new post-crisis paradigm. *SSRN, 47*, 1271. DOI: 10.2139/ssrn.2676553

Arner, D. W., Buckley, R. P., Zetzsche, D. A., & Veidt, R. (2020). Sustainability, FinTech and financial inclusion. *European Business Organization Law Review, 21*(1), 7–35. DOI: 10.1007/s40804-020-00183-y

Arsanjani, J. J., Mooney, P., Helbich, M., & Zipf, A. (2015). An exploration of future patterns of the contributions to OpenStreetMap and development of a Contribution Index. *Transactions in GIS, 19*(6), 896–914. DOI: 10.1111/tgis.12139

Arsiwala, A., Elghaish, F., & Zoher, M. (2023). Digital twin with Machine learning for predictive monitoring of CO2 equivalent from existing buildings. *Energy and Building, 284*, 112851. Advance online publication. DOI: 10.1016/j.enbuild.2023.112851

Arslanian, H., & Fischer, F. (2019). *The future of finance: The impact of FinTech, AI, and crypto on financial services*. Springer. DOI: 10.1007/978-3-030-14533-0

Ascarya, A. (2009). Lessons learned from repeated financial crises: An Islamic economic perspective. *Bulletin of Monetary Economics and Banking*, *12*(1), 27–74. DOI: 10.21098/bemp.v12i1.466

Asensio, J., Josa, I., Monserrat, A., & de la Fuente, A. (2023). 3D-printed concrete footbridges: An approach to assess the sustainability performance. *Structural Concrete*, *24*(6), 7705–7725. Advance online publication. DOI: 10.1002/suco.202201227

Ashta, A. (2018). News and trends in Fintech and digital microfinance: Why are European MFIs invisible? *FIIB Business Review*, *7*(4), 232–243. DOI: 10.1177/2319714518805183

Ashta, A., & Herrmann, H. (2021). Artificial intelligence and fintech: An overview of opportunities and risks for banking, investments, and microfinance. *Strategic Change*, *30*(3), 211–222. DOI: 10.1002/jsc.2404

Asmirajanti, M., Antia, A., & Dewi, R. (2023). "Implementation of Nursing Center in improving the quality of Nursing Higher Education in the era of Society 5.0: Systematic review." Jurnal Aisyah. *Jurnal Ilmu Kesehatan*, *8*(2). Advance online publication. DOI: 10.30604/jika.v8i2.1814

Astriana, L., Regina, R., & Yohanes, G. S. Y. (2024). THE IMPLEMENTATION OF SOCIETY 5.0 IN POLICY AND EDUCATIONAL STRATEGIES IN THE 21st CENTURY. In *PROSIDING SEMINAR NASIONAL PENELITIAN DAN PENGABDIAN KEPADA MASYARAKAT* (Vol. 3, pp. 115–130). SNPP.

Audrin, B., & Davoine, E. (2017). La fonction RH face à la numérisation des organisations: Le cas des outils de communication numérique. *Management & Avenir*, *92*(92), 15–39. DOI: 10.3917/mav.092.0015

Awang, Y., Taib, A., & Muda, N. (2020). Perceived challenges towards Education 4.0 implementation among academicians: A preliminary analysis. e-Academia Journal, 9(2).

Ayyagari, R., Grover, V., & Purvis, R. (2011). Technostress: Technological Antecedents and Implications. *Management Information Systems Quarterly*, *35*(4), 831–858. DOI: 10.2307/41409963

Bakirci, M. (2024). Enhancing air pollution mapping with autonomous UAV networks for extended coverage and consistency. *Atmospheric Research*, *306*, 107480. https://doi.org/https://doi.org/10.1016/j.atmosres.2024.107480. DOI: 10.1016/j.atmosres.2024.107480

Balogun, A. L., Marks, D., Sharma, R., Shekhar, H., Balmes, C., Maheng, D., Arshad, A., & Salehi, P. (2020). Assessing the Potentials of Digitalization as a Tool for Climate Change Adaptation and Sustainable Development in Urban Centres. *Sustainable Cities and Society*, *53*, 101888. Advance online publication. DOI: 10.1016/j.scs.2019.101888

Bandura, A. (1986). *Social Foundation of Thought and Action: a social cognitive theory*. Prentice –Hall.

Banker, R. D., Chang, H., & Kao, Y. (2002). Impact of Information Technology on Public Accounting Firm Productivity. *Journal of Information Systems*, *16*(2), 209–222. DOI: 10.2308/jis.2002.16.2.209

Banque de France (2018). L'impact des TIC et de la digitalisation sur la productivité et la part du travail dans la valeur ajoutée: enseignements à partir d'un échantillon d'entreprises françaises. Document de travail n°785.

Bansal, G., Rajgopal, K., Chamola, V., Xiong, Z., & Niyato, D. (2022). Healthcare in Metaverse: A Survey on Current Metaverse Applications in Healthcare. *IEEE Access : Practical Innovations, Open Solutions*, *10*, 119914–119946. Advance online publication. DOI: 10.1109/ACCESS.2022.3219845

Barnes, W., Gartland, M., & Stack, M. (2004). Old habits die hard: Path dependence and behavioural lock-in. *Journal of Economic Issues*, *38*(2), 371–377. DOI: 10.1080/00213624.2004.11506696

Barney, J. B. (1991). Firm resources and sustained competitive advantage. *Journal of Management*, *17*(1), 99–120. DOI: 10.1177/014920639101700108

Barney, J. B. (2001). Resource-Based Theories of Competitive Advantage: A Ten Year Retrospective on the Resource-Based View. *Journal of Management*, *27*(6), 643–650. DOI: 10.1177/014920630102700602

Barney, J. B., Ketchen, D. J.Jr, & Wright, M. (2021). Resource-Based Theory and the Value Creation Framework. *Journal of Management*, *47*(7), 1936–1955. DOI: 10.1177/01492063211021655

Baron, R. M., & Kenny, D. A. (1986). The moderator-mediator variable distinction in social psychological research: Conceptual, strategic, and statistical considerations. *Journal of Personality and Social Psychology*, *51*(6), 1173–1182. DOI: 10.1037/0022-3514.51.6.1173 PMID: 3806354

Barresi, A. (2023). Urban Digital Twin and urban planning for sustainable cities. *Techne : Journal of Technology for Architecture and Environment*, (25), 78–83. Advance online publication. DOI: 10.36253/techne-13568

Basova, Y., Dobrotvorskiy, S., Balog, M., Iakovets, A., Chelabi, M. A., & Zinchenko, A. (2023). Increasing SME supply chain resilience in the face of rapidly changing demand with 3D model visualisation. *International Journal of Mechatronics and Applied Mechanics*, *14*(5). Advance online publication. DOI: 10.17683/ijomam/issue14.5

Basu, R., Pal, S., & Ghosh, A. (2022). Blockchain in waste management: Case study of Indian startups. *Journal of Sustainable Development*, *12*(4), 98–112.

Batunanggar, S. (2019). *Fintech development and regulatory frameworks in Indonesia* (No. 1014). ADBI Working Paper Series.

Bauer, M. E. (2020). Remote Sensing of Environment: History, Philosophy, Approach and Contributions, 1969 –2019. *Remote Sensing of Environment*, *237*, 111522. Advance online publication. DOI: 10.1016/j.rse.2019.111522

Bayoumy, K., Gaber, M., Elshafeey, A., Mhaimeed, O., Dineen, E. H., Marvel, F. A., Martin, S. S., Muse, E. D., Turakhia, M. P., Tarakji, K. G., & Elshazly, M. B. (2021). Smart wearable devices in cardiovascular care: where we are and how to move forward. In *Nature Reviews Cardiology* (Vol. 18, Issue 8). DOI: 10.1038/s41569-021-00522-7

Beck, T., Chen, T., Lin, C., & Song, F. M. (2016). Financial innovation: The bright and the dark sides. *Journal of Banking & Finance*, *72*, 28–51. DOI: 10.1016/j.jbankfin.2016.06.012

Belfanti, F. *Creating shared value and clusters* (Doctoral dissertation, Università Carlo Cattaneo-LIUC).

Benga, B., & Elhamma, A. (2024). Navigating the Digital Frontier: A Literature Review on Business Digitalization. *European Scientific Journal*, *20*(10), 107–125. DOI: 10.19044/esj.2024.v20n10p107

Bennani, S. and Elhamma, A. (2015), La comptabilité en finance islamique selon les normes aaoifi. Editions universitaires européennes.

Bergquist, A. K., & Eriksson, L. (2019). Sober business: Shared value creation between the insurance industry and the temperance movement. *Business History*, *61*(2), 322–342. DOI: 10.1080/00076791.2017.1380627

Bergquist, A. K., & Lindmark, M. (2016). Sustainability and shared value in the interwar Swedish copper industry. *Business History Review*, *90*(2), 197–225. DOI: 10.1017/S0007680516000374

Bertolotto, M., McArdle, G., & Schoen-Phelan, B. (2020). Volunteered and crowd-sourced geographic information: The OpenStreetMap project. *Journal of Spatial Information Science*, *20*(20), 65–70. DOI: 10.5311/JOSIS.2020.20.659

Beschorner, T. (2014). Creating shared value: The one-trick pony approach. *Business Ethics Journal Review*, *1*(17), 106–112.

Beschorner, T., & Hajduk, T. (2017). Creating shared value. A fundamental critique. *Creating Shared Value–Concepts, Experience. Criticism*, •••, 27–37.

Bescos, P. L., & Cauvin, E. (2004). L'évaluation des performances dans les entreprises françaises: une étude empirique. *Actes du 25ème Congrès de l'AFC*, Orléans.

Bettinger, A. (1972). Fintech: A series of 40 time shared models used at Manufacturers Hanover Trust Company. *Interfaces*, •••, 62–63.

Bhattacharya, A. (2021). Digital Transformation in Indian SMEs: Challenges and Opportunities. *Journal of Business Studies*, *34*(2), 120–135.

Bhattacharya, A., & Roy, S. (2022). Green Mobility and Digital Technologies: The Role of the FAME India Scheme. *Journal of Sustainable Transportation*, *11*(3), 56–72.

Bibri, S. E., & Krogstie, J. (2020). Environmentally data-driven smart sustainable cities: Applied innovative solutions for energy efficiency, pollution reduction, and urban metabolism. *Energy Informatics*, *3*(1), 1–20. DOI: 10.1186/s42162-020-00130-8

Bierstaker, J. L., Burnaby, P., & Thibodeau, J. (2001). The impact of information technology on the audit process: An assessment of the state of the art and implications for the future. *Managerial Auditing Journal*, *16*(3), 159–164. DOI: 10.1108/02686900110385489

Bill Gates. (2014) Banking is changing. Impatient Optimists. *Bill & Melinda Gates Foundation Web site*.

Blake, J. (1999). Overcoming the value-action gap in environmental policy: Tensions between national policy and local experience. *Local Environment*, *4*(3), 257–278. DOI: 10.1080/13549839908725599

Blakstad, S., & Allen, R. (2018). FinTech revolution. *Cham, Switzerland: Springer*, *121*, 132. https://doi.org/DOI: 10.1007/978-3-319-76014-8

Bockstette, V., Pfitzer, M., & Smith, D. (2015). Banking on shared value. How banks profit by rethinking their purpose. FSG.: http://sharedvalue.org/

Bofondi, M., & Gobbi, G. (2017). The big promise of FinTech. *European economy*, (2), 107-119.

Bollaert, H., Lopez-de-Silanes, F., & Schwienbacher, A. (2021). Fintech and access to finance. *Journal of Corporate Finance*, *68*, 101941. https://doi.org/https://doi.org/10.1016/j.jcorpfin.2021.101941. DOI: 10.1016/j.jcorpfin.2021.101941

Bonilla, C., Brentan, B., Montalvo, I., Ayala-Cabrera, D., & Izquierdo, J. (2023). Digitalization of water distribution systems in small cities, a tool for verification and hydraulic analysis: A case study of Pamplona, Colombia. *Water (Switzerland)*. Advance online publication. DOI: 10.3390/w15213824

Bonnet, D., Westerman, G., & McAfee, A. (2014). *Leading Digital: Turning Technology into Business Transformation*. Harvard Business Review Press.

Borase, A. A., Bokil, S., & Sakhare, V. (2024). Geospatial solution for sustainable waste management: A case study. *Innovative Infrastructure Solutions*, *9*(6), 218. DOI: 10.1007/s41062-024-01539-w

Bos, C. (2018). *La transformation digitale, vers un management stratégique augmenté. Céline Bos, Ea Conseil & formation*. DIF.

Boss, D., Nelson, T., Winters, M., & Ferster, C. J. (2018). Using crowdsourced data to monitor change in spatial patterns of bicycle ridership. *Journal of Transport & Health*, *9*, 226–233. DOI: 10.1016/j.jth.2018.02.008

Botts, M., & Robin, A. (2007). *OpenGIS ® Sensor Model Language (SensorML) Implementation Specification*. Design.

Boumpa, E., Tsoukas, V., Gkogkidis, A., Spathoulas, G., & Kakarountas, A. (2022). Security and Privacy Concerns for Healthcare Wearable Devices and Emerging Alternative Approaches. *Lecture Notes of the Institute for Computer Sciences, Social-Informatics and Telecommunications Engineering, LNICST, 440 LNICST*. DOI: 10.1007/978-3-031-06368-8_2

Bouquin, H. (2001). Le contrôle de gestion. 5ème édition mise à jour, PUF, collection. *Gestion*.

Bouwman, H., Nikou, S., & de Reuver, M. (2019). Digitalization, business models, and SMEs: How do business model innovation practices improve performance of digitalizing SMEs? *Telecommunications Policy*, *43*(9), 101828. DOI: 10.1016/j.telpol.2019.101828

Boyer-Davis, S. (2019). Technostress in Accounting Professionals: A Quantitative Examination of the Differences Between Managers and Non-Managers. *Journal of Accounting and Finance*, *19*(2), 25–41.

BPS. B. P. S. (2018). Statistical yearbook of Indonesia 2018. In BPS-Statistics Indonesia. https://www.bps.go.id/publication/2018/07/03/5a963c1ea9b0fed6497d0845/

Bratu, S., & Sabău, R. I. (2022). Digital Commerce in the Immersive Metaverse Environment: Cognitive Analytics Management, Real-Time Purchasing Data, and Seamless Connected Shopping Experiences. *Linguistic and Philosophical Investigations*, *21*(0), 170. Advance online publication. DOI: 10.22381/lpi21202211

Brod, C. (1982). Managing technostress: Optimizing the use of computer technology. *The Personnel Journal*, *61*(10), 753–757. PMID: 10258012

Brod, C. (1984). *Technostress: The Human Cost of Computer Revolution*. Addison-Wesley.

Buchak, G., Matvos, G., Piskorski, T., & Seru, A. (2018). Fintech, regulatory arbitrage, and the rise of shadow banks. *Journal of Financial Economics*, *130*(3), 453–483. DOI: 10.1016/j.jfineco.2018.03.011

Budhathoki, N. R., Bruce, B., & Nedovic-Budic, Z. (2008). Reconceptualizing the role of the user of spatial data infrastructure. *GeoJournal*, *72*(3-4), 149–160. DOI: 10.1007/s10708-008-9189-x

Budhathoki, N. R., & Haythornthwaite, C. (2013). Motivation for open collaboration: Crowd and community models and the case of OpenStreetMap. *The American Behavioral Scientist*, *57*(5), 548–575. DOI: 10.1177/0002764212469364

Budziszewski, P. K. (2021). Entertainment Software Rating Board (ESRB). In *Encyclopedia of Video Games: The Culture, Technology, and Art of Gaming: 3 Volumes, Second Edition* (Vol. 1).

Burton, J., Kemp, D., Barnes, R., & Parmenter, J. (2024). A socio-spatial analysis of Australia's critical minerals endowment and policy implications. *Resources Policy*, *88*, 104448. Advance online publication. DOI: 10.1016/j.resourpol.2023.104448

Bu, Y., Li, H., & Wu, X. (2022). Effective regulations of FinTech innovations: The case of China. *Economics of Innovation and New Technology*, *31*(8), 751–769. DOI: 10.1080/10438599.2020.1868069

Büyüközkan, G., & Uztürk, D. (2024). Integrated design framework for smart agriculture: Bridging the gap between digitalization and sustainability. *Journal of Cleaner Production*, *449*, 141572. Advance online publication. DOI: 10.1016/j.jclepro.2024.141572

Cadag, J. R. D., & Gaillard, J. C. (2012). Integrating knowledge and actions in disaster risk reduction: The contribution of participatory mapping. *Area*, *44*(1), 100–109. DOI: 10.1111/j.1475-4762.2011.01065.x

Cai, C. W. (2018). Disruption of financial intermediation by FinTech: A review on crowdfunding and blockchain. *Accounting and Finance*, *58*(4), 965–992. DOI: 10.1111/acfi.12405

Califf, C., Sarker, S., & Sarker, S. (2020). The Bright and Dark Sides of Technostress: A Mixed-Methods Study Involving Healthcare IT. *Management Information Systems Quarterly*, *44*(2), 809–856. DOI: 10.25300/MISQ/2020/14818

Camarena-Martinez, J. L., Ochoa-Silva, B., & Wendlandt-Amezaga, T. R. (2016). Exploring the origins of creating shared value in the CSR literature. *International Journal of Business and Management*, *11*(12), 97–109. DOI: 10.5539/ijbm.v11n12p97

Campbell, S., Greenwood, M., Prior, S., Shearer, T., Walkem, K., Young, S., Bywaters, D., & Walker, K. (2020). Purposive sampling: Complex or simple? Research case examples. *Journal of Research in Nursing : JRN*, *25*(8), 652–661. DOI: 10.1177/1744987120927206 PMID: 34394687

Canali, S., Ferretti, A., Schiaffonati, V., & Blasimme, A. (2024). Wearable Technologies for Healthy Ageing: Prospects, Challenges, and Ethical Considerations. In *Journal of Frailty and Aging* (Vol. 13, Issue 2). DOI: 10.14283/jfa.2024.19

Canali, S., Schiaffonati, V., & Aliverti, A. (2022). Challenges and recommendations for wearable devices in digital health: Data quality, interoperability, health equity, fairness. *PLOS Digital Health*, *1*(10), e0000104. Advance online publication. DOI: 10.1371/journal.pdig.0000104 PMID: 36812619

Cannon, N. H., & Herda, D. N. (2016). Auditors' Organizational Commitment, Burnout and Turnover Intention: A Replication. *Behavioral Research in Accounting*, *28*(2), 69–74. DOI: 10.2308/bria-51455

Cao, F., Sun, J., & Yuan, R. (2019). Board directors with foreign experience and stock price crash risk: Evidence from China. *Journal of Business Finance & Accounting*, *46*(9-10), 1144–1170. https://corporatefinanceinstitute.com/resources/capital-markets/market-risk/. DOI: 10.1111/jbfa.12400

Casadesus-Masanell, R., & Zhu, F. (2013). Business Model Innovation and Competitive Imitation: The Case of Sponsor-Based Business Models. *Strategic Management Journal*, *34*(4), 464–482. DOI: 10.1002/smj.2022

Castejón Teruel, A. (2018). The rise of FinTech in the global financial markets.

Castellacci, F., & Lie, C. M. (2017). A taxonomy of green innovators: Empirical evidence from South Korea. *Journal of Cleaner Production, 143*, 1036–1047. Advance online publication. DOI: 10.1016/j.jclepro.2016.12.016

Cavallo, A., Cosenz, F., & Noto, G. (2023). Business model scaling and growth hacking in digital entrepreneurship. *Journal of Small Business Management*, •••, 1–28.

Cavazotte, F., Lemos, A. H., & Villadsen, K. (2014). Corporate smart phones: Professionals' conscious engagement in escalating work connectivity. *New Technology, Work and Employment, 29*, 72–87.

Cavelius, F., Endenich, Ch., & Zicari, A. (2018). L'impact de la digitalisation sur le rôle du controleur de gestion. Transitions numériques et informations comptables, May, Nantes, France. pp.cd-rom. ffhal-01907810f.

Cazals, F. (2015). *Stratégies digitales: La méthode des 6C*. Deboeck Supérieur.

Cerda, I. H., Therond, A., Moreau, S., Studer, K., Donjow, A. R., Crowther, J. E., Mazzolenis, M. E., Lang, M., Tolba, R., Gilligan, C., Ashina, S., Kaye, A. D., Yong, R. J., Schatman, M. E., & Robinson, C. L. (2024). Telehealth and Virtual Reality Technologies in Chronic Pain Management: A Narrative Review. In *Current Pain and Headache Reports* (Vol. 28, Issue 3). DOI: 10.1007/s11916-023-01205-3

Ch'ng, P.-C., Cheah, J., & Amran, A.Ch'ng. (2021). Eco-innovation practices and sustainable business performance: The moderating effect of market turbulence in the Malaysian technology industry. *Journal of Cleaner Production, 283*, 124556. DOI: 10.1016/j.jclepro.2020.124556

Chakrabarty, S., & Bass, A. E. (2014). Corporate governance in microfinance institutions: Board composition and the ability to face institutional voids. *Corporate Governance, 22*(5), 367–386. DOI: 10.1111/corg.12071

Chapellier, P. (1993). Pour un élargissement de l'approche contingente du système d'information comptable de la PME. Acte du Congrès de L'AFC.

Chatterjee, D., & Bose, P. (2022). Digital Innovation in Indian Agriculture: A Case Study of Agri-Tech Startups. *Indian Journal of Agriculture and Sustainability, 8*(1), 100–115.

Chawla, L. (1998). Significant life experiences revisited: A review of research on sources of pro-environmental sensitivity. *The Journal of Environmental Education, 29*(3), 3, 11–21. DOI: 10.1080/00958969809599114

Cheah, A., Amran, A., & Yahya, S. (2019). Internal oriented resources and social enterprises' performance: How can social enterprises help themselves before helping others? *Journal of Cleaner Production*, *211*, 607–619. DOI: 10.1016/j.jclepro.2018.11.203

Chege, S. M., & Wang, D. (2020). The influence of technology innovation on SME performance through environmental sustainability practices in Kenya. *Technology in Society*, *60*, 101210. DOI: 10.1016/j.techsoc.2019.101210

Chen, J., Chen, S., Fu, R., Li, D., Jiang, H., Wang, C., Peng, Y., Jia, K., & Hicks, B. J. (2022). Remote Sensing Big Data for Water Environment Monitoring: Current Status, Challenges, and Future Prospects. In *Earth's Future* (Vol. 10, Issue 2). DOI: 10.1029/2021EF002289

Chen, K. C. (2020). Implications of Fintech developments for traditional banks. *International journal of economics and financial issues, 10*(5), 227.

Cheng, M., & Qu, Y. (2020). Does bank FinTech reduce credit risk? Evidence from China. *Pacific-Basin Finance Journal*, *63*, 101398. DOI: 10.1016/j.pacfin.2020.101398

Chengoden, R., Victor, N., Huynh-The, T., Yenduri, G., Jhaveri, R. H., Alazab, M., Bhattacharya, S., Hegde, P., Maddikunta, P. K. R., & Gadekallu, T. R. (2023). Metaverse for Healthcare: A Survey on Potential Applications, Challenges and Future Directions. *IEEE Access : Practical Innovations, Open Solutions*, *11*, 12765–12795. Advance online publication. DOI: 10.1109/ACCESS.2023.3241628

Chen, L., Li, X., & Zhu, J. (2024). Carbon peak control for achieving net-zero renewable-based smart cities: Digital twin modeling and simulation. *Sustainable Energy Technologies and Assessments*, *65*, 103792. Advance online publication. DOI: 10.1016/j.seta.2024.103792

Chen, Q., Li, X., Zhang, Z., Zhou, C., Guo, Z., Liu, Z., & Zhang, H. (2023). Remote sensing of photovoltaic scenarios: Techniques, applications and future directions. *Applied Energy*, *333*, 120579. Advance online publication. DOI: 10.1016/j.apenergy.2022.120579

Chen, Y. R. R., Hung-Baesecke, C. J. F., Bowen, S. A., Zerfass, A., Stacks, D. W., & Boyd, B. (2020). The role of leadership in shared value creation from the public's perspective: A multi-continental study. *Public Relations Review*, *46*(1), 101749. DOI: 10.1016/j.pubrev.2018.12.006

Chesbrough, H. (2010). Business model innovation: Opportunities and barriers. *Long Range Planning*, *43*(2-3), 354–363. DOI: 10.1016/j.lrp.2009.07.010

Cheung, C. M. (2019). Panel report: The dark side of the digitization of the individual. *Internet Research, 29*(2), 274–288. DOI: 10.1108/INTR-04-2019-541

Chin, S.-W., Rubambiza, G., Zhao, Y., Malek, K., & Weatherspoon, H. (2024). Realtime optimization and management system (ROAM): A decision support system for digital agriculture systems. *Smart Agricultural Technology, 8*, 100452. Advance online publication. DOI: 10.1016/j.atech.2024.100452

Chung, K. H., & Zhang, H. (2011). Corporate governance and institutional ownership. *Journal of Financial and Quantitative Analysis, 46*(1), 247–273. DOI: 10.1017/S0022109010000682

Cialdini, R., Kallgren, C., & Reno, R. (1991). A focus theory of normative conduct: A theoretical refinement and re-evaluation of the role of norms in human behaviour. *Advances in Experimental Social Psychology, 24*, 201–234. DOI: 10.1016/S0065-2601(08)60330-5

CII (2023). "Green Manufacturing: AI in Water and Resource Optimization." Confederation of Indian Industry.

Claessens, S., & Laeven, L. (2004). Competition in the financial sector and growth: A cross-country perspective. In *Financial development and economic growth: Explaining the links* (pp. 66–105). Palgrave Macmillan UK. DOI: 10.1057/9780230374270_3

Clark, C., Maron, M., Patel, D., Radford, T., Soden, R. J., & Uithol, P. (2016). *Open mapping for the SDGs: a practical guide to launching and growing open mapping initiatives at the national and local levels* (No. 139458, pp. 1-27). The World Bank.

Clark, L. A., & Watson, D. (1999). Temperament: A new paradigm for trait psychology. Dans L. A. (Eds.), *Handbook of personality: Theory and research* (pp. 399–423). Guilford Press.

Clauss, T., Abebe, M., Tangpong, C., & Hock, M. (2021). Strategic Agility, Business Model Innovation, and Firm Performance: An Empirical Investigation. *IEEE Transactions on Engineering Management, 68*(3), 767–784. DOI: 10.1109/TEM.2019.2910381

Clauß, T., Bouncken, R. B., Laudien, S., & Sascha, K. (2020). Business model reconfiguration and innovation in smes: A mixed-method analysis from the electronics industry. *International Journal of Innovation Management, 24*(02), 2050015. DOI: 10.1142/S1363919620500152

Clerck, J. (2017). Digitalization, Digital Transformation [-SCOOP.]. *Differences: A Journal of Feminist Cultural Studies*, •••, i.

Coase, R. H. (1937). The nature ofthe firm. *Economica*, *4*(16), 386–405. DOI: 10.1111/j.1468-0335.1937.tb00002.x

Cockburn, T. (2024). Digital Transformation: Strategy, Execution, and Technology. *The Learning Organization*, *31*(3), 458–464. DOI: 10.1108/TLO-04-2024-307

Colangelo, G. (2022). Enforcing copyright through antitrust? The strange case of news publishers against digital platforms. *Journal of Antitrust Enforcement*. Advance online publication. DOI: 10.1093/jaenfo/jnab009

Coles, J. L., Daniel, N. D., & Naveen, L. (2008). Boards: Does one size fit all? *Journal of Financial Economics*, *87*(2), 329–356. DOI: 10.1016/j.jfineco.2006.08.008

Colesky, M., Hoepman, J.-H., & Hillen, C. (2016). *A critical analysis of privacy design strategies*. In 2016 IEEE Security and Privacy Workshops (SPW) (pp. 33-40). IEEE. DOI: 10.1109/SPW.2016.23

Cooper, C. L. (1998). *Job stress*. Oxford University Press.

Cooper, C. L., Dewe, P., & O'Driscoll, M. (2001). *Organizational Stress: A review and critique of theory, research, and applications*. Sage. DOI: 10.4135/9781452231235

Cooper-Martin, E., & Holbrook, M. B. (1993). Ethical consumption experiences and ethical space. In *L.McAlister et M.L. Rothschild (coord.), Advances in Consumer Research, 20* (pp. 113–118). Association for Consumer Research.

Corbett, F., & Spinello, E. (2020). Connectivism and leadership: Harnessing a learning theory for the digital age to redefine leadership in the twenty-first century. *Heliyon*, *6*(1), e03250. Advance online publication. DOI: 10.1016/j.heliyon.2020.e03250 PMID: 31993523

Corner, P. D., & Pavlovich, K. (2016). Shared value through inner knowledge creation. *Journal of Business Ethics*, *135*(3), 543–555. DOI: 10.1007/s10551-014-2488-x

Costa, P. T., & McCrae, R. R. (1985). *NEO personality inventory professional manual*. Psychological Assessment Resources, Inc.

Crane, A. (2001). Unpacking the ethical product. *Journal of Business Ethics*, *30*(4), 361–373. DOI: 10.1023/A:1010793013027

Crane, A., Palazzo, G., Spence, L. J., & Matten, D. (2014). Contesting the value of "creating shared value". *California Management Review*, *56*(2), 130–153. DOI: 10.1525/cmr.2014.56.2.130

Cumming, D. J., & Schwienbacher, A. (2021). Fintech venture capital. In *The Routledge Handbook of FinTech* (pp. 11–37). Routledge. DOI: 10.4324/9780429292903-3

Dagher, L., Shi, H., Zhao, Y., & Marrouche, N. F. (2020). Wearables in cardiology: Here to stay. *Heart Rhythm*, *17*(5), 889–895. Advance online publication. DOI: 10.1016/j.hrthm.2020.02.023 PMID: 32354455

Daily, C. M., Dalton, D. R., & Cannella, A. A.Jr. (2003). Corporate governance: Decades of dialogue and data. *Academy of Management Review*, *28*(3), 371–382. DOI: 10.2307/30040727

Danys, L., Zolotova, I., Romero, D., Papcun, P., Kajati, E., Jaros, R., Koudelka, P., Koziorek, J., & Martinek, R. (2022). Visible Light Communication and localization: A study on tracking solutions for Industry 4.0 and the Operator 4.0. *Journal of Manufacturing Systems*, *64*, 535–545. Advance online publication. DOI: 10.1016/j.jmsy.2022.07.011

Daood, A., & Menghwar, P. R. E. M. (2017). Understanding" creating shared value". In *EUROMED ACADEMY OF BUSINESS CONFERENCE BOOK OF PROCEEDINGS* (pp. 513-525). EuroMed Press.

Darmaji, D., Mustiningsih, M., & Arifin, I. "Quality management education in the industrial revolution era 4.0 and society 5.0." In *5th International Conference on Education and Technology (ICET 2019)*, pp. 565-570. Atlantis Press, 2019. https://doi.org/DOI: 10.2991/icet-19.2019.141

Day, A., Paquet, S., Scott, N., & Hambley, L. (2012). Perceived information and communication technology (ICT) demands on employee outcomes: The moderating effect of organizational ICT support. *Journal of Occupational Health Psychology*, *17*(4), 473–491. DOI: 10.1037/a0029837 PMID: 23066697

De Sardan, J.P.O. (1995). The Politics of the Field, Investigation. Brussels, Belgium: Academia Bruylant, Collection Anthropologie prospective.

Degrossi, L. C., Porto de Albuquerque, J., Santos Rocha, R. D., & Zipf, A. (2018). A taxonomy of quality assessment methods for volunteered and crowdsourced geographic information. *Transactions in GIS*, *22*(2), 542–560. DOI: 10.1111/tgis.12329 PMID: 29937686

Dekhili, S. (2016). Mass retailers: What legitimacy to market ecological products from the point of view of consumers? *Management Avenir*, (5), 55–77. DOI: 10.3917/mav.087.0055

Dent, J. F. (1990). Strategy, organization and control: Some possibilities for accounting research. *Accounting, Organizations and Society*, *15*(1/2), 3–25. DOI: 10.1016/0361-3682(90)90010-R

Depitre, B. C., & Havre, L. (2000). Sustainable development and consumer citizenship. 1st International Congess of Marketing Tendencies in Europe.

Desreumaux, A. (1998), Théorie des organisations. éd. EMS.

Devinney, T. M., Auger, P., Eckhardt, G., & Birtchnell, T. (2006). The other CSR: Consumer social responsibility.

Diaz, I., Chiaburu, D. S., Zimmerman, R. D., & Boswell, W. R. (2012). Communication technology: Pros and cons of constant connection to work. *Journal of Vocational Behavior, 80*(2), 500–508. DOI: 10.1016/j.jvb.2011.08.007

Dietrick, T. A. (2021). Biometric Monitoring Devices: Modern Solutions to Protecting Athletes' Data Privacy. *Pittsburgh Journal of Technology Law & Policy, 21*(1). Advance online publication. DOI: 10.5195/tlp.2021.245

Donnelly, D. P., Quirin, J. J., & O'Bryan, D. (2003). Auditor acceptance of dysfunctional audit behavior: An explanatory model using auditors' personal characteristics. *Behavioral Research in Accounting, 15*(1), 87–110. DOI: 10.2308/bria.2003.15.1.87

Dorn, D. (2017). La montée en puissance des machines: Comment l'ordinateur a changé le travail. *Revue Française des Affaires Sociales, 1*, 35–63.

Downes, L., & Nunes, P. F. (2013). Big-Bang Disruption. *Harvard Business Review, 91*(3), 44–56.

Dudézert, A. (2018). *La Transformation digitale des entreprises*. La Découverte.

Dudhat, A., Lestari Santoso, N. P., Santoso, S., & Setiawati, R. (2021). Blockchain in Indonesia University: A Design Viewboard of Digital Technology Education. *APTISI Transactions on Technopreneurship, 3*(1), 68–80. Advance online publication. DOI: 10.34306/att.v3i1.146

Durlević, U., Novković, I., Carević, I., Valjarević, D., Marjanović, A., Batoćanin, N., Krstić, F., Stojanović, L., & Valjarević, A. (2023). Sanitary landfill site selection using GIS-based on a fuzzy multi-criteria evaluation technique: A case study of the City of Kraljevo, Serbia. *Environmental Science and Pollution Research International, 30*(13), 37961–37980. Advance online publication. DOI: 10.1007/s11356-022-24884-8 PMID: 36576628

Edwards, J. R., & Cooper, C. L. (1990). The person€nvironment fit approach to stress: Recurring problems and some suggested solutions. *Journal of Organizational Behavior, 11*(4), 293–307. DOI: 10.1002/job.4030110405

Eklinder-Frick, J., Perna, A., & Fremont, V. H. J. (2023). "Guest editorial": Understanding digital transformation from an inter-organisational network perspective. *Journal of Business and Industrial Marketing*, *38*(6), 1245–1250. DOI: 10.1108/JBIM-06-2023-605

ElHaffar, G., Durif, F., & Dubé, L. (2020). Towards closing the attitude-intention-behavior gap in green consumption: A narrative review of the literature and an overview of future research directions. *Journal of Cleaner Production*, *275*, 122556. DOI: 10.1016/j.jclepro.2020.122556

Elhamma, A. (2011). Recherche d'une congruence entre les outils du contrôle de gestion et leurs facteurs de contingence au sein des entreprises au Maroc. Thèse de Doctorat, Université Mohammed V, Rabat Maroc.

Elhamma, A. (2023). Impact of mandatory IFRS adoption on foreign direct investment: the moderating role of conflict of interest regulation. Journal of Financial Reporting and Accounting, Vol. ahead-of-print No. ahead-of-print. https://doi.org/ DOI: 10.1108/JFRA-04-2022-0145

Elhamma, A. (2012). The activity based costing in morocco: Adoption and diffusion. *Arabian Journal of Business and Management Review*, *1*(6), 33–45. DOI: 10.12816/0002111

Elhamma, A. (2013). Performance de la comptabilité par activités: Perceptions des responsables d'entreprises. *La Revue des Sciences de Gestion*, (263-264), 227–232.

Elhamma, A. (2014). Performance du Balanced Scorecard: Perception des responsables d'entreprises. *Revue Internationale de Management et de Stratégie*, *5*(2), 1–9.

Elhamma, A. (2015). La comptabilité des produits financiers islamiques: Normes AAOIFI vs. IFRS. *Revue de Management et de Stratégie*, *1*(2), 10–22.

Elhamma, A. (2015). Perceived benefits of ABC implementation in Moroccan enterprises: Results of an empirical study. American Journal of Business. *Economics and Management*, *3*(2), 24–28.

Elhamma, A. (2015). The relationship between budgetary evaluation, firm size and performance. *Journal of Management Development*, *34*(8), 973–986. DOI: 10.1108/JMD-06-2014-0053

Elhamma, A. (2023), Numérisation du contrôle de gestion en fonction du secteur d'activité: résultats d'une étude empirique, Moroccan Journal of Entrepreneurship, Innovation and Management, 8 (1&2), 59-68. DOI: https://doi.org/DOI: 10.48396/IMIST.PRSM/mjeim-v8i1%20&%202.43254

Elhamma, A. (2023). Digitalisation et incertitude environnementale: cas du contrôle de gestion des entreprises marocaines. Revue Économie, Gestion et Société, 1 (39). https://doi.org/DOI: 10.48382/IMIST.PRSM/regs-v1i39.42390

Elhamma, A. (2023). The relationship between organisational decentralisation, balanced scorecard and its perceived benefits in Moroccan SMEs. International Journal of Accounting. *Auditing and Performance Evaluation*, *19*(2), 185–202. DOI: 10.1504/IJAAPE.2023.132384

Elhamma, A. (2024). Determinants of national IFRS adoption: Evidence from the Middle East and North Africa region. International Journal of Accounting. *Auditing and Performance Evaluation*, *20*(1-2), 69–90. DOI: 10.1504/IJAAPE.2024.135535

Elhamma, A., & El-Moumane, R. (2023). Impact de la taille sur la digitalisation du contrôle de gestion des entreprises marocaines: résultats d'une enquête. Alternatives Managériales Economiques, 5 (3), 182-199. DOI: https://doi.org/DOI: 10.48374/IMIST.PRSM/ame-v5i3.41916

Elhamma, A., & El-Moumane, R. (2023). Impact of Firm Size on Digitalization of Management Control: Evidence from Morocco. International Journal of Management. *Accounting & Economics*, *10*(6), 412–424. DOI: 10.5281/zenodo.8216014

Elhamma, A., & Lassaad, B. M. (2017). Liens entre participation budgétaire, taille et performance: Cas des entreprises au Maroc. *Revue Congolaise de Gestion*, *24*(2), 43–62. DOI: 10.3917/rcg.024.0043

Elhamma, A., & Moalla, M. (2015). Impact of uncertainty and decentralization on activity-based costing use. *International Journal of Accounting and Economics Studies*, *3*(2), 148–155. DOI: 10.14419/ijaes.v3i2.4817

Elhamma, A., & Zhang, Yi. (2013). The relationship between activity-based costing, business strategy and performance in Moroccan enterprises. *Journal of Accounting and Management Information Systems*, *12*(1), 22–38.

Elhazmiri, B., Naveed, N., Anwar, M. N., & Haq, M. I. U. (2022). The role of additive manufacturing in industry 4.0: An exploration of different business models. *Sustainable Operations and Computers*. Advance online publication. DOI: 10.1016/j.susoc.2022.07.001

Elwood, S. (2010). Geographic information science: Emerging research on the societal implications of the geospatial web. *Progress in Human Geography*, *34*(3), 349–357. DOI: 10.1177/0309132509340711

Emmanuel, C., Otley, D., & Merchant, K. A. (1990). *Accounting for Management Control*. Chapman and Hall. DOI: 10.1007/978-1-4899-6952-1

EnCashea. (2021). *Digital Platforms for Recycling and the Circular Economy*. Retrieved from https://www.encashea.com

Eshet-Alkalai, Y. (2012). Thinking in the digital era: A revised model for digital literacy. *Issues in Informing Science and Information Technology*, *9*, 267–276.

Ezawa, I. D., Hollon, S. D., & Robinson, N. (2023). Examining Predictors of Depression and Anxiety Symptom Change in Cognitive Behavioral Immersion: Observational Study. *JMIR Mental Health*, *10*, e42377. Advance online publication. DOI: 10.2196/42377 PMID: 37450322

Fabian, P. S., Kwon, H. H., Vithanage, M., & Lee, J. H. (2023). Modeling, challenges, and strategies for understanding impacts of climate extremes (droughts and floods) on water quality in Asia: A review. In *Environmental Research* (Vol. 225). DOI: 10.1016/j.envres.2023.115617

Fähndrich, J. (2023). A literature review on the impact of digitalisation on management control. *Journal of Management Control*, *34*(1), 9–65. DOI: 10.1007/s00187-022-00349-4

Falcão, D., & Roseira, C. (2022). Mapping the socially responsible consumption gap research: Review and future research agenda. *International Journal of Consumer Studies*, *46*(5), 1718–1760. DOI: 10.1111/ijcs.12803

Falchuk, B., Loeb, S., & Neff, R. (2018). The Social Metaverse: Battle for Privacy. *IEEE Technology and Society Magazine*, *37*(2), 52–61. Advance online publication. DOI: 10.1109/MTS.2018.2826060

Fernández-Miguel, A., García-Muiña, F. E., Jiménez-Calzado, M., Melara San Román, P., Fernández del Hoyo, A. P., & Settembre-Blundo, D. (2024). Boosting business agility with additive digital molding: An Industry 5.0 approach to sustainable supply chains. *Computers & Industrial Engineering*, *192*, 110222. Advance online publication. DOI: 10.1016/j.cie.2024.110222

Fernández-Portillo, A., Almodóvar-González, M., Sánchez-Escobedo, M. C., & Coca-Pérez, J. L. (2022). The role of innovation in the relationship between digitalisation and economic and financial performance. A company-level research. *European Research on Management and Business Economics*, *28*(3), 100190. DOI: 10.1016/j.iedeen.2021.100190

Fernando, J., Chiappetta Jabbour, C. J., & Wah, W.-X. (2019). Pursuing green growth in technology firms through the connections between environmental innovation and sustainable business performance: Does service capability matter? *Resources, Conservation and Recycling*, *141*, 8–20. DOI: 10.1016/j.resconrec.2018.09.031

Ferreras-Méndez, J. L., Newell, S., Fernández-Mesa, A., & Alegre, J. (2015). Depth and breadth of external knowledge search and performance: The mediating role of absorptive capacity. *Industrial Marketing Management*, *47*, 86–97. DOI: 10.1016/j.indmarman.2015.02.038

Ferreras-Méndez, J. L., Olmos-Peñuela, J., Salas-Vallina, A., & Alegre, J. (2021). Entrepreneurial orientation and new product development performance in SMEs: The mediating role of business model innovation. *Technovation*, *108*, 1–13, 102325. DOI: 10.1016/j.technovation.2021.102325

Flick, U. (2007). The SAGE Qualitative Research Kit (8 cols). London, Angleterre. *Sage (Atlanta, Ga.)*.

Flipkart. (2023). *Eliminating Single-use Plastic through AI-powered Eco-Packaging*. Retrieved from https://www.flipkart.com

Floridi, L., & Taddeo, M. (2016). What is data ethics? *Philosophical Transactions. Series A, Mathematical, Physical, and Engineering Sciences*, *374*(2083), 20160360. DOI: 10.1098/rsta.2016.0360 PMID: 28336805

Folkman, S., Lazarus, R., Dunkel-Schetter, D., Delongis, A., & Gruen, R. (1986). Dynamics of a stressful encounter: Cognitive appraisal, coping and encounter outcomes. *Journal of Personality and Social Psychology*, *50*(5), 992–1003. DOI: 10.1037/0022-3514.50.5.992 PMID: 3712234

Ford, E., Milne, R., & Curlewis, K. (2023). Ethical issues when using digital biomarkers and artificial intelligence for the early detection of dementia. In *Wiley Interdisciplinary Reviews*. Data Mining and Knowledge Discovery., DOI: 10.1002/widm.1492

Foss, N. J., & Saebi, T. (2017). Fifteen Years of Research on Business Model Innovation: How Far Have We Come, and Where Should We Go? *Journal of Management*, *43*(1), 200–227. DOI: 10.1177/0149206316675927

Francisco, M., & Linnér, B.-O. (2023). AI and the governance of sustainable development: An idea analysis of the European Union, the United Nations, and the World Economic Forum. Environmental Science and Policy. Advance online publication. DOI: 10.1016/j.envsci.2023.103590

François-Lecompte, A. (2003), Towards a better understanding of socially responsible consumption, 19th Congress of the French Marketing Association, Tunis May 2003.

François-Lecompte, A. (2005), Socially Responsible Consumption: Proposal and Validation of an Integrative Conceptual Framework, Thesis for the Doctorate in Management Sciences, Pierre Mendes-France University.

Francois-Lecompte, A., & Roberts, J. A. (2006). Developing a measure of socially responsible consumption in France. *Marketing Management Journal, 16*(2), 50–66.

François-Lecompte, A., & Valette-Florence, P. (2004) Proposal of a Scale for Measuring Socially Responsible Consumption, *20th Congress of the French Marketing Association*, Saint Malo, May 2004.

Francois-Lecompte, A., & Valette-Florence, P. (2006). Getting to know the socially responsible consumer. *Decisions Marketing, 41*, 67–79.

Gadeyne, N., Verbruggen, M., Delanoeije, J., & De Cooman, R. (2018). All wired, all tired? Work-related ICT-use outside work hours and work-to-home conflict: The role of integration preference, integration norms and work demands. *Journal of Vocational Behavior, 107*, 86–99. DOI: 10.1016/j.jvb.2018.03.008

Gai, K., Qiu, M., & Sun, X. (2018). A survey on FinTech. *Journal of Network and Computer Applications, 103*, 262–273.

Gan, W., Dao, M. S., Zettsu, K., & Sun, Y. "Iot-based multimodal analysis for smart education: Current status, challenges and opportunities." In *Proceedings of the 3rd ACM Workshop on Intelligent Cross-Data Analysis and Retrieval*, pp. 32-40. 2022. https://doi.org/DOI: 10.1145/3512731.3534208

Gaskin, J. E. (2020). *Structural Equation Modeling*. MyEducator.

Gavette, H., McDonald, C. L., Kostick-Quenet, K., Mullen, A., Najafi, B., & Finco, M. G. (2023). Advances in prosthetic technology: A perspective on ethical considerations for development and clinical translation. *Frontiers in Rehabilitation Sciences, 4*, 1335966. Advance online publication. DOI: 10.3389/fresc.2023.1335966 PMID: 38293290

Gay, C., & Szostak, B. L. (2019). *Innovation and Creativity in SMEs, Challenges, Evolutions and Prospects*. British Library ISTE Ltd and John Wiley & Sons, Inc. DOI: 10.1002/9781119513742

George, G., Merrill, R. K., & Schillebeeckx, S. J. D. (2021). Digital Sustainability and Entrepreneurship: How Digital Innovations Are Helping Tackle Climate Change and Sustainable Development. *Entrepreneurship Theory and Practice, 45*(5), 999–1027. Advance online publication. DOI: 10.1177/1042258719899425

Gervais, M. (2000). Contrôle de gestion, édition. *Economica.*

Ghosh, S., Sinha, P., & Jha, A. (2022). Artificial intelligence and sustainability: Applications and challenges. *Energy Research Journal, 25*(3), 200–215.

Gomber, P., Kauffman, R. J., Parker, C., & Weber, B. W. (2018). On the Fintech Revolution: Interpreting the forces of innovation, disruption, and transformation in financial services. *Journal of Management Information Systems*, *35*(1), 220–265. DOI: 10.1080/07421222.2018.1440766

Gong, C., & Ribiere, V. (2021). Developing a unified definition of digital transformation. *Technovation*, *102*, 102217. DOI: 10.1016/j.technovation.2020.102217

Goodchild, M. F. (2007). Citizens as sensors: The world of volunteered geography. *GeoJournal*, *69*(4), 211–221. DOI: 10.1007/s10708-007-9111-y

Goodchild, M. F. (2008). The use cases of digital earth. *International Journal of Digital Earth*, *1*(1), 31–42. DOI: 10.1080/17538940701782528

Goodchild, M. F., & Glennon, J. A. (2010). Crowdsourcing geographic information for disaster response: A research frontier. *International Journal of Digital Earth*, *3*(3), 231–241. DOI: 10.1080/17538941003759255

Goranson, C., Thihalolipavan, S., & di Tada, N. (2012). VGI and Public Health: Possibilities and Pitfalls. Crowdsourcing Geographic Knowledge: Volunteered Geographic Information (VGI). *Theory into Practice*, 329–340.

Graham, C. C. (2024). The role of Geographic Information Systems in mitigating plastics pollution in the Global South—A spatial analysis of recycling facilities in Costa Rica. *The Science of the Total Environment*, *937*, 173396. https://doi.org/https://doi.org/10.1016/j.scitotenv.2024.173396. DOI: 10.1016/j.scitotenv.2024.173396 PMID: 38796014

Graser, K., Walzer, A. N., Hunhevicz, J., Jähne, R., Seiler, F., Wüst, R., & Hall, D. M. (2023). Qualitative technology evaluation of digital fabrication with concrete: Conceptual framework and scoreboard. *Automation in Construction*, *154*, 104964. Advance online publication. DOI: 10.1016/j.autcon.2023.104964

Green, K. R., & Chewning, H. L. (2020). The fault in our systems: LMS as a vehicle for critical pedagogy. *TechTrends*, *64*(3), 423–431. DOI: 10.1007/s11528-020-00480-w

Grinberger, A. Y., Minghini, M., Yeboah, G., Juhász, L., & Mooney, P. (2022). Bridges and barriers: An exploration of engagements of the research community with the OpenStreetMap community. *ISPRS International Journal of Geo-Information*, *11*(1), 54.

Grover, P., Kar, A. K., & Dwivedi, Y. K. (2022). Understanding artificial intelligence adoption in operations management: Insights from the review of academic literature and social media discussions. *Annals of Operations Research*, *308*(1-2), 177–213. DOI: 10.1007/s10479-020-03683-9

Guillaudeux, M., Rousseau, O., Petot, J., Bennis, Z., Dein, C. A., Goronflot, T., Vince, N., Limou, S., Karakachoff, M., Wargny, M., & Gourraud, P. A. (2023). Patient-centric synthetic data generation, no reason to risk re-identification in biomedical data analysis. *NPJ Digital Medicine*, *6*(1), 37. Advance online publication. DOI: 10.1038/s41746-023-00771-5 PMID: 36899082

Gunasekera, C., & Balasubramani, R. (2020). *Use of Information Communication Technology by School Teachers in Information Provision: An analysis of Sri Lankan perspective*. Library Philosophy & Practice.

Guo, H., Guo, A., & Ma, H. (2022). Inside the black box: How business model innovation contributes to digital start-up performance. *Journal of Innovation & Knowledge*, *7*(2), 100188. DOI: 10.1016/j.jik.2022.100188

Guo, H., Tang, J., Su, Z., & Katz, J. A. (2017). Opportunity recognition and SME, performance: The mediating effect of business model innovation. *R & D Management*, *47*(3), 431–442. DOI: 10.1111/radm.12219

Guo, Y., Tang, Q., Darkwa, J., Wang, H., Su, W., Tang, D., & Mu, J. (2024). Multi-objective integrated optimization of geothermal heating system with energy storage using digital twin technology. *Applied Thermal Engineering*, *252*, 123685. Advance online publication. DOI: 10.1016/j.applthermaleng.2024.123685

Gupta, K., Jain, V., & Singh, S. (2021). The role of blockchain in creating sustainable supply chains. *International Journal of Logistics Management*, *32*(2), 320–340.

Gupta, N., & Kumar, S. (2021). Digital Sustainability in India's IT Industry: A Case Study of Wipro and Infosys. *International Journal of Information Systems*, *17*(2), 44–59.

Habib-ur-Rahman, M., Ahmad, A., Raza, A., Hasnain, M. U., Alharby, H. F., Alzahrani, Y. M., ... & El Sabagh, A. (2022). Impact of climate change on agricultural production; Issues, challenges, and opportunities in Asia. *Frontiers in Plant Science*, *13*, 925548.

Hafsi, M., & Assar, S. (2017). Le rôle de la modélisation d'entreprise dans la transformation numérique: Une étude exploratoire. 22ème colloque de l'AIM (Association Information & Management), May 2017, Paris, France. ffhal-01656840f

Hagen, E. (2020). Sustainability in OpenStreetMap Building a More Stable Ecosystem in OSM for Development and Humanitarianism.

Hair, J., Black, W., Babin, B., & Anderson, R. (2010). *Multivariate data analysis* (7th ed.). Prentice-Hall, Inc.

Haklay, M. (2010). How good is volunteered geographical information? A comparative study of OpenStreetMap and Ordnance Survey datasets. *Environment and Planning. B, Planning & Design*, *37*(4), 682–703. DOI: 10.1068/b35097

Haklay, M., Basiouka, S., Antoniou, V., & Ather, A. (2010). How many volunteers does it take to map an area well? The validity of Linus' law to volunteered geographic information. *The Cartographic Journal*, *47*(4), 315–322. DOI: 10.1179/000870410X12911304958827

Hakobyan, L., Monforte-Gómez, B., Moliner-Martínez, Y., Molins-Legua, C., & Campíns-Falcó, P. (2022). Improving sustainability of the Griess reaction by reagent stabilization on PDMS membranes and ZnNPs as reductor of nitrates: Application to different water samples. *Polymers*, *14*(3), 464. Advance online publication. DOI: 10.3390/polym14030464 PMID: 35160454

Hall, M., & Smith, D. (2009). Mentoring and turnover intentions in public accounting firms: A research note. *Accounting, Organizations and Society*, *34*(6-7), 695–704. DOI: 10.1016/j.aos.2008.11.003

Hamalainen, M., & Salmi, A. (2023). Digital transformation in a cross-laminated timber business network. *Journal of Business and Industrial Marketing*, *38*(6), 1251–1265. Advance online publication. DOI: 10.1108/JBIM-01-2022-0003

Hancock, A. (2016). *A digital leader – what on earth is that? Retrieved from*https://digileaders.com/adrian-hancock/

Hartmann, M., Oriani, R., & Bateman, H. (2013). The Performance Effect of Business Model Innovation: an Empirical Analysis of Pension Funds. *35th DRUID Celebration Conference*, Barcelona, Spain

Hartmann, P. M., Zaki, M., Feldmann, N., & Neely, A. (2016). Capturing value from big data a taxonomy of data-driven business models used by start-up firms. *International Journal of Operations & Production Management*, *36*(10), 1382–1406. DOI: 10.1108/IJOPM-02-2014-0098

Hassanin, M. A., Salem, A. E., Helal, M. Y., Elshawarbi, N. N., Ahmed, I. S., & Mansour, N. (2023). The power of integration towards sustainable performance: A model to minimize technostress among frontline restaurant employees by combining job and employee resources. *Geo Journal of Tourism and Geosites*, *49*(3), 934–945. Advance online publication. DOI: 10.30892/gtg.49310-1094

Havele, A., Polys, N., & Behr, J. (2023). Building 3D Web Interoperability for the Metaverse. *Proceedings - Web3D 2023: 28th International Conference on Web3D Technology*. DOI: 10.1145/3611314.3623584

Heidenstrøm, N., & Hebrok, M. (2022). Towards realizing the sustainability potential within digital food provisioning platforms: The case of meal box schemes and online grocery shopping in Norway. *Sustainable Production and Consumption, 29*, 831–850. Advance online publication. DOI: 10.1016/j.spc.2021.06.030

Heikkilä, M., Saarni, J., & Saurama, A. (2022). Innovation in Smart Ports: Future Directions of Digitalization in Container Ports. *Journal of Marine Science and Engineering, 10*(12), 1925. Advance online publication. DOI: 10.3390/jmse10121925

Heikkilä, P., Schmalfuß, F., Honka, A., Kaasinen, E., Mach, S., & Väänänen, K. (2018). Quantified Factory Worker - Expert Evaluation and Ethical Considerations of Wearable Self-tracking Devices. *ACM International Conference Proceeding Series*. DOI: 10.1145/3275116.3275119

Heinonen, H. T., Semenov, A., Veijalainen, J., & Hamalainen, T. (2022). *A survey on technologies which make Bitcoin greener or more justified*. IEEE., DOI: 10.1109/ACCESS.2022.3190891

Hemphill, T. A. (2023). The 'Metaverse' and the challenge of responsible standards development. *Journal of Responsible Innovation, 10*(1), 2243121. Advance online publication. DOI: 10.1080/23299460.2023.2243121

Herda, D. N., & Lavelle, J. J. (2012). The Auditor-Audit Firm Relationship and Its effect on Burnout and Turnover Intention. *Accounting Horizons, 26*(4), 707–723. DOI: 10.2308/acch-50181

Herfort, B., Eckle, M., de Albuquerque, J. P., & Zipf, A. (2015, May). Towards assessing the quality of volunteered geographic information from OpenStreetMap for identifying critical infrastructures. In *ISCRAM*.

Herfort, B., Lautenbach, S., Porto de Albuquerque, J., Anderson, J., & Zipf, A. (2021). The evolution of humanitarian mapping within the OpenStreetMap community. *Scientific reports, 11*(1), 3037. https://doi.org/DOI: 10.1038/s41598-021-82404-z

Hesselmann, F., & Kallinikos, J. (2022). The responsible organization in the digital age: Corporate digital responsibility and its challenges. *Information Systems Journal, 32*(2), 213–233. DOI: 10.1111/isj.12342

Hess, T., Matt, C., Benlian, A., & Wiesböck, F. (2016). Options for Formulating a Digital Transformation Strategy. *MIS Quarterly Executive, 15*(2), 103–119.

Hikmat, H. (2022). The Readiness of Education in Indonesia in Facing The Society Era 5.0. *Jurnal Basicedu, 6*(2), 2953–2961. DOI: 10.31004/basicedu.v6i2.2526 10

Hinsby, K., Négrel, P., de Oliveira, D., Barros, R., Venvik, G., Ladenberger, A., Griffioen, J., Piessens, K., Calcagno, P., Götzl, G., Broers, H. P., Gourcy, L., van Heteren, S., Hollis, J., Poyiadji, E., Čápová, D., & Tulstrup, J. (2024). Mapping and understanding Earth: Open access to digital geoscience data and knowledge supports societal needs and UN sustainable development goals. *International Journal of Applied Earth Observation and Geoinformation*, *130*, 103835. https://doi.org/ https://doi.org/10.1016/j.jag.2024.103835. DOI: 10.1016/j.jag.2024.103835

Hobfoll, S. E., & Shirom, A. (1993). Stress and burnout in work organizations. Dans R. G. (Ed.) (Éd.), *Handbook of organization behavior* (pp. 41-61). New York: Dekker.

Hodson, J., Dale, A., Jost, F., & Clifton-Ross, J. (2020). Sustainability issue communication and student social media engagement: Recommendations for climate communicators. *Journal of Digital and Social Media Marketing*, *8*(3), 221–234. DOI: 10.69554/LIHR6053

Hoe, S. L. (2023). Digital transformation strategy, execution, and technology, Taylor & Francis Group, CRC Press.

Holmes, S., & Nicholls, D. (1989). Modelling the accounting information requirement of small business. *Accounting and Business Research*, *19*(74), 143–150.

Holstein, K., Wortman Vaughan, J., Daumé, H.III, Dudik, M., & Wallach, H. (2019). Improving fairness in machine learning systems: What do industry practitioners need? *Proceedings of the 2019 CHI Conference on Human Factors in Computing Systems*, 1-16. https://doi.org/DOI: 10.1145/3290605.3300830

Hoosain, M. S., Paul, B. S., Doorsamy, W., & Ramakrishna, S. (2023). The influence of circular economy and 4IR technologies on the climate–water–energy–food nexus and the SDGs. *Water (Basel)*, *15*(4), 787. Advance online publication. DOI: 10.3390/w15040787

Hoosain, M. S., Paul, B. S., Kass, S., & Ramakrishna, S. (2023). Tools Towards the Sustainability and Circularity of Data Centers. *Circular Economy and Sustainability*, *3*(1), 173–197. Advance online publication. DOI: 10.1007/s43615-022-00191-9 PMID: 35791435

Horak, J., Voumik, L. C., & Popescu, G. H. (2023). Remote Sensing Data Fusion Techniques, Multimodal Behavioral Predictive and Mobile Location Analytics, and Spatial Cognition and Context Awareness Algorithms in the Metaverse Economy. *Linguistic and Philosophical Investigations*, *22*(0), 77. Advance online publication. DOI: 10.22381/lpi2220235

Horne, M., Hill, A., Murells, T., & Ugail, H. Irving, Chinnadorai, R., & Hardy, M. (2020). Using avatars in weight management settings: A systematic review. In *Internet Interventions* (Vol. 19). DOI: 10.1016/j.invent.2019.100295

Hosamo, H. H., Nielsen, H. K., Kraniotis, D., Svennevig, P. R., & Svidt, K. (2023). Digital Twin framework for automated fault source detection and prediction for comfort performance evaluation of existing non-residential Norwegian buildings. *Energy and Building*, *281*, 112732. Advance online publication. DOI: 10.1016/j.enbuild.2022.112732

Hosta, M., & Zabkar, V. (2021). Antecedents of environmentally and socially responsible sustainable consumer behavior. *Journal of Business Ethics*, *171*(2), 273–293. DOI: 10.1007/s10551-019-04416-0

Hsieh, Y., & Wang, M. (2012). The moderating role of personality in HRM from the influence of job stress on job burnout perspective. *International Management Review*, *8*(2), 5–18.

Hulsen, T. (2023). Applications of the metaverse in medicine and healthcare. *Advances in Laboratory Medicine/Avances En Medicina de Laboratorio, 0.*

Huong, P. T., Cherian, J., Hien, N. T., Sial, M. S., Samad, S., & Tuan, B. A. (2021). Environmental management, green innovation, and social–open innovation. *Journal of Open Innovation*, *7*(1), 89. Advance online publication. DOI: 10.3390/joitmc7010089

Hussain, A., Ahmed, F., Siddiqi, Z., Basit, S. A., & Nasim, S. (2015). Factors Creating Conflict between Sales and Operational Teams in the Banking Industry. *International Journal of Research in Organizational Behavior and Human Resource Management*, *3*(3), 18–28.

Hussein, L. A., Baharudin, A. S., Jayaraman, K., & Kiumarsi, S. H. A. I. A. N. (2019). B2B e-commerce technology factors with mediating effect perceived usefulness in Jordanian manufacturing SMES. *Journal of Engineering Science and Technology*, *14*(1), 411–429.

Hwang, Y., Shin, D., & Lee, H. (2023). Students' perception on immersive learning through 2D and 3D metaverse platforms. *Educational Technology Research and Development*, *71*(4), 1687–1708. Advance online publication. DOI: 10.1007/s11423-023-10238-9 PMID: 37359489

Hyun, W. (2023, February). Study on standardization for interoperable metaverse. In 2023 25th International Conference on Advanced Communication Technology (ICACT) (pp. 319-322). IEEE.

Icela, L., González-Pérez, R.-M. M. S., & Antonio, E.-G. J. (2023). Education 4.0 Maturity Models for Society 5.0: Systematic literature review. *Cogent Business & Management, 10*(3), 2256095. DOI: 10.1080/23311975.2023.2256095

Ilin, V., Ivetić, J., & Simić, D. (2017). Understanding the determinants of e-business adoption in ERP-enabled firms and non-ERP-enabled firms: A case study of the Western Balkan Peninsula. *Technological Forecasting and Social Change, 125*, 206–223. DOI: 10.1016/j.techfore.2017.07.025

Imtiaz, N. M., Subramaniam, M., & Sathiyasekar, K. (2023). Enhancing Cloud Security through Asymmetrical AES-EDDSA and Hyperledger Integration Algorithms for Environmental Sustainability. *Journal of Environmental Protection and Ecology*. Advance online publication. DOI: 10.1007/s11356-022-21699-5

Indian Government's Cybersecurity Policy. (2020). *Challenges in IoT Adoption and Cybersecurity Risks*. Retrieved from https://www.meity.gov.in

Infosys (2022). "Circular Economy and AI in Operations." Infosys Sustainability Report 2022.

Islam, S. M. S., Yeşilköy, S., Baydaroğlu, Ö., Yıldırım, E., & Demir, I. (2024). State-level multidimensional agricultural drought susceptibility and risk assessment for agriculturally prominent areas. *International Journal of River Basin Management*, 1–18. Advance online publication. DOI: 10.1080/15715124.2024.2304546

Jain, S. (2020). Make in India: A framework for sustainable development. *The Journal of Industrial Economics, 14*(1), 78–90.

Janvrin, D., Bierstaker, J., & Jordan, D. (2008, March). An Examination of Audit Information Technology Use and Perceived Importance. *Accounting Horizons, 22*(1), 1–21. DOI: 10.2308/acch.2008.22.1.1

Jelokhani-Niaraki, M., Bastami Mofrad, R., Yazdanpanah Dero, Q., Hajiloo, F., & Sadeghi-Niaraki, A. (2020). A volunteered geographic information system for monitoring and managing urban crimes: A case study of Tehran, Iran. *Police Practice and Research, 21*(6), 547–561. DOI: 10.1080/15614263.2019.1644175

Jelovac, D., Ljubojevic, C., & Ljubojevic, L. (2022). HPC in business: The impact of corporate digital responsibility on building digital trust and responsible corporate digital governance. *Digital Policy, Regulation and Governance, 24*(6), 485–497. DOI: 10.1108/DPRG-11-2020-0164

Jiayu, W., & Wang, Z. (2024). Economic integration through renewable energy and digital currency in RCEP. *Economic Change and Restructuring*, *57*(2), 58. Advance online publication. DOI: 10.1007/s10644-024-09646-5

Jin, T., & Han, X. (2024). Robotic arms in precision agriculture: A comprehensive review of the technologies, applications, challenges, and future prospects. *Computers and Electronics in Agriculture*, *221*, 108938. Advance online publication. DOI: 10.1016/j.compag.2024.108938

Joe, H. E., Yun, H., Jo, S. H., Jun, M. B. G., & Min, B. K. (2018). A review on optical fiber sensors for environmental monitoring. In *International Journal of Precision Engineering and Manufacturing - Green Technology* (Vol. 5, Issue 1). DOI: 10.1007/s40684-018-0017-6

Johnson, P. A., & Sieber, R. E. (2017). The Geoweb for community-based organizations: Tool development, implementation, and sustainability in an era of Google Maps. *The Journal of Community Informatics*, *13*(1). Advance online publication. DOI: 10.15353/joci.v13i1.3295

Jones, A.III, Norman, C. S., & Wier, B. (2010). Healthy Lifestyle as a Coping Mechanism for Role Stress in Public Accounting. *Behavioral Research in Accounting*, *22*(1), 21–41. DOI: 10.2308/bria.2010.22.1.21

Joseph, D., Ng, K.-Y., Koh, C., & Ang, S. (2007). Turnover of information technology professionals: A narrative review, meta-analytic structural equation modeling, and model development. *Management Information Systems Quarterly*, *31*(3), 3. DOI: 10.2307/25148807

Kačerová, I., Kubr, J., Hořejší, P., & Kleinová, J. (2022). Ergonomic Design of a Workplace Using Virtual Reality and a Motion Capture Suit. *Applied Sciences (Basel, Switzerland)*, *12*(4), 2150. Advance online publication. DOI: 10.3390/app12042150

Kadirvelu, B., Gavriel, C., Nageshwaran, S., Chan, J. P. K., Nethisinghe, S., Athanasopoulos, S., Ricotti, V., Voit, T., Giunti, P., Festenstein, R., & Faisal, A. A. (2023). A wearable motion capture suit and machine learning predict disease progression in Friedreich's ataxia. *Nature Medicine*, *29*(1), 86–94. Advance online publication. DOI: 10.1038/s41591-022-02159-6 PMID: 36658420

Kala, N. (2022). Revolutionizing medical education with metaverse. International Journal of Scientific Research in Computer Science. *Engineering and Information Technology*, *8*(4), 26–32.

Kaleel, M., & Zahir, I. (2016). Web Based Land Information System for Nintavur Divisional Secretariat Division (DSD), Sri Lanka. *Journal of Geography. Environment and Earth Science International*, *5*(4), 1–6.

Kamyab, H., Khademi, T., Chelliapan, S., SaberiKamarposhti, M., Rezania, S., Yusuf, M., Farajnezhad, M., Abbas, M., Hun Jeon, B., & Ahn, Y. (2023). The latest innovative avenues for the utilization of artificial Intelligence and big data analytics in water resource management. *Results in Engineering*, *20*, 101566. Advance online publication. DOI: 10.1016/j.rineng.2023.101566

Kane, G. C., Palmer, D., Phillips, A. N., Kiron, D., & Buckley, N. (2015). *Strategy, not technology, drives digital transformation*. MIT Sloan Management Review and Deloitte University Press.

Kangara, C. T. C., Gocha, M., Tsokota, T., & Marovah, T. "Assessing Readiness for Teaching and Learning Using Icts in Zimbabwean Secondary Schools in Gweru Distrct, Zimbabwe." (2022).https://doi.org/DOI: 10.21203/rs.3.rs-1652431/v1

Kanthi, N. S., & Purwanto, T. H. (2016, November). Application of OpenStreetMap (OSM) to support the mapping village in Indonesia. In *IOP Conference Series: Earth and Environmental Science* (Vol. 47, No. 1, p. 012003). IOP Publishing. DOI: 10.1088/1755-1315/47/1/012003

Kaplan, R. S., & Norton, D. P. (1992). The balanced scorecard, measures that drive performance. *Harvard Business Review*, (January-February), 71–79. PMID: 10119714

Kapoor, R. (2022). AI-Driven Energy Solutions for India's Smart Grids. *Energy Studies Journal*, *15*(3), 89–102.

Kazungu, I., Panga, F. P., & Mchopa, A. (2015). Impediments to adoption of e-marketing by Tanzanian small and medium sized enterprises: An explanatory model. International Journal of Economics, Commerce and Management, III, 6, 587-597.

Keche, K. (2021). *Relevancy of new higher education approaches in 'Second Republic Zimbabwe*. Higher Education-New Approaches to Accreditation, Digitalization, and Globalization in the Age of Covid.

Kemp, K. (2014). Open Geospatial Consortium (OGC). In *Encyclopedia of Geographic Information Science*. DOI: 10.4135/9781412953962.n152

Kgoroebutswe, T. K., Makate, N., Fillinger, U., Mpho, M., Segoea, G., Sangoro, P. O., Mutero, C. M., Chanda, E., Ntebela, D., Mogopa, M., Mosweunyane, T., & Nkya, T. E. (2020). Vector control for malaria elimination in Botswana: Progress, gaps and opportunities. *Malaria Journal*, *19*(1), 1–12. DOI: 10.1186/s12936-020-03375-6 PMID: 32843037

Khaimovich, I., Ramzaev, V., & Chumak, V. (2020). Data modelling for analysis of readness of municipal education in industry 5.0. *CEUR Workshop Proceedings*, *2667*, 1–4.

Khan, M. A., Hussain, A., Ali, M. M., & Tajummul, M. A. (2022). Assessing the impact of liquidity on the value of assets return. [GBMR]. *Global Business and Management Research*, *14*(1), 54–76. DOI: 10.32890/gbmr2022.14.1.4

Khan, M. A., Khan, R., Al-Zghoul, T. M., Khan, A., Hussain, A., Baarimah, A. O., & Arshad, M. A. (2024). Optimizing municipal solid waste management in urban Peshawar: A linear mathematical modeling and GIS approach for efficiency and sustainability. *Case Studies in Chemical and Environmental Engineering*, *9*, 100704. https://doi.org/https://doi.org/10.1016/j.cscee.2024.100704. DOI: 10.1016/j.cscee.2024.100704

Khedhaouria, A., & Cucchi, A. (2019). Technostress creators, personality traits, and job burnout: A fuzzy-set configurational analysis. *Journal of Business Research*, *101*, 349–361. DOI: 10.1016/j.jbusres.2019.04.029

Khelifi, L., & Mignotte, M. (2020). Deep Learning for Change Detection in Remote Sensing Images: Comprehensive Review and Meta-Analysis. *IEEE Access : Practical Innovations, Open Solutions*, *8*, 126385–126400. Advance online publication. DOI: 10.1109/ACCESS.2020.3008036

Knapskog, M., & Browne, M. (2022). Sensors securing sustainable digital urban logistics—A practitioner's perspective. *Frontiers in Future Transportation*. Advance online publication. DOI: 10.3389/ffutr.2022.993411

Kofos, A., Ubacht, J., Rukanova, B., Korevaar, G., Kouwenhoven, N., & Tan, Y.-H. (2022). Circular economy visibility evaluation framework. *Journal of Responsible Technology*, *10*, 100026. Advance online publication. DOI: 10.1016/j.jrt.2022.100026

Ko, L. S. C., Moro, S., Bury, J., Vickers, T., Sachsenhauser, B., & Mönnig, S. (2021). Rheology and setting control of concrete for digital construction. *ACI Materials Journal*, *118*(4), 43–54. DOI: 10.14359/51733121

Koltsios, S., Fokaides, P., Georgali, P.-Z., Tsolakis, A. C., Chatzipanagiotidou, P., Klumbytė, E., Jurelionis, A., Šeduikytė, L., Kontopoulos, C., Malavazos, C., Panteli, C., Sušnik, M., Cebrat, G., Ioannidis, D., & Tzovaras, D. (2022). An enhanced framework for next-generation operational buildings energy performance certificates. *International Journal of Energy Research*, *46*(14), 12543–12563. DOI: 10.1002/er.8517

Kopp, J., Preis, J., Žák, P., & Vogt, D. (2024). Mapping the Environmental Quality of University Campus Areas for the Needs of Blue-Green Infrastructure Planning. In *The Contribution of Universities Towards Education for Sustainable Development* (pp. 211–231). Springer. DOI: 10.1007/978-3-031-49853-4_13

Korucuk, S., Aytekin, A., Ecer, F., Karamaşa, Ç., & Zavadskas, E. K. (2022). Assessing Green Approaches and Digital Marketing Strategies for Twin Transition via Fermatean Fuzzy SWARA-COPRAS. *Axioms*, *11*(12), 709. DOI: 10.3390/axioms11120709

Kostner, M. K., Zanfei, A., Alberizzi, J. C., Renzi, M., Righetti, M., & Menapace, A. (2023). Micro hydro power generation in water distribution networks through the optimal pumps-as-turbines sizing and control. *Applied Energy*, *351*, 121802. Advance online publication. DOI: 10.1016/j.apenergy.2023.121802

Kotarba, M. (2017). Measuring digitalization: Key metrics. *Foundations of Management*, *9*(1), 123–138. DOI: 10.1515/fman-2017-0010

Koutsovili, E. I., Tzoraki, O., Kalli, A. A., Provatas, S., & Gaganis, P. (2023). Participatory approaches for planning nature-based solutions in flood vulnerable landscapes. *Environmental Science & Policy*, *140*, 12–23. Advance online publication. DOI: 10.1016/j.envsci.2022.11.012

Kranz, J., Zeiss, R., Beck, R., Gholami, R., Sarker, S., Watson, R. T., & Whitley, E. A. (2022). Practicing what we preach? Reflections on more sustainable and responsible IS research and teaching practices. *Communications of the Association for Information Systems*, *49*(1), 115–132. DOI: 10.17705/1CAIS.05138

Kraus, S. J. (1995). Attitudes and the Prediction of Behavior – a Meta-Analysis of the Empirical Literature. *Personality and Social Psychology Bulletin*, *21*(1), 58–75. DOI: 10.1177/0146167295211007

Külling, N., Adde, A., Lambiel, A., Wicki, S., Guisan, A., Grêt-Regamey, A., & Lehmann, A. (2024). Nature's contributions to people and biodiversity mapping in switzerland: Spatial patterns and environmental drivers. *Ecological Indicators*, *163*, 112079. DOI: 10.1016/j.ecolind.2024.112079

Kumar, N., Singh, S. K., Mishra, V. N., Reddy, G. O., & Bajpai, R. K. (2018). Open-source satellite data and GIS for land resource mapping. Geospatial Technologies in Land Resources Mapping, *Monitoring and Management*, 185-200.

Kumar, A., & Sharma, T. (2021). Blockchain and Circular Economy: Case Studies from Indian Corporations. *Indian Journal of Technology and Sustainability*, *9*(4), 66–81.

Kumar, K., & Al-Besher, A. (2022). IoT enabled e-learning system for higher education. *Measurement. Sensors*, *24*, 100480. DOI: 10.1016/j.measen.2022.100480

Kumar, P., Sharma, S. K., & Dutot, V. (2023). Artificial intelligence (AI)-enabled CRM capability in healthcare: The impact on service innovation. *International Journal of Information Management*, *69*, 102598.

Kumar, R., & Patel, A. (2021). Digital technologies and the SDGs: A study of Indian corporations. *Sustainable Business Review*, *33*(2), 112–130.

Kumar, S., Shukla, M., & Rao, P. (2020). IoT in energy management: The case of Larsen & Toubro. *Engineering and Technology Journal*, *15*(4), 190–198.

Kumar, V., Vrat, P., & Shankar, R. (2022). *Factors Influencing the Implementation of Industry 4.0 for Sustainability in Manufacturing*. Global Journal of Flexible Systems Management., DOI: 10.1007/s40171-022-00312-1

Kurniawan, T. A., Othman, M. H. D., Liang, X., Goh, H. H., Gikas, P., Kusworo, T. D., Anouzla, A., & Chew, K. W. (2023). Decarbonization in waste recycling industry using digitalization to promote net-zero emissions and its implications on sustainability. *Journal of Environmental Management*, *338*, 117765. Advance online publication. DOI: 10.1016/j.jenvman.2023.117765 PMID: 36965421

Kyvik, O. (2018). The global mindset: A must for international innovation and entrepreneurship. *The International Entrepreneurship and Management Journal*, *14*(2), 309–327.

Ladwein, R. (1999). *Consumer and buyer behavior*. Economica.

Lahane, S., Paliwal, V., & Kant, R. (2023). Evaluation and ranking of solutions to overcome the barriers of Industry 4.0 enabled sustainable food supply chain adoption. Cleaner Logistics and Supply Chain. Advance online publication. DOI: 10.1016/j.clscn.2023.100116

Land, S., van der, , Land, S., van der, , & Schouten, A., Hooff, van den, & Feldberg, F. (2011). Modeling the Metaverse: A Theoretical Model of Effective Team Collaboration.... *Journal of Virtual Worlds Research*, *4*(3).

Larrinaga, F., Pérez, A., Aldalur, I., Hernández, J. L., Izkara, J. L., & de Viteri, P. S. (2021). A holistic and interoperable approach towards the implementation of services for the digital transformation of smart cities: The case of Vitoria-Gasteiz (Spain). *Sensors (Basel)*, *21*(23), 8061. Advance online publication. DOI: 10.3390/s21238061 PMID: 34884064

Larsen & Toubro. (2023). "Digital Twin Technology in Energy Efficiency. Retrieved from https://www.lnt.com

Latifi, M.-A., Nikou, S., & Bouwman, H. (2021). Business model innovation and firm performance: Exploring causal mechanisms in SMEs. *Technovation*, *107*, 102274. DOI: 10.1016/j.technovation.2021.102274

Lazaroiu, A. C., Roscia, M., Dancu, V. S., & Balaban, G. (2024). Social impact of decarbonization objectives through smart homes: Survey and analysis. *Renewable Energy*, *230*, 120872. Advance online publication. DOI: 10.1016/j.renene.2024.120872

Lazarus, R., & Folkman, S. (1984). *Stress, Appraisal, and Coping*. Springer.

Ledro, C., Nosella, A., & Dalla Pozza, I. (2023). Integration of AI in CRM: Challenges and guidelines. *Journal of Open Innovation*, *9*(4), 100151. DOI: 10.1016/j.joitmc.2023.100151

Lee, T., & Mitchell, T. (1994). An alternative approach: The unfolding model of voluntary employee turnover. . *Academy of Management Review*, 19(1), 51–89. Récupéré sur http://dx.doi.org/DOI: 10.5465/amr.1994.9410122008

Leung, L. (2011). Effects of ICT connectedness, permeability, flexibility, and negative spillovers on burnout and job and family satisfaction. *Human Technology*, *7*(3), 250–267. DOI: 10.17011/ht/urn.2011112211714

Li, J., Huang, X., Tu, L., Zhang, T., & Wang, L. (2022). A review of building detection from very high resolution optical remote sensing images. In *GIScience and Remote Sensing* (Vol. 59, Issue 1). DOI: 10.1080/15481603.2022.2101727

Li, X., & Heng, Q. (2021, June). Design of mobile learning resources based on new blended learning: a case study of superstar learning app. In 2021 IEEE 3rd International Conference on Computer Science and Educational Informatization (CSEI) (pp. 333-338). IEEE.

Liang, J., Li, G., Zhang, F., Fan, D., & Luo, H. (2023). Benefits and challenges of the educational metaverse: Evidence from quantitative and qualitative data. *Journal of Educational Technology Development and Exchange*, *16*(1), 71–91. Advance online publication. DOI: 10.18785/jetde.1601.04

Lichtenthaler, U. (2020). Corporate digital responsibility: A framework for success in the digital age. *The Journal of Business Strategy*, *41*(6), 31–37.

Lin, H., Wan, S., Gan, W., Chen, J., & Chao, H. C. (2022, December). Metaverse in education: Vision, opportunities, and challenges. In 2022 IEEE International Conference on Big Data (Big Data) (pp. 2857-2866). IEEE.

Linton, J. D., & Walsh, J. P. (2008). The open source movement in commercial software: A game theoretic analysis. *Management Science*, *54*(7), 1301–1315. DOI: 10.1287/mnsc.1070.0856

Lin, Y., Wang, Q.-J., & Zheng, M.-Q. (2023). Nexus Among Digital Economy, Green Innovation, and Green Development: Evidence from China. *Emerging Markets Finance & Trade*, •••, 1–20. DOI: 10.1080/1540496X.2023.2258260

Lippert, K., Khan, M. N. R., Rabbi, M. M., Dutta, A., & Cloutier, R. (2021). A Framework of Metaverse for Systems Engineering. *Proceedings of 2021 IEEE International Conference on Signal Processing, Information, Communication and Systems, SPICSCON 2021*. DOI: 10.1109/SPICSCON54707.2021.9885722

Lipton, Z. C. (2018). The mythos of model interpretability. *Communications of the ACM*, *61*(10), 36–43. DOI: 10.1145/3233231

Li, S., Zhou, T., Yang, H., & Wang, P. (2023). Blockchain-based secure storage and access control scheme for supply chain ecological business data: A case study of the automotive industry. *Sensors (Basel)*, *23*(16), 7036. Advance online publication. DOI: 10.3390/s23167036 PMID: 37631574

Lisnawati, L., Aryati, T., & Gunawan, J. (2024). Implementation of digital innovation on sustainability performance: The moderating role of green accounting in the industrial sector. *Eastern-European Journal of Enterprise Technologies*. DOI: 10.15587/1729-4061.2024.298639

Liu, Y., & Siau, K. L. (2023). Human-AI Interaction and AI Avatars. *Lecture Notes in Computer Science (Including Subseries Lecture Notes in Artificial Intelligence and Lecture Notes in Bioinformatics), 14059 LNCS*. DOI: 10.1007/978-3-031-48057-7_8

Liu, C., & Duan, D. (2020). Spatial inequality of bus transit dependence on urban streets and its relationships with socioeconomic intensities: A tale of two megacities in China. *Journal of Transport Geography*, *86*, 102768. DOI: 10.1016/j.jtrangeo.2020.102768

Liu, X., Zeng, X., & Chen, H. (2018). Exploring the determinants of citizen participation in voluntary geographic information initiatives. *International Journal of Geographical Information Science*, *32*, 1423–1440.

Liu, Y., Ma, C., & Huang, Z. (2023). Can the digital economy improve green total factor productivity? An empirical study based on Chinese urban data. *Mathematical Biosciences and Engineering*, *20*(4), 6866–6893. DOI: 10.3934/mbe.2023296 PMID: 37161132

Li, Y., Chung, S.-H., Wen, X., & Zhou, S. (2023). Towards the sustainable economy through digital technology: A drone-aided after-sales service scheduling model. *Applied Soft Computing*, *138*, 110202. Advance online publication. DOI: 10.1016/j.asoc.2023.110202

Li, Z., Ma, J., Jiang, F., Zhang, S., & Tan, Y. (2024). Assessing the impacts of urban morphological factors on urban building energy modeling based on spatial proximity analysis and explainable machine learning. *Journal of Building Engineering*, *85*, 108675. Advance online publication. DOI: 10.1016/j.jobe.2024.108675

Lombardot, E., & Mugel, O. (2017). Proposal of an explanatory model of the gap between intention and responsible behaviour in the context of food purchase. Review of the responsible organization, 12(1), 17-33.

Lopez, D., & Peters, G. (2012). The Effect of Workload Compression on Audit Quality. *Auditing*, *31*(4), 139–165. DOI: 10.2308/ajpt-10305

Lowe, D. J., Bierstaker, J. L., Janvrin, D. J., & Jenkins, J. G. (2017). Information Technology in an Audit Context: Have the Big 4 Lost Their Advantage? *Accounting Publications*, 32(1), 87-107. doi:https://lib.dr.iastate.edu/acct_pubs/19

Luis, S. (2023). Can Central Bank Digital Currencies be green and sustainable? *Green Finance*, *5*(4), 603–623. DOI: 10.3934/GF.2023023

Luong, N. A. M., & Wang, L. (2019). Factors Influencing E-commerce Usage within Internationalisation: A study of Swedish small and medium-sized fashion retailers.

Lutkevich, B. (2019). What is HIPAA (Health Insurance Portability and Accountability Act)? In *WhatIs.com*.

Mahdiraji, H. A., Yaftiyan, F., Abbasi-Kamardi, A., Jafari-Sadeghi, V., Sahut, J.-M., & Dana, L.-P. (2023). A synthesis of boundary conditions with adopting digital platforms in SMEs: An intuitionistic multi-layer decision-making framework. *The Journal of Technology Transfer*, *48*(5), 1723–1751. Advance online publication. DOI: 10.1007/s10961-023-10028-8

Mahindra & Mahindra. (2022). *AI-driven Sustainability Solutions*. Retrieved from https://www.mahindra.com

Maier, C., Laumer, S., Wirth, J., & Weitzel, T. (2019). Technostress and the hierarchical levels of personality: A two-wave study with multiple data samples. *European Journal of Information Systems*, *28*(5), 496–522. DOI: 10.1080/0960085X.2019.1614739

Major, L., Francis, G. A., & Tsapali, M. (2021). The effectiveness of technology-supported personalised learning in low-and middle-income countries: A meta-analysis. *British Journal of Educational Technology, 52*(5), 1935–1964. DOI: 10.1111/bjet.13116

Malaysia, B. N. (2016). *Financial technology regulatory sandbox framework.* Bank Negara Malaysia., https://www.bnm.gov.my/index.php?ch=57&p-g=137&ac=533&bb=file

Marakarkandy, B., Yajnik, N., & Dasgupta, C. (2017). Enabling internet banking adoption: An empirical examination with an augmented technology acceptance model (TAM). *Journal of Enterprise Information Management, 30*(2), 263–294. DOI: 10.1108/JEIM-10-2015-0094

Maria, M., Shahbodin, F., & Pee, N. C. (2018). "Malaysian higher education system towards industry 4.0–current trends overview." In AIP Conference Proceedings, vol. 2016, no. 1. AIP Publishing, https://doi.org/DOI: 10.1063/1.5055483

MarketsandMarkets. (2023). *Metaverse in Healthcare Market.* https://www.marketsandmarkets.com/Market-Reports/metaverse-in-healthcare-market-225839181.html

Martin, K. E. (2019). Ethical implications and accountability of algorithms. *Journal of Business Ethics, 160*(4), 835–850. DOI: 10.1007/s10551-018-3921-3

Marti, P., Massari, S., & Recupero, A. (2023). *Transformational design for food systems: Cultural, social and technological challenges.* International Journal of Food Design., DOI: 10.1386/ijfd_00053_1

Marzouk, M., Ayman, R., Alwan, Z., & Elshaboury, N. (2022). Green building system integration into project delivery utilising BIM. *Environment, Development and Sustainability, 24*(5), 6467–6480. Advance online publication. DOI: 10.1007/s10668-021-01712-6

Masanet, E., Shehabi, A., Lei, N., Smith, S., & Koomey, J. (2020). Recalibrating global data center energy-use estimates. *Science, 367*(6481), 984–986. DOI: 10.1126/science.aba3758 PMID: 32108103

Massung, E., Coyle, D., Cater, K. F., Jay, M., & Preist, C. (2013, April). Using crowdsourcing to support pro-environmental community activism. In *Proceedings of the SIGCHI Conference on human factors in Computing systems* (pp. 371-380). DOI: 10.1145/2470654.2470708

Matarazzo, M., Penco, L., Profumo, G., & Quaglia, R. (2021). Digital transformation and customer value creation in Made in Italy SMEs: A dynamic capabilities perspective. *Journal of Business Research, 123*, 642–656. DOI: 10.1016/j.jbusres.2020.10.033

Matt, C., Hess, T., & Benlian, A. (2015). Digital Transformation Strategies, Business and In-formation Systems Engineering. *Business & Information Systems Engineering*, *57*(5), 339–343. DOI: 10.1007/s12599-015-0401-5

McCarthy, A. M., Maor, D., McConney, A., & Cavanaugh, C. (2023). Digital transformation in education: Critical components for leaders of system change. *Social Sciences & Humanities Open*, *8*(1), 100479. DOI: 10.1016/j.ssaho.2023.100479

McCray, N. (2018). Mapping Energy Access in Rural Tanzania: 2017 Summer Internship with the World Resources Institute.

McCray, N. (2018). Mapping Energy Access in Rural Tanzania: 2017 Summer Internship with the World Resources Institute. https://commons.clarku.edu/idce_masters_papers/203

McLafferty, S. L., & Wang, F. (2012). Spatial disparities in access to nursing home facilities in Illinois: Implications for long-term care policy. *The Gerontologist*, *52*, 219–230.

Medoh, C. N., & Telukdarie, A. (2020). Logistics optimisation: A cyber physical model. *International Journal of Business Analytics*, *7*(1), 66–79. DOI: 10.4018/IJBAN.2020010104

Mehrabi, N., Morstatter, F., Saxena, N., Lerman, K., & Galstyan, A. (2021). A survey on bias and fairness in machine learning. *ACM Computing Surveys*, *54*(6), 1–35. DOI: 10.1145/3457607

Mehta, P., & Kapoor, R. (2020). Bridging the Digital Divide: The Role of Infrastructure in India's Digital Future. *Indian Economic Review*, *15*(3), 45–59.

Mena, A. R., Ceballos, H. G., & Alvarado-Uribe, J. (2022). Measuring Indoor Occupancy through Environmental Sensors: A Systematic Review on Sensor Deployment. In *Sensors* (Vol. 22, Issue 10). DOI: 10.3390/s22103770

Menghwar, P. S., & Daood, A. (2021). Creating shared value: A systematic review, synthesis and integrative perspective. *International Journal of Management Reviews*, *23*(4), 466–485. https://www.dawn.com/. DOI: 10.1111/ijmr.12252

Merin-Rodrigañez, J., Dasí, A., & Alegre, J. (2024). Digital transformation and firm performance in innovative SMEs: The mediating role of business model innovation. *Technovation, 134*, 103027. DOI: 10.1016/j.technovation.2024.103027

Meszaros, J., Minari, J., & Huys, I. (2022). The future regulation of artificial intelligence systems in healthcare services and medical research in the European Union. *Frontiers in Genetics, 13*, 927721. Advance online publication. DOI: 10.3389/fgene.2022.927721 PMID: 36267404

Meyssonnier, F., & Pourtier, F. (2006). Les ERP changent-ils le contrôle de gestion? *Comptabilité Contrôle Audit, 12*(1), 45–64. DOI: 10.3917/cca.121.0045

Miles, M. B., & Huberman, M. A. (2003). *Analyse des données qualitatives*. De Boeck Supérieur.

Minghini, M., Antoniou, V., Fonte, C. C., Estima, J., Olteanu-Raimond, A. M., See, L., & Lupia, F. (2017). The relevance of protocols for VGI collection. In *Mapping and the citizen sensor* (pp. 223–247). Ubiquity Press.

Ministry of Electronics & IT. (2021). *Digital India: Transforming India into a digitally empowered society*. Government of India.

Miranda, J., Navarrete, C., Noguez, J., Molina-Espinosa, J.-M., Ramírez-Montoya, M.-S., Navarro-Tuch, S. A., Bustamante-Bello, M.-R., Rosas-Fernández, J.-B., & Molina, A. (2021). The core components of education 4.0 in higher education: Three case studies in engineering education. *Computers & Electrical Engineering, 93*, 107278. DOI: 10.1016/j.compeleceng.2021.107278

Mirbabaie, M., Stieglitz, S., & Volkeri, S. (2016, January). Volunteered geographic information and its implications for disaster management. In *2016 49th Hawaii International Conference on System Sciences (HICSS)* (pp. 207-216). IEEE. DOI: 10.1109/HICSS.2016.33

Mirghani, T. (2020). The Growing Demand for Education in Saudi Arabia: How Effective Is Borrowing Educational Models from the West? *Journal of Education and Learning, 9*(6), 59. Advance online publication. DOI: 10.5539/jel.v9n6p59

Mitra, S. (2021). Organizational Resistance to Change: Implications for Digital Transformation in India. *Journal of Management Studies, 48*(1), 87–102.

Mitra, S., & Joshi, A. (2022). Blockchain and Supply Chain Transparency in India's Energy Sector. *Journal of Energy and Sustainability, 12*(2), 110–125.

Mkansi, M. (2022). E-business adoption costs and strategies for retail micro businesses. *Electronic Commerce Research, 22*(4), 1153–1193.

Mobasheri, A., Zipf, A., & Francis, L. (2018). OpenStreetMap data quality enrichment through awareness raising and collective action tools—Experiences from a European project. *Geo-Spatial Information Science*, *21*(3), 234–246. DOI: 10.1080/10095020.2018.1493817

Mobo, F. D., & Ahmad, M. (2024). Spatial Data-Driven Citizen Engagement in the Metaverse. In Guo, Y. (Ed.), *Emerging Developments and Technologies in Digital Government* (pp. 181–203). IGI Global., DOI: 10.4018/979-8-3693-2363-2.ch010

MOH. (2024). *Seha Virtual Hospital*. https://www.moh.gov.sa/en/Ministry/Projects/Pages/Seha-Virtual-Hospital.aspx

Mohtaramzadeh, M., Ramayah, T., & Jun-Hwa, C. (2018). B2B E-commerce adoption in Iranian manufacturing companies: Analyzing the moderating role of organizational culture. *International Journal of Human-Computer Interaction*, *34*(7), 621–639. DOI: 10.1080/10447318.2017.1385212

Molari, L., Coppolino, F. S., & García, J. J. (2021). Arundo donax: A widespread plant with great potential as sustainable structural material. *Construction & Building Materials*, *268*, 121143. Advance online publication. DOI: 10.1016/j.conbuildmat.2020.121143

Montalbano, G., & Santi, G. (2023). Sustainability of Temporary Housing in Post-Disaster Scenarios: A Requirement-Based Design Strategy. *Buildings (Basel, Switzerland)*, *13*(12), 2952. DOI: 10.3390/buildings13122952

Mooney, P., & Minghini, M. (2017). A Review of OpenStreetMap Data. In Foody, G., See, L., Fritz, S., Mooney, P., Olteanu-Raimond, A.-M., Fonte, C. C., & Antoniou, V. (Eds.), *Mapping and the Citizen Sensor* (pp. 37–59). Ubiquity Press., DOI: 10.5334/bbf

Mooney, P., Minghini, M., Foody, G. M., See, L., Fritz, S., Mooney, P., & Antoniou, V. (2017). *A review of OpenStreetMap data*. Mapping and the Citizen Sensor.

Moore, J. E. (2001). One Road to Turnover: An Examination of Work Exhaustion in Technology Professionals. *Management Information Systems Quarterly*, *24*(1), 141–168. DOI: 10.2307/3250982

Mousavinezhad, S., Choi, Y., Khorshidian, N., Ghahremanloo, M., & Momeni, M. (2024). Air quality and health co-benefits of vehicle electrification and emission controls in the most populated United States urban hubs: Insights from New York, Los Angeles, Chicago, and Houston. *The Science of the Total Environment*, *912*, 169577. Advance online publication. DOI: 10.1016/j.scitotenv.2023.169577 PMID: 38154628

Muchielli, A. (2009). *Dictionary of qualitative methods in the humanities and social sciences* (3rd ed.). Armand Colin.

Mukarram, M. M. T., Kafy, A.-A., Mukarram, M. M. T., Rukiya, Q. U., Almulhim, A. I., Das, A., Fattah, M. A., Rahman, M. T., & Chowdhury, M. A. (2023). Perception of coastal citizens on the prospect of community-based rainwater harvesting system for sustainable water resource management. *Resources, Conservation and Recycling, 198*, 107196. Advance online publication. DOI: 10.1016/j.resconrec.2023.107196

Mutanga, P., Nezandonyi, J., & Bhukuvhani, C. (2018). Enhancing Engineering Education through Technological Pedagogical and Content Knowledge (TPACK): A Case Study. *International Journal of Education and Development Using Information and Communication Technology, 14*(3), 38–49.

Mynko, O., Bonheure, M., Amghizar, I., Brown, D. J., Chen, L., Marin, G. B., Freitas de Alvarenga, R., Civancik Uslu, D., Dewulf, J., & Van Geem, K. M. (2023). Electrification of steam cracking as a pathway to reduce the impact of the petrochemical industry on climate change. *Journal of Cleaner Production, 427*, 139208. Advance online publication. DOI: 10.1016/j.jclepro.2023.139208

Myntra. (2023). "*Pre-Loved: Fostering Circular Fashion Economy.*" Retrieved from https://www.myntra.com

Nagpal, P., Singh, A., & Sharma, D. (2020). Smart meters and IoT in Indian cities: A sustainable solution. *International Journal of Urban Planning, 12*(1), 58–67.

Nair, K. (2021). Data Privacy and Cybersecurity Challenges in India's Digital Economy. *Cybersecurity Review, 22*(1), 98–115.

Nambisan, S. (2009). Platforms for collaboration: The case of the virtual worlds industry. *Academy of Management Review, 34*(1), 32–49. DOI: 10.5465/amr.2009.35732578

Nambisan, S., Lyytinen, K., Majchrzak, A., & Song, M. (2017). Digital innovation management: Reinventing innovation management research in a digital world. *Management Information Systems Quarterly, 41*(1), 223–238. DOI: 10.25300/MISQ/2017/41:1.03

Narayan, R., & Bose, M. (2021). Skill India Mission: Preparing the Workforce for the Digital Age. *Journal of Human Resource Development, 14*(1), 77–91.

Nasiri, M., Ukko, J., Saunila, M., & Rantala, T. (2020). Managing the digital supply chain: The role of smart technologies. *Technovation, 96–97*, 102121. DOI: 10.1016/j.technovation.2020.102121

NASSCOM. (2023). *AI and Digital Transformation in the Retail Sector: Flipkart Case Study*. NASSCOM.

Natera Orozco, L. G., Deritei, D., Vancso, A., & Vasarhelyi, O. (2020). Quantifying life quality as walkability on urban networks: The case of Budapest. In *Complex Networks and Their Applications VIII: Volume 2 Proceedings of the Eighth International Conference on Complex Networks and Their Applications COMPLEX NETWORKS 2019 8* (pp. 905-918). Springer International Publishing.

Neis, P., & Zielstra, D. (2014). Recent Developments and Future Trends in Volunteered Geographic Information Research: The Case of OpenStreetMap. *Future Internet*, *6*(1), 76–106. DOI: 10.3390/fi6010076

Neis, P., Zielstra, D., & Zipf, A. (2011). The street network evolution of crowdsourced maps: OpenStreetMap in Germany 2007–2011. *Future Internet*, *4*(1), 1–21. DOI: 10.3390/fi4010001

Ngongang, D. (2010). Analyse de la pratique des coûts dans les PMI camerounaises. Revue libanaise de gestion et d'économie, 5.

Nguyen, T. P., Nguyen, H., & Ngo, H. Q. T. (2023). Toward a sustainable transition in automated production: Enabling the vision-based approach and synchronous control for textile surface inspection systems. *Textile Research Journal*, *93*(23-24), 5391–5415. Advance online publication. DOI: 10.1177/00405175231199257

Niknam, A., Sarli, R., Taherizadeh, M., Attarroshan, S., & Pourmansouri, F. (2024). REDD implementation for greenhouse gas reduction and climate change mitigation in Hyrcanian forests: A case study of the Kojoor Watershed, Northern Iran. *Environmental Monitoring and Assessment*, *196*(5), 474. DOI: 10.1007/s10661-024-12616-z PMID: 38662125

Nikolaou, G., Neocleous, D., Christou, A., Kitta, E., & Katsoulas, N. (2020). Implementing sustainable irrigation in water-scarce regions under the impact of climate change. In *Agronomy* (Vol. 10, Issue 8). DOI: 10.3390/agronomy10081120

Nouri, H., & Parker, R. (2013, June). Career growth opportunities and employee turnover intentions in public accounting firms. *The British Accounting Review*, *45*(2), 138–148. DOI: 10.1016/j.bar.2013.03.002

Nouri, H., & Parker, R. J. (2020). Turnover in public accounting firms: A literature review. *Managerial Auditing Journal*, *35*(2), 294–321. DOI: 10.1108/MAJ-03-2018-1823

Ntamo, D., Lopez-Montero, E., Mack, J., Omar, C., Highett, M. I., Moss, D., Mitchell, N., Soulatintork, P., Moghadam, P. Z., & Zandi, M. (2022). Industry 4.0 in action: Digitalisation of a continuous process manufacturing for formulated products. *Digital Chemical Engineering*, *3*, 100025. Advance online publication. DOI: 10.1016/j.dche.2022.100025

Nuutinen, M., Kaasinen, E., Hyvärinen, J., Mölsä, A., & Siltanen, S. (2022). *Making a building smart with a co-created and continuously evolving enjoyable service entity—Insights from a collaborative study*. Smart Cities., DOI: 10.3390/smartcities5010001

O'brien, R. M. (2007). A caution regarding rules of thumb for variance inflation factors. *Quality & Quantity*, *41*(5), 673–690. DOI: 10.1007/s11135-006-9018-6

Obaideen, K., Albasha, L., Iqbal, U., & Mir, H. (2024). *Wireless power transfer: Applications, challenges, barriers, and the role of AI in achieving sustainable development goals - A bibliometric analysis*. Energy Strategy Reviews., DOI: 10.1016/j.esr.2024.101376

Okumus, D., Gunbeyaz, S. A., Kurt, R. E., & Turan, O. (2024). An Approach to Advance Circular Practices in the Maritime Industry through a Database as a Bridging Solution. *Sustainability (Basel)*, *16*(1), 453. Advance online publication. DOI: 10.3390/su16010453

Otto, D., & Kerres, M. (2022). Increasing sustainability in open learning: Prospects of a distributed learning ecosystem for open educational resources. *Frontiers in Education*, *7*, 866917. Advance online publication. DOI: 10.3389/feduc.2022.866917

Ouellette, J. A., & Wood, W. (1998). Habit and intention in everyday life: The multiple processes by which past behavior predicts future behavior. *Psychological Bulletin*, *124*(1), 54–74. DOI: 10.1037/0033-2909.124.1.54

Owida, A., Galal, N. M., & Elrafie, A. (2022). Decision-making framework for a resilient sustainable production system during COVID-19: An evidence-based research. *Computers & Industrial Engineering*, *164*, 107905. Advance online publication. DOI: 10.1016/j.cie.2021.107905 PMID: 34975207

Ozili, P. K. (2023). Using Central Bank Digital Currency to Achieve the Sustainable Development Goals. SSRN *Electronic Journal*. DOI: 10.2139/ssrn.4370181

Paithankar, D. N., Pabale, A. R., Kolhe, R. V., William, P., & Yawalkar, P. M. (2023). Framework for implementing air quality monitoring system using LPWA-based IoT technique. *Measurement. Sensors*, *26*, 100709. Advance online publication. DOI: 10.1016/j.measen.2023.100709

Pandey, R., Mehta, D., Kumar, V., & Prakash Pradhan, R. (2024). Quantifying soil erosion and soil organic carbon conservation services in indian forests: A RUSLE-SDR and GIS-based assessment. *Ecological Indicators, 163*, 112086. https://doi.org/https://doi.org/10.1016/j.ecolind.2024.112086. DOI: 10.1016/j.ecolind.2024.112086

Panek, J., & Netek, R. (2019). Collaborative mapping and digital participation: A tool for local empowerment in developing countries. *Information (Basel), 10*(8), 255. DOI: 10.3390/info10080255

Pan, G., & Seow, P. (2016). Preparing accounting graduates for digital revolution: A critical review of information technology competencies and skills development. *Journal of Education for Business, 91*(3), 166–175. DOI: 10.1080/08832323.2016.1145622

Pan, S. L., Carter, L., Tim, Y., & Sandeep, M. S. (2022). Digital sustainability, climate change, and information systems solutions: Opportunities for future research. *International Journal of Information Management, 63*, 102444. Advance online publication. DOI: 10.1016/j.ijinfomgt.2021.102444

Pardamean, B., Soeparno, H., Budiarto, A., Mahesworo, B., & Baurley, J. (2020). Quantified self-using consumer wearable device: Predicting physical and mental health. *Healthcare Informatics Research, 26*(2), 83–92. Advance online publication. DOI: 10.4258/hir.2020.26.2.83 PMID: 32547805

Parhi, S., Joshi, K., Gunasekaran, A., & Sethuraman, K. (2022). Reflecting on an empirical study of the digitalization initiatives for sustainability on logistics: The concept of sustainable logistics 4.0. *Cleaner Logistics and Supply Chain*. DOI: 10.1016/j.clscn.2022.100058

Parida, V., Sjödin, D., & Reim, W. (2019). Reviewing Literature on Digitalization, Business Model Innovation, and Sustainable Industry: Past Achievements and Future Promises. *Sustainability (Basel), 11*(2), 391. DOI: 10.3390/su11020391

Pasewark, W., & Viator, R. (2006). Sources of work-family conflict in the accounting profession. *Behavioral Research in Accounting, 18*(1), 147–165. DOI: 10.2308/bria.2006.18.1.147

Patel, A., & Rathi, M. (2021). Corporate Training for Sustainability Leadership: The Case of Reliance Industries. *Corporate Leadership Review, 18*(1), 90–105.

Patel, K. J., & Patel, H. J. (2018). Adoption of internet banking services in Gujarat: An extension of TAM with perceived security and social influence. *International Journal of Bank Marketing, 36*(1), 147–169. DOI: 10.1108/IJBM-08-2016-0104

Paudel, B., & Thapa, R. B. (2018). Community mapping for disaster risk reduction and management: A review. *International Journal of Disaster Risk Reduction, 31*, 1099–1112.

Pauwels, K., & Weiss, A. (2008). Moving from free to fee: How online firms market to change their business model successfully. *Journal of Marketing*, *72*(3), 14–31. DOI: 10.1509/JMKG.72.3.014

Pérez, L. I. G., María, S. R. M., & Francisco, J. G. P. (2022). Habilitadores tecnológicos 4.0 para impulsar la educación abierta: Aportaciones para las recomendaciones de la UNESCO. *RIED-Revista Iberoamericana de Educación a Distancia*, *25*(2), 23–43. DOI: 10.5944/ried.25.2.33088

Pock, T. (2007). Contingency-based Design of Management Control Systems. Doctoral Thesis, University of St. Gallen Graduate School of Business Administration, Economics, Law, and Social Sciences (HSG).

Poggi, F., & Amado, M. (2024). The spatial dimension of energy consumption in cities. *Energy Policy*, *187*, 114023. Advance online publication. DOI: 10.1016/j.enpol.2024.114023

Pooyandeh, M., & Sohn, I. (2023). Smart Lithium-Ion Battery Monitoring in Electric Vehicles: An AI-Empowered Digital Twin Approach. *Mathematics*, *11*(23), 4865. Advance online publication. DOI: 10.3390/math11234865

Power, T. (2021). *Smart Grids and Energy Efficiency Initiatives*. Retrieved from https://www.tatapower.com

Power, T. (2021). Annual [." Tata Power.]. *Sustainability Report*, •••, 2021.

Power, T. (2022). *Smart Grid and AI-Powered Energy Solutions*. Tata Power.

Priem, R. L., Wenzel, M., & Koch, J. (2018). Business models and demand-side strategy: Putting value creation for consumers center stage. *Long Range Planning*, *51*(1), 22–31. DOI: 10.1016/j.lrp.2017.07.007

Pu, G., Wong, W.-K., Du, Q., Al Shraah, A., Alromaihi, A., & Muda, I. (2024). Asymmetric impact of natural resources, fintech, and digital banking on climate change and environmental sustainability in BRICS countries. *Resources Policy*, *91*, 104872. Advance online publication. DOI: 10.1016/j.resourpol.2024.104872

Purdy, M. (2022). How the Metaverse Could Change Work. In *Harvard Business Review*.

Quadir, B., Chen, N.-S., & Isaias, P. (2022). Analyzing the educational goals, problems and techniques used in educational big data research from 2010 to 2018. *Interactive Learning Environments, 30*(8), 1539–1555. DOI: 10.1080/10494820.2020.1712427

Qu, J., Kizil, M. S., Yahyaei, M., & Knights, P. F. (2024). Developing a digital twin for a laboratory ball mill operation – a step towards mining metaverse. *Mining Technology, 133*(1), 3–16. Advance online publication. DOI: 10.1177/25726668231222990

Ragu-nathan, T. S., Tarafdar, M., Ragu-nathan, B. S., & Tu, Q. (2008). The consequences of technostress for end users in organizations: Conceptual development and empirical validation. *Information Systems Research, 19*(4), 417–433. DOI: 10.1287/isre.1070.0165

Rahi, P., Sood, S. P., Kalhotra, S. K., Khan, I. R., & Dandotiya, M. (2023). Artificial Intelligence of Things (AloT) and metaverse technology for brain health, mental health, and wellbeing. In *Contemporary Applications of Data Fusion for Advanced Healthcare Informatics*. DOI: 10.4018/978-1-6684-8913-0.ch019

Rahimi, F. B., Levy, R. M., Boyd, J. E., & Dadkhahfard, S. (2018). Human behaviour and cognition of spatial experience; a model for enhancing the quality of spatial experiences in the built environment. *International Journal of Industrial Ergonomics, 68*, 245–255. DOI: 10.1016/j.ergon.2018.08.002

Rajaguru, S. (2021). Forced and Unplanned Digital Transformation of Education in Sri Lanka during [Crisis: A Case Study.]. *COVID*, •••, 19.

Raj, N. S., & Renumol, V. G. (2022). A systematic literature review on adaptive content recommenders in personalized learning environments from 2015 to 2020. *Journal of Computers in Education, 9*(1), 113–148. DOI: 10.1007/s40692-021-00199-4

Rakhmawati, D., & Sartono, K. E. (2023). Implementation Of Character Education At Civic Education In 5.0 Era On Fifth Grade State Elementary EDUCATION VIDYA QASANA. *PROGRES PENDIDIKAN, 4*(1), 32–37. DOI: 10.29303/prospek.v4i1.315

Ramesh Kumar, C., & Chitra, M. P. (2022). Design and implementation of pipelined SDF FFT architecture for sustainable industrial noise suppression in digital hearing aids. *Sustainable Energy Technologies and Assessments, 49*, 101858. Advance online publication. DOI: 10.1016/j.seta.2021.101858

RamHormozi, H. (2019). *The Anatomy of Consumerism: The Story of Excess, Greed, Self-Indulgence, Wealth Accumulation, Insurmountable Waste, and Environmental Degradation*. FriesenPress.

Ramírez-Montoya, M.-S., & Lugo-Ocando, J. (2020). Systematic review of mixed methods in the framework of educational innovation. *Comunicar*, *28*(65), 9–20. DOI: 10.3916/C65-2020-01

Ramón, J., Campaña, A., Renteria, N., & Intriago, M. (2023). Research of the Development of Green Central Bank Digital Currency, Cbdc. *Social Science Research Network*. DOI: 10.2139/ssrn.4412456

Ranjan, P., Verma, A., & Sharma, V. (2022). AI-powered energy management: Tata Power's case study. *Journal of Clean Energy*, *9*(2), 85–100.

Rashed, A., & Mutis, I. (2023). Trends of integrated project delivery implementations viewed from an emerging innovation framework. *Engineering, Construction, and Architectural Management*, *30*(3), 989–1014. Advance online publication. DOI: 10.1108/ECAM-06-2021-0516

Rashid, N. (2020). Meeting refinery wastewater challenges through membrane-based biological treatment complemented by an integrated asset sustainability program. *Desalination and Water Treatment*, *176*, 18–23. Advance online publication. DOI: 10.5004/dwt.2020.25489

Razzaq, A., Sharif, A., Ozturk, I., & Skare, M. (2023). Asymmetric influence of digital finance and renewable energy technology innovation on green growth in China. *Renewable Energy*, *202*, 310–319. DOI: 10.1016/j.renene.2022.11.082

Reddy, V., ... (2021). "Blockchain Technology in Plastic Waste Management: A Case Study of Hindustan Unilever." *Journal of Circular Economy*, 3(2), 50-68.

Reio, T. G.Jr, & Shuck, B. (2015). Exploratory factor analysis: Implications for theory, research, and practice. *Advances in Developing Human Resources*, *17*(1), 12–25. DOI: 10.1177/1523422314559804

Reis, J., Amorim, M., Melao, N., Cohen, Y., & Rodrigues, M. (2020). Digitalization: A Literature Review and Research Agenda. In book: Proceedings on 25th International Joint Conference on Industrial Engineering and Operations Management – IJCIEOM, 443-456. www.doi//10.1007/978-3-030-43616-2_47

Reis, S., Seto, E., Northcross, A., Quinn, N. W. T., Convertino, M., Jones, R. L., Maier, H. R., Schlink, U., Steinle, S., Vieno, M., & Wimberly, M. C. (2015). Integrating modelling and smart sensors for environmental and human health. *Environmental Modelling & Software*, *74*, 238–246. Advance online publication. DOI: 10.1016/j.envsoft.2015.06.003 PMID: 26644778

Ren, L., Zhang, W., Wang, Y., Wang, H., Yang, H., Yao, P., & Zhu, Z. (2024). Distribution characteristics and assessment of wind energy resources in the coastal areas of Guangdong. *Sustainable Horizons*, *9*, 100081. Advance online publication. DOI: 10.1016/j.horiz.2023.100081

Ribeiro, A., Vieira, V., Alves, L., & Maciel, C. (2024). VISHnu: An approach to support the personalization of self-expressive avatars using context-awareness. *International Journal of Human-Computer Studies*, *185*, 103243. Advance online publication. DOI: 10.1016/j.ijhcs.2024.103243

Ritala, P., & Hurmelinna-Laukkanen, P. (2013). Incremental and radical innovation in coopetition—The role of absorptive capacity and appropriability. *Journal of Product Innovation Management*, *30*(1), 154–169. DOI: 10.1111/j.1540-5885.2012.00956.x

Ritter, T., & Pedersen, C. L. (2020). Digitization capability and the digitalization of business models in business-to-business firms: Past, present, and future. *Industrial Marketing Management*, *86*, 180–190. DOI: 10.1016/j.indmarman.2019.11.019

Robert, B. (2022). Healthcare Diagnosis and Treatment in the Metaverse: Remote Sensing Algorithms, Networked Wearable Devices, and Virtual Patient Data. *American Journal of Medical Research (New York, N.Y.)*, *9*(2), 41. Advance online publication. DOI: 10.22381/ajmr9220223

Robinson, L., Cotten, S. R., Ono, H., Quan-Haase, A., Mesch, G., Chen, W., & Stern, M. J. (2015). Digital inequalities and why they matter. *Information Communication and Society*, *18*(5), 569–582. DOI: 10.1080/1369118X.2015.1012532

Röck, M., Passer, A., & Allacker, K. (2024). SLiCE: An open building data model for scalable high-definition life cycle engineering, dynamic impact assessment, and systematic hotspot analysis. *Sustainable Production and Consumption*, *45*, 450–463. Advance online publication. DOI: 10.1016/j.spc.2024.01.005

Rodríguez-Abitia, G., & Bribiesca-Correa, G. (2021). Assessing digital transformation in universities. *Future Internet*, *13*(2), 52. DOI: 10.3390/fi13020052

Rogers, E.M. (2003). Diffusion of innovations.

Ross, J. W., Beath, C. M., & Sebastian, I. M. (2017). Digitized ≠ Digital. *MIT CISR Research Briefings*, *18*(10), 1–3.

Roux, N., & Noûs, C. (2021). The choice of common spaces in the inhabited, ecological and solidarity support. Sustainable development and territories. Economics, geography, politics, law, sociology, 12(2).

Rumetshofer, T., Straka, K., & Fischer, J. (2024). How the digital product passport can lead the plastics industry towards a circular economy—A case study from bottle caps to frisbees. *Polymers*, *16*(10), 1420. Advance online publication. DOI: 10.3390/polym16101420 PMID: 38794613

Rusman, A., Mas'udi, M. M., Hermoyo, R. P., Yarno, Y., Yunianti, S., & Rafsanjani, H. (2023, June). Education transformation in 5.0 society development era. In AIP Conference Proceedings (Vol. 2727, No. 1). AIP Publishing.

Saberi, S., Kouhizadeh, M., Sarkis, J., & Shen, L. (2019). Blockchain technology and its relationships to sustainable supply chain management. *International Journal of Production Research*, *57*(7), 2117–2135. DOI: 10.1080/00207543.2018.1533261

Sabherwal, R., Jeyaraj, A., & Chowa, C. (2006). Information system success: Individual and organizational determinants. *Management Science*, *52*(12), 1849–1864. DOI: 10.1287/mnsc.1060.0583

Sadanand, A., Nagarajan, R. V., & Devadas, M. (2021). The façade wall: A focus on the green architecture of Laurie Baker's houses. *International Journal of Energy Production and Management*, *6*(3), 277–293. Advance online publication. DOI: 10.2495/EQ-V6-N3-277-293

Sahabuddin, M., Sakib, M. N., Rahman, M. M., Jibir, A., Fahlevi, M., Aljuaid, M., & Grabowska, S. (2023). The evolution of FinTech in scientific research: A bibliometric analysis. *Sustainability*, *15*(9), 7176.

Saksonova, S., & Kuzmina-Merlino, I. (2017). Fintech as financial innovation–The possibilities and problems of implementation.

Salim, W., Wijaya, N., Ramadhan, F., & Iman, H. K. (2024). Spatial vulnerability assessment of climate-related disasters in the Rebana Metropolitan Coastal Area, West Java Province. *IOP Conference Series. Earth and Environmental Science*, *1318*(1), 12008. DOI: 10.1088/1755-1315/1318/1/012008

Salmon, D., Babbitt, C. W., Babbitt, G. A., & Wilmer, C. E. (2021). A framework for modeling fraud in E-waste management. *Resources, Conservation and Recycling*, *169*, 105613. Advance online publication. DOI: 10.1016/j.resconrec.2021.105613

Samiha, Y. T., Handayani, T., Razaq, A., Fithriyah, M., Fitri, A., & Anshari, M. (2022, March). Implementation of Education 4.0 as sustainable decisions for a sustainable development. In 2022 International conference on decision aid sciences and applications (DASA) (pp. 846-850). IEEE.

San Cornelio, G., Martorell, S., & Ardèvol, E. (2023). "My goal is to make sustainability mainstream": Emerging visual narratives on the environmental crisis on Instagram. *Frontiers in Communication*. Advance online publication. DOI: 10.3389/fcomm.2023.1265466

Sánchez-Torres, J. A., Canada, F.-J. A., Sandoval, A. V., & Alzate, J.-A. S. (2018). E-banking in Colombia: Factors favouring its acceptance, online trust and government support. *International Journal of Bank Marketing*, *36*(1), 170–183. DOI: 10.1108/IJBM-10-2016-0145

Santos, E. G., Wiederhecker, H. C., Lopes, L. E., & Marini, M. Â. (2023). Equivalence of citizen science and scientific data for modelling species distribution of birds from a tropical savanna. *Austral Ecology*, *48*(8), 2171–2184. Advance online publication. DOI: 10.1111/aec.13454

Sá, P., Silva, P. C., Peixinho, J., Figueiras, A., & Rodrigues, A. V. (2023). Sustainability at play: Educational design research for the development of a digital educational resource for primary education. *Social Sciences (Basel, Switzerland)*, *12*(7), 407. Advance online publication. DOI: 10.3390/socsci12070407

Sart, G. (2022). Impact of Higher Education and Globalization on Sustainable Development in the New EU Member States. *Sustainability (Basel)*, *14*(19), 11916. DOI: 10.3390/su141911916

Sarwatt, D. S., Lin, Y., Ding, J., Sun, Y., & Ning, H. (2024). Metaverse for Intelligent Transportation Systems (ITS): A Comprehensive Review of Technologies, Applications, Implications, Challenges and Future Directions. *IEEE Transactions on Intelligent Transportation Systems*, *25*(7), 6290–6308. Advance online publication. DOI: 10.1109/TITS.2023.3347280

Saucier, G., & Ostendorf, F. (1999). Hierarchical subcomponents of the Big Five personality factors: A cross-languagereplication. *Journal of Personality and Social Psychology*, *76*(4), 613–627. DOI: 10.1037/0022-3514.76.4.613 PMID: 10234848

Saurette, D. D., Heck, R. J., Gillespie, A. W., Berg, A. A., & Biswas, A. (2024). Sample Size Optimization for Digital Soil Mapping: An Empirical Example. *Land (Basel)*, *13*(3), 365. Advance online publication. DOI: 10.3390/land13030365

Schlecht, L., Schneider, S., & Buchwald, A. (2021). The prospective value creation potential of Blockchain in business models: A Delphi study. *Technological Forecasting and Social Change*, *166*, 120601. DOI: 10.1016/j.techfore.2021.120601

Schmidt, D., Casagranda, L. F., Butturi, M. A., & Sellitto, M. A. (2024). Digital Technologies, Sustainability, and Efficiency in Grain Post-Harvest Activities: A Bibliometric Analysis. *Sustainability (Basel), 16*(3), 1244. Advance online publication. DOI: 10.3390/su16031244

Schröder-Bergen, S., Glasze, G., Michel, B., & Dammann, F. (2022). De/colonizing OpenStreetMap? Local mappers, humanitarian and commercial actors and the changing modes of collaborative mapping. *GeoJournal, 2022*(87), 5051–5066. DOI: 10.1007/s10708-021-10547-7

Schwartz-Belkin, I., & Portman, M. E. (2023). A review of geospatial technologies for improving Marine Spatial Planning: Challenges and opportunities. In *Ocean and Coastal Management* (Vol. 231). DOI: 10.1016/j.ocecoaman.2022.106280

Scott, W. R. (2008). *Institutions and organizations: Ideas and interests*. Sage Publications.

Sehra, S. S., Singh, J., Rai, H. S., & Anand, S. S. (2020). Extending processing toolbox for assessing the logical consistency of OpenStreetMap data. *Transactions in GIS, 24*(1), 44–71. DOI: 10.1111/tgis.12587

Sen, R., & Gupta, V. (2022). Sustainability and Digital Education in Indian Institutes of Technology. *Journal of Higher Education Studies, 9*(1), 22–34.

Shahzad, A., Zahrullail, N., Akbar, A., Mohelska, H., & Hussain, A. (2022). COVID-19's Impact on Fintech Adoption: Behavioral Intention to Use the Financial Portal. *Journal of Risk and Financial Management, 15*(10), 428. DOI: 10.3390/jrfm15100428

Shahzad, M., Qu, Y., Zafar, A. U., & Appolloni, A. (2021). Does the interaction between the knowledge management process and sustainable development practices boost corporate green innovation? *Business Strategy and the Environment, 30*(8), 4206–4222. Advance online publication. DOI: 10.1002/bse.2865

Sharif, A., Brahim, M., Dogan, E., & Tzeremes, P. (2023). Analysis of the spillover effects between green economy, clean and dirty cryptocurrencies. *Energy Economics, 120*, 106594. DOI: 10.1016/j.eneco.2023.106594

Sharma, A., & Gupta, M. (2022). Green Technologies and Policy Gaps in India: A Comparative Analysis. *Indian Journal of Policy Research, 11*(2), 34–48.

Sharma, A., & Kumar Tiwari, M. (2023). Digital twin design and analytics for scaling up electric vehicle battery production using robots. *International Journal of Production Research, 61*(24), 8512–8546. Advance online publication. DOI: 10.1080/00207543.2022.2152896

Sharma, D., Thapar, S., Jain, D., & Sachdeva, K. (2024). Mapping the Spatiotemporal Variability of Particulate Matter Pollution in Delhi: Insights from Land Use Regression Modelling. *Photonirvachak (Dehra Dun)*, *52*(6), 1329–1346. Advance online publication. DOI: 10.1007/s12524-024-01879-1

Sharma, G. D., Shahbaz, M., Singh, S., Chopra, R., & Cifuentes-Faura, J. (2023). Investigating the nexus between green economy, sustainability, bitcoin and oil prices: Contextual evidence from the United States. *Resources Policy*, *80*, 103168. DOI: 10.1016/j.resourpol.2022.103168

Sharma, K., Kumar, R., Kumar, A., Balabantaray, S., & Arora, M. (2024). A digital ecosystem for sustainable fruit supply chain in Uttarakhand: A comprehensive review. *Environment, Development and Sustainability*. Advance online publication. DOI: 10.1007/s10668-023-04142-8

Sharma, K., & Rao, S. (2022). Eco-packaging solutions in Indian e-commerce: A case study of Flipkart. *Journal of Business and Sustainability*, *14*(2), 143–158.

Sharma, M.. (2020). Indore Smart City: A Model for IoT-Driven Sustainability. *International Journal of Smart Cities*, *6*(2), 112–126.

Sharma, M., Joshi, S., & Govindan, K. (2023). Overcoming barriers to implement digital technologies to achieve sustainable production and consumption in the food sector: A circular economy perspective. *Sustainable Production and Consumption*, *39*, 203–215. Advance online publication. DOI: 10.1016/j.spc.2023.04.002

Sharma, N., Saharia, M., & Ramana, G. V. (2024). High resolution landslide susceptibility mapping using ensemble machine learning and geospatial big data. *Catena*, *235*, 107653. Advance online publication. DOI: 10.1016/j.catena.2023.107653

Shaw, D., Newholm, T., & Dickinson, R. (2006). Consumption as voting: An exploration of consumer empowerment. *European Journal of Marketing*, *40*(9/10), 1049–1067. DOI: 10.1108/03090560610681005

Shekar, P. R., & Mathew, A. (2024). GIS-based assessment of soil erosion and sediment yield using the revised universal soil loss equation (RUSLE) model in the Murredu Watershed, Telangana, India. *HydroResearch, 7*, 315–325. https://doi.org/https://doi.org/10.1016/j.hydres.2024.05.003

Shinde, S. P., Barai, V. N., Gavit, B. K., Kadam, S. A., Atre, A. A., Pande, C. B., Pal, S. C., Radwan, N., Tolche, A. D., & Elkhrachy, I. (2024). Assessment of groundwater potential zone mapping for semi-arid environment areas using AHP and MIF techniques. *Environmental Sciences Europe*, *36*(1), 87. DOI: 10.1186/s12302-024-00906-9

Shin, S., Kim, H., Yoo, J., & Park, M. (2023). The Effects of Metaverse Avatar Identification on Immersion, Vicarious Pleasure, and Fashion Brand Item Sharing Intention. *Journal of the Korean Society of Clothing and Textiles*, *47*(3). Advance online publication. DOI: 10.5850/JKSCT.2023.47.3.492

Shui, T., Hu, J., Yang, K., Kang, H., Rui, H., & Wang, B. (2023). Cell-Free Networking for Integrated Data and Energy Transfer: Digital Twin Based Double Parameterized DQN for Energy Sustainability. *IEEE Transactions on Wireless Communications*, *22*(11), 8035–8049. Advance online publication. DOI: 10.1109/TWC.2023.3258143

Silvestre, B. S., & Ţîrcă, D. M. (2019). Innovations for sustainable development: Moving toward a sustainable future. In *Journal of Cleaner Production* (Vol. 208). DOI: 10.1016/j.jclepro.2018.09.244

Singh, A., & Hess, T. (2017). How chief digital officers promote the digital transformation of their companies. *MIS Quarterly Executive*, *16*, 1–17.

Singh, A., Klarner, P., & Hess, T. (2020). How do chief digital officers pursue digital transformation activities? The role of organization design parameters. *Long Range Planning*, *53*(3), 101890. DOI: 10.1016/j.lrp.2019.07.001

Singh, A., & Patel, D. (2021). Digital India and Smart Cities: A Pathway to Sustainability. *Indian Journal of Public Policy*, *16*(4), 143–159.

Smith, K. J., Emerson, D. J., & Boster, C. R. (2018, September). An examination of reduced audit quality practices within the beyond the role stress model. *Managerial Auditing Journal*, *33*(8/9), 736–759. DOI: 10.1108/MAJ-07-2017-1611

Smith, T., & Boers, N. (2023). Global vegetation resilience linked to water availability and variability. *Nature Communications*, *14*(1), 498. Advance online publication. DOI: 10.1038/s41467-023-36207-7 PMID: 36717585

Snoussi, N., & Elhamma, A. (2022). Adoption du Balanced Scorecard par les PME: Une étude exploratoire dans le contexte marocain. Alternatives Managériales Economiques 4 (1), 158-179. https://doi.org/DOI: 10.48374/IMIST.PRSM/ame-v4i1.30471

Solís, P., McCusker, B., Menkiti, N., Cowan, N., & Blevins, C. (2018). Engaging global youth in participatory spatial data creation for the UN sustainable development goals: The case of open mapping for malaria prevention. *Applied Geography (Sevenoaks, England)*, *98*, 143–155. DOI: 10.1016/j.apgeog.2018.07.013

Soluk, J., Kammerlander, N., & Darwin, S. (2021). Digital entrepreneurship in developing countries: The role of institutional voids. *Technological Forecasting and Social Change*, *170*, 120876. DOI: 10.1016/j.techfore.2021.120876

Solutions, Z. (2022). *AI-based Energy Management for Commercial Buildings*. Retrieved from https://www.zenatix.com

Somani, S. N., Yu, K. M., Chiu, A. G., Sykes, K. J., & Villwock, J. A. (2022). Consumer Wearables for Patient Monitoring in Otolaryngology: A State of the Art Review. In *Otolaryngology - Head and Neck Surgery (United States)* (Vol. 167, Issue 4). DOI: 10.1177/01945998211061681

Songling, Y., Ishtiaq, M., Anwar, M., & Ahmed, H. (2018). The role of government support in sustainable competitive position and firm performance. *Sustainability (Basel)*, *10*(10), 3495. DOI: 10.3390/su10103495

Song, Y., Gong, Y., & Song, Y. (2024). The impact of digital financial development on the green economy: An analysis based on a volatility perspective. *Journal of Cleaner Production*, *434*, 140051–140051. DOI: 10.1016/j.jclepro.2023.140051

Sponem, S. (2002). L'explication de la diversité des pratiques budgétaires: une approche contingente. Actes du 23ème Congrès de l'AFC, Toulouse, mai.

Srai, J., & Lorentz, H. (2019). Developing design principles for the digitalisation of purchasing andsupply management. *Journal of Purchasing and Supply Management*, *25*(1), 78–98. DOI: 10.1016/j.pursup.2018.07.001

Srivastava, R., Mishra, A., & Gupta, N. (2021). Predictive maintenance using AI in Indian manufacturing: Opportunities and challenges. *Journal of Industrial Engineering*, *21*(1), 51–66.

Srivastava, S. C., Chandra, S., & Shirish, A. (2015). Technostress creators and job outcomes: Theorising the moderating influence of personality traits. *Information Systems Journal*, *25*(4), 355–401. DOI: 10.1111/isj.12067

Štampach, R., Herman, L., Trojan, J., Tajovská, K., & Řezník, T. (2021). Humanitarian mapping as a contribution to achieving sustainable development goals: Research into the motivation of volunteers and the ideal setting of mapathons. *Sustainability (Basel)*, *13*(24), 13991. DOI: 10.3390/su132413991

Suhluli, S. A., & Ali Khan, S. M. F. (2022). Determinants of user acceptance of wearable IoT devices. *Cogent Engineering*, *9*(1), 2087456. Advance online publication. DOI: 10.1080/23311916.2022.2087456

Sulu, S., Ceylan, A., & Kaynak, R. (2010, July). Work Alienation as a Mediator of the Relationship between Organizational Injustice and Organizational Commitment: Implications for Healthcare Professionals. *International Journal of Business and Management*, *5*(8), 27–38. DOI: 10.5539/ijbm.v5n8p27

Sungkawati, E. (2024). Opportunities and challenges: adopting "blue-green economy" terms to achieve SDGs. Revenue Journal: Management and Entrepreneurship, 2(1), 01-13.

Sun, X., & Ye, B. (2023). The functional differentiation of brain–computer interfaces (BCIs) and its ethical implications. *Humanities & Social Sciences Communications, 10*(1), 878. Advance online publication. DOI: 10.1057/s41599-023-02419-x

Suthakaran, S., Withanage, A., Gunawardhane, M., & Gunatilake, J. (2018, December). A flood risk assessment based on an OpenStreetMap application: a case study in Manmunai North Divisional Secretariat of Batticaloa, Sri Lanka. In *FOSS4G Asia 2018 conference. Department of Town and Country Planning, University of MoratuwaMorawa. Sri Lanka* (pp. 02-05).

Suthakaran, S., Jayakody, S., Subasinghe, S., Seneviratne, N., & Alahakoon, R. (2022). Mapping the Flood Risk Exposure Using Open-Source Geospatial Tools and Techniques: A Case of Gampaha Divisional Secretariat Division, Sri Lanka. *Journal of Geoscience and Environment Protection, 10*(10), 18–31. DOI: 10.4236/gep.2022.1010002

Sweeney, J., & Summers, S. (2002). The Effect of the Busy Season Workload on Public Accountants' Job Burnout. *Behavioral Research in Accounting, 14*(1), 223–245. DOI: 10.2308/bria.2002.14.1.223

Swider, B. W., & Zimmerman, R. D. (2010). Born to burnout: A meta-analytic path model of personality, job burnout, and work outcomes. *Journal of Vocational Behavior, 76*(3), 487–506. DOI: 10.1016/j.jvb.2010.01.003

Tang, C., Yi, W., Occhipinti, E., Dai, Y., Gao, S., & Occhipinti, L. G. (2024). A roadmap for the development of human body digital twins. *Nature Reviews Electrical Engineering, 1*(3), 199–207. Advance online publication. DOI: 10.1038/s44287-024-00025-w

Tanir, T., Yildirim, E., Ferreira, C. M., & Demir, I. (2024). Social vulnerability and climate risk assessment for agricultural communities in the United States. *The Science of the Total Environment, 908*, 168346. Advance online publication. DOI: 10.1016/j.scitotenv.2023.168346 PMID: 37939966

Tan, Z., Wang, C., Yan, C., Zhou, M., & Jiang, C. (2020). Protecting privacy of location-based services in road networks. *IEEE Transactions on Intelligent Transportation Systems, 22*(10), 6435–6448. DOI: 10.1109/TITS.2020.2992232

Tanzania, N. F. P. A., & Tanzania, U. N. F. P. A. (2020). *Fact Sheet: FGM in the United Republic of Tanzania*. UNFPA., Available from https://tanzania.unfpa.org/en/publications/fact-sheet-fgm-united-republic-tanzania

Tarafdar, M., Gupta, A., & Turel, O. (2015). Editorial: Special Issue on "dark side of information technology use": An Introduction and a framework for research. *Information Systems Journal*, *25*(3), 161–170. DOI: 10.1111/isj.12070

Tarafdar, M., Pullins, E. B., & Ragu-Nathan, T. S. (2015). Technostress: Negative effect on performance and possible mitigations. *Information Systems Journal*, *25*(2), 103–132. DOI: 10.1111/isj.12042

Tarafdar, M., Tu, Q., Ragu-Nathan, B. S., & Ragu-Nathan, T. S. (2007). The Impact of Technostress on Role Stress and Productivity. *Journal of Management Information Systems*, *24*(1), 301–328. DOI: 10.2753/MIS0742-1222240109

Tarafdar, M., Tu, Q., & Ragu-Nathan, T. S. (2010). Impact of Technostress on End-User Satisfaction and Performance. *Journal of Management Information Systems*, *27*(3), 303334. DOI: 10.2753/MIS0742-1222270311

Tarafdar, M., Tu, Q., Ragu-Nathan, T. S., & Ragu-Nathan, B. S. (2011). Crossing to the Dark Side: Examining Creators, Outcomes, and Inhibitors of Technostress. *Communications of the ACM*, *54*(9), 113–120. DOI: 10.1145/1995376.1995403

Teece, D. J. (2007). Explicating dynamic capabilities: The nature and microfoundations of (sustainable) enterprise performance. *Strategic Management Journal*, *28*(13), 1319–1350. DOI: 10.1002/smj.640

Teece, D. J. (2010). Business models, business strategy and innovation. *Long Range Planning*, *43*(2-3), 172–194. DOI: 10.1016/j.lrp.2009.07.003

Ter Hoeven, C. L., van Zoonen, W., & Fonner, K. L. (2016). The practical paradox of technology: The influence of communication technology use on employee burnout and engagement. *Communication Monographs*, *83*(2), 239–263. DOI: 10.1080/03637751.2015.1133920 PMID: 27226694

Terés-Zubiaga, J., González-Pino, I., Álvarez-González, I., & Campos-Celador, Á. (2023). Multidimensional procedure for mapping and monitoring urban energy vulnerability at regional level using public data: Proposal and implementation into a case study in Spain. *Sustainable Cities and Society*, *89*, 104301. Advance online publication. DOI: 10.1016/j.scs.2022.104301

TERI. (2022). *Sustainability and Digital Technologies: A Survey of Indian Corporations*. The Energy and Resources Institute.

Togo, M., & Gandidzanwa, C. P. (2021). The role of Education 5.0 in accelerating the implementation of SDGs and challenges encountered at the University of Zimbabwe. *International Journal of Sustainability in Higher Education*, *22*(7), 1520–1535. DOI: 10.1108/IJSHE-05-2020-0158

Trabelsi, E. (2024). Transition to Sustainable Environment and Economic Growth in Tunisia: An ARDL Approach. *World Development Sustainability*, 100165.

Tu, T. T., & Hoang, H. Y. (2023). Applications of Geographic Information System (GIS) in Environmental Management. *Scientific Collection «InterConf»*.

Tutusaus, S., Schwartz, K., & Smit, S. (2018). The ambiguity of innovation drivers: The adoption of information and communication technologies by public water utilities. *Journal of Cleaner Production*, *171*, S79–S85. DOI: 10.1016/j.jclepro.2016.08.002

Ul Haq, I., Maneengam, A., Chupradit, S., & Huo, C. (2022). Are green bonds and sustainable cryptocurrencies truly sustainable? Evidence from a wavelet coherence analysis. *Economic Research-Ekonomska Istraživanja*, 1–20. DOI: 10.1080/1331677X.2022.2080739

Umar, M., & Safi, A. (2023). Do green finance and innovation matter for environmental protection? A case of OECD economies. *Energy Economics*, *119*, 106560. Advance online publication. DOI: 10.1016/j.eneco.2023.106560

UNFPA. (2018). Crowdsourced maps, East and Southern Africa, *Tanzania*. 2018. https://esaro.unfpa.org/en/news/girls-escaping-fgm-rural-tanzania-crowdsourced-maps-show-way-safety

Unilever, H. (2022). *Blockchain and Circular Economy in Packaging*.Retrieved from https://www.hul.co.in

Upadhyaya, S., Rao, S., & Rao, M. (2024). Assessment of wind and wave energy potential along the Indian coast. *Cogent Engineering*, *11*(1), 2316950. Advance online publication. DOI: 10.1080/23311916.2024.2316950

Urbinati, A., Manelli, L., Frattini, F., & Bogers, M. L. A. M. (2022). The digital transformation of the innovation process: Orchestration mechanisms and future research directions. *Innovation (North Sydney, N.S.W.)*, *24*(1), 65–85. DOI: 10.1080/14479338.2021.1963736

Vasarhelyi, M. A., Kogan, A., & Tuttle, B. M. (2015). Big Data in Accounting: An Overview. *Accounting Horizons*, *29*(2), 381–396. DOI: 10.2308/acch-51071

Veerubhotla, A., Krantz, A., Ibironke, O., & Pilkar, R. (2022). Wearable devices for tracking physical activity in the community after an acquired brain injury: A systematic review. In *PM and R* (Vol. 14, Issue 10). DOI: 10.1002/pmrj.12725

Venkatesan, P., & Chakraborty, S. (2023). Blockchain for sustainability in Indian FMCG: The case of Hindustan Unilever. *Journal of Business and Technology*, 19(3), 78-93.

Verhagen, M., de Reuver, M., & Bouwman, H. (2023). Implementing business models into operations: Impact of business model implementation on performance. *IEEE Transactions on Engineering Management*, *70*(1), 173–183. DOI: 10.1109/TEM.2020.3046365

Verplanken, B., & Wood, W. (2006). Interventions to break and create consumer habits. *Journal of Public Policy & Marketing*, *25*(1), 90–103. DOI: 10.1509/jppm.25.1.90

Vial, G. (2021). Understanding digital transformation: a review and a research agenda. In Hinterhuber, A., Vescovi, T., & Checchinato, F. (Eds.), *Managing Digital Transformation: Understanding the Strategic Process* (1st ed.). Routledge. DOI: 10.4324/9781003008637-4

Wang, S., Zhou, Y., Zhang, X., Wang, Y., Yang, Y., Shang, Y., Chen, Y., & Shi, X. (2024). Mapping and resource evaluation of deep high-temperature geothermal resources in the Jiyang Depression, China. *Energy Geoscience*, 100320. https://doi.org/https://doi.org/10.1016/j.engeos.2024.100320

Wang, C., Lu, Y. C., & Song, S. R. (2024). Geothermal feasibility analysis inside Yangmingshan National Park, Taiwan. *Geothermics*, *116*, 102834. Advance online publication. DOI: 10.1016/j.geothermics.2023.102834

Wang, S.-J., & Park, S. Y. (2023). Disaster Education in Hospitals using Metaverse: Focusing on COVID-19. *Prehospital and Disaster Medicine*, *38*(S1), s85. Advance online publication. DOI: 10.1017/S1049023X23002431

Wang, T., Gan, V. J. L., Hu, D., & Liu, H. (2022). Digital twin-enabled built environment sensing and monitoring through semantic enrichment of BIM with SensorML. *Automation in Construction*, *144*, 104625. Advance online publication. DOI: 10.1016/j.autcon.2022.104625

Wang, Y., Sun, G., Wu, Y., Wang, S., Yue, X., & Zhang, H. (2024). Urban population density and energy conservation: Empirical evidence from 276 cities in China. *Heliyon*, *10*(5), e26882. Advance online publication. DOI: 10.1016/j.heliyon.2024.e26882 PMID: 38434365

Warden, C. A., Chen, J. F., & Yen, W. H. (2024). Metaverse Servicescape: Emotional Response to Virtual Retail Design. *International Journal of Human-Computer Interaction*. Advance online publication. DOI: 10.1080/10447318.2024.2322200

Warner, K. S. R., & Wäger, M. (2019). Building dynamic capabilities for digital transformation: An ongoing process of strategic renewal. *Long Range Planning*, *52*(3), 326–349. Advance online publication. DOI: 10.1016/j.lrp.2018.12.001

Warren Jr., J. D., Moffitt, K. C. and Byrnes, P. (2015). How Big Data Will Change Accounting. 29(2), 397-407.

Webster, F. E.Jr. (1975). determining the characteristics of socially responsible consumer. *The Journal of Consumer Research*, *2*(December), 188–196. DOI: 10.1086/208631

Weinberger, M. (2022). What Is Metaverse?—A Definition Based on Qualitative Meta-Synthesis. *Future Internet*, *14*(11), 310. Advance online publication. DOI: 10.3390/fi14110310

Weslati, O., & Serbaji, M. M. (2024). Spatial assessment of soil erosion by water using RUSLE model, remote sensing and GIS: A case study of Mellegue Watershed, Algeria–Tunisia. *Environmental Monitoring and Assessment*, *196*(1), 14. Advance online publication. DOI: 10.1007/s10661-023-12163-z PMID: 38055082

Wesolowski, A., Eagle, N., Noor, A. M., Snow, R. W., Buckee, C. O., & Simeone, A. (2014). The impact of biases in mobile phone ownership on estimates of human mobility. *Journal of the Royal Society, Interface*, *2014*(11), 20120986. PMID: 23389897

Westerman, G., Bonnet, D., & McAfee, A. (2014). The nine elements of digital transformation, available at: https:// sloanreview.mit.edu/article/the-nine-elements-of digital transformation.

Westerman, G., Bonnett, D., & McAffee, A. (2014). *Gagner avec le digital*. Editions Diatein.

Willis, K. S., & Cross, E. (2022). Investigating the potential of EDA data from biometric wearables to inform inclusive design of the built environment. *Emotion, Space and Society*, *45*, 100906. Advance online publication. DOI: 10.1016/j.emospa.2022.100906

Wirtz, B. W., Göttel, V., & Daiser, P. (2016). Business model innovation: Development, concept and future research directions. *Journal of Business Models*, *4*(1), 1–28.

World Bank (2022). "Digital Technologies for SME Growth: Insights from India." World Bank Group Report.

World Bank. (2013). *Diagnostic Assessment of Select Environmental Challenges in India*. Retrieved from https://www.worldbank.org

Wu, J. Y., Ching, C. T. S., Wang, H. M. D., & De Liao, L. (2022). Emerging Wearable Biosensor Technologies for Stress Monitoring and Their Real-World Applications. In *Biosensors* (Vol. 12, Issue 12). DOI: 10.3390/bios12121097

Wu, M., Mahajan, V., & Balasubramanian, S. (2003). An analysis of e-business adoption and its impact on business performance. *Journal of Technological Advancements*, *31*(4), 425–447. DOI: 10.1177/0092070303255379

Xie, J., Ma, H., Zhou, Z., & Hanying, T. (2017). Work-Related Use of Information and Communication Technologies after Hours (W_ICTs) and Emotional Exhaustion: A Mediated Moderation Model. *Computers in Human Behavior*. Advance online publication. DOI: 10.1016/j.chb.2017.10.023

Xin, C., Fan, S., Mbanyele, W., & Shahbaz, M. (2023). Towards inclusive green growth: Does digital economy matter? *Environmental Science and Pollution Research International*, *30*(27), 70348–70370. DOI: 10.1007/s11356-023-27357-8 PMID: 37148510

Yadav, S., Samadhiya, A., Kumar, A., Luthra, S., & Pandey, K. K. (2024). Nexus between fintech, green finance and natural resources management: Transition of BRICS nation industries from resource curse to resource blessed sustainable economies. *Resources Policy*, *91*, 104903–104903. DOI: 10.1016/j.resourpol.2024.104903

Yagoub, M. M. (2015). Public perception on disaster management using volunteered geographic information (VGI): Case of UAE. *ISPRS Annals of the Photogrammetry, Remote Sensing and Spatial Information Sciences*, *2*(W2), 241–246. DOI: 10.5194/isprsannals-II-2-W2-241-2015

Yang, X., Huang, M., Luo, L., Guo, H., & Zhu, C. (2023). Efficient Panoramic Video Coding for Immersive Metaverse Experience. *IEEE Network*, *37*(6), 58–66. Advance online publication. DOI: 10.1109/MNET.2023.3319958

Yan, J., Chen, X., Chen, Y., & Liang, D. (2020). Multistep prediction of land cover from dense time series remote sensing images with temporal convolutional networks. *IEEE Journal of Selected Topics in Applied Earth Observations and Remote Sensing*, *13*, 5149–5161. DOI: 10.1109/JSTARS.2020.3020839

Yan, J., Li, G., Qi, G., Qiao, H., Nie, Z., Huang, C., & Yao, X. (2021). Landscape ecological risk assessment of farming-pastoral ecotone in China based on terrain gradients. *Human and Ecological Risk Assessment*, *27*(8), 2124–2141. DOI: 10.1080/10807039.2021.1956300

Yasin, E. H., Siddig, A. A., Deiab, E. E., Kornel, C., Hasoba, A., & Osman, A. (2023). *Forest Degradation in Dryland Ecosystems of Sudan: Review of the Causes, Consequences, Assessment Methods, and Potential Solutions*. Mitigating Global Climate Change-Enhancing Adaptation, Evaluation, and Restoration of Mountain Ecosystems.

Ye, W., Wong, W.-K., Arnone, G., Nassani, A. A., Haffar, M., & Faiz, M. F. (2023). Cryptocurrency and green investment impact on global environment: A time series analysis. *International Review of Economics & Finance*, *86*, 155–169. Advance online publication. DOI: 10.1016/j.iref.2023.01.030

Yoon, S., & Nam, Y. (2024). Metaverse engagement and Korea travel intentions: Understanding affordances, presence, and place attachment among Brazilian ZEPETO users. *Journal of Destination Marketing & Management*, *31*, 100865. Advance online publication. DOI: 10.1016/j.jdmm.2024.100865

Yoon, T. E., & George, J. F. (2013). Why aren't organizations adopting virtual worlds? *Computers in Human Behavior*, *29*(3), 772–790.

Zaiem, I. (2005). The ecological behaviour of the consumer. La revue des sciences de gestion, (4), 75-88.

Zeina, K., Eyad, A.-M., Janahan, T., Richard, J., & Guy, P. (2023). *The Future of Healthcare in the Metaverse*. PWC. https://www.pwc.com/m1/en/industries/healthcare/the-future-of-healthcare-in-the-metaverse.html

Zerbe, W. J., & Paulhus, D. L. (1987). Socially desirable responding in organizational behavior: A reconception. *Academy of Management Review*, *12*(2), 250–264. DOI: 10.2307/258533

Zhang, K. Q., Chen, H. H., Tang, L. Z., & Qiao, S. (2022). Green Finance, Innovation and the Energy-Environment-Climate Nexus. *Frontiers in Environmental Science*, *10*, 879681. Advance online publication. DOI: 10.3389/fenvs.2022.879681

Zhang, S., Bai, M., Wang, X., Peng, X., Chen, A., & Peng, P. (2023). Remote sensing technology for rapid extraction of burned areas and ecosystem environmental assessment. *PeerJ*, *11*, e14557. Advance online publication. DOI: 10.7717/peerj.14557 PMID: 36778148

Zhang, X., Estoque, R. C., Murayama, Y., & Ranagalage, M. (2021). Capturing urban heat island formation in a subtropical city of China based on Landsat images: Implications for sustainable urban development. *Environmental Monitoring and Assessment, 193*(3), 1–13. DOI: 10.1007/s10661-021-08890-w PMID: 33587190

Zhang, Y., Ma, X., Pang, J., Xing, H., & Wang, J. (2023). The impact of digital transformation of manufacturing on corporate performance. The mediating effect of business model innovation and the moderating effect of innovation capability. *Research in International Business and Finance*, *64*, 101890. DOI: 10.1016/j.ribaf.2023.101890

Zhang, Z., Liu, N., & Zhao, L. (2024). Spatio-temporal evolution and driving factors of waste disposal facilities in China. *Journal of Environmental Planning and Management*, *67*(8), 1805–1829. Advance online publication. DOI: 10.1080/09640568.2023.2182187

Zhang, Z., Zhang, G., & Li, L. (2023). The spatial impact of atmospheric environmental policy on public health based on the mediation effect of air pollution in China. *Environmental Science and Pollution Research International*, *30*(55), 116584–116600. Advance online publication. DOI: 10.1007/s11356-022-21501-6 PMID: 35779217

Zhao, S., Tu, K., Ye, S., Tang, H., Hu, Y., & Xie, C. (2023). Land Use and Land Cover Classification Meets Deep Learning: A Review. In *Sensors (Basel, Switzerland)* (Vol. 23, Issue 21). DOI: 10.3390/s23218966

Zhe, C., Huilan, G., Jiang, W., & Zhongyi, H. (2023). The Ideal and Reality of Metaverse: User Perception of VR Products Based on Review Mining. *Data Analysis and Knowledge Discovery*, *7*(1). Advance online publication. DOI: 10.11925/infotech.2096-3467.2022.0371

Zheng, Z., Zhao, X., Zhang, H., Liu, B., & Liu, Y. (2023). AvatarReX: Real-Time Expressive Full-body Avatars. *ACM Transactions on Graphics*, *42*(4), 1–19. Advance online publication. DOI: 10.1145/3592101

Zhou, P., Liu, Y., & Huang, Y. (2020). IoT in sustainable manufacturing: Global trends and challenges. *Journal of Sustainable Manufacturing*, *29*(2), 97–110.

Zook, M., Graham, M., Shelton, T., & Gorman, S. (2010). Volunteered geographic information and crowdsourcing disaster relief: A case study of the Haitian earthquake. *World Medical & Health Policy*, *2*(2), 7–33. DOI: 10.2202/1948-4682.1069

Zott, C., & Ami, R. (2017). Business Model Innovation: How to Create Value in a Digital World. *NIM Marketing Intelligence Review*, *9*(1), 18–23. DOI: 10.1515/gfkmir-2017-0003

Zott, C., Amit, R., & Massa, L. (2011). The Business Model: Recent Developments and Future Research. *Journal of Management*, *37*(4), 1019–1042. DOI: 10.1177/0149206311406265

Zvarikova, K., Michalikova, K. F., & Rowland, M. (2022). Retail Data Measurement Tools, Cognitive Artificial Intelligence Algorithms, and Metaverse Live Shopping Analytics in Immersive Hyper-Connected Virtual Spaces. *Linguistic and Philosophical Investigations*, *21*(0), 9. Advance online publication. DOI: 10.22381/lpi2120221

About the Contributors

Afef Khalil is a researcher and an assistant Professor of Accounting at theUniversity of Manouba (ISCAE), Tunisia. She is the author of several books and publications in international journals. She is a reviewer and an Editorial board member of several journals.

Hosn el Woujoud Bousselmi is a researcher and an assistant Professor of Business Administration at the University of Carthage (FSEGN), Tunisia. She is the author of many articles.

Imen Ben Slimene, Associate Professor in Finance and Accounting at the Upper-Alsace University- UHA (France) and a researcher at the Research Center in Management of Organizations (CREGO-EA 7317). She is the author of several papers and books in international journals, contributed to various book chapters, and served as an editor for numerous books in the accounting and finance domain. She is a reviewer and editor board member of several journals.

***

Syeda Fizza Abbas is a distinguished academician with an illustrious career spanning over 18 years in higher education, specializing in accounting and finance. Currently serving as the Head of Department (Accounting and Finance) at Kinnaird College for Women, Lahore, Pakistan, Syeda Fizza Abbas has been a pivotal member of the institution since 2006. Apart from teaching, Syeda Fizza Abbas contributes significantly to academic leadership through research supervision and curriculum development, shaping the educational landscape in their field. With a robust academic background, Syeda Fizza Abbas holds an MPhil in Commerce from the University of Central Punjab, Lahore, where she achieved a remarkable CGPA of 3.85/4.00, alongside earning a Gold Medal in MSc Banking & Finance from Government College University, Lahore. Syeda Fizza Abbas is renowned for her research prowess, with 18 publications in esteemed journals and presentations at 22 international conferences. Notably, her research on derivatives in Pakistani banks earned acclaim as a Co-Principal Investigator in a HEC SRGP Project in 2019. Awarded for her scholarly contributions, Syeda Fizza Abbas received the Best Paper Awards at prestigious international conferences, underscoring her expertise in analyzing capital structure dynamics in emerging market economies amidst political instability and exchange rate volatility.

Yousuf Aboya is working as a senior lecturer in the Department of Economics at the Institute of Business Management. He has an M.Phil. in Economics from the Institute of Business Management (IoBM) and an M.A in Economics from the University of Karachi. He is a Ph.D. scholar at IoBM. He has nine years of teaching experience at various business institutions in Karachi. His research interests are in Monetary Economics, Macroeconomics & International Trade. He has some research publications in reputable journals to his credit. He has also presented papers at various conferences.

Muhammad Danyal is a research scholar who completed his MPhil finance degree at Lyallpur Business School at GC University Faisalabad, Pakistan. He is a visiting Lecturer at different colleges. He has teaching and research experience of more than two years in Accounting and Finance.

Munir Ahmad is a seasoned professional in the realm of Spatial Data Infrastructure (SDI), Geo-Information Productions, Information Systems, and Information Governance, boasting over 25 years of dedicated experience in the field. With a PhD in Computer Science, Dr. Ahmad's expertise spans Spatial Data Production, Management, Processing, Analysis, Visualization, and Quality Control. Throughout his career, Dr. Ahmad has been deeply involved in the development and deployment of SDI systems specially in the context of Pakistan, leveraging his proficiency in Spatial Database Design, Web, Mobile & Desktop GIS, and Geo Web Services Architecture. His contributions to Volunteered Geographic Information (VGI) and Open Source Geoportal & Metadata Portal have significantly enriched the geospatial community. As a trainer and researcher, Dr. Ahmad has authored over 50 publications, advancing the industry's knowledge base and fostering innovation in Geo-Tech, Data Governance, and Information Infrastructure, and Emerging Technologies. His commitment to Research and Development (R&D) is evident in his role as a dedicated educator and mentor in the field.

Muhammad Akbar holds a BSc in Agricultural Engineering from Bahauddin Zakariya University, Multan, and an MSc in Water Resources Engineering from the Centre of Excellence in Water Resources Engineering at UET Lahore. He is currently working as a Field Engineer/Consultant at MM Pakistan. His research interests include climate change impacts on hydrological patterns, flood risk management, and sustainable solutions for water resources. He has conducted significant research on hydraulic modeling and natural flood storage to mitigate flooding risks.

Mounir Alkhalaf, holds a Master's degree from ESC Rennes School of Business. He is currently preparing a PhD, he worked in several French digital companies and published some research in the field of the role of artificial intelligence in the selection and recruitment of human resources. In addition to Artificial Intelligence and Business Models in Global Large Corporations as Meta, X . Internet of Things (IoT) Applications in Business Operations.

Taher Alkhalaf is currently an Associate Professor in the Faculty of Business Administration at several public and private universities. He obtained his PhD in Management Sciences from University of Caen Normandy (Institute of Business Administration, IAE Caen), France. He has more than ten years of experience in the academic field, scientific research methodology and statistical software SPSS-AMOS, Structural Equation Modeling (SEM), PLS.mart. WarpPLS. He has published a number of papers and participated in a number of forums on Human Resource Management, Innovation and Entrepreneurship.

Sinda Ben Sedrine Doghri, Ph.D. in Management Sciences from the Toulouse School of Management in France. She is an associate professor of the Doctoral and research master's degree in administration and business strategy. My research interests include Knowledge Management, Innovation, Strategic Management of Entreprises, Human Resources Management,Digital transformation,Leadership ... She published extensively in academic journals and participated in several international conferences such as International Business Information Management Association (IBIMA), International Association of Strategic Management (AIMS) . she is head of the management, human resources and law department at the Higher Institute of Management of Tunis(Tunis University)

Bimol Chandra Das is a postgraduate student at Trine University in USA, pursuing a Master's degree in Business Analytics. He earned his B.Sc. in Statistics from the University of Dhaka, Bangladesh, in 2019. His research interests include Machine Learning and AI in Business, Predictive Analytics, Big Data Analytics, Data Visualization, Optimization Techniques, Consumer Behavior Analysis, Supply Chain Analytics, Financial Analytics, and Marketing Analytics. He is actively involved in research projects focused on sustainability in the healthcare and transportation sectors. His findings have been published in several peer-reviewed international journals and conferences.

Omar Durrah is an Associate Professor and Chairperson of Management Department, College of Commerce and Business Administration, Dhofar University, Oman. He holds a PhD in management and a Master's degree in Management. He is a Fellow of Higher Education Academy (FHEA), Advance HE, U.K. His researches focus on behavioral, psychological, and organizational subjects, In addition to entrepreneurship. He has 33 papers indexed in Scopus and web of science in many journals like: Psychological Reports, Current Psychology, Management Research Review, International Journal of Entrepreneurial Behavior & Research, Digital Policy, Regulation and Governance, and European Journal of Innovation Management. He serves as a member of the editorial board/scientific committees of several peer reviewed research journals and conferences. Durrah won the National Research Award in Oman 2021.

Askar Garad, a Yemeni scholar based in Indonesia, earned his Doctoral Degree in Management from Universitas Muhammadiyah Yogyakarta. He now serves as a lecturer and researcher at Universitas Muhammadiyah Yogyakarta

Al Iyoob is a well-known academician who hails from Sri Lanka. I am a Lecture in Geography at South Eastern University of Sri Lanka. My contributions to the field of Geography are, and I have received recognition for my work both nationally and internationally.

Marium Azad is a Ph.D. scholar who completed her MPhil degree at Punjab University Lahore, Pakistan. She is a Lecturer at the National University of Modern Languages, Mirpur, Pakistan. She has more than 12 years of teaching and research experience in Business Education.

Arsalan Haneef Malik is an academician and experienced professional in accounting and finance. He is affiliated with the Institute of Business Management (IoBM) Karachi, Pakistan. With a PhD from the University of Malaysia Sarawak, he has published extensively in the social sciences in highly reputed journals. Among his research areas are financial inclusion, financial stability, institutional quality, and environmental and social sustainability. He inspires and mentors students to think critically and apply their knowledge to real-world situations. Arsalan Haneef Malik is committed to academic excellence and shaping the next generation of financial professionals.

Farah Naz is an accomplished academic with a passion for research and teaching. Holding a Ph.D. in Finance from the University of Central Punjab, Lahore, she has dedicated her career to advancing knowledge in the field of accounting and finance . Dr. Naz brings over a decade of teaching experience, currently serving as an Assistant Professor at Kinnaird College for Women, Lahore, Pakistan. Dr. Naz's research interests span various areas of finance, including capital markets, risk management, and corporate governance. She has authored numerous articles in esteemed international journals, addressing topics such as intellectual capital efficiency, volatility forecasting, and the nexus of capital, risk, and liquidity in banking. Dr. Naz's scholarly contributions have earned recognition from prestigious organizations and institutions, including Scopus, ABDC, and ESCI. With a commitment to excellence in both academia and research, Dr. Farah Naz continues to inspire and mentor the next generation of scholars while making significant contributions to the advancement of knowledge in her field.

Eze Emmanuel Onyemaechi is a Nigerian researcher with a passion for innovative scientific inquiry. He holds a Bachelor's degree in Microbiology from Federal University Wukari, Nigeria, and is currently pursuing a Master's degree in Public Health at Sechenov University, Moscow. As a young researcher, Eze is driven by a curiosity to explore novel fields of study and contribute meaningfully to the scientific community. His research interests span across various disciplines, with a focus on Clinical medicine, Pharmacoepidemiology, Green energy etc. Eze is committed to advancing knowledge and improving public health outcomes through his research endeavors.

Manoj Kumar Rao is an accomplished Assistant Professor at Department of Management Studies, J.D. College of Engineering and Management, Nagpur. With a diverse academic background including Ph.D. in Finance, UGC NET in Management, MBA, LLB, PGDIR, and PGDIT, he brings a wealth of knowledge to his role. With a remarkable teaching career spanning over 15 years at the post-graduate level, Dr. Rao is recognized for his profound expertise in the fields of finance and account. His scholarly contributions extend beyond the classroom, as evidenced by the publication of 17 research papers in reputable National and International journals, including SCOPUS indexed journals. Dr. Rao's commitment to advancing knowledge is further demonstrated through the authorship of Three Books. Notably, his innovative thinking has resulted in Two Patents published at both the National and International levels. His multifaceted accomplishments make him a valuable asset to the academic and research community.

Muhammad Rehan is an accomplished academic with expertise in Accounting and Finance. He holds a Ph.D. in Accounting and Finance from Tokat Gaziosmanpaşa University, Turkey, and has additional qualifications including a Master in Management Sciences (Finance), an MBA in Finance from Mohammad Ali Jinnah University, and an MA in Islamic Banking and Finance from the

University of Karachi. Currently serving as an Assistant Professor in the Department of Accounting & Finance at the Institute of Business Management (IoBM), Karachi, Dr. Rehan has published 11 research papers in high-impact journals including Scopus, Web of Science, and HEC-recognized categories. His research interests span corporate finance, green finance, Islamic finance, behavioral finance, and sustainable development. He has also been actively involved in various equality, diversity, and inclusion initiatives and has a keen interest in geopolitical conflicts such as the Russia-Ukraine war.

Awais Rehman is a Finance, Law, and Islamic Finance expert, holding a PhD in Finance, MS Finance, LLB, and MSc in Economics. With over 5 years of experience, he has excelled as an Assistant Professor, and Lecturer and also in the applied corporate world as Factory Manager. Driven by a passion for research, he has published in esteemed journals, focusing on Financial inclusion, Islamic finance, and behavioral finance.

Ahsan Riaz graduated from the Asia Pacific University of Technology & Innovation, Malaysia, with a Ph.D. in corporate finance and a merit award. Dr. Ahsan Riaz is an Assistant Professor at Lyallpur Business School GC University Faisalabad, Pakistan. He has vast teaching and research experience of more than 14 years in Accounting and Finance. He has authored many research articles and is an editorial board member of the Asian Institute of Research for Economics and Business Quarterly Reviews. He is also a reviewer of many reputable journals like Sustainability (MDPI), Sustainability Accounting, Management and Policy Journal (Emerald) Asian Social Science, International Business Research, and the International Journal of Economics and Finance of the Canadian Center of Science and Education (CCSE). He is an expert in quantitative analysis and a professional Eviews, Gretl, Jamovi and Vos-Viewer trainer.

Pujita Roy is a highly accomplished professional with a Bachelor in Dental Surgery from the University of Dhaka, Bangladesh. She completed her internship at the prestigious Holy Family Red Crescent Hospital in Dhaka, where she honed her clinical skills. With a deep passion for research, Pujita pursued a Master's in Public Health at North South University, where she also engaged in a research internship, further fueling her drive to contribute to global health. Pujita is known for her innovative thinking and her commitment to pushing the boundaries of traditional practice. She is not content to serve only one community but is determined to make a difference on a global scale. Pujita's dedication to her work is matched only by her kindness and empathy, making her a compassionate and thoughtful individual who genuinely cares about the well-being of others. Her passion for research and her desire to serve the world make her a truly inspiring figure.

Jan Vrba holds a Bachelor's Degree in Social Affairs from the Czech Republic, a Master's Degree in Politics and Administration from Poland, and a Doctorate in Human Resources from the United States. He is currently the Vice Dean for International Cooperation at the Faculty of Administration and Economic Studies in Uherské Hradiště, Akademia Jagiellońska w Toruniu. As a dedicated researcher, Jan focuses on global social and welfare systems, exploring their economics, sustainability, and impact on business and management. He has a particular expertise in East Asian and Southeast Asian countries. In addition to his research, Jan is fluent in Czech, Japanese, English, and Slovak.

Rida Zahid is a super skilled and hardworking doctor who got her MBBS degree from Capital Medical University in Beijing, China. She boosted her skills with a one-year clinical internship at Beijing Chaoyang Hospital, which is one of the best hospitals around. There, she got loads of practical experience, which let her use what she learned in her books in real life. While studying at Capital Medical University, Rida learned a ton about medical stuff. The school had cool facilities and taught her all about different areas of medicine. She did awesome in her classes because she's focused on being a great doctor. Her internship at Beijing Chaoyang Hospital was intense. She worked with some of the best doctors, saw complicated medical treatments, and helped take care of lots of different patients. This didn't just make her better at medical stuff; it also made her more confident and ready to tackle tough medical problems. Rida loves learning new things in medicine and always tries to stay up to date by going to workshops, seminars, and conferences. She wants to use the newest medical info to help her patients as best as she can. Besides her job, Rida is all about helping people stay healthy and improving healthcare for everyone, especially those who don't get much medical help. She works on health projects, helps out at clinics, and teaches people about staying healthy. She also fights for better healthcare laws to make things better for everyone. Rida Zahid is all about caring, helping, and being excellent in her job as a doctor. She works super hard for her patients, keeps learning new things, and helps her community be healthier. She plans to keep on making a big difference in medicine, helping both people and whole communities get better.

Index

A

B

C

D

E

F

G

H

I

L

M

N

O

P

Q

S

T

V

W

www.ingramcontent.com/pod-product-compliance
Lightning Source LLC
LaVergne TN
LVHW080344011026
849161LV00009B/2185